fushigi yûgi™

The Mysterious Play
VOL. 17: DEMON

Story & Art By
YUU WATASE

FUSHIGI YÛGI
THE MYSTERIOUS PLAY
VOL. 17:DEMON
SHÔJO EDITION

STORY AND ART BY YUU WATASE

Editor's Note: At the author's request, the spelling of Ms. Watase's first name has been changed from "Yû," as it has appeared on previous VIZ publications, to "Yuu."

English Adaptation/William Flanagan
Touch-up & Lettering/Bill Spicer
Touch-up Assistance/Walden Wong
Design/Hidemi Sahara
Editor/Frances E. Wall

Managing Editor/Annette Roman
Director of Production/Noboru Watanabe
Vice President of Publishing/Alvin Lu
Sr. Director of Acquisitions/Rika Inouye
Vice President of Sales & Marketing/Liza Coppola
Publisher/Hyoe Narita

Printed in Canada

Published by VIZ Media, LLC
P.O. Box 77010
San Francisco, CA 94107

Shôjo Edition
10 9 8 7 6 5 4 3 2 1
First printing, December 2005

www.viz.com
store.viz.com

PARENTAL ADVISORY
FUSHIGI YÛGI is rated T+ for Older Teen and is recommended
for ages 16 and up. This volume contains realistic and fantasy
violence and sexual situations.

CONTENTS

STORY THUS FAR

In the winter of her third year of middle school, Miaka was whisked away into the pages of a mysterious old book called THE UNIVERSE OF THE FOUR GODS and began a dual existence as an ordinary schoolgirl in modern Japan and a priestess of the god Suzaku in a fictional version of ancient China. Miaka fell in love with Tamahome, one of the Celestial Warriors of Suzaku responsible for the protection of the priestess. Miaka's best friend Yui was also sucked into the world of the book and became the priestess of Seiryu, the bitter enemy of Suzaku and Miaka. After clashing repeatedly with the corrupt and vengeful Seiryu Celestial Warriors, Miaka summoned Suzaku and vanquished her enemies, reconciled with Yui, and saved the earth from destruction. In the end, Suzaku granted Miaka one impossible wish: for Tamahome to be reborn as a human in the real world so that the two lovers would never again be separated.

Miaka enters Yotsubadai High School and plans to settle into a normal life with her beloved Tamahome, who is now called Taka Sukunami. But Suzaku returns to give Miaka a new mission: She must re-enter THE UNIVERSE OF THE FOUR GODS and find seven special stones that contain Taka's memories from his former life as Tamahome…or her soulmate could disappear forever! With the help of the reunited Warriors of Suzaku, Miaka and Taka are able to recover four of the stones. But the demon-god Tenkô says he will stop at nothing to thwart their quest, and his minions repeatedly terrorize Miaka and Taka! After returning from their latest journey into the world of the book, Taka and Miaka discover that they have been missing from the real world for months. Miaka's family is furious, and Taka returns to his apartment alone, only to be attacked by Tenkô's servant Miiru. Miaka runs after Taka, but when she arrives at his building, she sees the apartment complex explode into flames as Tenkô's image rises above the scene of destruction!

THE UNIVERSE OF THE FOUR GODS is based on ancient Chinese legend, but Japanese pronunciation of Chinese names differs slightly from their Chinese equivalents. Here is a short glossary of the Japanese pronunciation of the Chinese names in this graphic novel:

CHINESE	JAPANESE	PERSON OR PLACE	MEANING
Lu-Hou	Rokô	Nuriko's brother	Backbone Lord
Mei-Song	Miisû	A monster	Bewitching Heights
Lai Lai	Nyan Nyan	A demigod	Daughter (x2)
Lian-Fahg	Renhô	A monster	Collect Beauty
Shi-Hang Lian	Shigyo Ren	Transfer student	Worship-Journey Collect
Han-gui Fei-gao	Kanki Hikô	Tenkô's servant	Drought Spirit Fly Shore
Jia-Pao	Kahô	A village	Add Cloak
Shao-Huan	Shôka	A little girl	Small Flower
Miao Nioh-An	Myo Ju-An	Mitsukake's name	Miracle Peaceful Life
Fang-Zhun	Hôjun	Chichiri's name	Fragrant Accordance

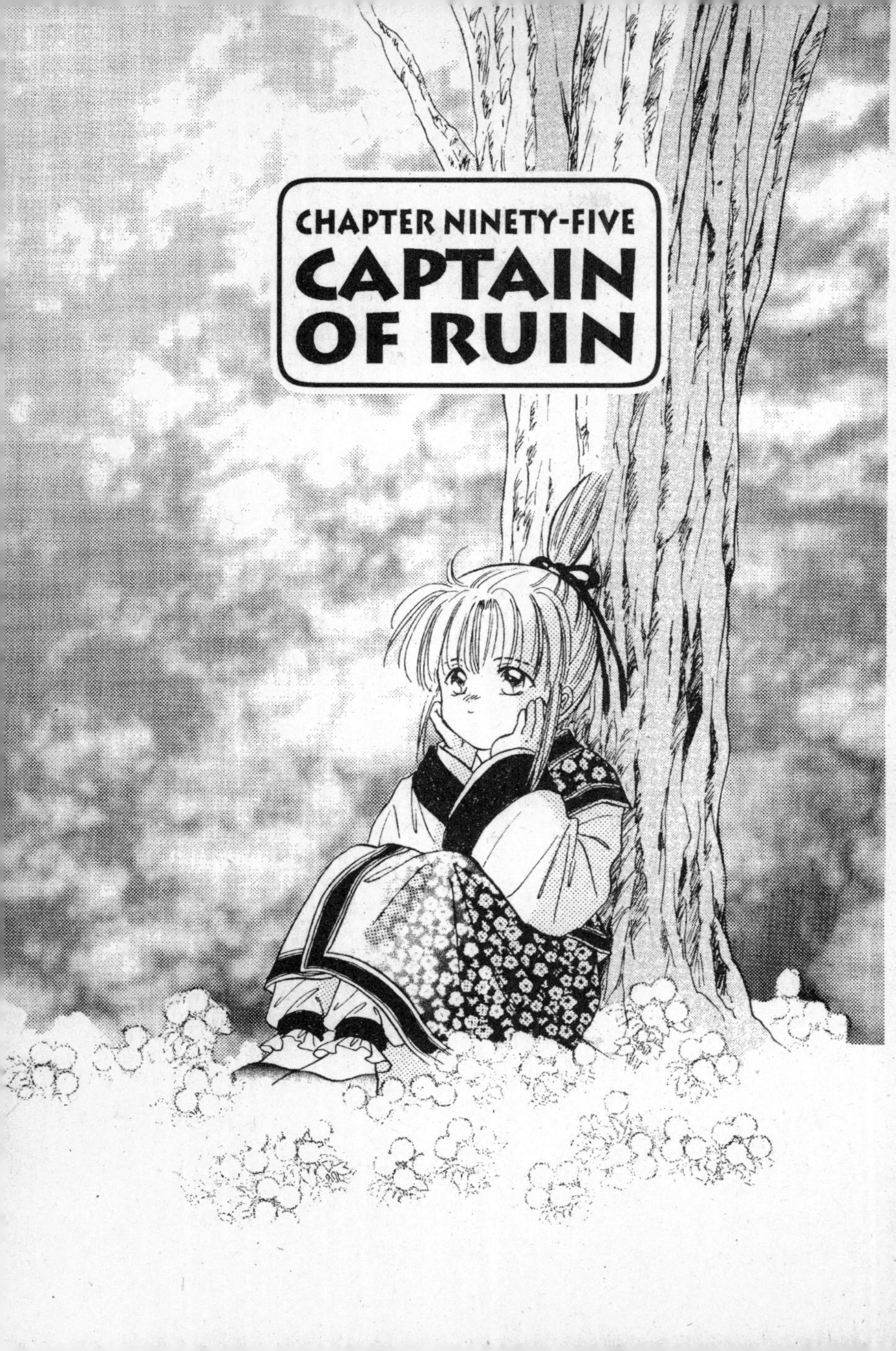
CHAPTER NINETY-FIVE
CAPTAIN OF RUIN

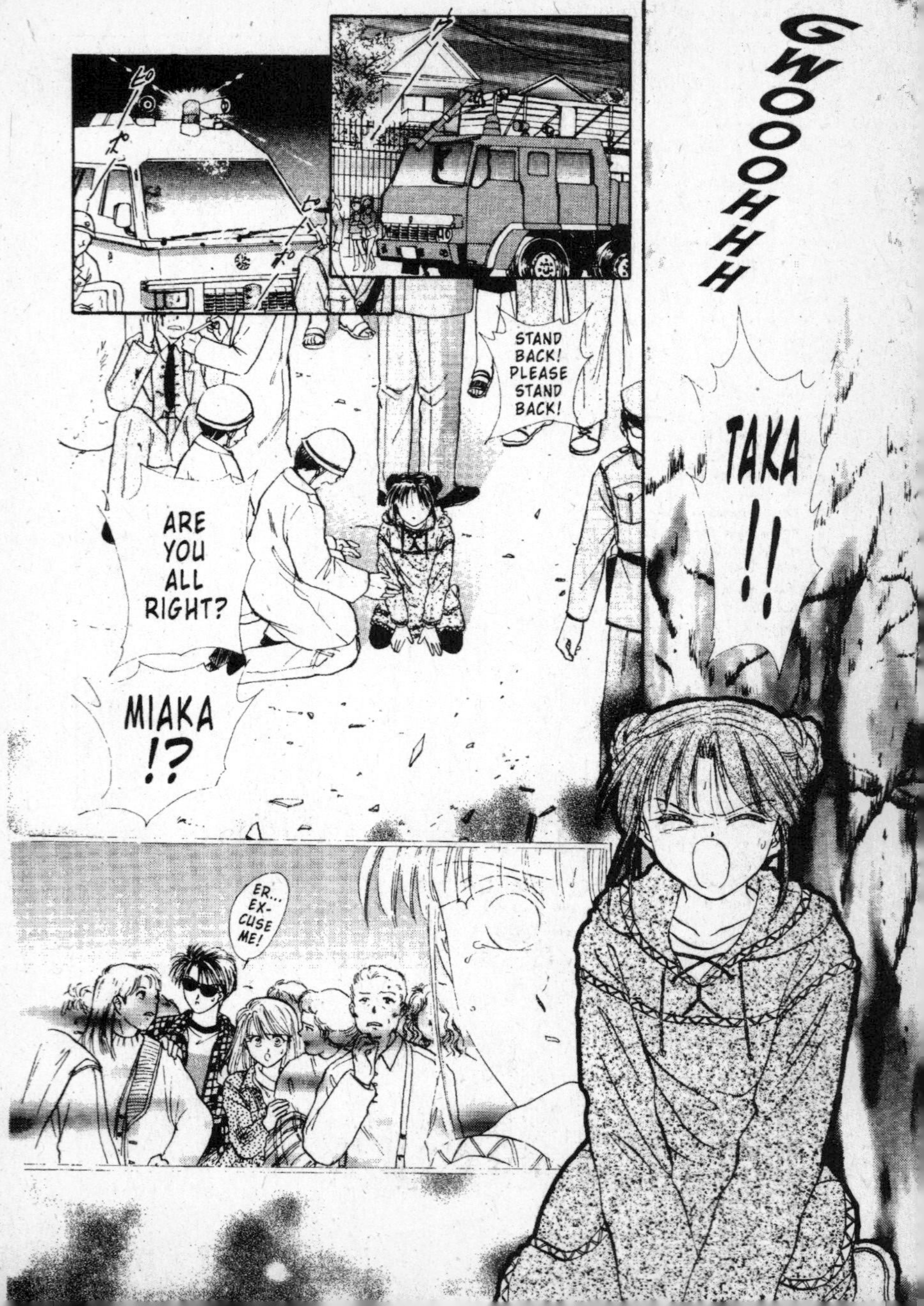
GWOOOOHHHH
TAKA !!
STAND BACK! PLEASE STAND BACK!
ARE YOU ALL RIGHT?
MIAKA !?
ER... EX-CUSE ME!

Volume 17. Ah, volume 17... Volume 17. Ah!
Hello, this is Watase. *Feeling a little sleepy.*
Hmm... By the time this is published, the anime will have finished its run. I'll comment on that in the next volume. *It's only March (1996) while I'm writing this.* Oh, and thanks to all of you, *Fushigi Yûgi* volumes 1-16 have sold a total of over 10 million books! *Thank you all so much!*
Enough of that! Watase is cutting this off! In both the good and the bad meanings of the word! *(What am I talking about?)*
FY, part 2. I've always called it "Part 2," but in my heart I've called it a "side story" or a "sequel." The main story was from volume 1 to volume 13... at least that's how I feel about it. *Because Part 2 is so short!* Now Part 2...was done by request (with Suzaku as the main god, and with a lot of comings and goings from the real world...). My biggest motivation was that I wanted to draw more of the celestial warriors!! So I agreed and got started. I loved the feel of volume 4, and I wanted to try that again! In Part 1, the situation was so dire and everyone had to be so heroic, there was no time for any real fun between the warriors (although I forced some in there! ☺). I was so happy that I could draw some exciting, crowded scenes after so long. *However...* in the last installment, chapter 94, something missed the mark. And it looks like something big and bad is headed this way. ☺ So just as I was thinking that I would do as I like, the characters started acting the way they wanted to! *Okay guys, have fun and... sorry.*
And the bad way I cut things off is... Around January, I kept on missing deadlines, I never got enough sleep, my stomach hurt, my stress was building, and everything was feeling terrible! When I was mentally and physically at my worst, right in the middle of work, I cut it off. I pulled the trigger............(vacation).....................☺ You're just one big dummy, now arntcha? is what they'd say in my home accent.

That was really an awful thing to do to my assistants.

YUI... ...?
YOU *DID* COME BACK! THANK GOD!
THIS IS A REAL SHOCK! WHAT'S...
MIAKA! WHERE'S TAKA? HE DIDN'T...
NO...
NO, TAKA ISN'T ...
TAKA ISN'T DEAD !!
MIAKA, HANG IN THERE, OKAY?

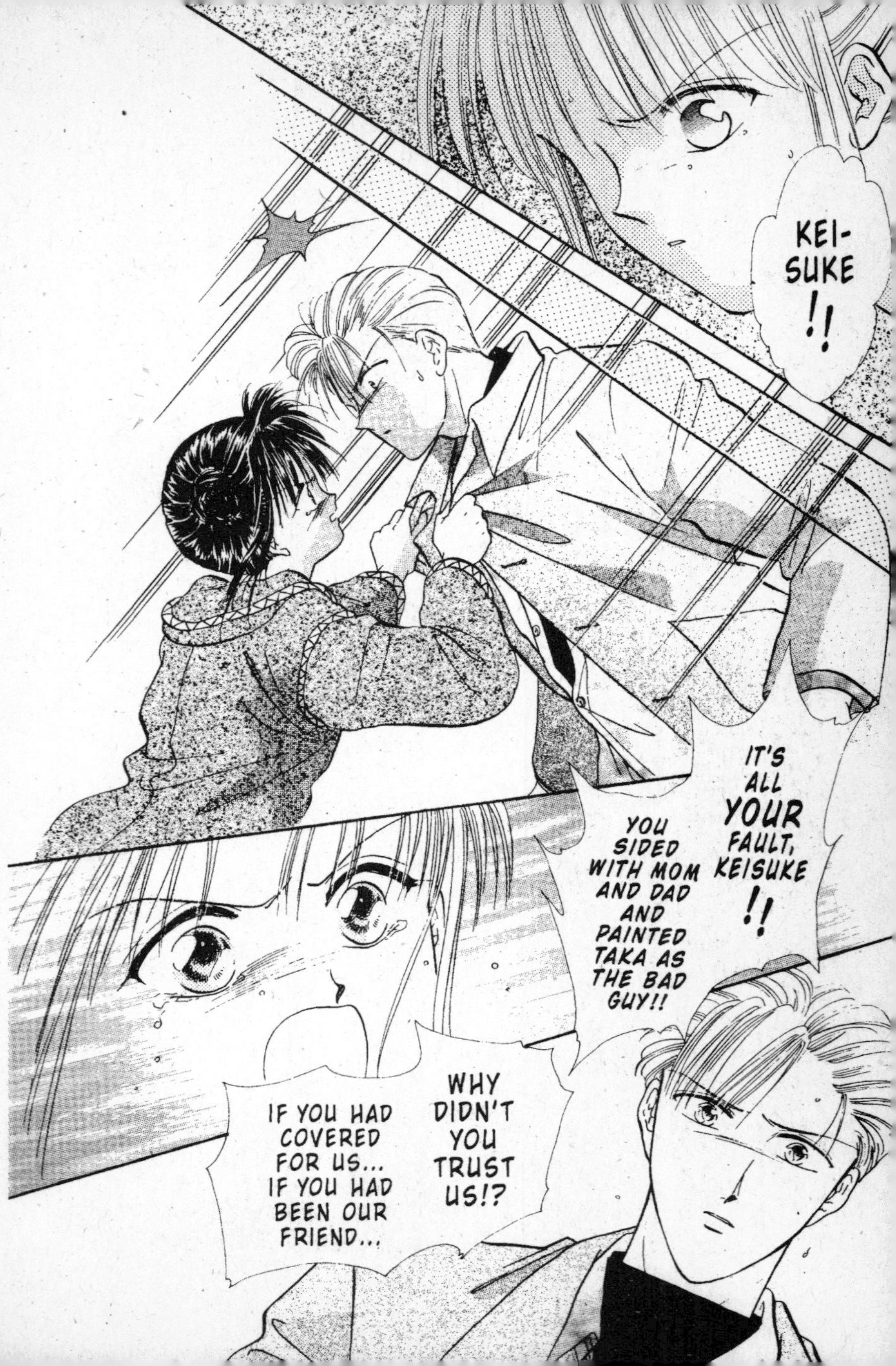
KEI-SUKE !!
IT'S ALL YOUR FAULT, KEISUKE !!
YOU SIDED WITH MOM AND DAD AND PAINTED TAKA AS THE BAD GUY!!
WHY DIDN'T YOU TRUST US!?
IF YOU HAD COVERED FOR US... IF YOU HAD BEEN OUR FRIEND...

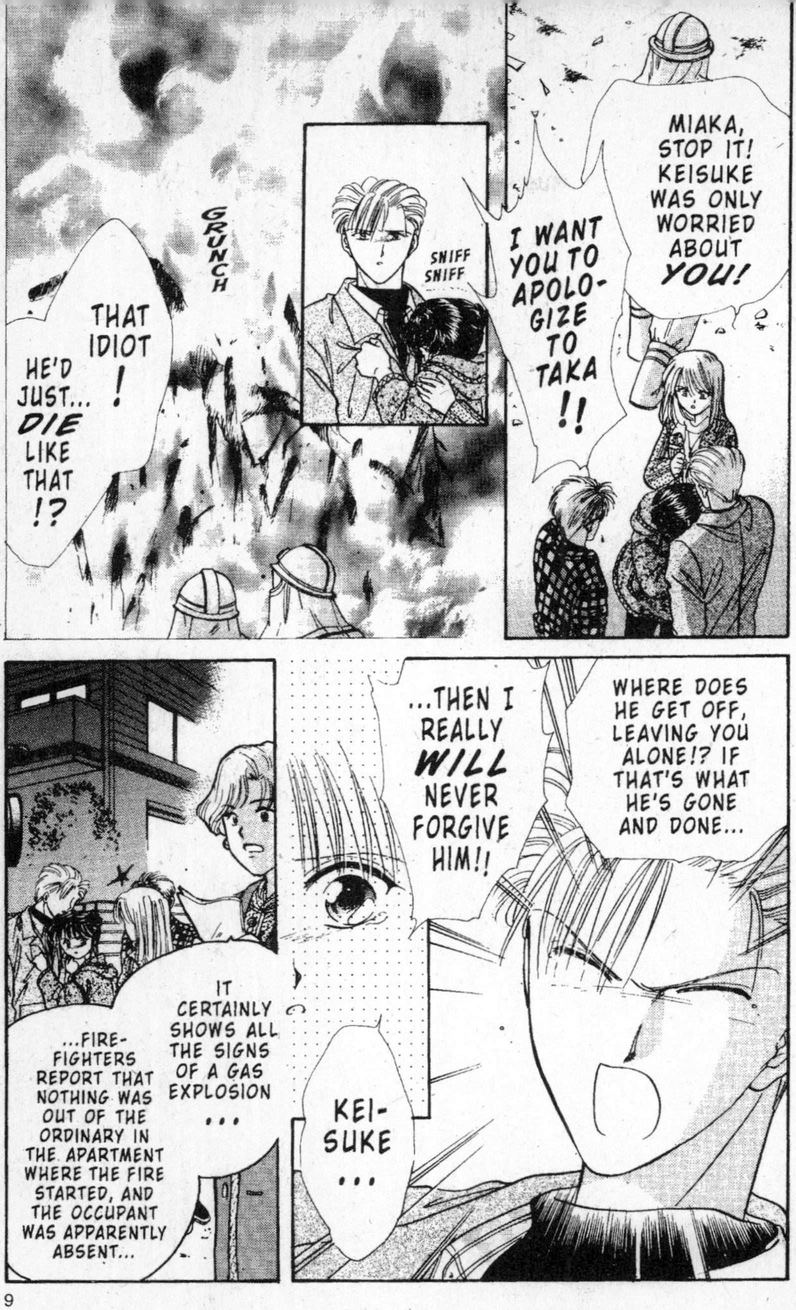
MIAKA, STOP IT! KEISUKE WAS ONLY WORRIED ABOUT *YOU!*
I WANT YOU TO APOLOGIZE TO TAKA!!
SNIFF SNIFF
GRUNCH
THAT IDIOT!
HE'D JUST... *DIE* LIKE THAT!?
WHERE DOES HE GET OFF, LEAVING YOU ALONE!? IF THAT'S WHAT HE'S GONE AND DONE...
...THEN I REALLY *WILL* NEVER FORGIVE HIM!!
KEI-SUKE...
IT CERTAINLY SHOWS ALL THE SIGNS OF A GAS EXPLOSION...
...FIRE-FIGHTERS REPORT THAT NOTHING WAS OUT OF THE ORDINARY IN THE APARTMENT WHERE THE FIRE STARTED, AND THE OCCUPANT WAS APPARENTLY ABSENT...

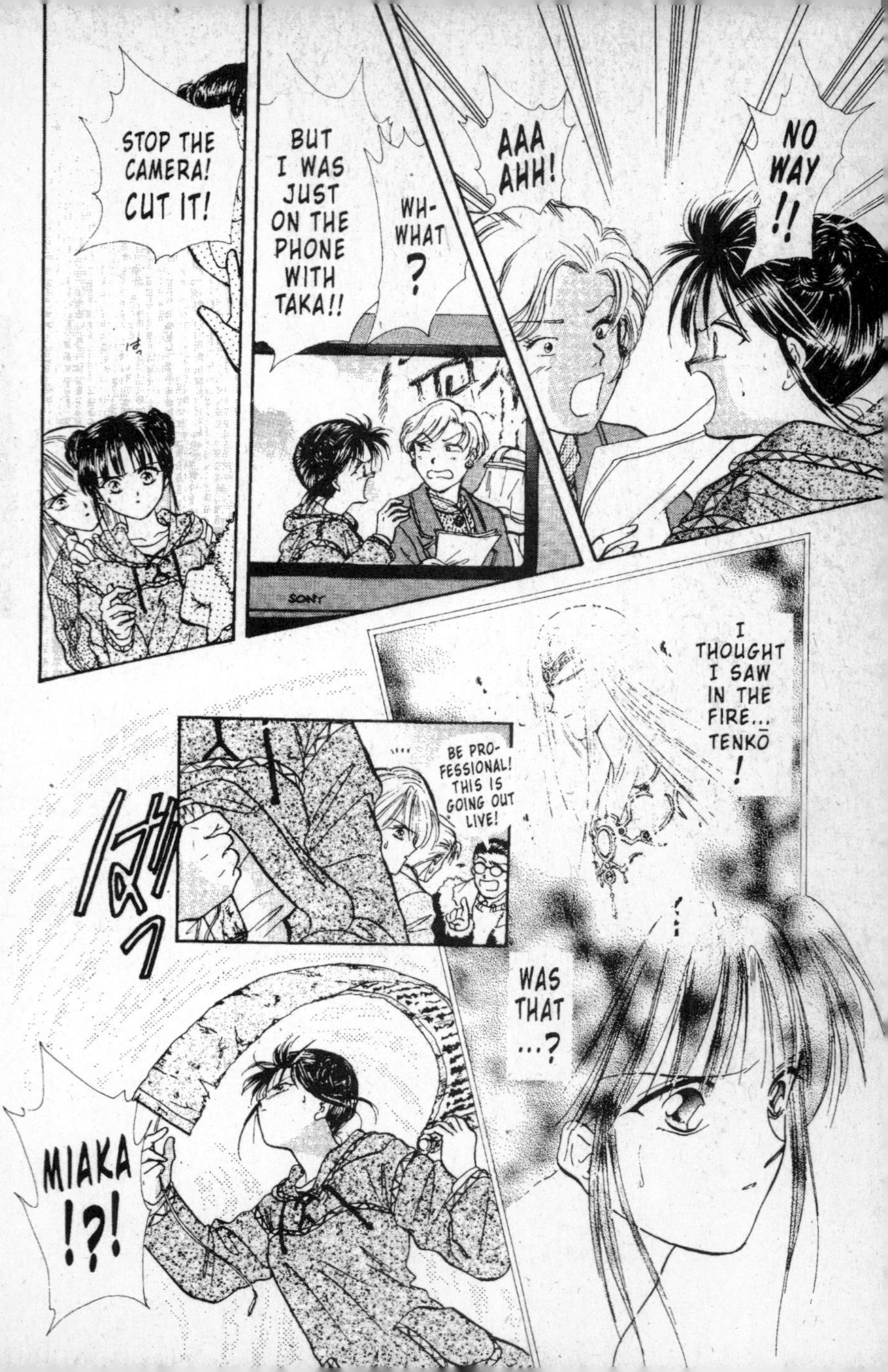
NO WAY !!
AAA AHH!
WH-WHAT ?
BUT I WAS JUST ON THE PHONE WITH TAKA!!
STOP THE CAMERA! CUT IT!
SONY
I THOUGHT I SAW IN THE FIRE... TENKŌ!
...
WAS THAT ...?
...
BE PRO-FESSIONAL! THIS IS GOING OUT LIVE!
MIAKA !?!

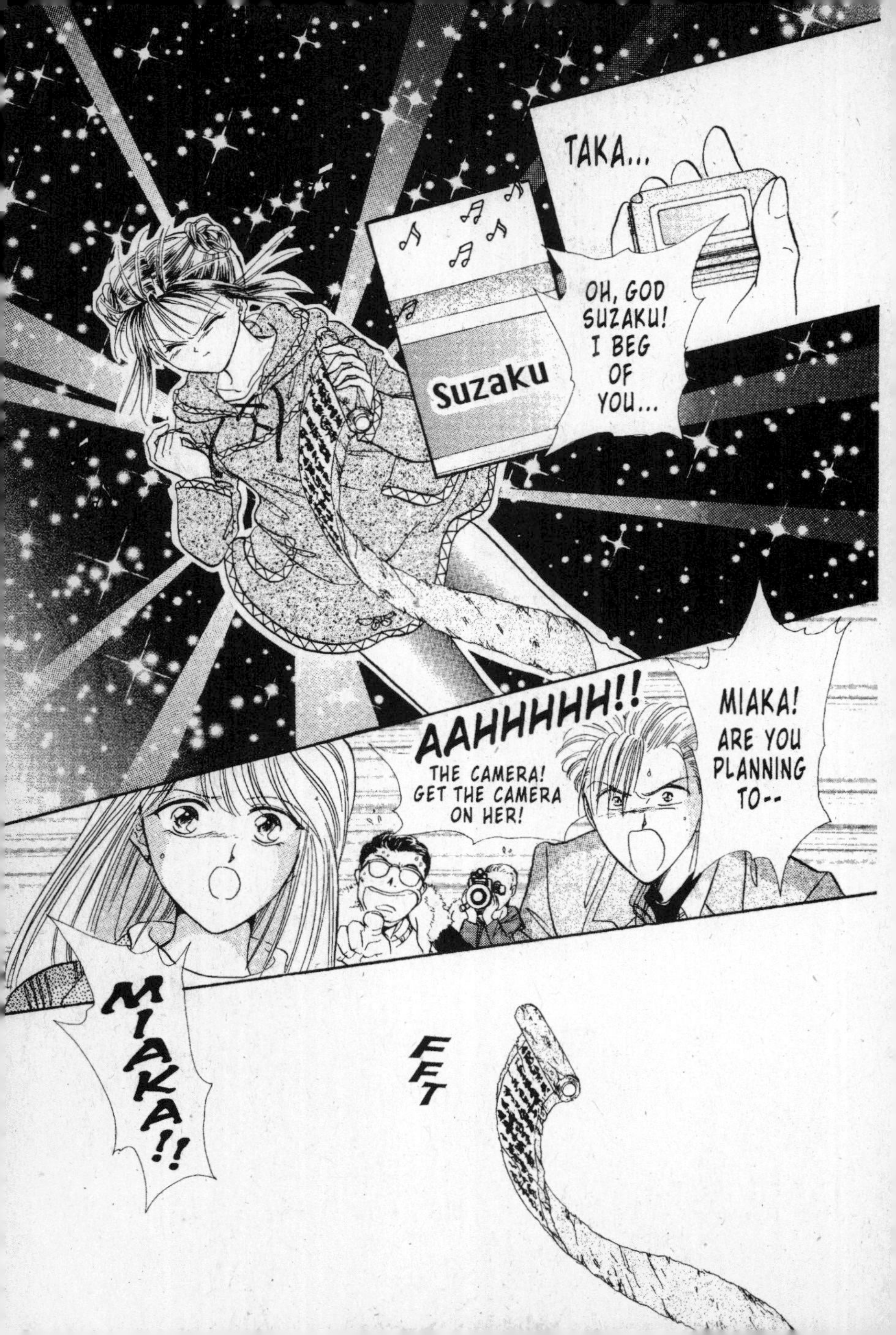

TAKA...
OH, GOD SUZAKU! I BEG OF YOU...
Suzaku
MIAKA! ARE YOU PLANNING TO--
AAHHHHH!!
THE CAMERA! GET THE CAMERA ON HER!
FFT
MIAKA!!

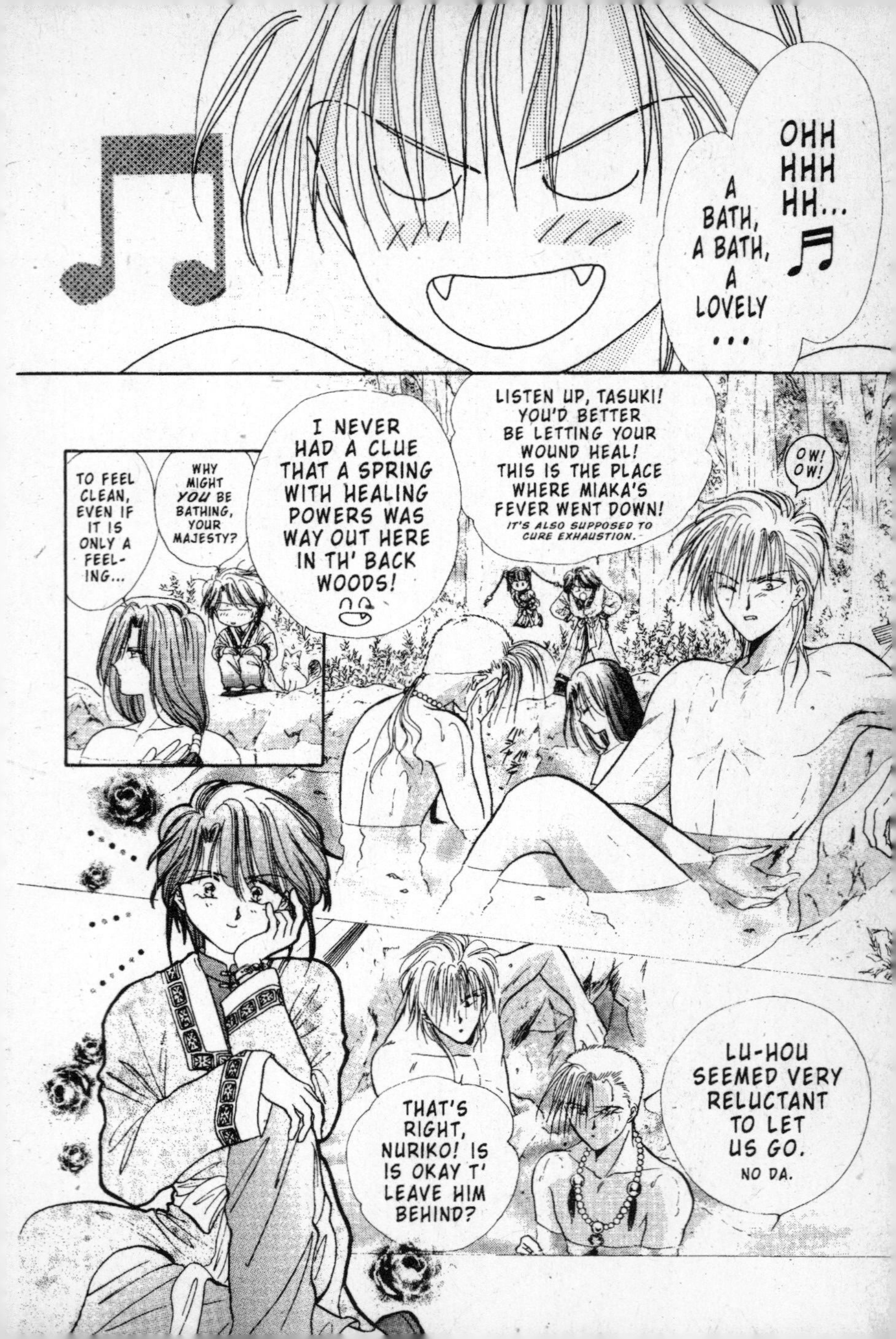
OHHHHHHH...
A BATH, A BATH, A LOVELY ...
OW! OW!
LISTEN UP, TASUKI! YOU'D BETTER BE LETTING YOUR WOUND HEAL! THIS IS THE PLACE WHERE MIAKA'S FEVER WENT DOWN!
IT'S ALSO SUPPOSED TO CURE EXHAUSTION.
I NEVER HAD A CLUE THAT A SPRING WITH HEALING POWERS WAS WAY OUT HERE IN TH' BACK WOODS!
WHY MIGHT YOU BE BATHING, YOUR MAJESTY?
TO FEEL CLEAN, EVEN IF IT IS ONLY A FEEL-ING...
LU-HOU SEEMED VERY RELUCTANT TO LET US GO.
NO DA.
THAT'S RIGHT, NURIKO! IS IS OKAY T' LEAVE HIM BEHIND?

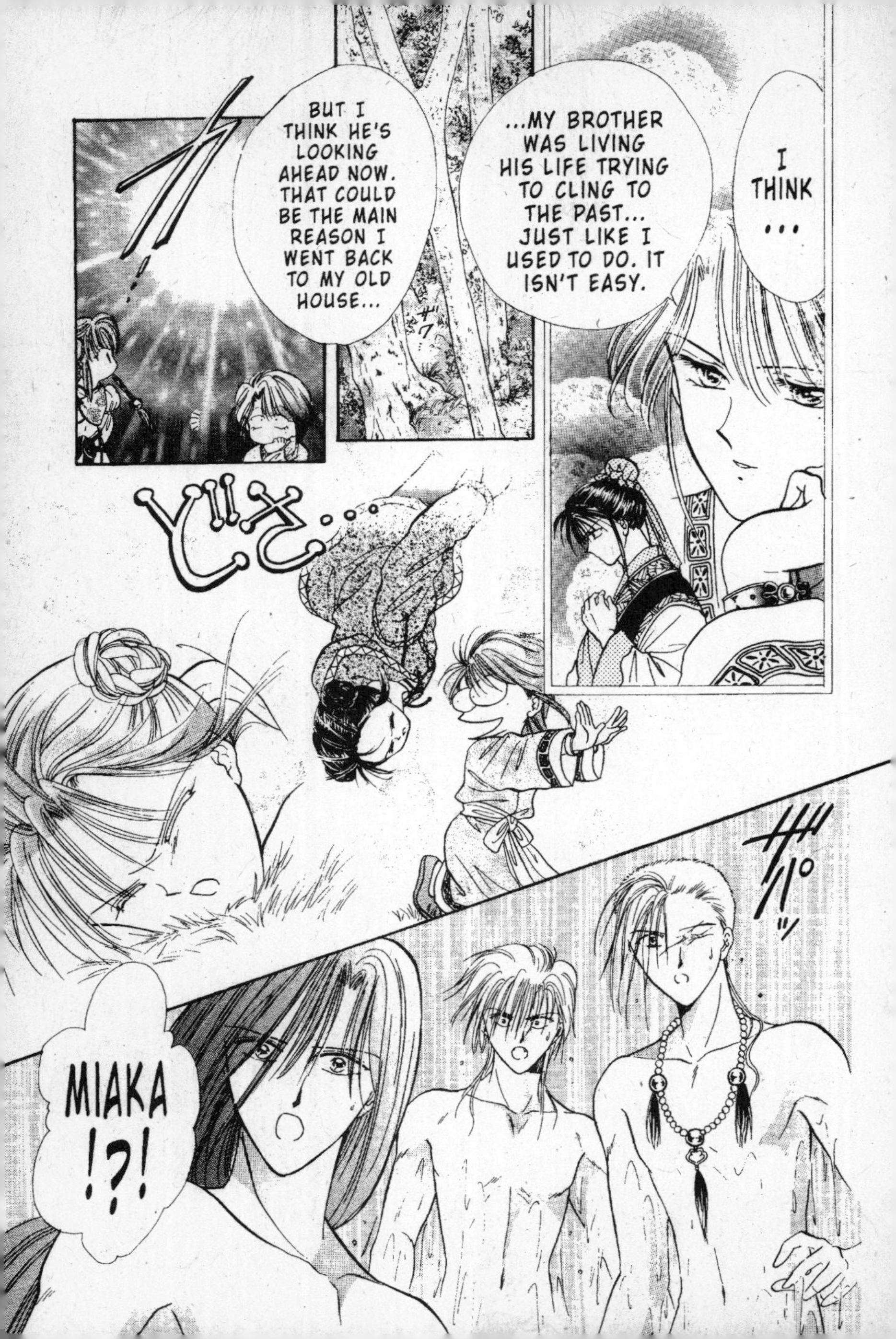

I THINK...
...MY BROTHER WAS LIVING HIS LIFE TRYING TO CLING TO THE PAST... JUST LIKE I USED TO DO. IT ISN'T EASY.
BUT I THINK HE'S LOOKING AHEAD NOW. THAT COULD BE THE MAIN REASON I WENT BACK TO MY OLD HOUSE...
どさ…
ザパッ
MIAKA !?!

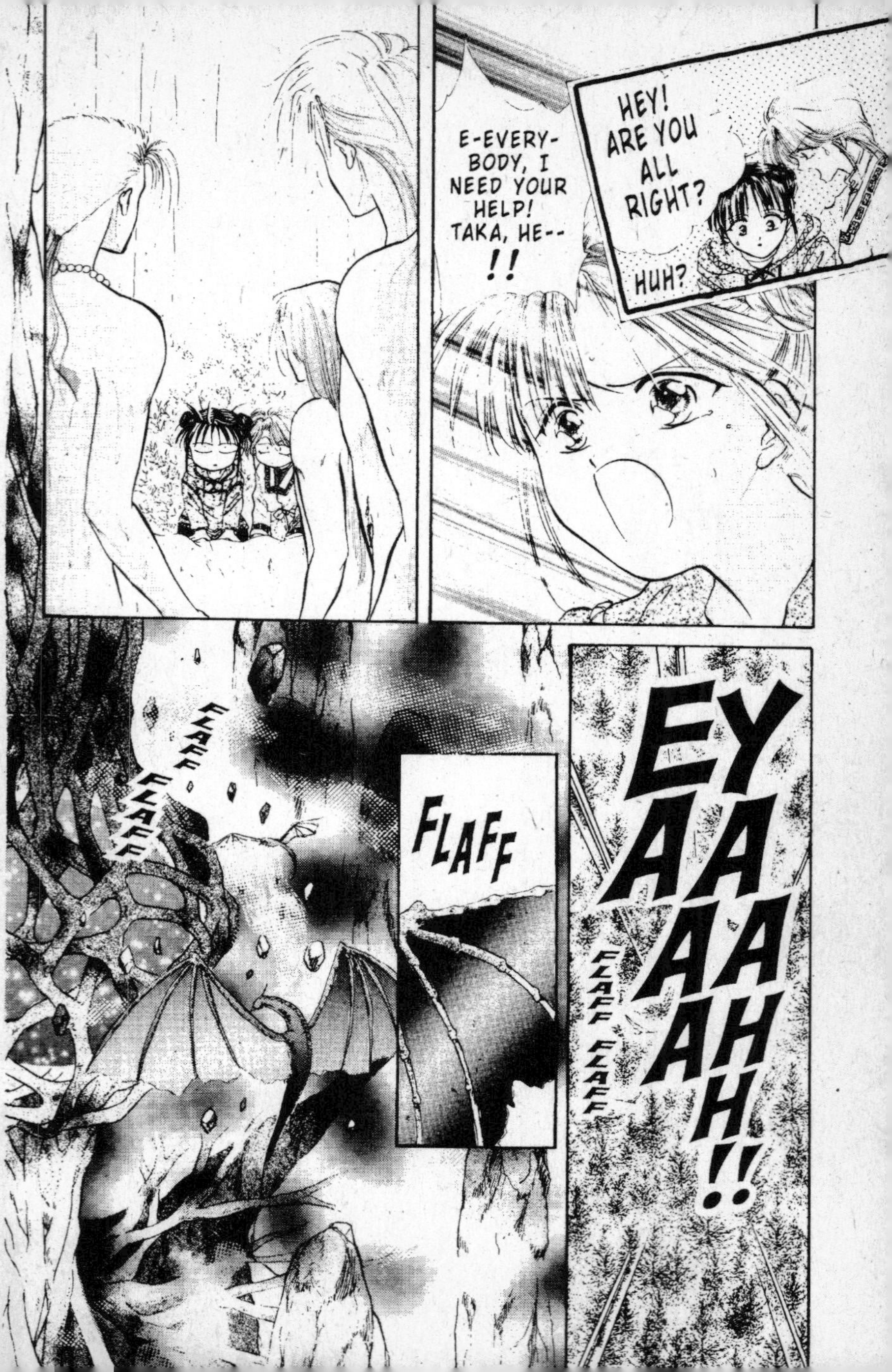
HEY! ARE YOU ALL RIGHT?
HUH?
E-EVERY-BODY, I NEED YOUR HELP! TAKA, HE--
!!
EYAAAAAAHH!!
FLAFF FLAFF
FLAFF
FLAFF FLAFF FLAFF

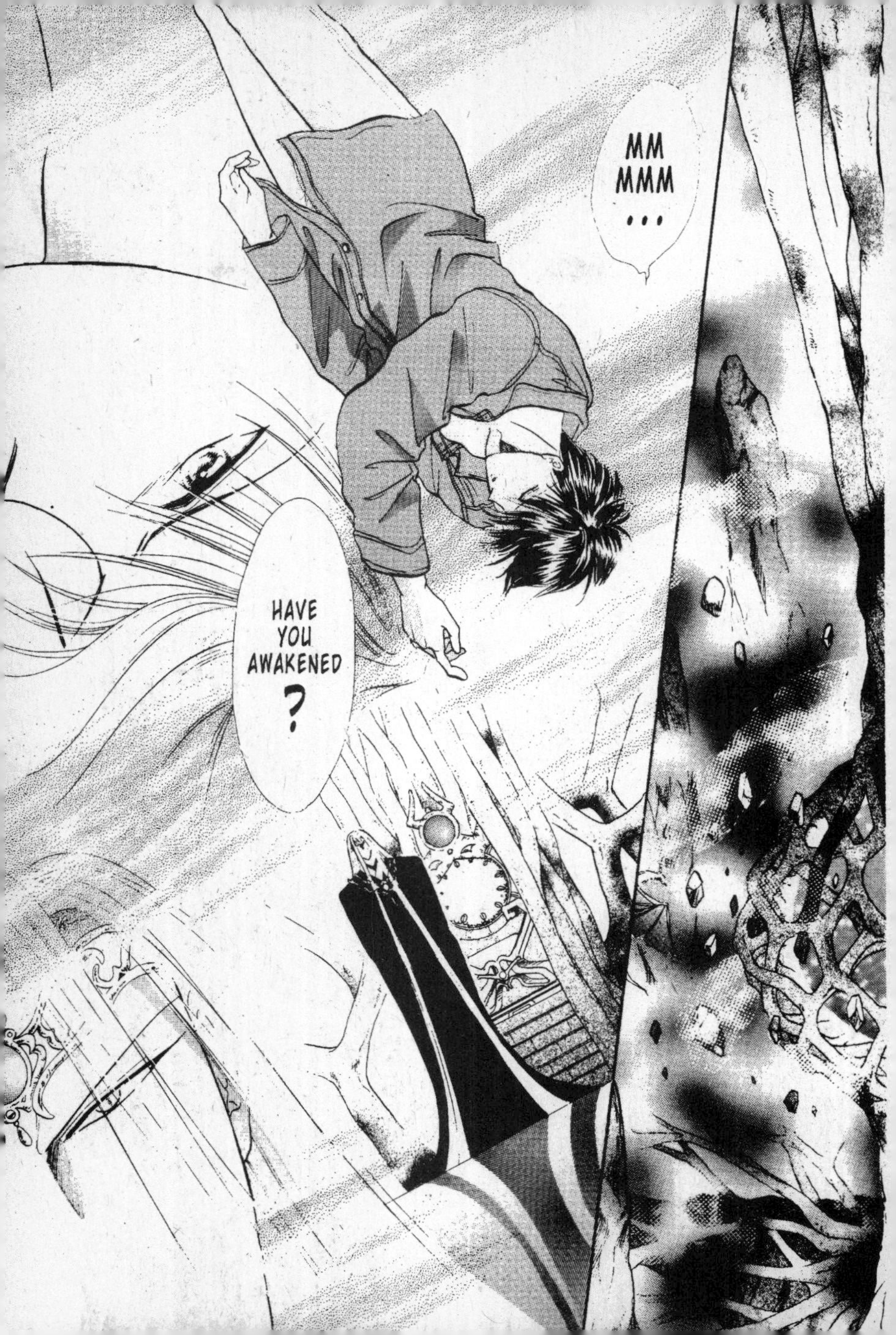
MM MMM...
HAVE YOU AWAKENED?

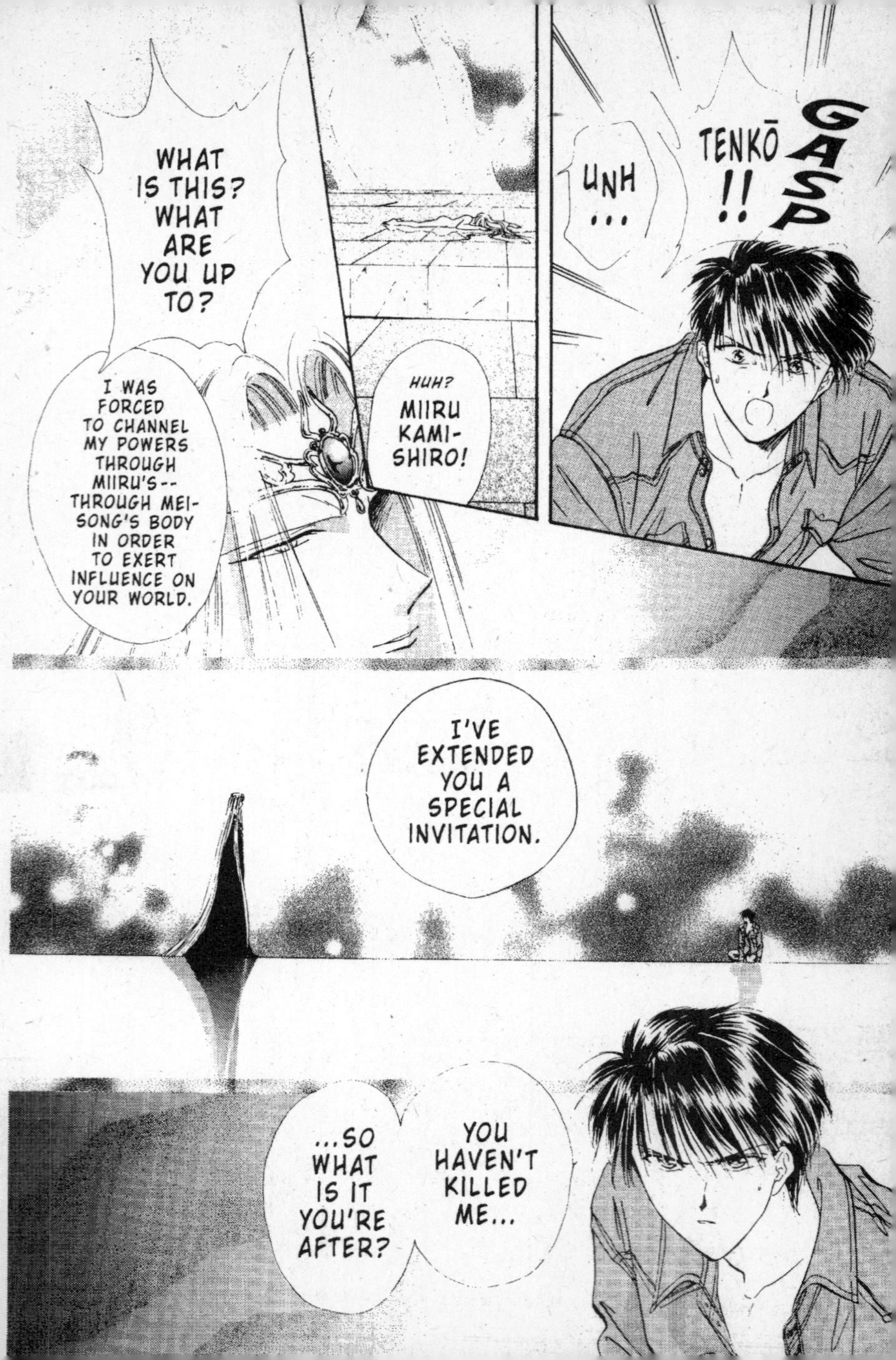
GASP
TENKŌ!!
UNH...
HUH? MIIRU KAMI-SHIRO!
WHAT IS THIS? WHAT ARE YOU UP TO?
I WAS FORCED TO CHANNEL MY POWERS THROUGH MIIRU'S-- THROUGH MEI-SONG'S BODY IN ORDER TO EXERT INFLUENCE ON YOUR WORLD.
I'VE EXTENDED YOU A SPECIAL INVITATION.
YOU HAVEN'T KILLED ME...
...SO WHAT IS IT YOU'RE AFTER?

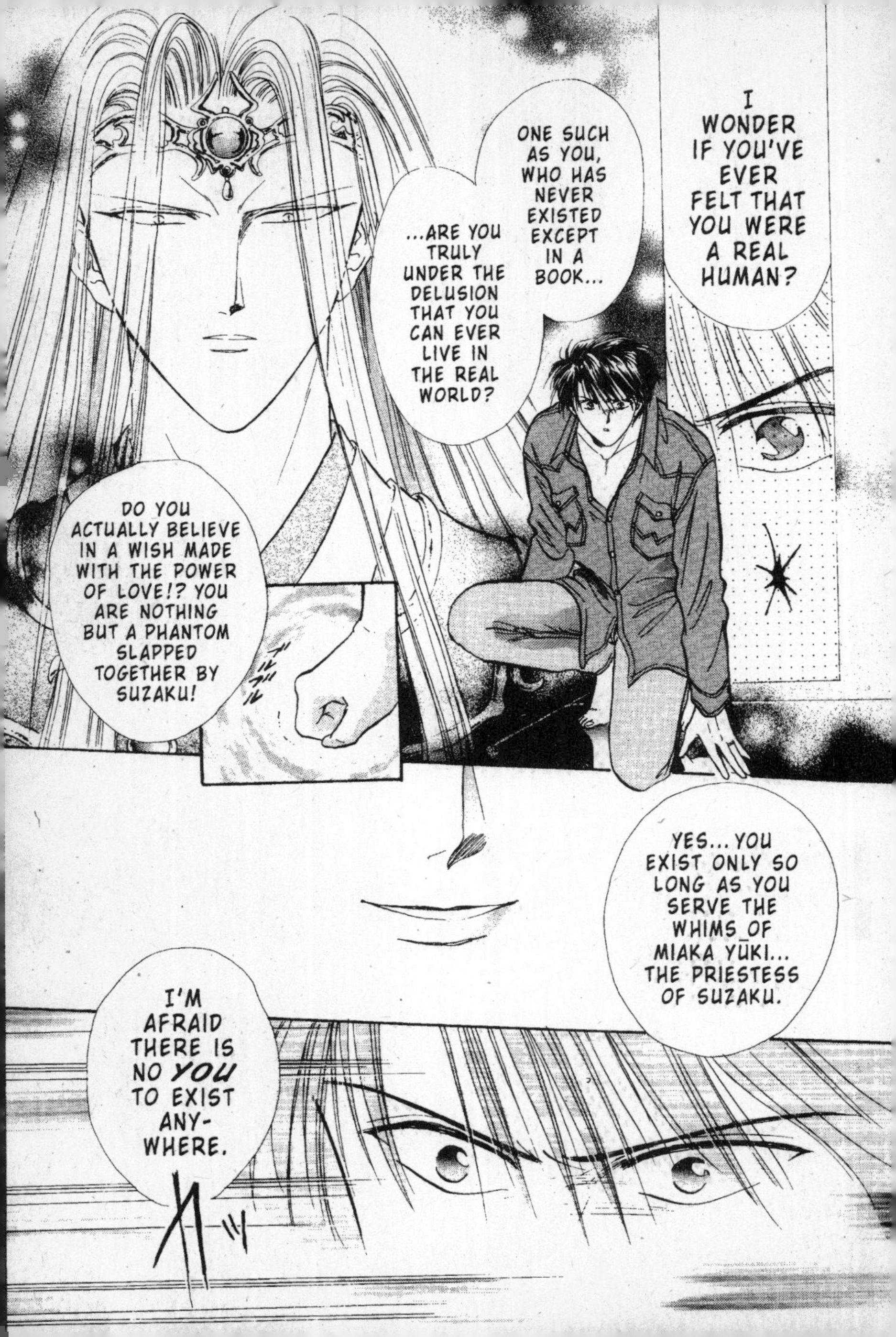
I WONDER IF YOU'VE EVER FELT THAT YOU WERE A REAL HUMAN?
ONE SUCH AS YOU, WHO HAS NEVER EXISTED EXCEPT IN A BOOK...
...ARE YOU TRULY UNDER THE DELUSION THAT YOU CAN EVER LIVE IN THE REAL WORLD?
DO YOU ACTUALLY BELIEVE IN A WISH MADE WITH THE POWER OF LOVE!? YOU ARE NOTHING BUT A PHANTOM SLAPPED TOGETHER BY SUZAKU!
YES... YOU EXIST ONLY SO LONG AS YOU SERVE THE WHIMS OF MIAKA YŪKI... THE PRIESTESS OF SUZAKU.
I'M AFRAID THERE IS NO *YOU* TO EXIST ANYWHERE.

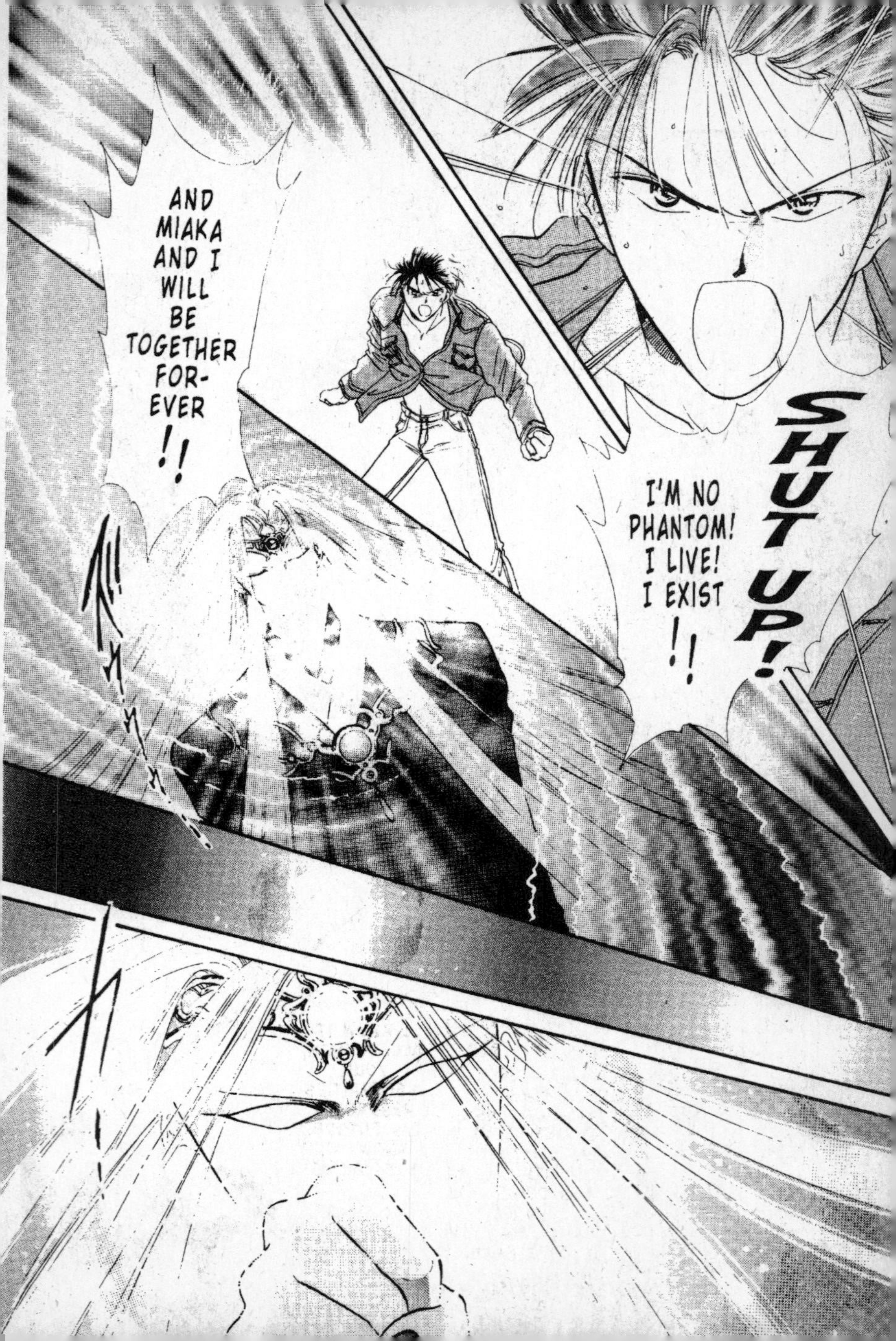
SHUT UP!
I'M NO PHANTOM! I LIVE! I EXIST!!
AND MIAKA AND I WILL BE TOGETHER FOR-EVER!!

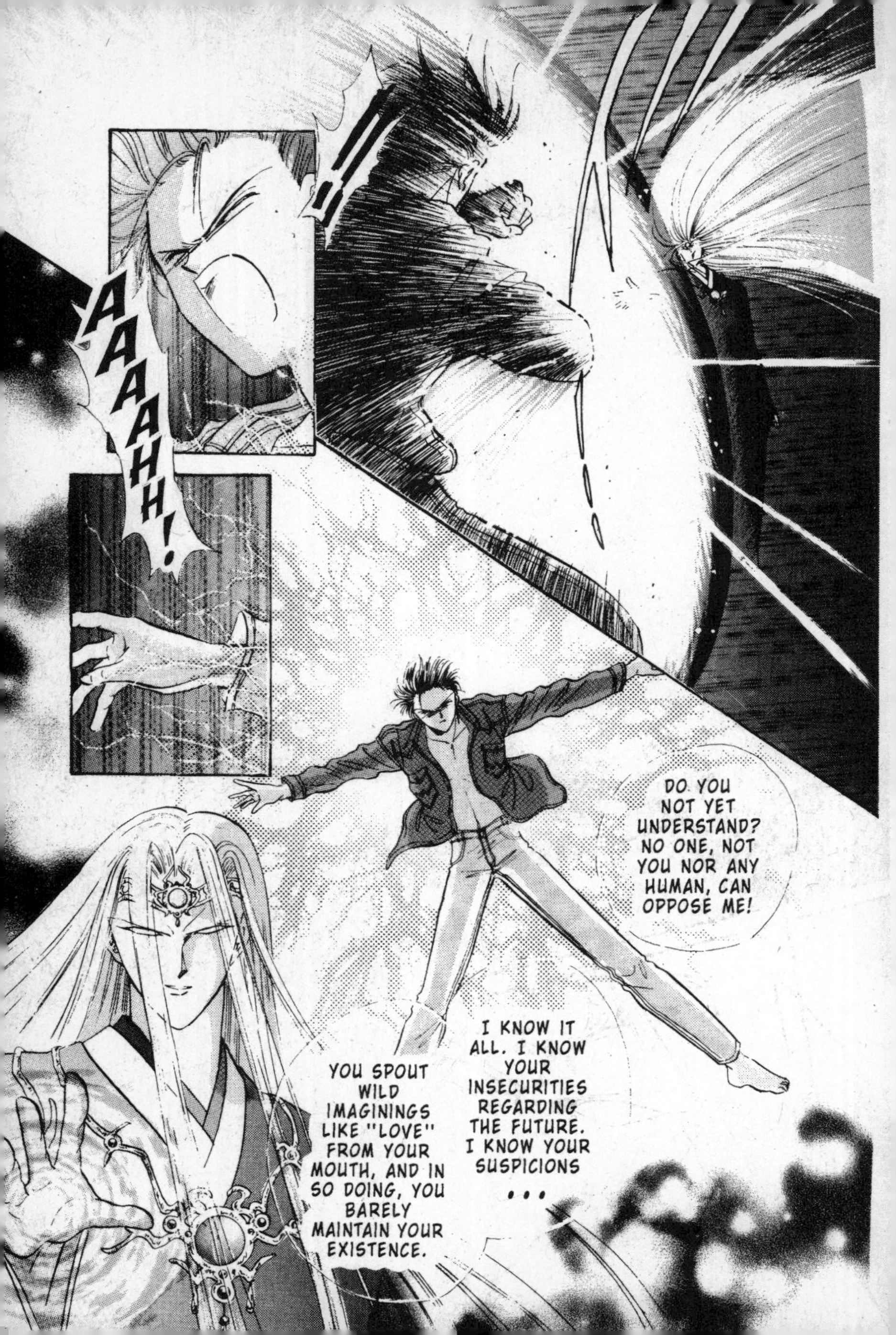
AAAAHH!
DO YOU NOT YET UNDERSTAND? NO ONE, NOT YOU NOR ANY HUMAN, CAN OPPOSE ME!
I KNOW IT ALL. I KNOW YOUR INSECURITIES REGARDING THE FUTURE. I KNOW YOUR SUSPICIONS ...
YOU SPOUT WILD IMAGININGS LIKE "LOVE" FROM YOUR MOUTH, AND IN SO DOING, YOU BARELY MAINTAIN YOUR EXISTENCE.

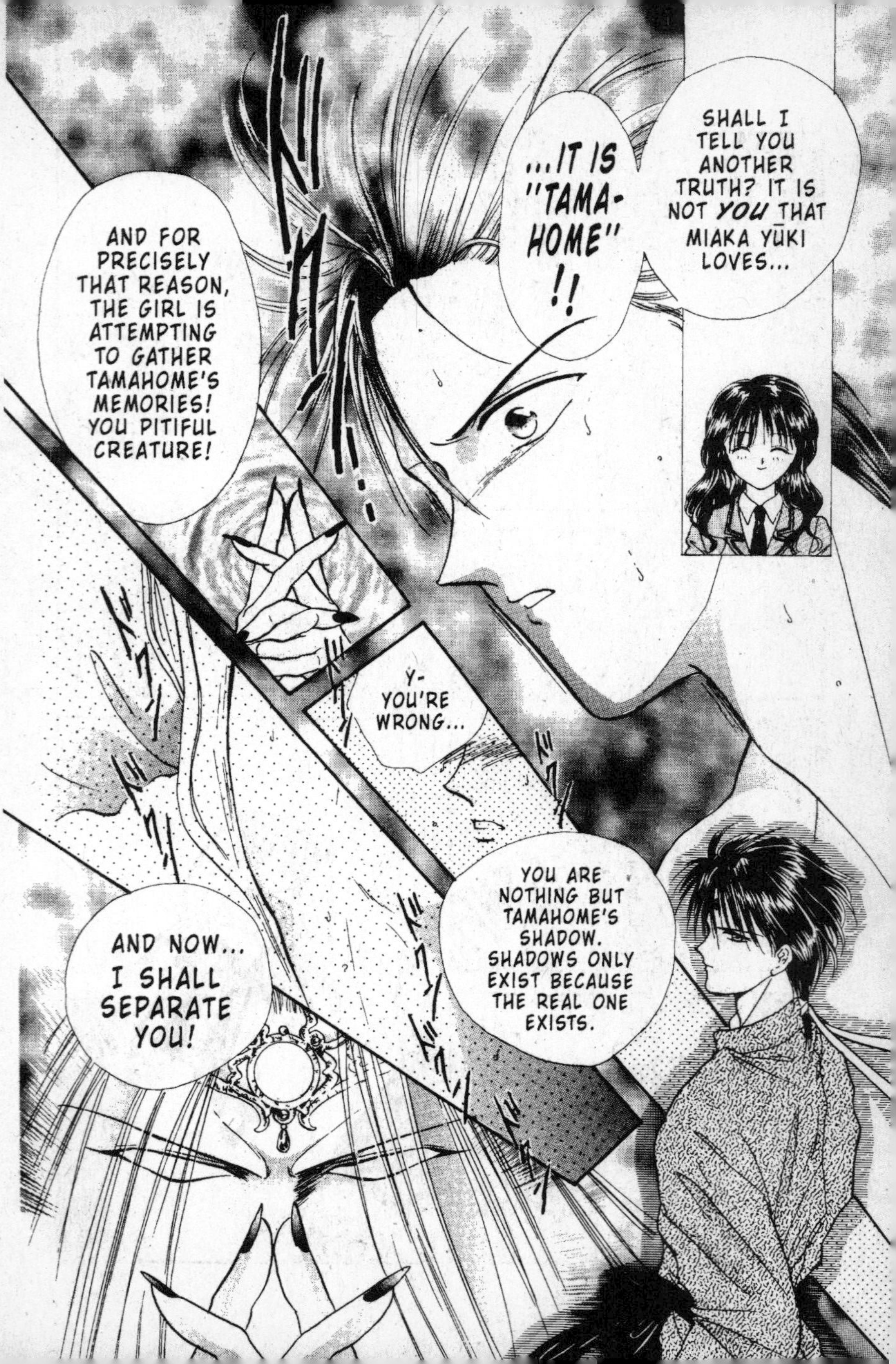
SHALL I TELL YOU ANOTHER TRUTH? IT IS NOT *YOU* THAT MIAKA YŪKI LOVES...
...IT IS "TAMAHOME"!!
AND FOR PRECISELY THAT REASON, THE GIRL IS ATTEMPTING TO GATHER TAMAHOME'S MEMORIES! YOU PITIFUL CREATURE!
Y-YOU'RE WRONG...
YOU ARE NOTHING BUT TAMAHOME'S SHADOW. SHADOWS ONLY EXIST BECAUSE THE REAL ONE EXISTS.
AND NOW... I SHALL SEPARATE YOU!

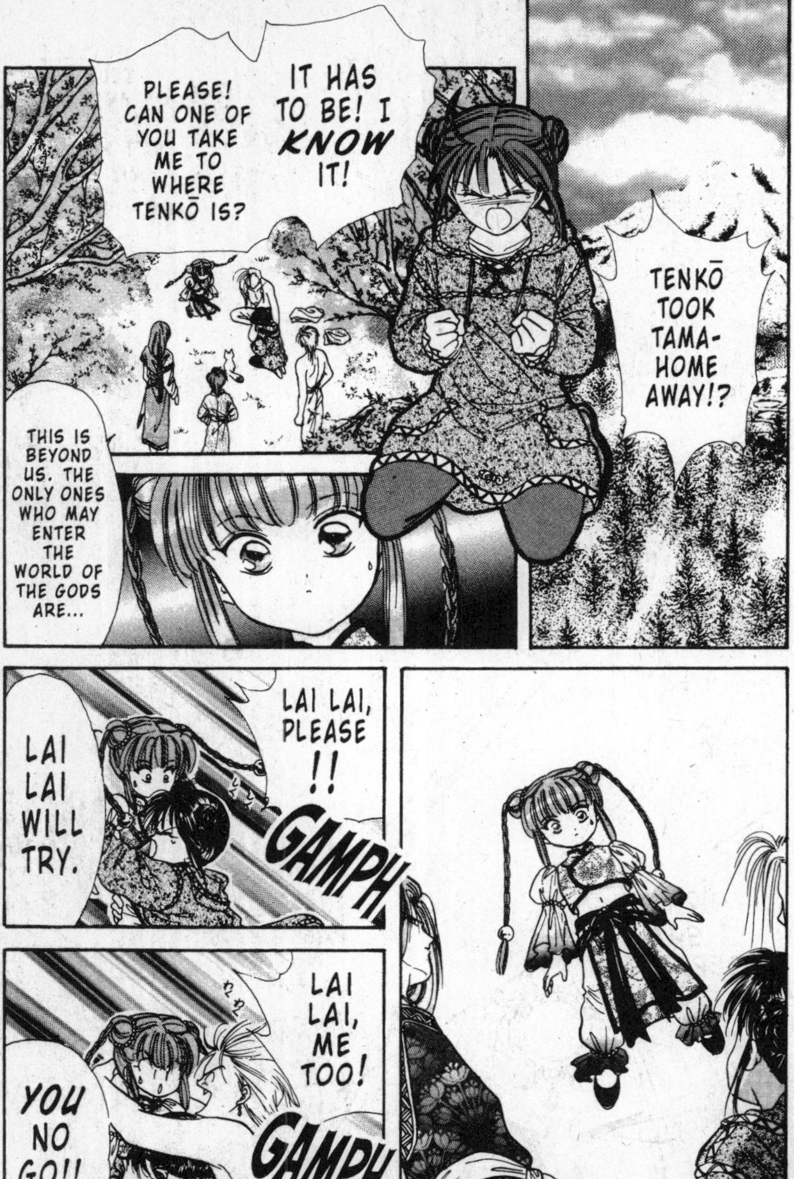
TENKŌ TOOK TAMA-HOME AWAY!?
IT HAS TO BE! I *KNOW* IT!
PLEASE! CAN ONE OF YOU TAKE ME TO WHERE TENKŌ IS?
THIS IS BEYOND US. THE ONLY ONES WHO MAY ENTER THE WORLD OF THE GODS ARE...
LAI LAI, PLEASE!!
LAI LAI WILL TRY.
GAMPH
LAI LAI, ME TOO!
YOU NO GO!!
GAMPH

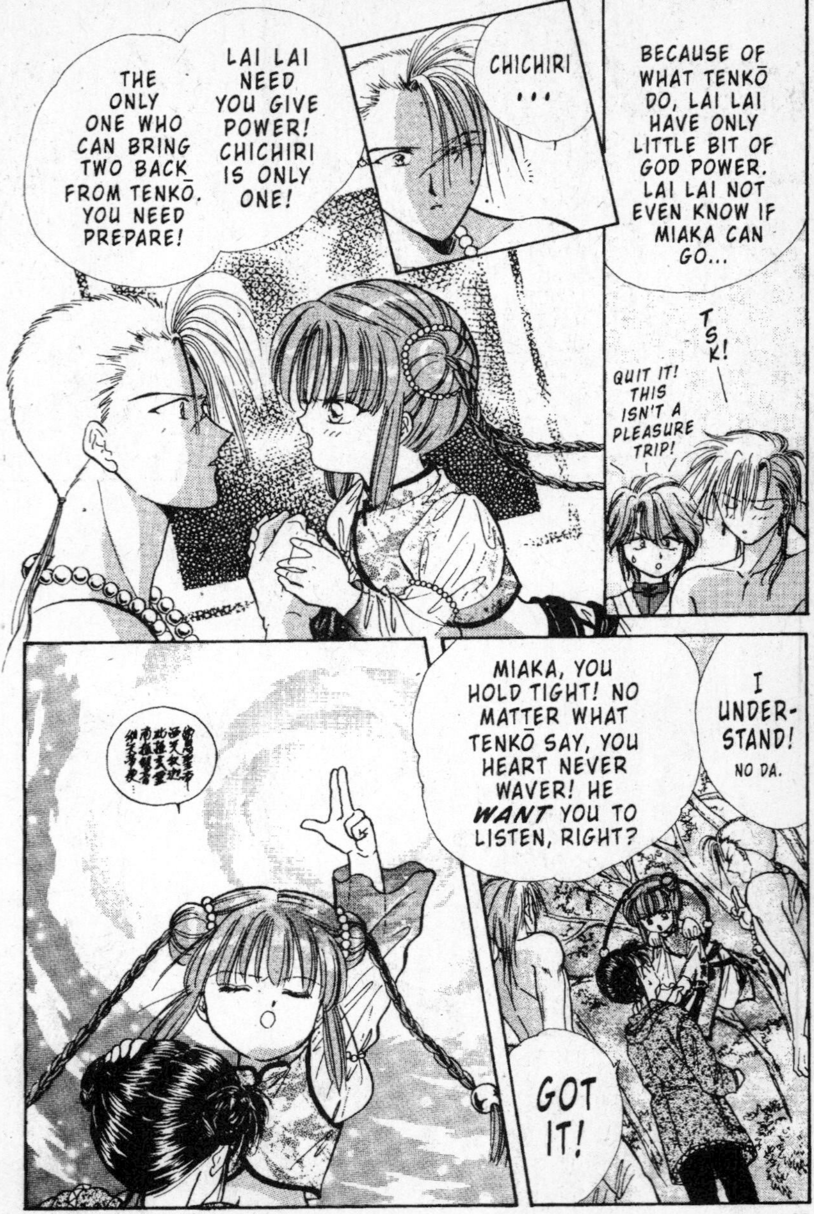
BECAUSE OF WHAT TENKŌ DO, LAI LAI HAVE ONLY LITTLE BIT OF GOD POWER. LAI LAI NOT EVEN KNOW IF MIAKA CAN GO...
TSK!
QUIT IT! THIS ISN'T A PLEASURE TRIP!
CHICHIRI ...
LAI LAI NEED YOU GIVE POWER! CHICHIRI IS ONLY ONE!
THE ONLY ONE WHO CAN BRING TWO BACK FROM TENKŌ. YOU NEED PREPARE!
I UNDER-STAND! NO DA.
MIAKA, YOU HOLD TIGHT! NO MATTER WHAT TENKŌ SAY, YOU HEART NEVER WAVER! HE WANT YOU TO LISTEN, RIGHT?
GOT IT!

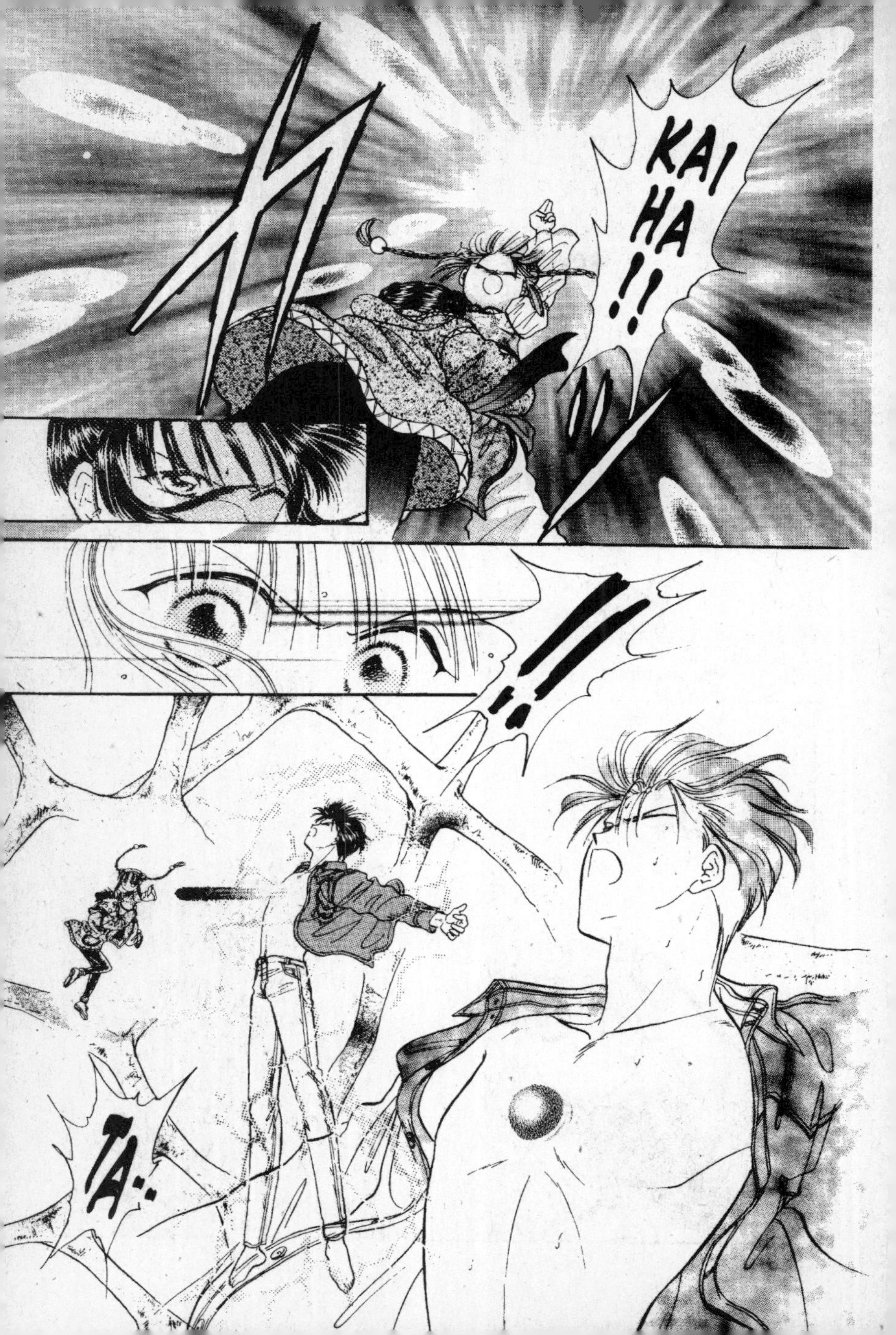
KAI HA!!
!!
TA-..

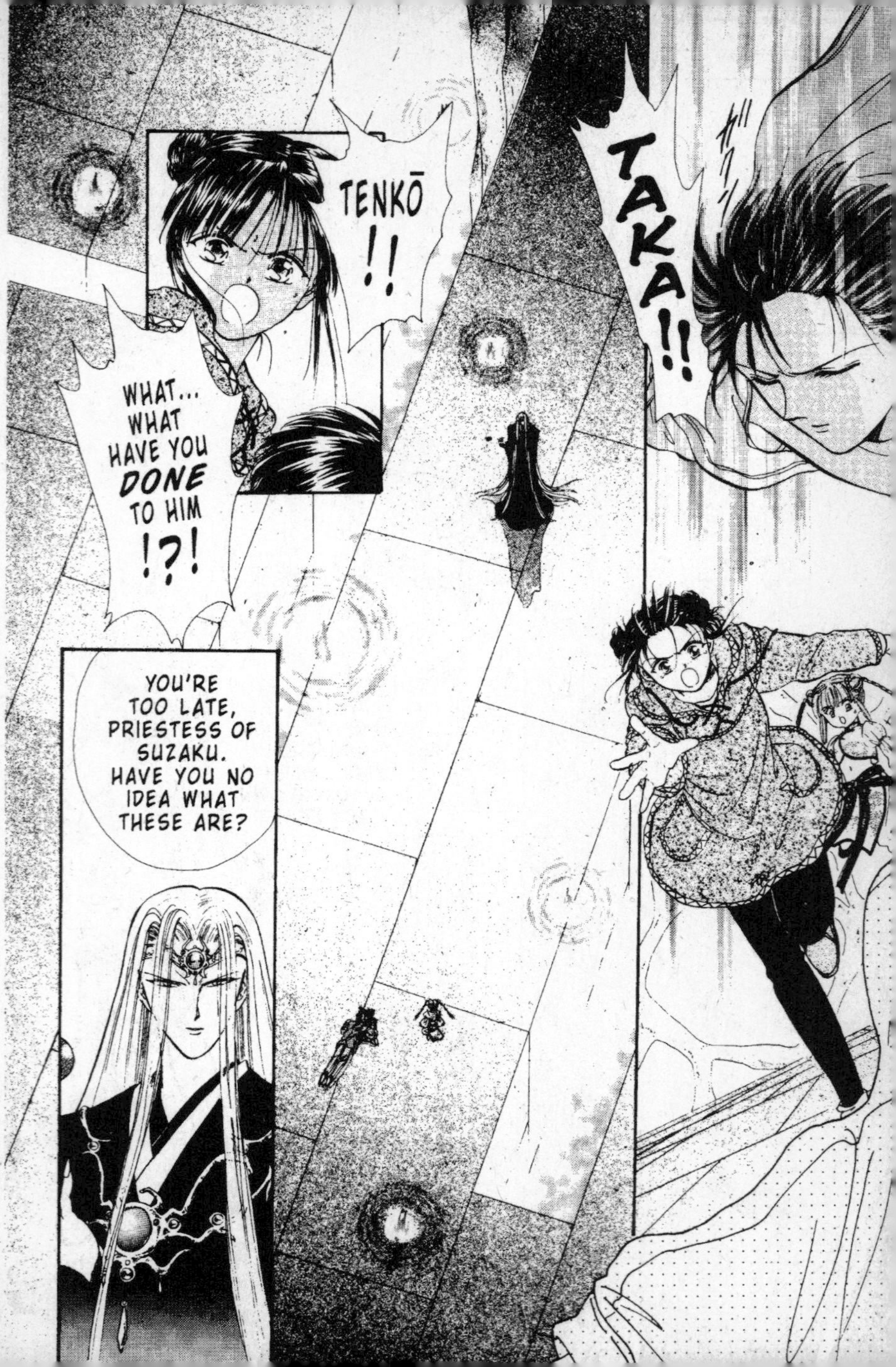
TAKA!!
TENKŌ!!
WHAT... WHAT HAVE YOU DONE TO HIM!?!
YOU'RE TOO LATE, PRIESTESS OF SUZAKU. HAVE YOU NO IDEA WHAT THESE ARE?

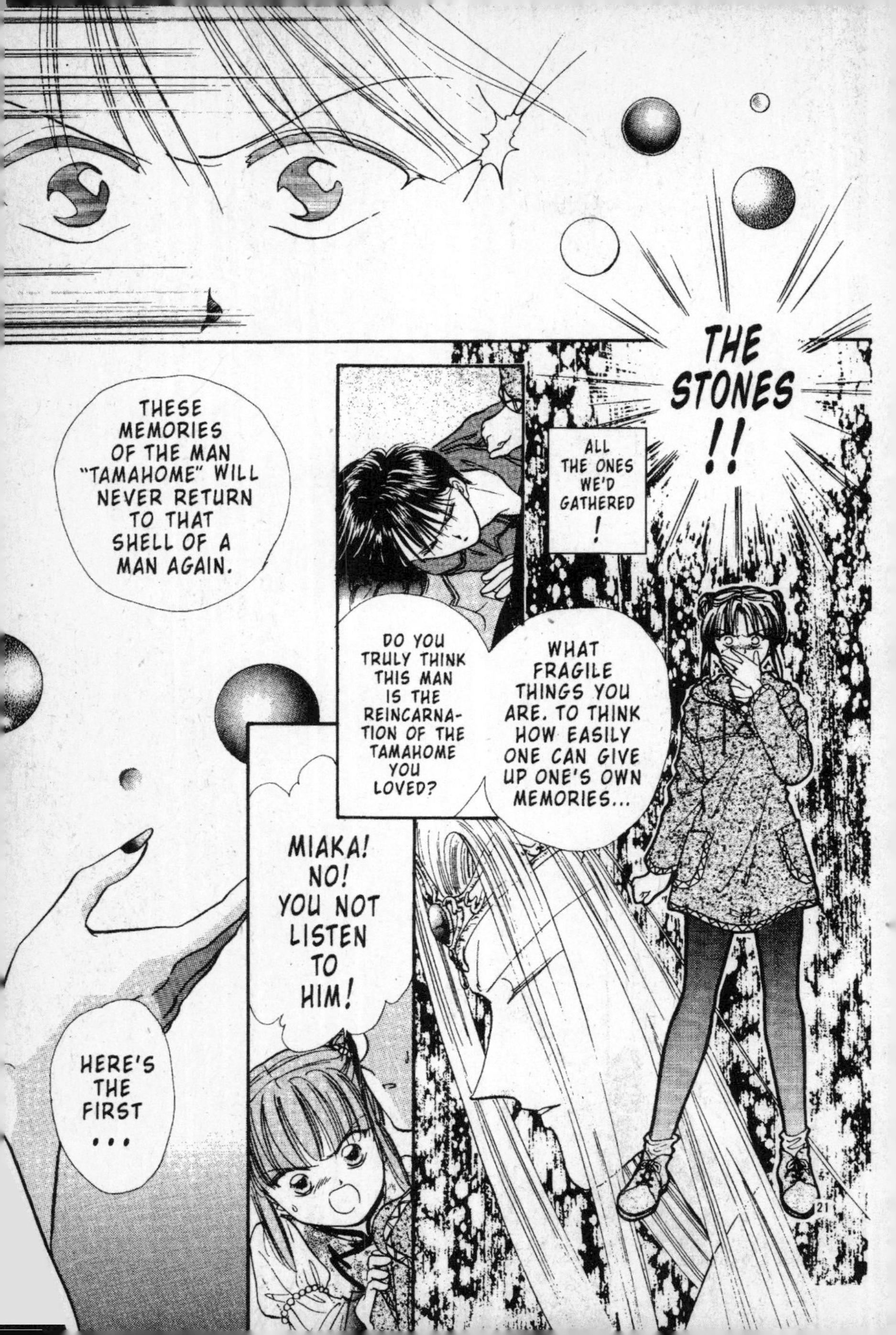
THE STONES !!
ALL THE ONES WE'D GATHERED !
WHAT FRAGILE THINGS YOU ARE. TO THINK HOW EASILY ONE CAN GIVE UP ONE'S OWN MEMORIES...
DO YOU TRULY THINK THIS MAN IS THE REINCARNATION OF THE TAMAHOME YOU LOVED?
MIAKA! NO! YOU NOT LISTEN TO HIM!
THESE MEMORIES OF THE MAN "TAMAHOME" WILL NEVER RETURN TO THAT SHELL OF A MAN AGAIN.
HERE'S THE FIRST ...

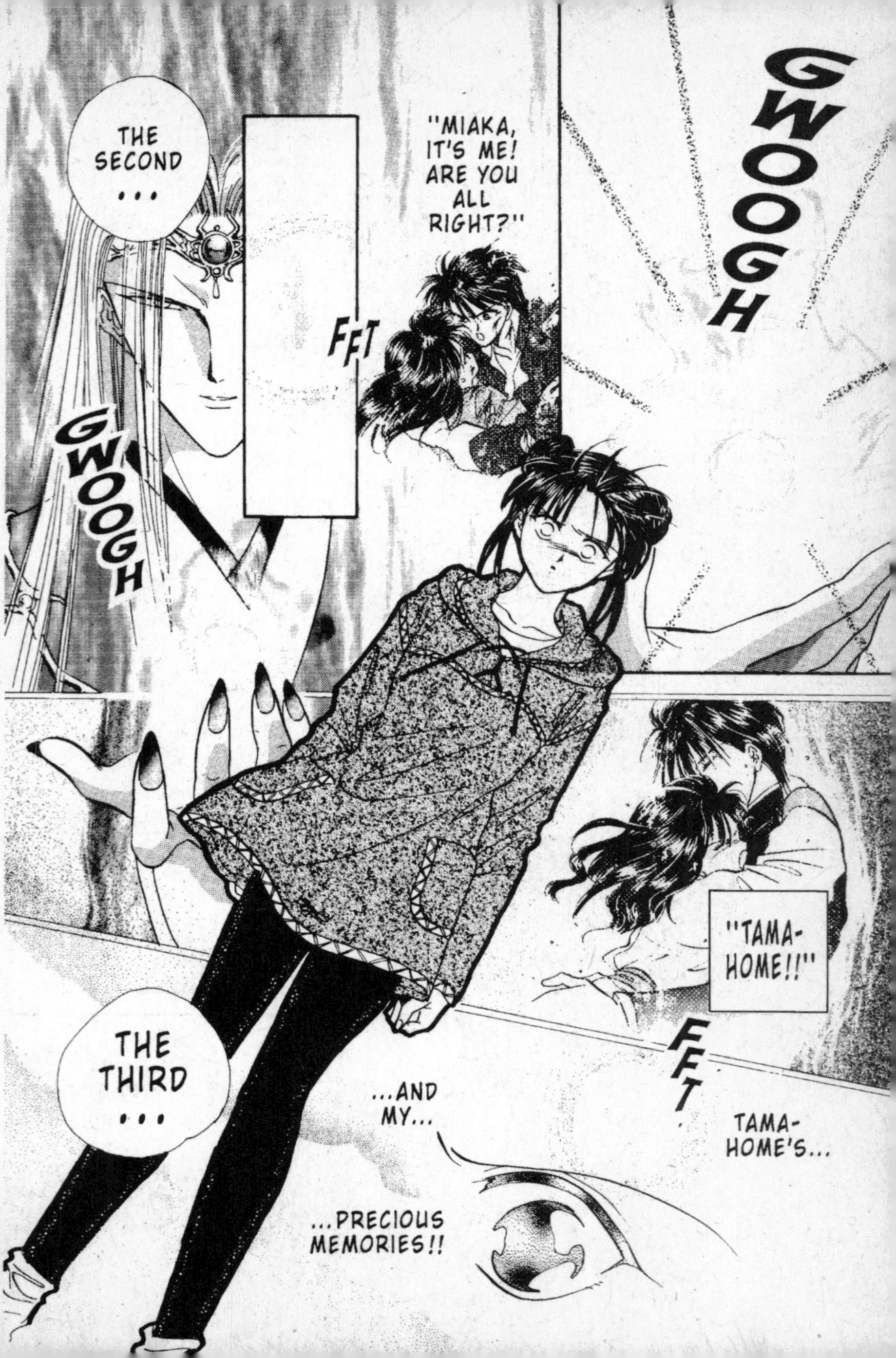
GWOOGH
"MIAKA, IT'S ME! ARE YOU ALL RIGHT?"
FFT
THE SECOND ...
GWOOGH
"TAMA-HOME!!"
FFT
TAMA-HOME'S...
...AND MY...
THE THIRD ...
...PRECIOUS MEMORIES!!

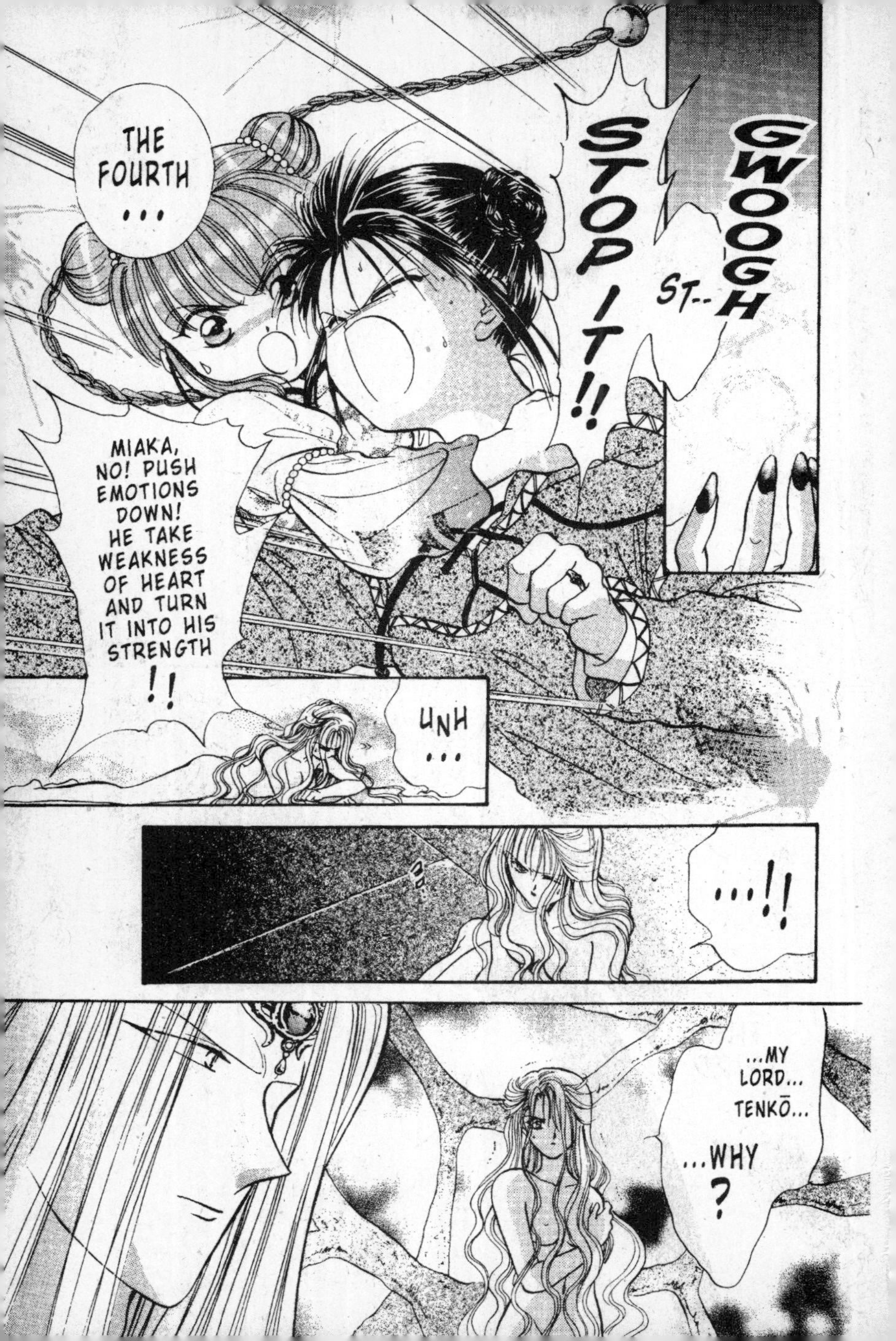
GWOOGH
ST--
STOP IT!!
THE FOURTH ...
MIAKA, NO! PUSH EMOTIONS DOWN! HE TAKE WEAKNESS OF HEART AND TURN IT INTO HIS STRENGTH!!
UNH ...
...!!
...MY LORD... TENKŌ...
...WHY?

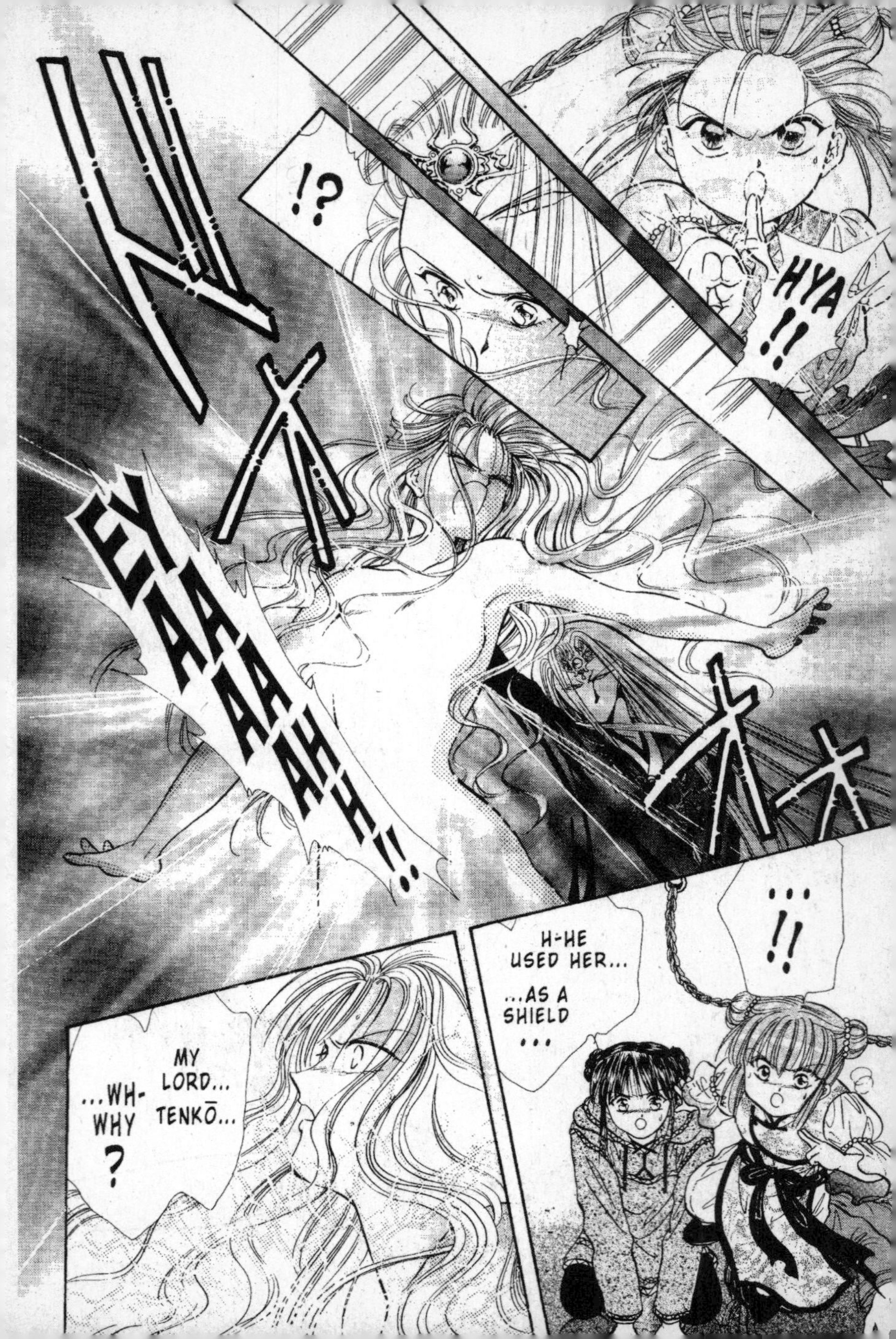
HYA!!
!?
EYAAAAHH!!
...!!
H-HE USED HER...
...AS A SHIELD...
MY LORD... TENKŌ...
...WH-WHY?

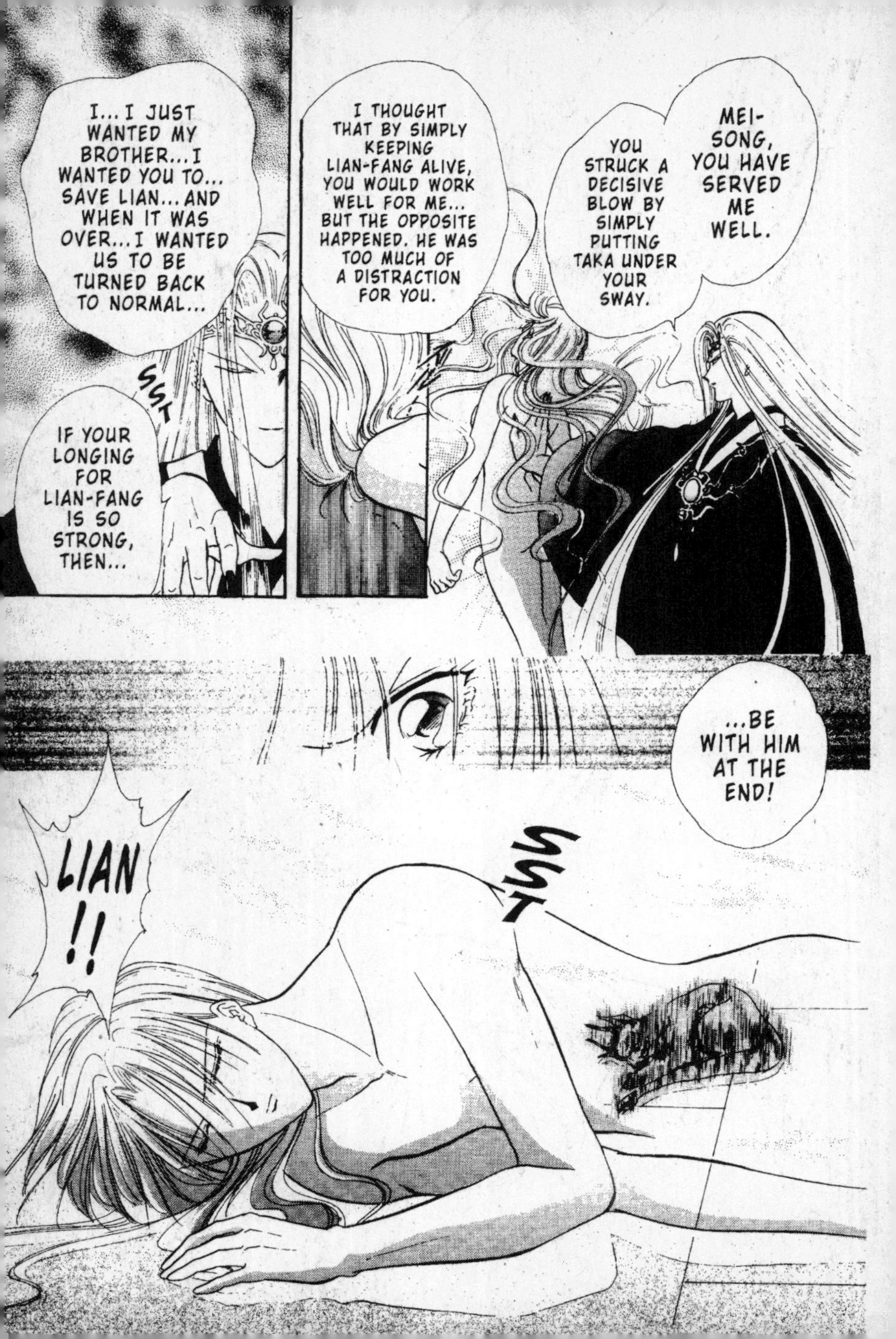
MEI-SONG, YOU HAVE SERVED ME WELL.
YOU STRUCK A DECISIVE BLOW BY SIMPLY PUTTING TAKA UNDER YOUR SWAY.
I THOUGHT THAT BY SIMPLY KEEPING LIAN-FANG ALIVE, YOU WOULD WORK WELL FOR ME... BUT THE OPPOSITE HAPPENED. HE WAS TOO MUCH OF A DISTRACTION FOR YOU.
I... I JUST WANTED MY BROTHER... I WANTED YOU TO... SAVE LIAN... AND WHEN IT WAS OVER... I WANTED US TO BE TURNED BACK TO NORMAL...
SST
IF YOUR LONGING FOR LIAN-FANG IS SO STRONG, THEN...
...BE WITH HIM AT THE END!
SST
LIAN!!

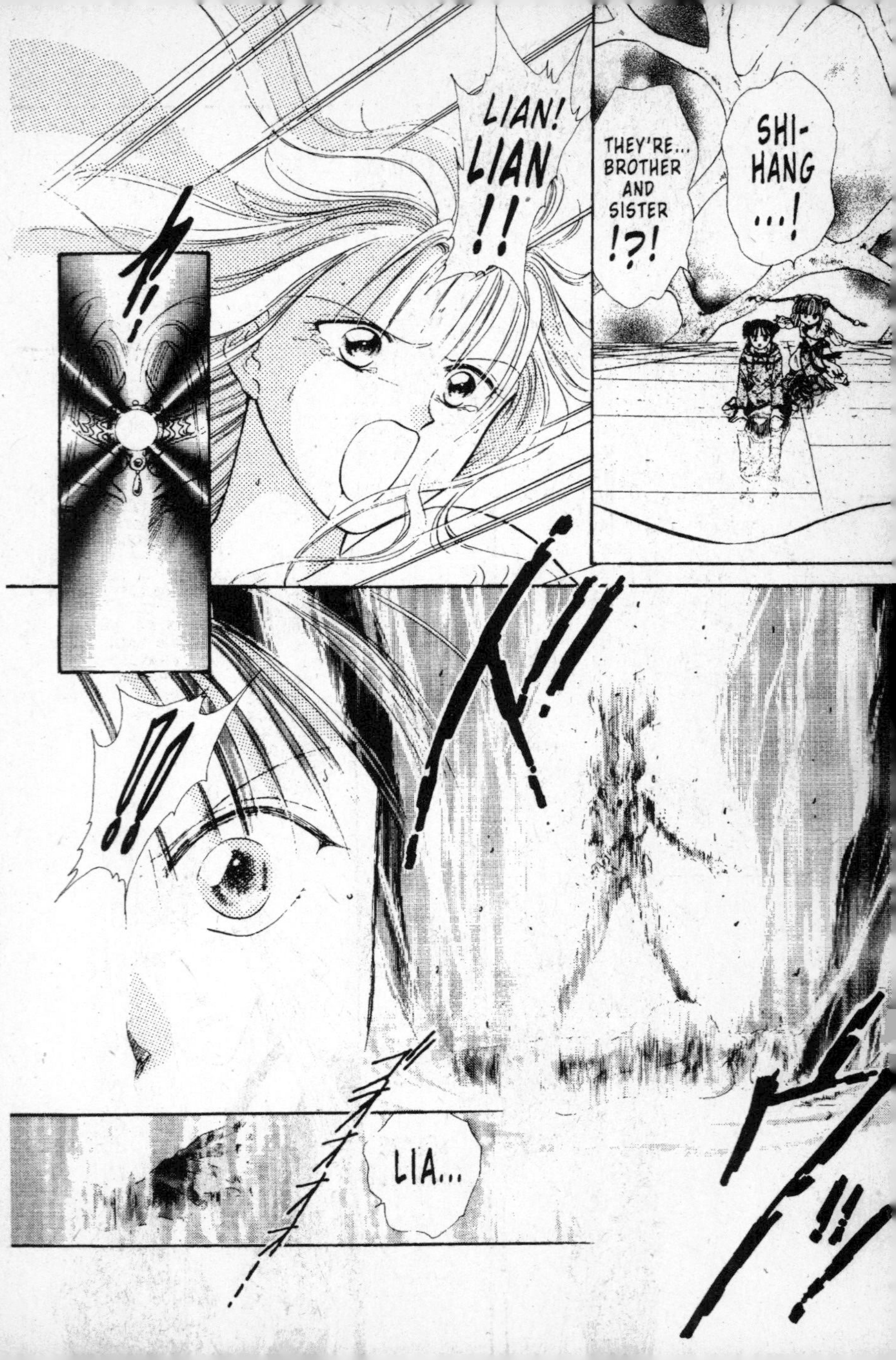
SHI-HANG ...!
THEY'RE... BROTHER AND SISTER !?!
LIAN! LIAN !!
LIA...

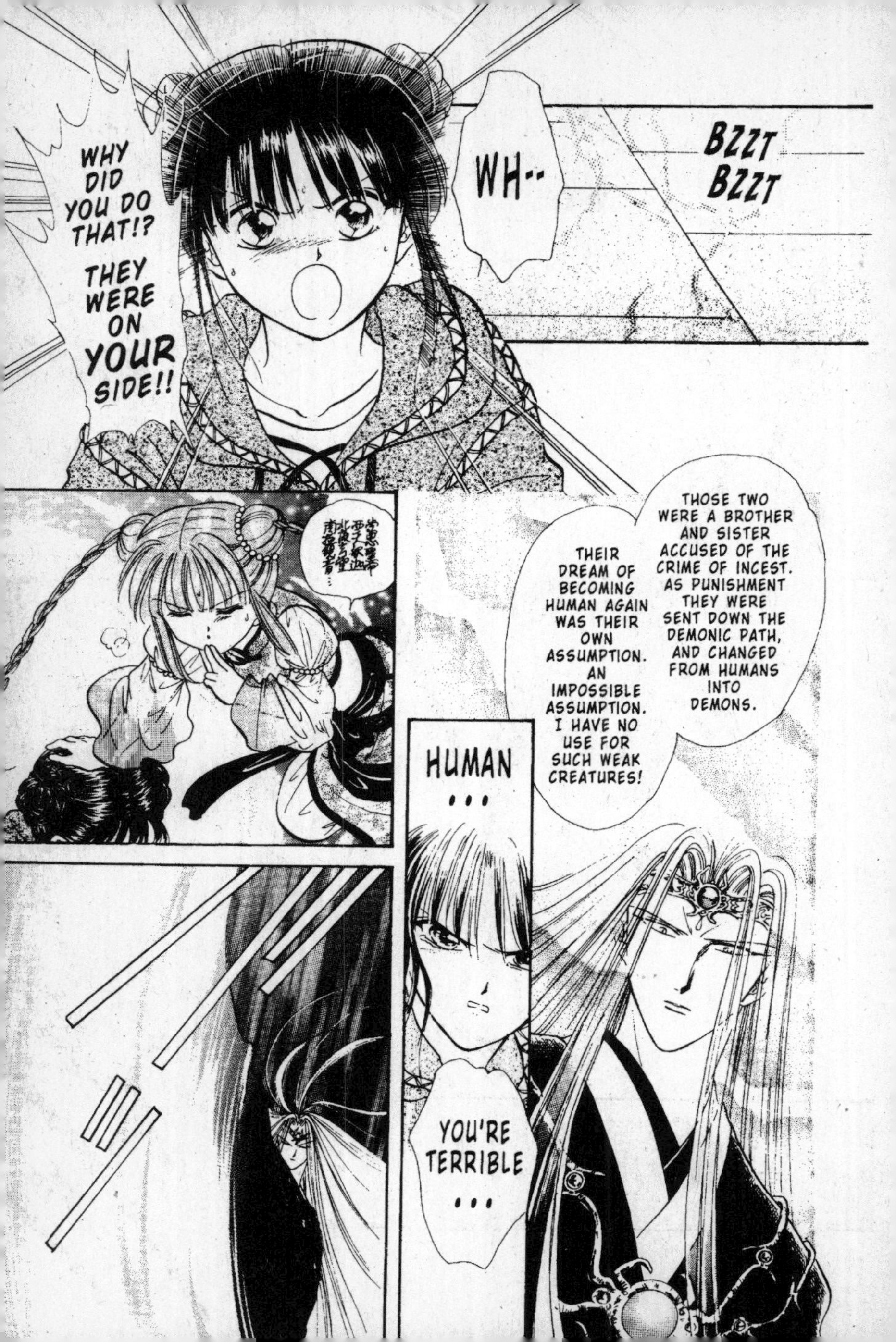
BZZT
BZZT
WH--
WHY DID YOU DO THAT!?
THEY WERE ON YOUR SIDE!!
THOSE TWO WERE A BROTHER AND SISTER ACCUSED OF THE CRIME OF INCEST. AS PUNISHMENT THEY WERE SENT DOWN THE DEMONIC PATH, AND CHANGED FROM HUMANS INTO DEMONS.
THEIR DREAM OF BECOMING HUMAN AGAIN WAS THEIR OWN ASSUMPTION. AN IMPOSSIBLE ASSUMPTION. I HAVE NO USE FOR SUCH WEAK CREATURES!
HUMAN ...
YOU'RE TERRIBLE ...

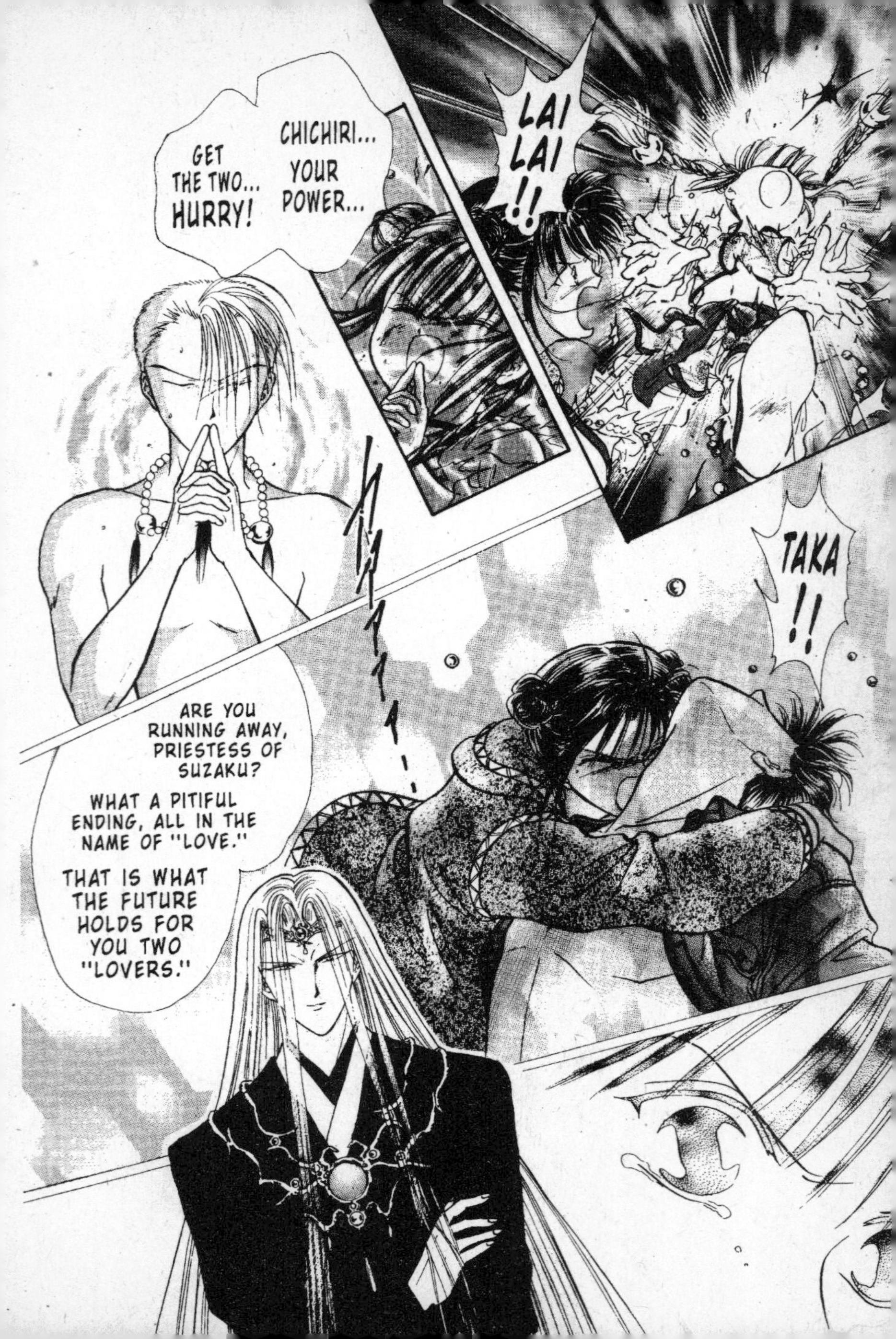
LAI LAI!!
CHICHIRI... YOUR POWER...
GET THE TWO... HURRY!
TAKA!!
ARE YOU RUNNING AWAY, PRIESTESS OF SUZAKU?
WHAT A PITIFUL ENDING, ALL IN THE NAME OF "LOVE."
THAT IS WHAT THE FUTURE HOLDS FOR YOU TWO "LOVERS."

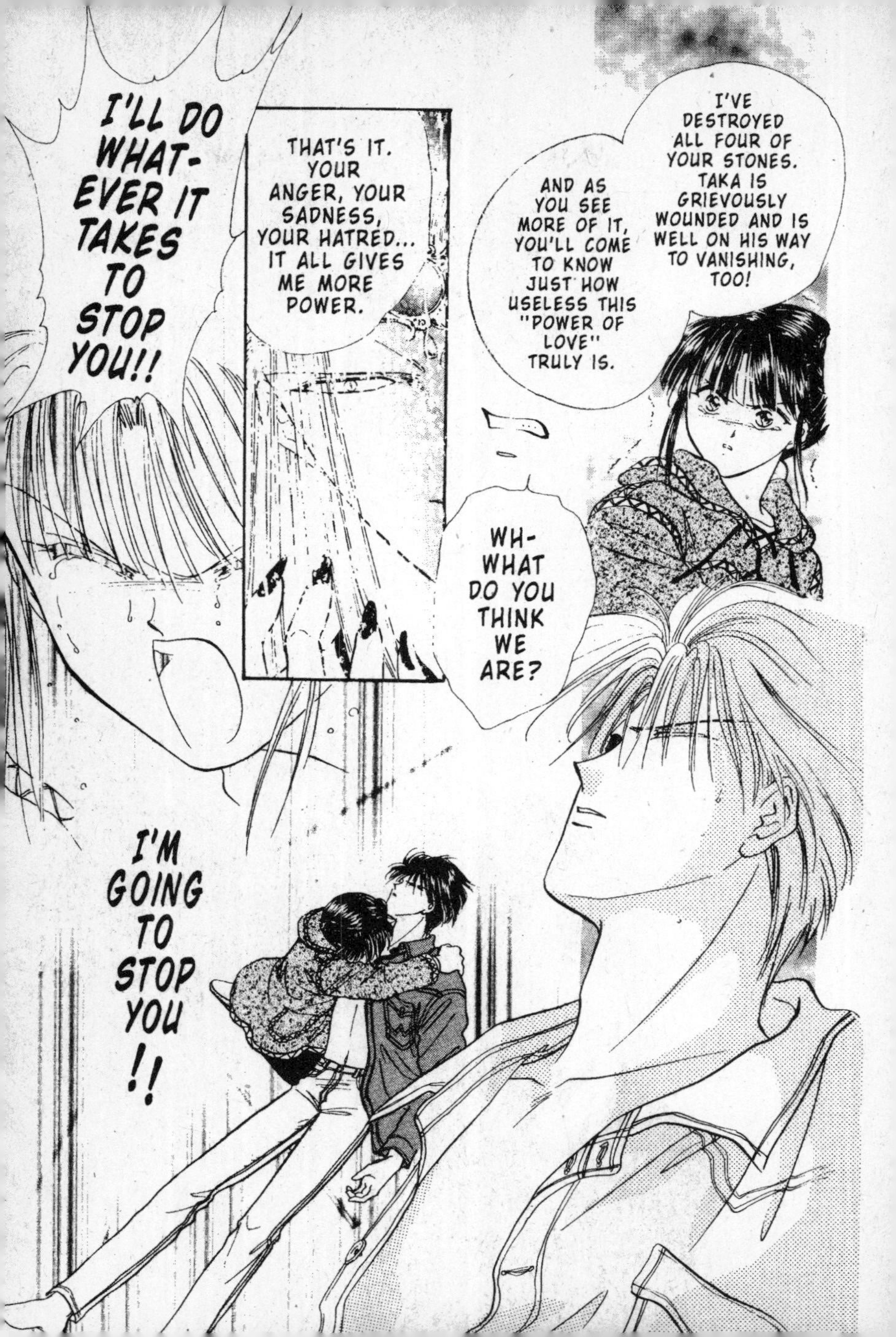
I'VE DESTROYED ALL FOUR OF YOUR STONES. TAKA IS GRIEVOUSLY WOUNDED AND IS WELL ON HIS WAY TO VANISHING, TOO!
AND AS YOU SEE MORE OF IT, YOU'LL COME TO KNOW JUST HOW USELESS THIS "POWER OF LOVE" TRULY IS.
THAT'S IT. YOUR ANGER, YOUR SADNESS, YOUR HATRED... IT ALL GIVES ME MORE POWER.
WH-WHAT DO YOU THINK WE ARE?
I'LL DO WHAT-EVER IT TAKES TO STOP YOU!!
I'M GOING TO STOP YOU!!

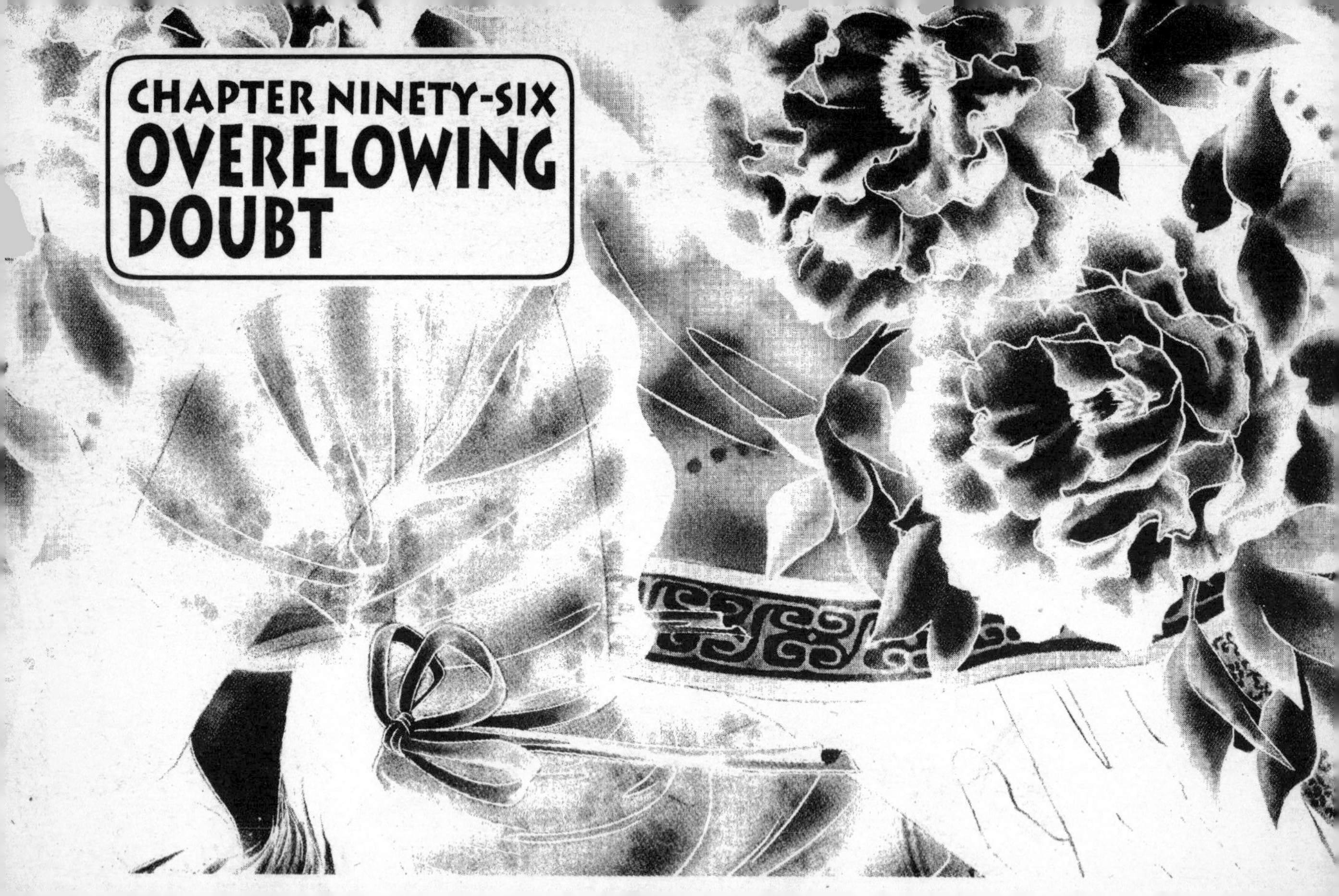
CHAPTER NINETY-SIX
OVERFLOWING
DOUBT

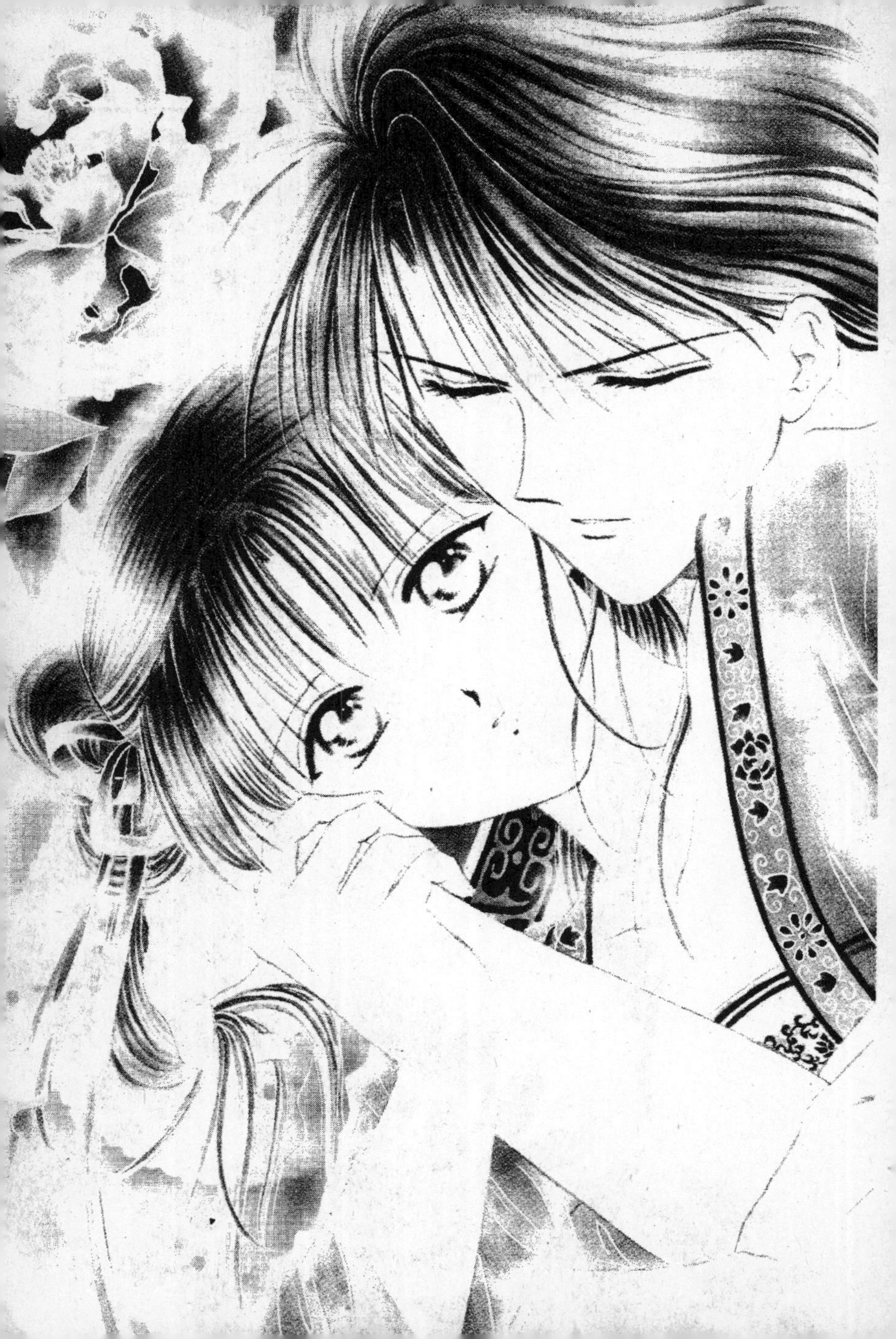

THE TWINS, BY REQUEST→

DEPICTING A SCENE IF THEY BOTH WERE ALIVE TODAY (OF COURSE, ONE IS STILL ALIVE, BUT...). (THE 17-YEAR OLD VERSION)

What happens when I use an art pen.

AMIBOSHI
SUBOSHI

I get a lot of calls to trot out Amiboshi again! But as I said previously, this is the story of Suzaku, Part 2, and please accept it as such.
A Suboshi fan said "Poor Suboshi" at the way he died, but it was just karma coming around. In other words, each of them were rewarded or punished as each of their actions warranted.
Suboshi's feelings for Yui never came to anything, but in the end, he even took on his brother's karma.
And Amiboshi... I keep telling you the way he talked to Miaka in volume 10 wasn't born out of romantic feelings! (The images made an impression, but that didn't represent his true feelings. I drew it in an erotic way as a bonus for the fans.) Personally, I think that Amiboshi gives off the feel of a rabbit... rabbit!?

The anime conveyed that very well!

PET PET
PAT PAT
THE OUTSIDE IS PRETTY AND SOFT, BUT THERE'S A CERTAIN SADNESS INSIDE.

I wonder if Suboshi is always doing things like that...? It's no good! No one can ever come between those brothers. They're best together!! ...I think. And now, the two are one. Amiboshi's happiness is a testament to Suboshi's spirit. Amiboshi will always remember Suboshi in the bottom of his heart. And when the day comes when he can remember fully... at that time, he'll be a truly mature and strong person. He'll be ready to handle the truth and accept it. Even when Amiboshi was acting as a spy, he always had in mind that Suboshi lived under Nakago, and even if he wanted to betray Nakago, he couldn't. (Nakago is so evil!) The Suzaku warriors really came to like him. If Amiboshi ever heard that Suboshi murdered Tamahome's family, he'd be in despair at the news. One reader said, "I notice that the twins bring out characteristics of the other. Amiboshi brought out the cruelty of Suboshi, and Suboshi brought out the gentleness of Amiboshi." Heh, heh, heh!

In the CD album "Seiryu no Gyakushuhen" ("Revenge of Seiryu Chapter"), Amiboshi's song made me cry. But I wanted Suboshi to sing it! Suboshi's song made me laugh. I mean, it was so cool, but the lyrics are so straightforward. How could he ever bring himself to sing that to Yui? ☺ All the other songs were great! And Hotohori's... Tomo didn't get a song! Sniff, sniff!

Buy the CD!

In all honesty, although their ways of showing love may have been wrong, they both felt their love very deeply.

THANK YOU FOR PUTTING NAKAGO ON THE COVER! THANK YOU!! AND SO, NEXT TIME, I'LL TALK ABOUT NAKAGO...

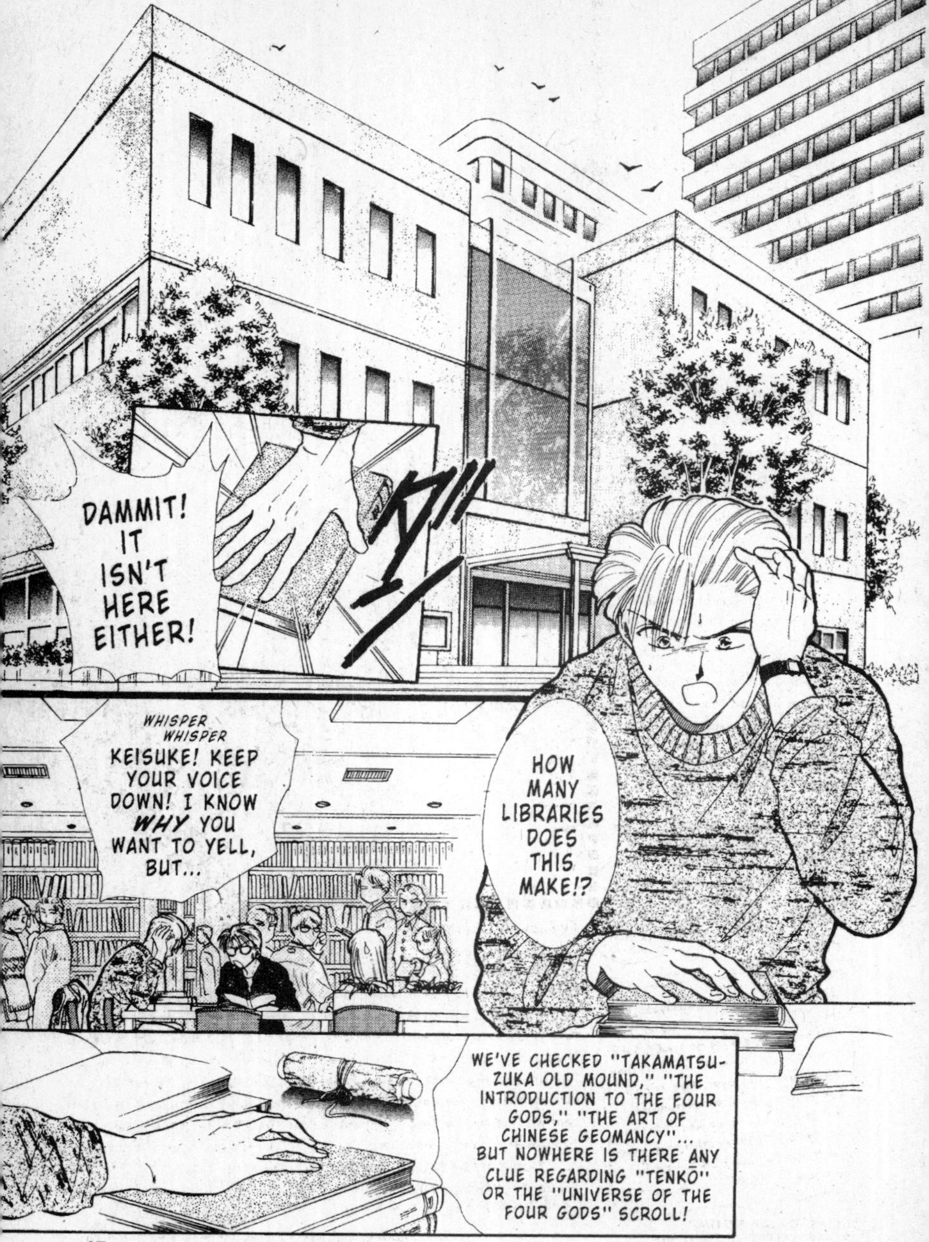
DAMMIT! IT ISN'T HERE EITHER!
HOW MANY LIBRARIES DOES THIS MAKE!?
WHISPER WHISPER
KEISUKE! KEEP YOUR VOICE DOWN! I KNOW *WHY* YOU WANT TO YELL, BUT...
WE'VE CHECKED "TAKAMATSU-ZUKA OLD MOUND," "THE INTRODUCTION TO THE FOUR GODS," "THE ART OF CHINESE GEOMANCY"... BUT NOWHERE IS THERE ANY CLUE REGARDING "TENKŌ" OR THE "UNIVERSE OF THE FOUR GODS" SCROLL!

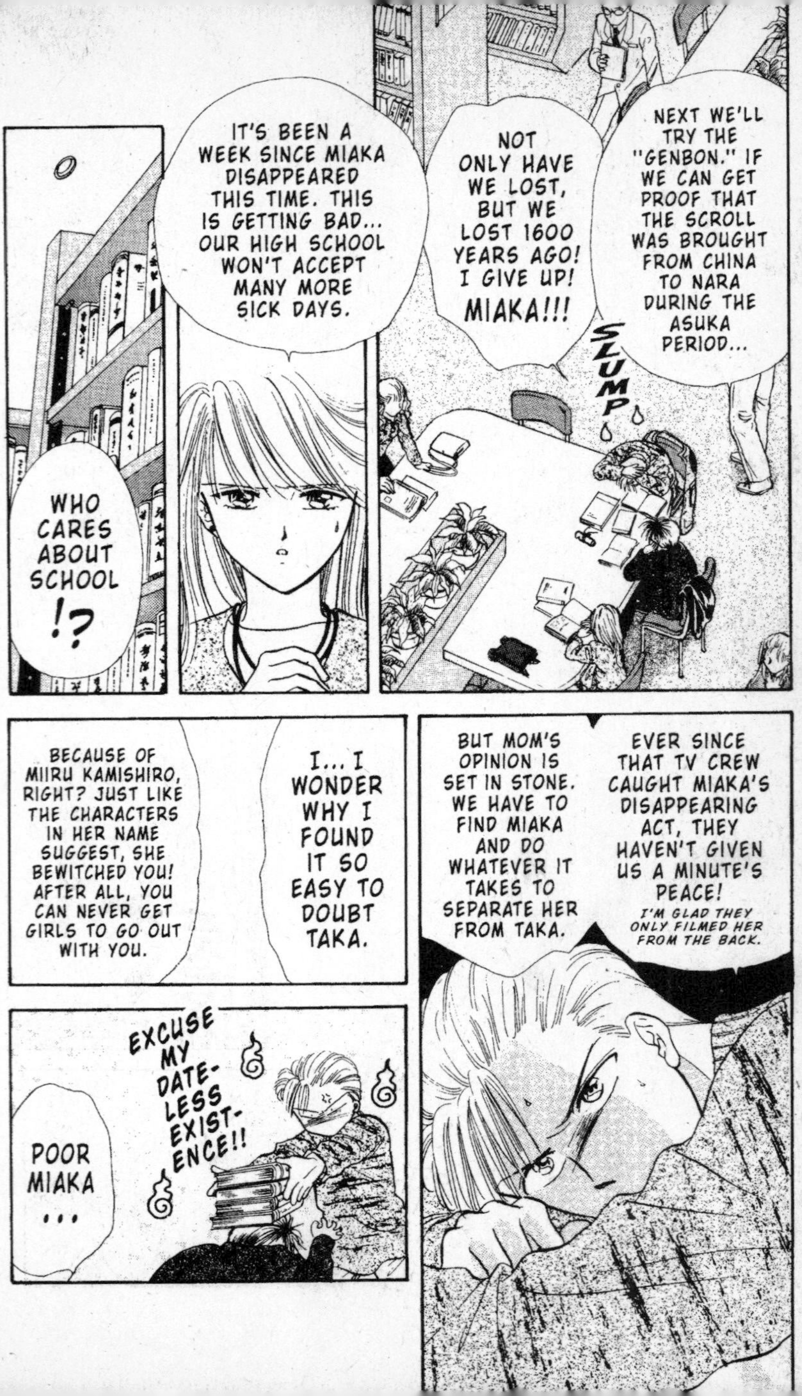
NEXT WE'LL TRY THE "GENBON." IF WE CAN GET PROOF THAT THE SCROLL WAS BROUGHT FROM CHINA TO NARA DURING THE ASUKA PERIOD...
NOT ONLY HAVE WE LOST, BUT WE LOST 1600 YEARS AGO! I GIVE UP! MIAKA!!!
SLUMP
IT'S BEEN A WEEK SINCE MIAKA DISAPPEARED THIS TIME. THIS IS GETTING BAD... OUR HIGH SCHOOL WON'T ACCEPT MANY MORE SICK DAYS.
WHO CARES ABOUT SCHOOL !?
EVER SINCE THAT TV CREW CAUGHT MIAKA'S DISAPPEARING ACT, THEY HAVEN'T GIVEN US A MINUTE'S PEACE!
I'M GLAD THEY ONLY FILMED HER FROM THE BACK.
BUT MOM'S OPINION IS SET IN STONE. WE HAVE TO FIND MIAKA AND DO WHATEVER IT TAKES TO SEPARATE HER FROM TAKA.
I... I WONDER WHY I FOUND IT SO EASY TO DOUBT TAKA.
BECAUSE OF MIIRU KAMISHIRO, RIGHT? JUST LIKE THE CHARACTERS IN HER NAME SUGGEST, SHE BEWITCHED YOU! AFTER ALL, YOU CAN NEVER GET GIRLS TO GO OUT WITH YOU.
EXCUSE MY DATE-LESS EXIST-ENCE!!
POOR MIAKA ...

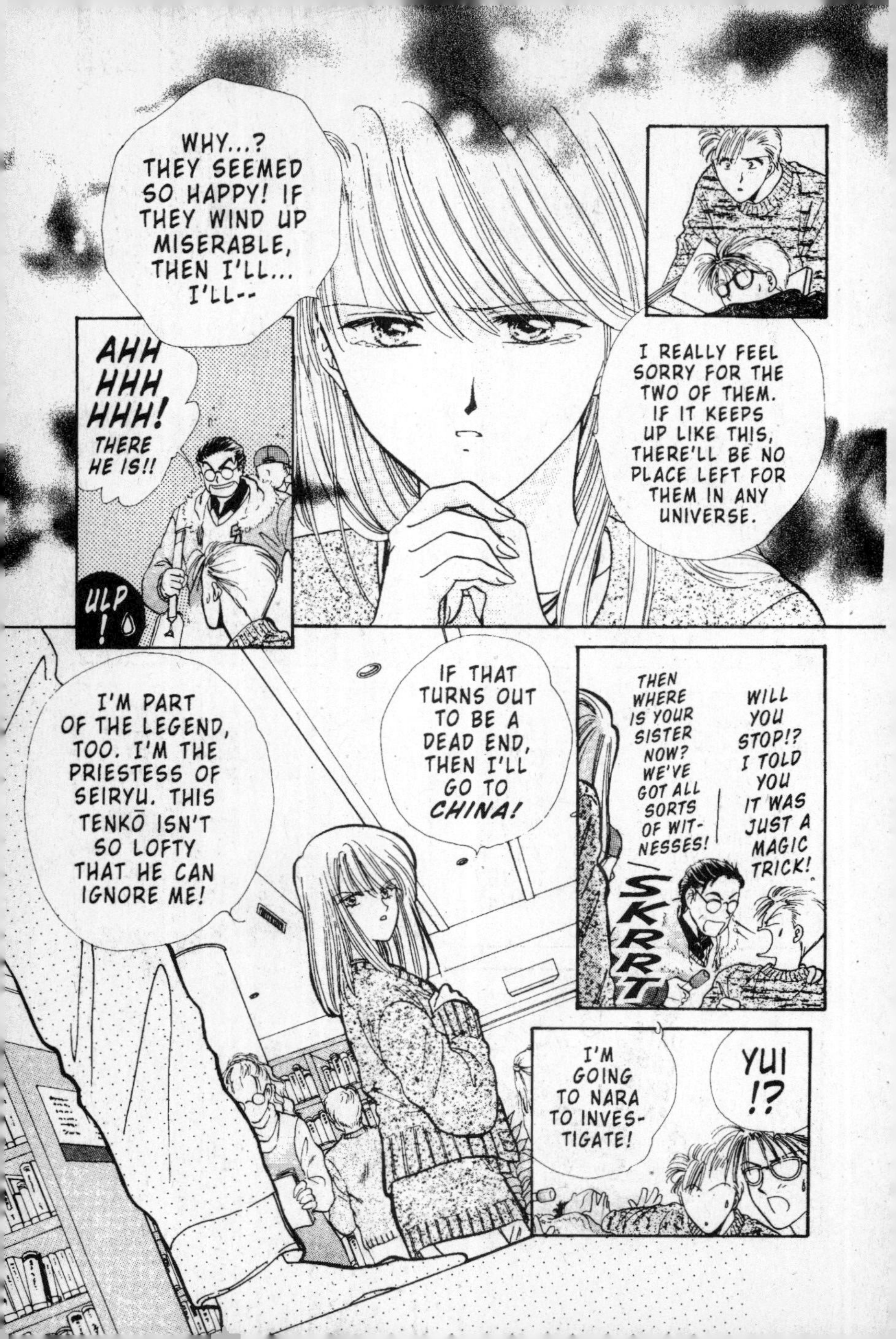
WHY...? THEY SEEMED SO HAPPY! IF THEY WIND UP MISERABLE, THEN I'LL... I'LL--
I REALLY FEEL SORRY FOR THE TWO OF THEM. IF IT KEEPS UP LIKE THIS, THERE'LL BE NO PLACE LEFT FOR THEM IN ANY UNIVERSE.
AHHHHHHHH! THERE HE IS!!
ULP!
WILL YOU STOP!? I TOLD YOU IT WAS JUST A MAGIC TRICK!
THEN WHERE IS YOUR SISTER NOW? WE'VE GOT ALL SORTS OF WITNESSES!
SKRRT
YUI!?
I'M GOING TO NARA TO INVESTIGATE!
IF THAT TURNS OUT TO BE A DEAD END, THEN I'LL GO TO CHINA!
I'M PART OF THE LEGEND, TOO. I'M THE PRIESTESS OF SEIRYU. THIS TENKŌ ISN'T SO LOFTY THAT HE CAN IGNORE ME!

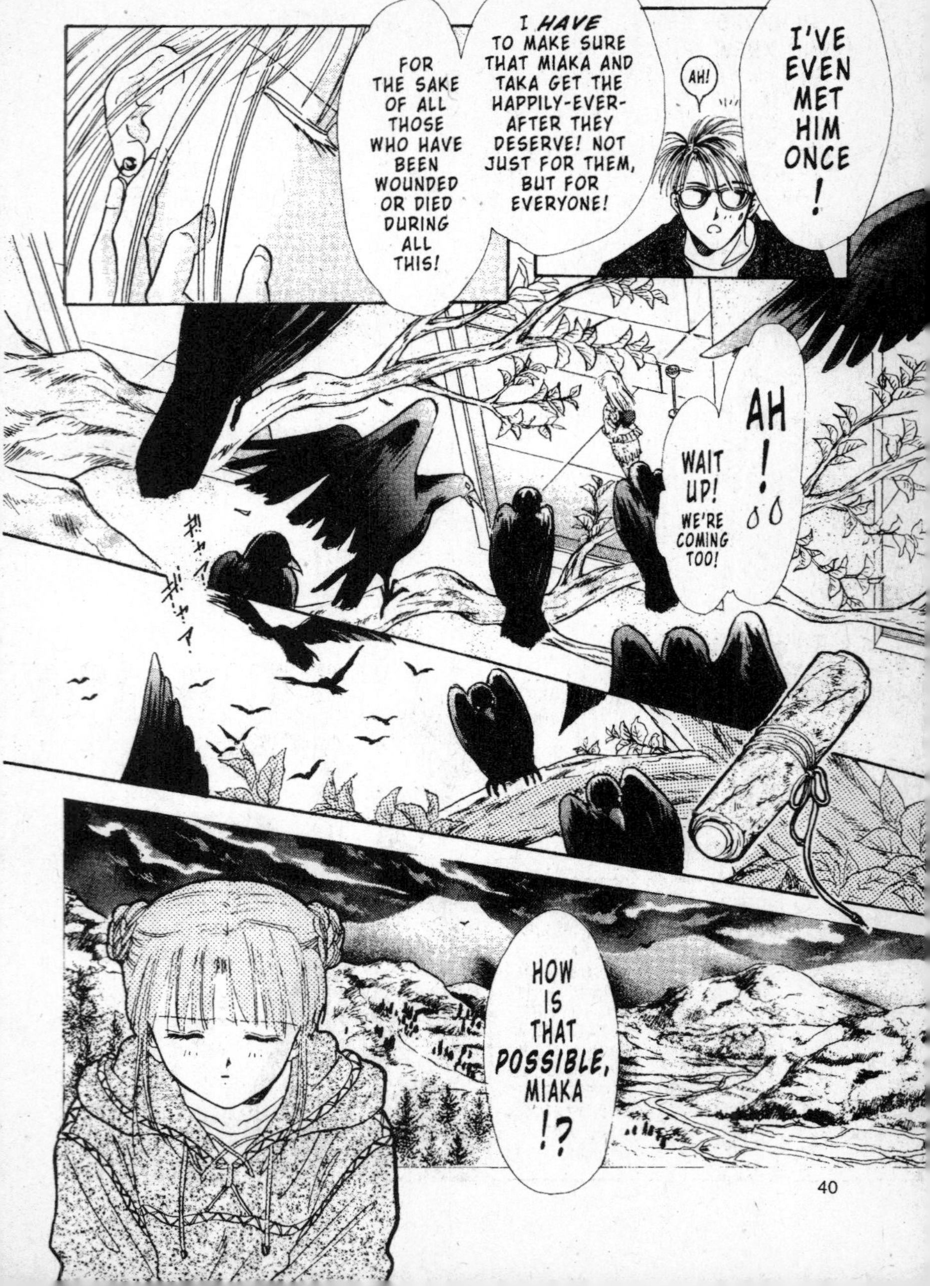
I'VE EVEN MET HIM ONCE!
AH!
I *HAVE* TO MAKE SURE THAT MIAKA AND TAKA GET THE HAPPILY-EVER-AFTER THEY DESERVE! NOT JUST FOR THEM, BUT FOR EVERYONE!
FOR THE SAKE OF ALL THOSE WHO HAVE BEEN WOUNDED OR DIED DURING ALL THIS!
AH!
WAIT UP! WE'RE COMING TOO!
HOW IS THAT *POSSIBLE*, MIAKA!?

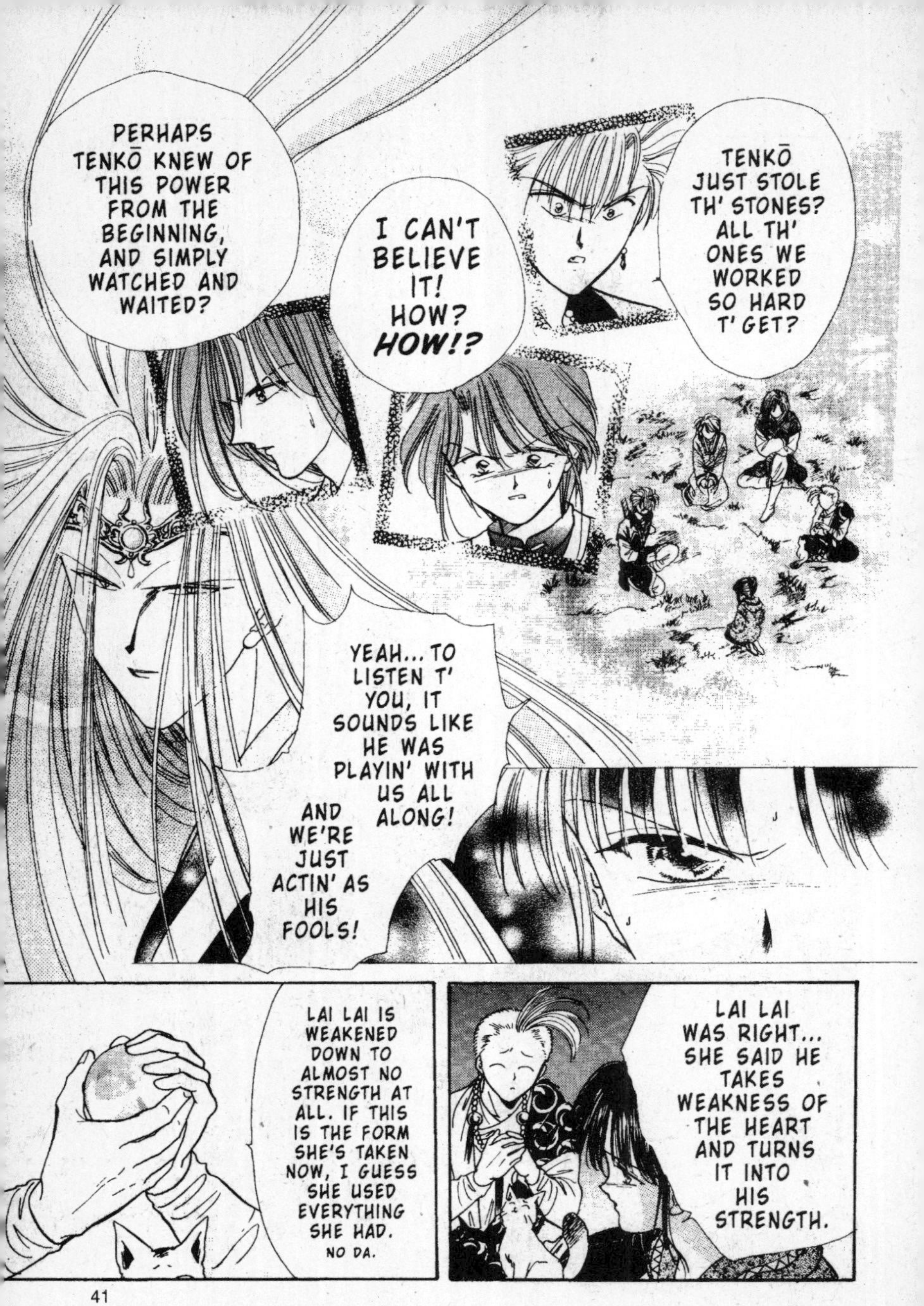
TENKŌ JUST STOLE TH' STONES? ALL TH' ONES WE WORKED SO HARD T' GET?
I CAN'T BELIEVE IT! HOW? *HOW!?*
PERHAPS TENKŌ KNEW OF THIS POWER FROM THE BEGINNING, AND SIMPLY WATCHED AND WAITED?
YEAH... TO LISTEN T' YOU, IT SOUNDS LIKE HE WAS PLAYIN' WITH US ALL ALONG!
AND WE'RE JUST ACTIN' AS HIS FOOLS!
LAI LAI WAS RIGHT... SHE SAID HE TAKES WEAKNESS OF THE HEART AND TURNS IT INTO HIS STRENGTH.
LAI LAI IS WEAKENED DOWN TO ALMOST NO STRENGTH AT ALL. IF THIS IS THE FORM SHE'S TAKEN NOW, I GUESS SHE USED EVERYTHING SHE HAD. NO DA.

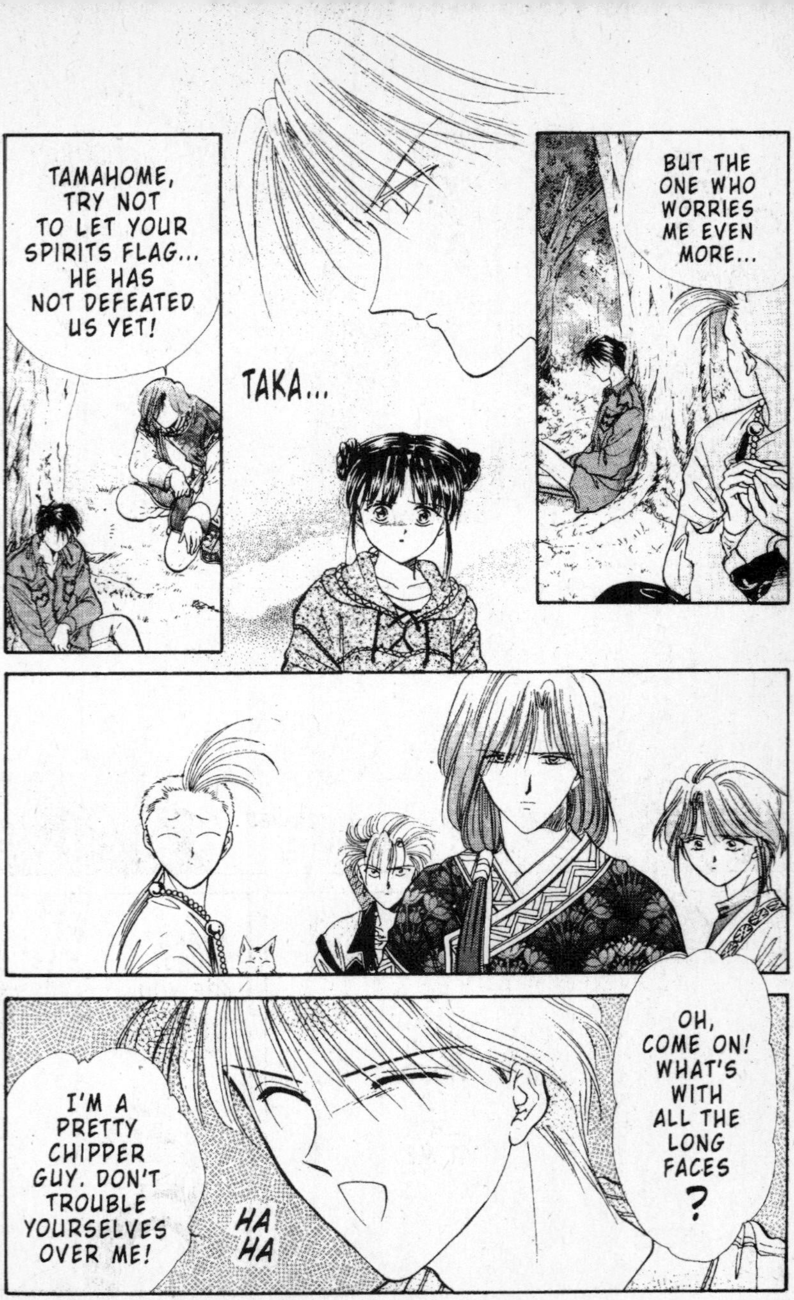
BUT THE ONE WHO WORRIES ME EVEN MORE...
TAKA...
TAMAHOME, TRY NOT TO LET YOUR SPIRITS FLAG... HE HAS NOT DEFEATED US YET!
OH, COME ON! WHAT'S WITH ALL THE LONG FACES?
HA HA
I'M A PRETTY CHIPPER GUY. DON'T TROUBLE YOURSELVES OVER ME!

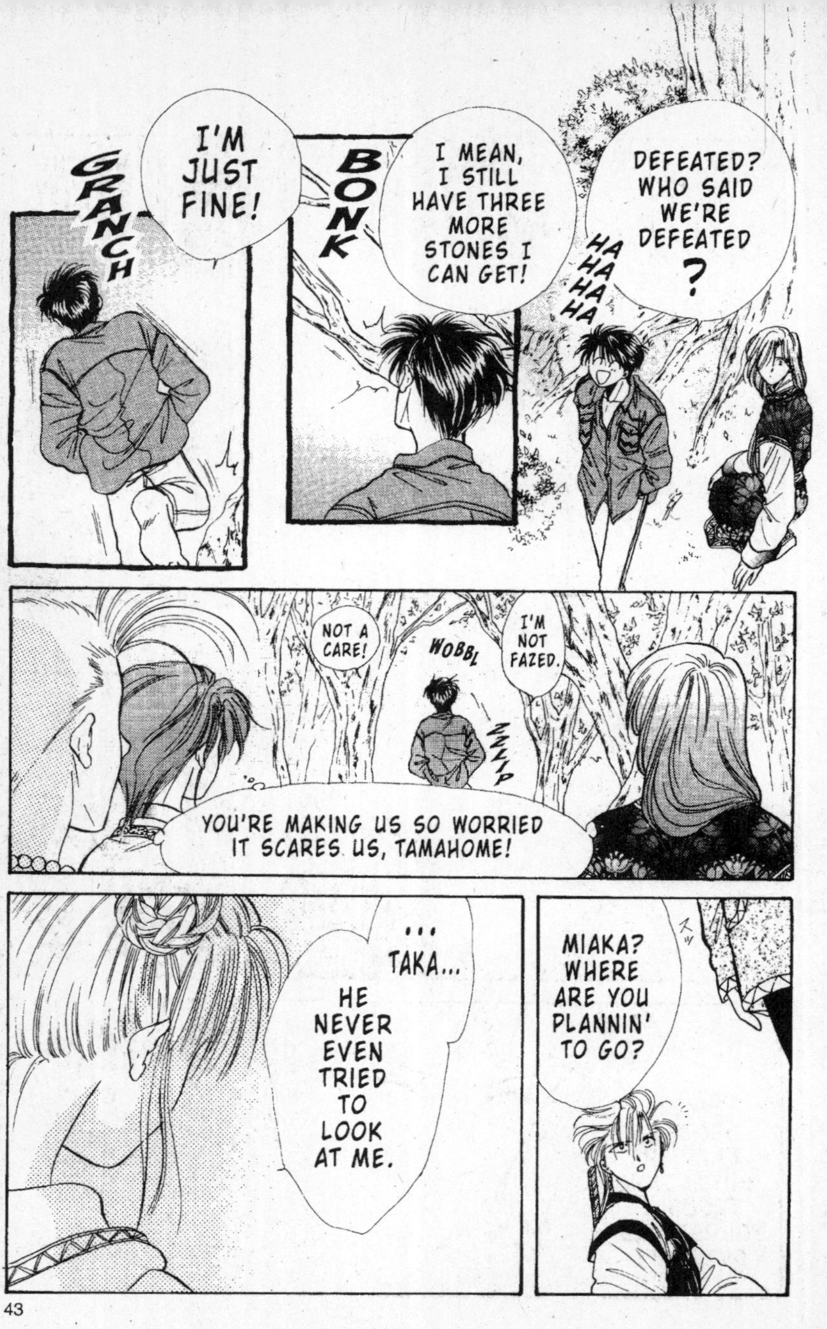
HA HA HA HA
DEFEATED? WHO SAID WE'RE DEFEATED?
BONK
I MEAN, I STILL HAVE THREE MORE STONES I CAN GET!
GRANCH
I'M JUST FINE!
I'M NOT FAZED.
WOBBL
NOT A CARE!
ZZLIP
YOU'RE MAKING US SO WORRIED IT SCARES US, TAMAHOME!
スッ
MIAKA? WHERE ARE YOU PLANNIN' TO GO?
... TAKA...
HE NEVER EVEN TRIED TO LOOK AT ME.

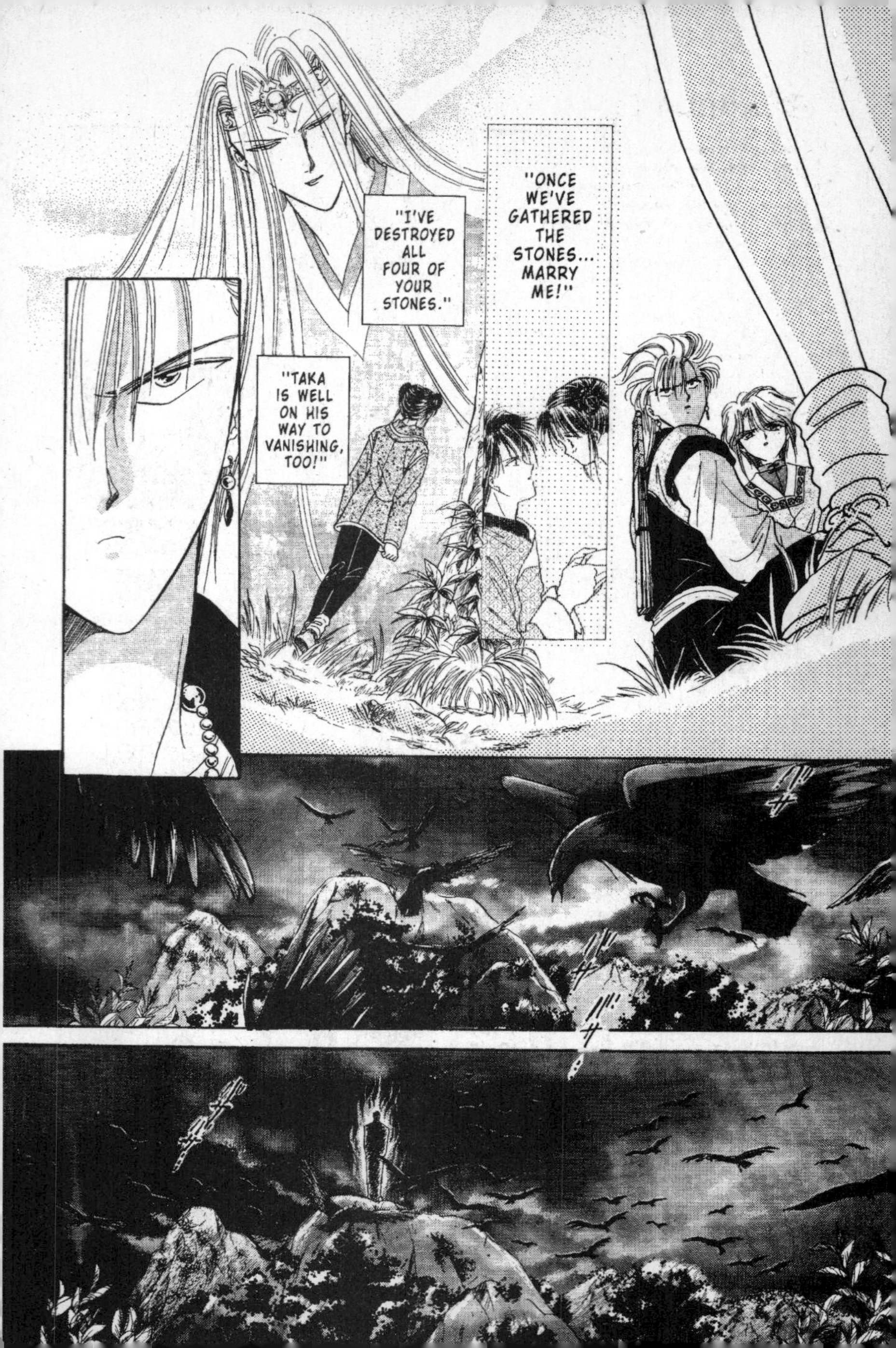
"ONCE WE'VE GATHERED THE STONES... MARRY ME!"
"I'VE DESTROYED ALL FOUR OF YOUR STONES."
"TAKA IS WELL ON HIS WAY TO VANISHING, TOO!"

HEH
WAA!!
WHAT THE...? THE WIND SUDDENLY GOT REAL STRONG!
!!
THAT SMELL ...
WHAT IS IT, CHICHIRI ?

Demon

"Aw, I sent off my letter ages ago, and ***no reply ever comes!!*** " To those fans who feel this, please don't be angry. *I'm positively worn out!* Maybe I'm the only one you write to, but I get cardboard boxes with a thousand letters in each every month! And I feel so relieved when I can finally make the time to read them. I'm sorry, everyone! At least I make every effort to read them! Umm...and even if you put, "Read by X-month, X-day," it still won't help. There have been times when I was only able to open mail long after such deadlines had passed. And please! People who send sign boards or requests for signed pictures... I'm sorry, but I can't do it! I can't even send your pictures back. I'm so sorry! Don't do it even as a joke! Not unless you want me to drop dead from exhaustion! *I keep hearing from the people around me that I look like I'm about to collapse. Isn't that an awful thing to say?*
Now, on to the next subject! (Oh! If you don't already know what goes on in this story, then come back and read this later.) About Tasuki! There was a day when news of Tasuki's rampage spread throughout the entire nation of Japan... *Really!?* Well... among the Tasuki fans (a friend calls them fanatics), the • reaction • was • unbelievable. ☺ And many people across the land heard the scream of indignation. (Okay, that's kind of an exaggeration. It's just written that way to create an image.) There were some good points to the reaction: The guy lost a little of his overwhelming popularity! It's a little scary. The incident certainly split the "angry" fans and the "overjoyed" fans into two distinct groups. As for what Miaka did... (there's a lot of jealousy going around). According to some of the letters I've received, the reaction ranges from "This is what I've been waiting for!" through "With Tasuki's history, what the hell is going on!?" ☺ and finally to people who are angry at Tasuki himself. (He does love her.) One person said, "I'd like you to sympathize with the plight of true love and stop placing obstacles between Miaka and Tama!" *That's so cute!*

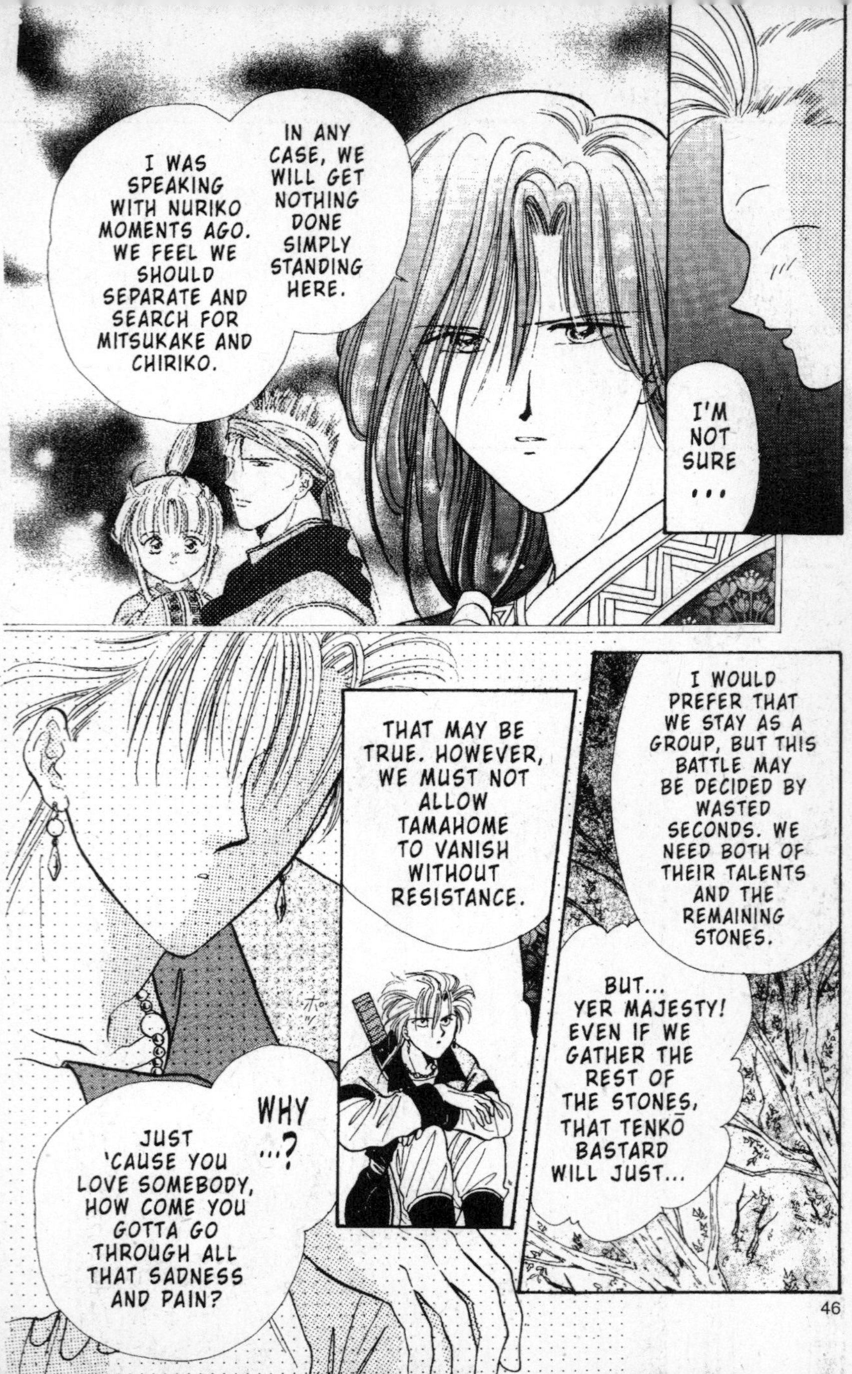

I'M NOT SURE ...
IN ANY CASE, WE WILL GET NOTHING DONE SIMPLY STANDING HERE.
I WAS SPEAKING WITH NURIKO MOMENTS AGO. WE FEEL WE SHOULD SEPARATE AND SEARCH FOR MITSUKAKE AND CHIRIKO.
I WOULD PREFER THAT WE STAY AS A GROUP, BUT THIS BATTLE MAY BE DECIDED BY WASTED SECONDS. WE NEED BOTH OF THEIR TALENTS AND THE REMAINING STONES.
BUT... YER MAJESTY! EVEN IF WE GATHER THE REST OF THE STONES, THAT TENKŌ BASTARD WILL JUST...
THAT MAY BE TRUE. HOWEVER, WE MUST NOT ALLOW TAMAHOME TO VANISH WITHOUT RESISTANCE.
WHY ...?
JUST 'CAUSE YOU LOVE SOMEBODY, HOW COME YOU GOTTA GO THROUGH ALL THAT SADNESS AND PAIN?

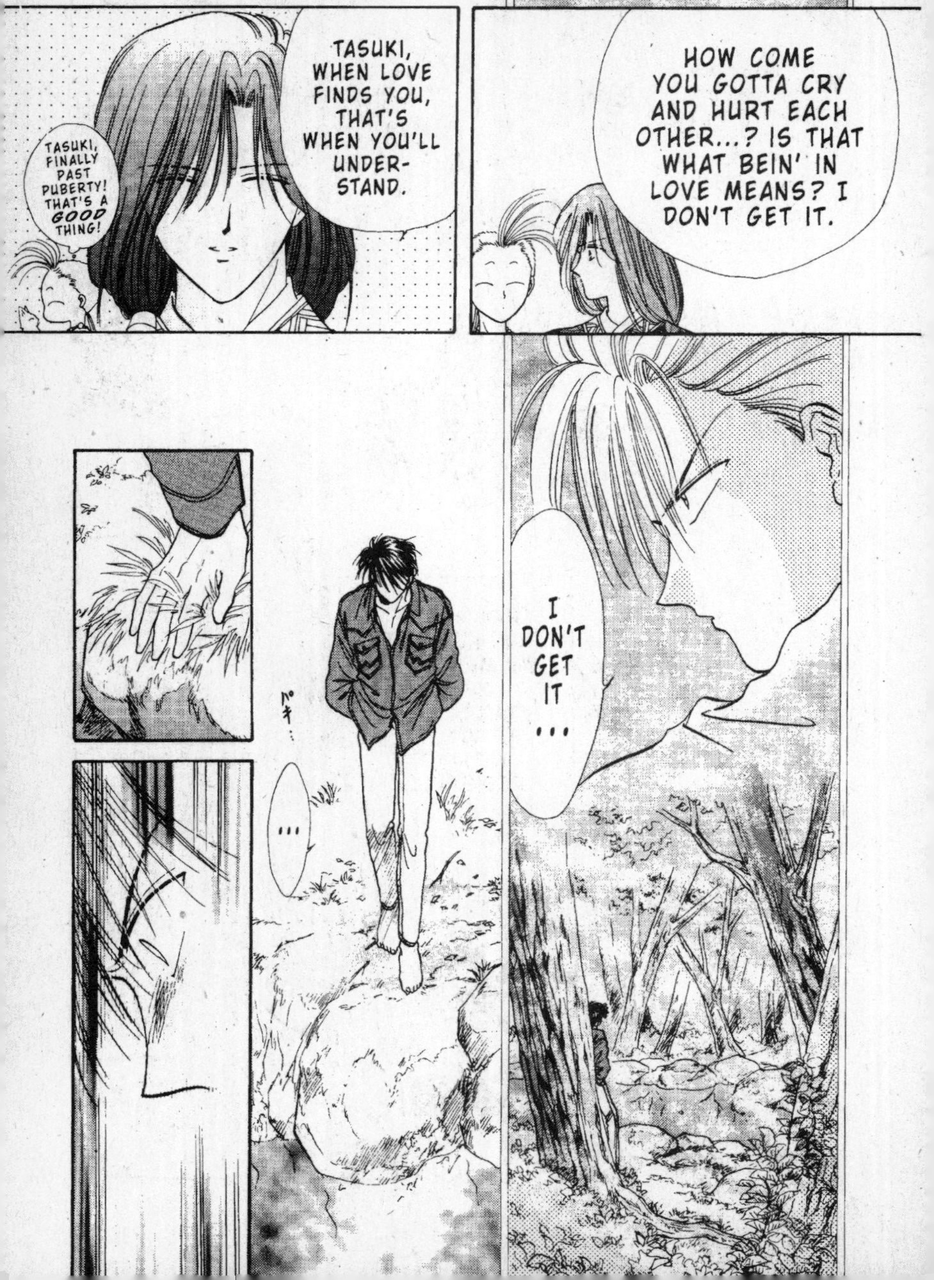
HOW COME YOU GOTTA CRY AND HURT EACH OTHER...? IS THAT WHAT BEIN' IN LOVE MEANS? I DON'T GET IT.
TASUKI, WHEN LOVE FINDS YOU, THAT'S WHEN YOU'LL UNDER-STAND.
TASUKI, FINALLY PAST PUBERTY! THAT'S A GOOD THING!
I DON'T GET IT ...
...
パキ…

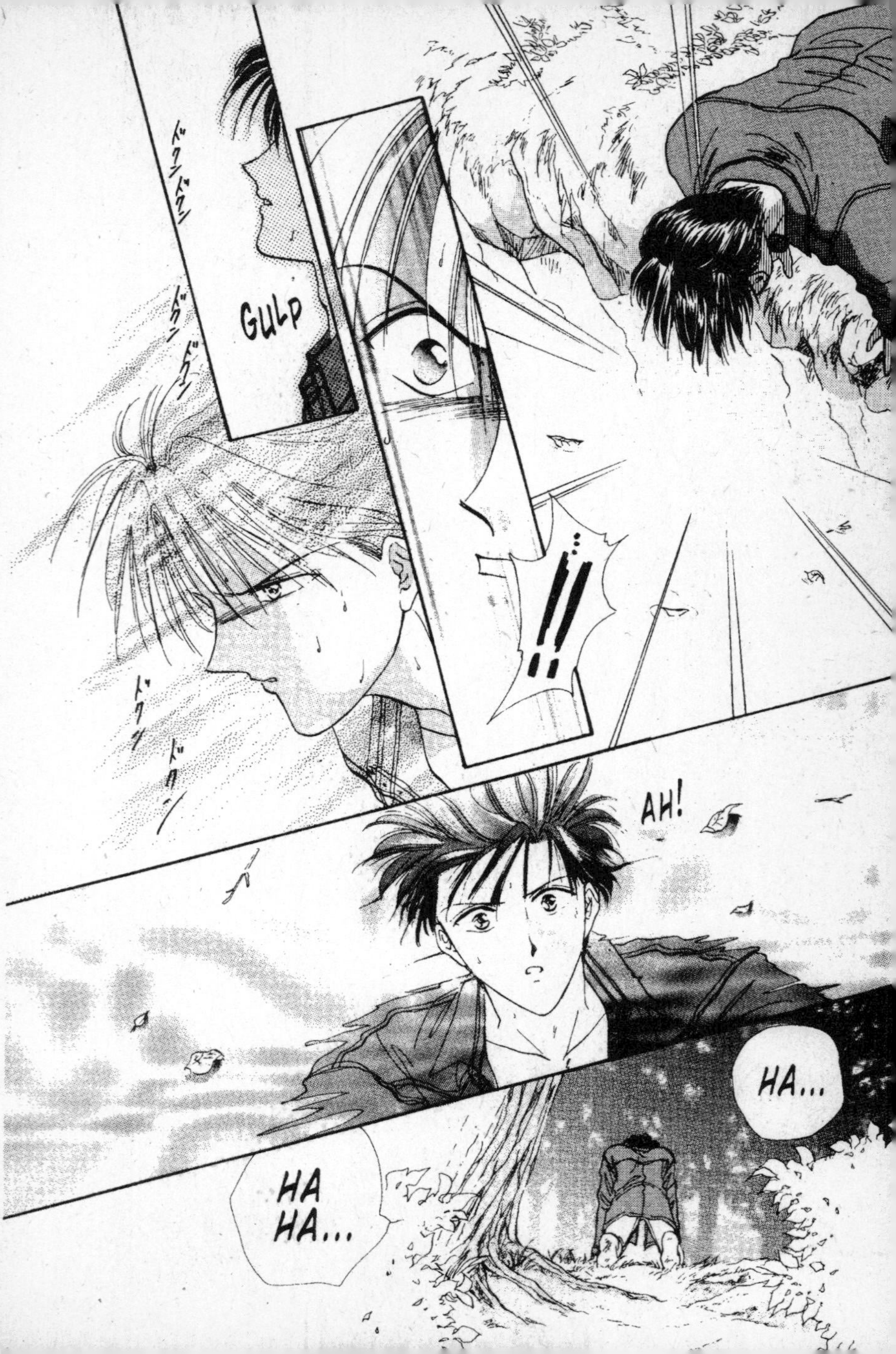

!!
GULP
AH!
HA...
HA HA...

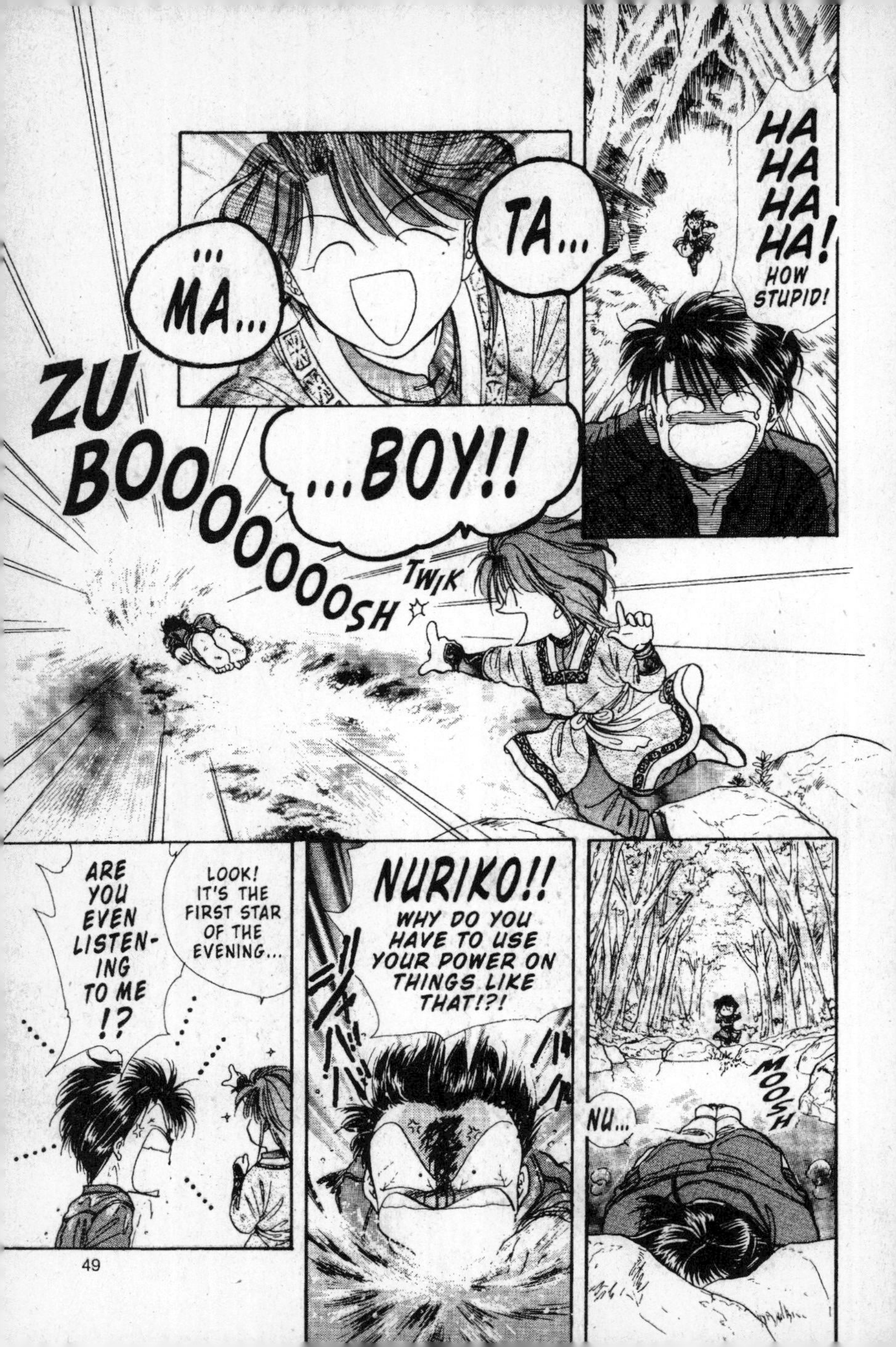
HA HA HA HA! HOW STUPID!
TA...
MA...
...BOY!!
ZU BOOOOOOOOOSH
TWIK
MOOSH
NU...
NURIKO!! WHY DO YOU HAVE TO USE YOUR POWER ON THINGS LIKE THAT!?!
LOOK! IT'S THE FIRST STAR OF THE EVENING...
ARE YOU EVEN LISTEN-ING TO ME !?

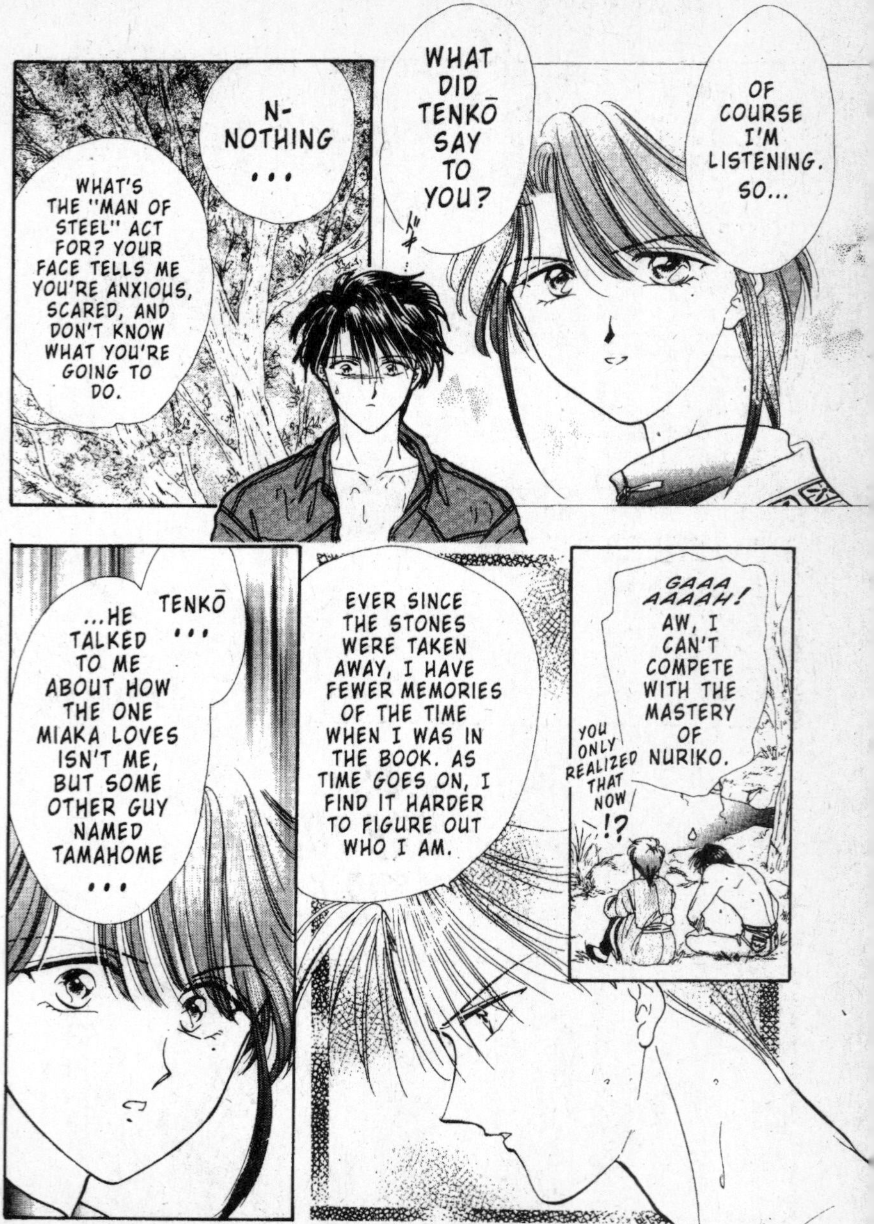
OF COURSE I'M LISTENING. SO...
WHAT DID TENKŌ SAY TO YOU?
N-NOTHING...
WHAT'S THE "MAN OF STEEL" ACT FOR? YOUR FACE TELLS ME YOU'RE ANXIOUS, SCARED, AND DON'T KNOW WHAT YOU'RE GOING TO DO.
GAAA AAAAH! AW, I CAN'T COMPETE WITH THE MASTERY OF NURIKO.
YOU ONLY REALIZED THAT NOW!?
EVER SINCE THE STONES WERE TAKEN AWAY, I HAVE FEWER MEMORIES OF THE TIME WHEN I WAS IN THE BOOK. AS TIME GOES ON, I FIND IT HARDER TO FIGURE OUT WHO I AM.
TENKŌ...
...HE TALKED TO ME ABOUT HOW THE ONE MIAKA LOVES ISN'T ME, BUT SOME OTHER GUY NAMED TAMAHOME...

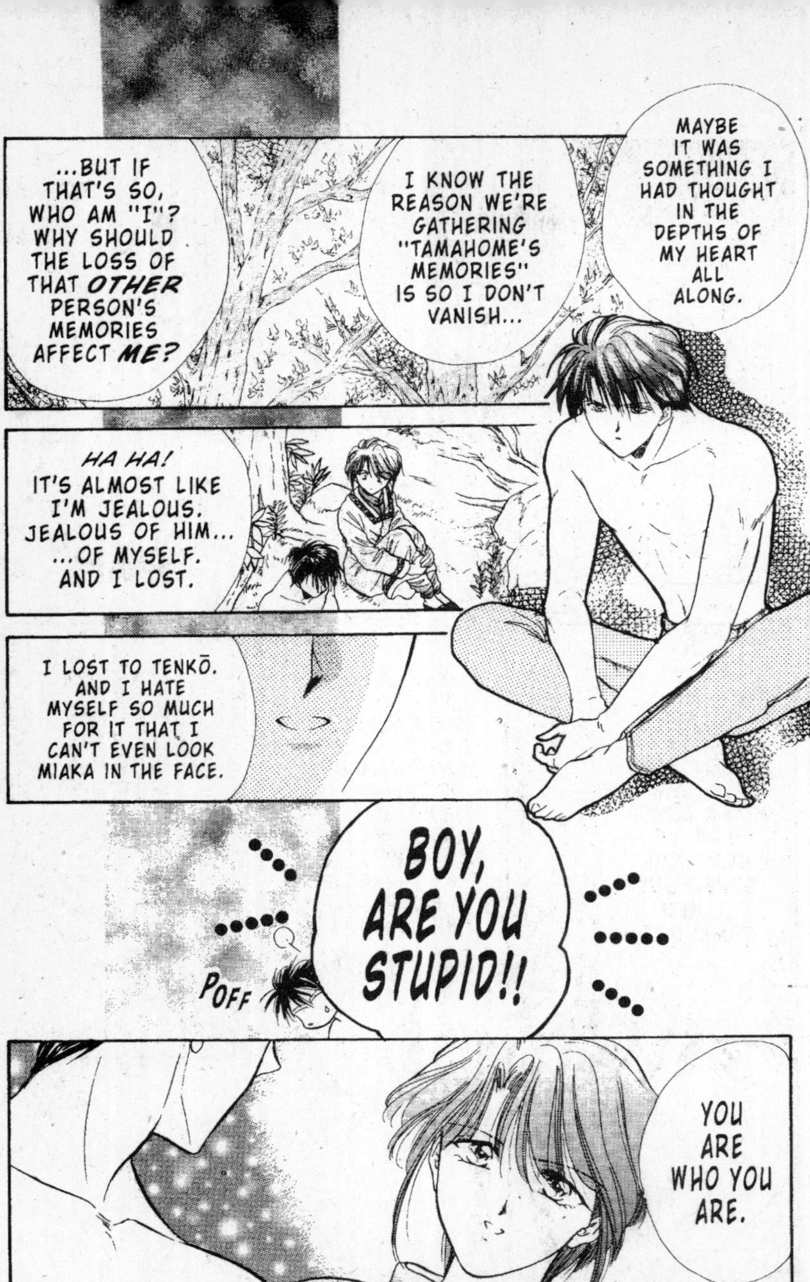
MAYBE IT WAS SOMETHING I HAD THOUGHT IN THE DEPTHS OF MY HEART ALL ALONG.
I KNOW THE REASON WE'RE GATHERING "TAMAHOME'S MEMORIES" IS SO I DON'T VANISH...
...BUT IF THAT'S SO, WHO AM "I"? WHY SHOULD THE LOSS OF THAT *OTHER* PERSON'S MEMORIES AFFECT *ME*?
HA HA! IT'S ALMOST LIKE I'M JEALOUS. JEALOUS OF HIM... ...OF MYSELF. AND I LOST.
I LOST TO TENKŌ. AND I HATE MYSELF SO MUCH FOR IT THAT I CAN'T EVEN LOOK MIAKA IN THE FACE.
BOY, ARE YOU STUPID!!
POFF
YOU ARE WHO YOU ARE.

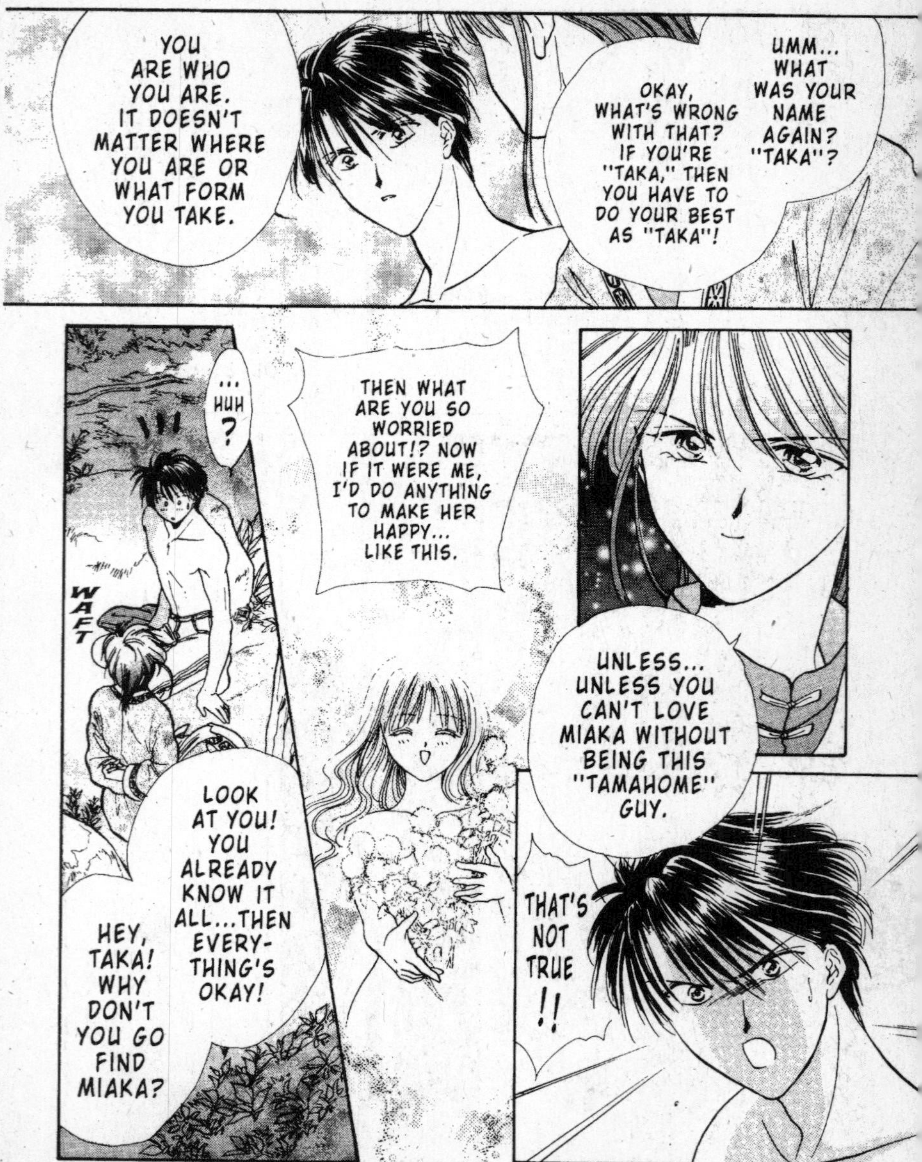
UMM... WHAT WAS YOUR NAME AGAIN? "TAKA"?
OKAY, WHAT'S WRONG WITH THAT? IF YOU'RE "TAKA," THEN YOU HAVE TO DO YOUR BEST AS "TAKA"!
YOU ARE WHO YOU ARE. IT DOESN'T MATTER WHERE YOU ARE OR WHAT FORM YOU TAKE.
THEN WHAT ARE YOU SO WORRIED ABOUT!? NOW IF IT WERE ME, I'D DO ANYTHING TO MAKE HER HAPPY... LIKE THIS.
UNLESS... UNLESS YOU CAN'T LOVE MIAKA WITHOUT BEING THIS "TAMAHOME" GUY.
THAT'S NOT TRUE!!
LOOK AT YOU! YOU ALREADY KNOW IT ALL...THEN EVERY-THING'S OKAY!
HEY, TAKA! WHY DON'T YOU GO FIND MIAKA?
WAFT
...HUH?

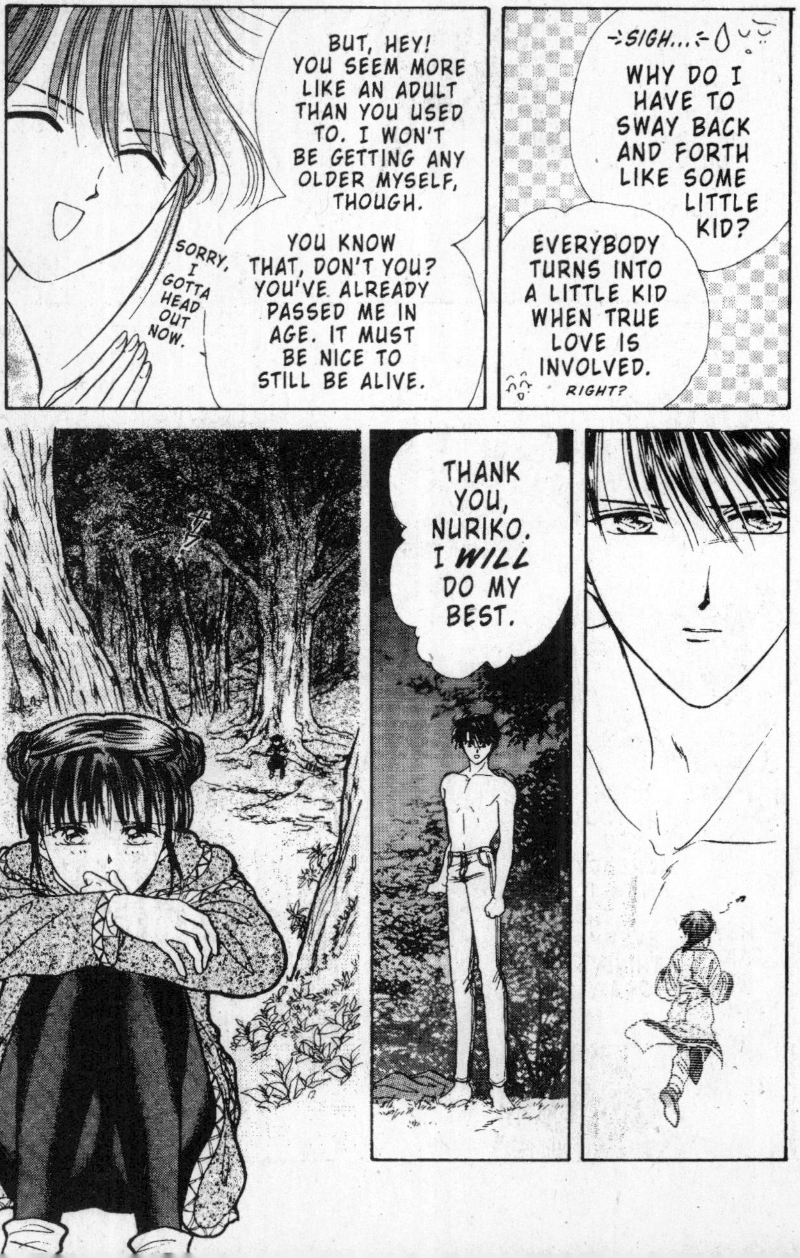
SIGH...
WHY DO I HAVE TO SWAY BACK AND FORTH LIKE SOME LITTLE KID?
EVERYBODY TURNS INTO A LITTLE KID WHEN TRUE LOVE IS INVOLVED.
RIGHT?
BUT, HEY! YOU SEEM MORE LIKE AN ADULT THAN YOU USED TO. I WON'T BE GETTING ANY OLDER MYSELF, THOUGH.
YOU KNOW THAT, DON'T YOU? YOU'VE ALREADY PASSED ME IN AGE. IT MUST BE NICE TO STILL BE ALIVE.
SORRY, I GOTTA HEAD OUT NOW.
THANK YOU, NURIKO. I *WILL* DO MY BEST.

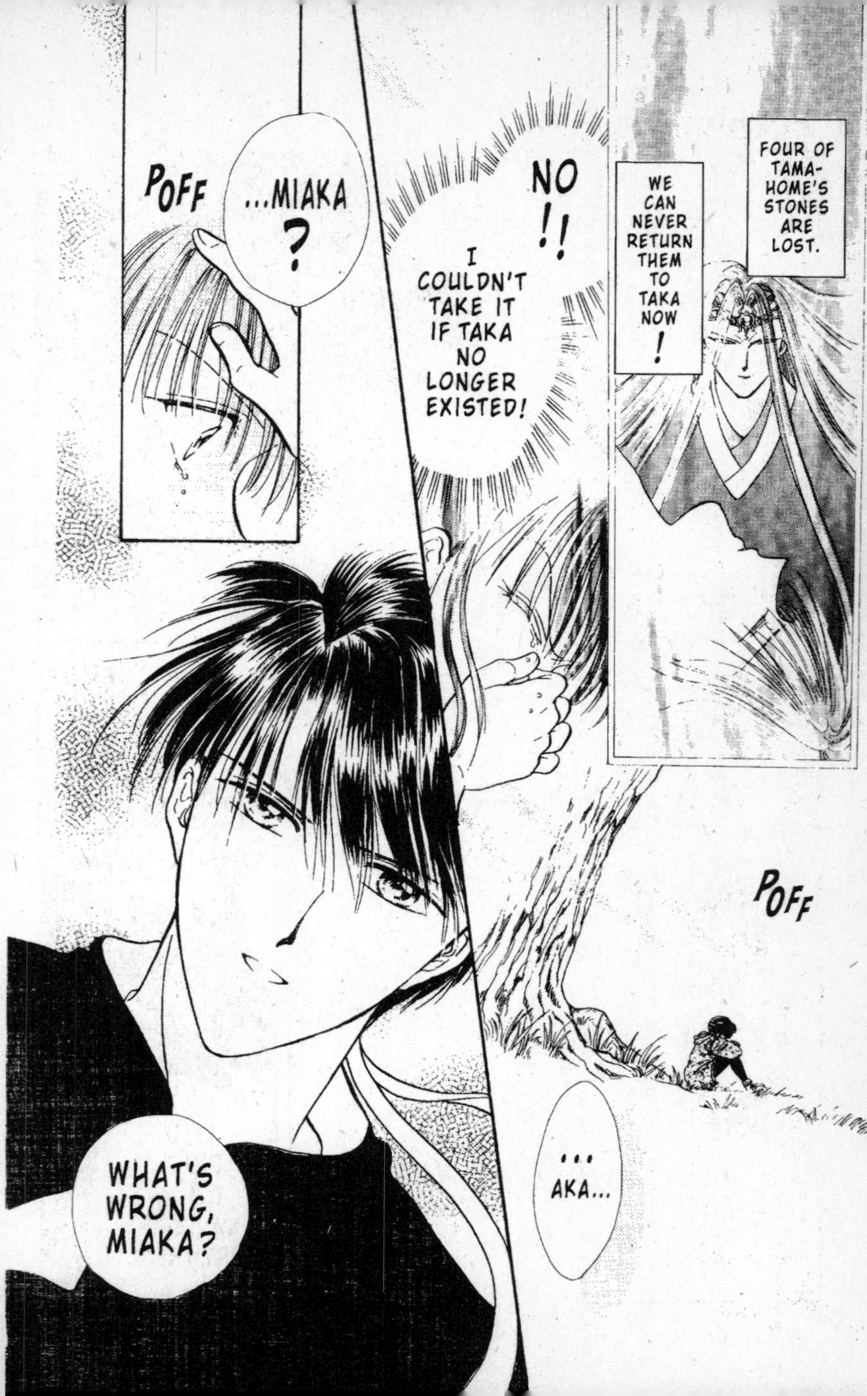
FOUR OF TAMA-HOME'S STONES ARE LOST.
WE CAN NEVER RETURN THEM TO TAKA NOW!
NO!!
I COULDN'T TAKE IT IF TAKA NO LONGER EXISTED!
...MIAKA?
POFF
POFF
...AKA...
WHAT'S WRONG, MIAKA?

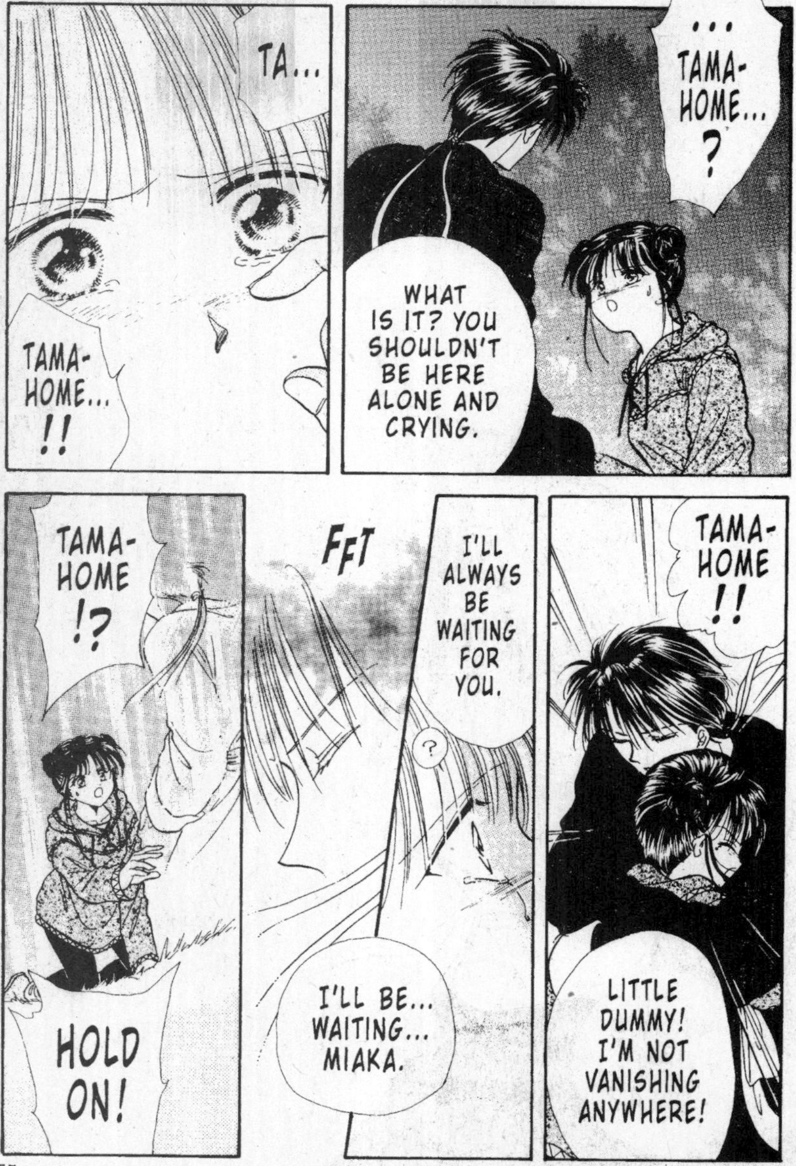
... TAMA-HOME... ?
WHAT IS IT? YOU SHOULDN'T BE HERE ALONE AND CRYING.
TA...
TAMA-HOME... !!
TAMA-HOME !!
LITTLE DUMMY! I'M NOT VANISHING ANYWHERE!
I'LL ALWAYS BE WAITING FOR YOU.
?
FFT
I'LL BE... WAITING... MIAKA.
TAMA-HOME !?
HOLD ON!

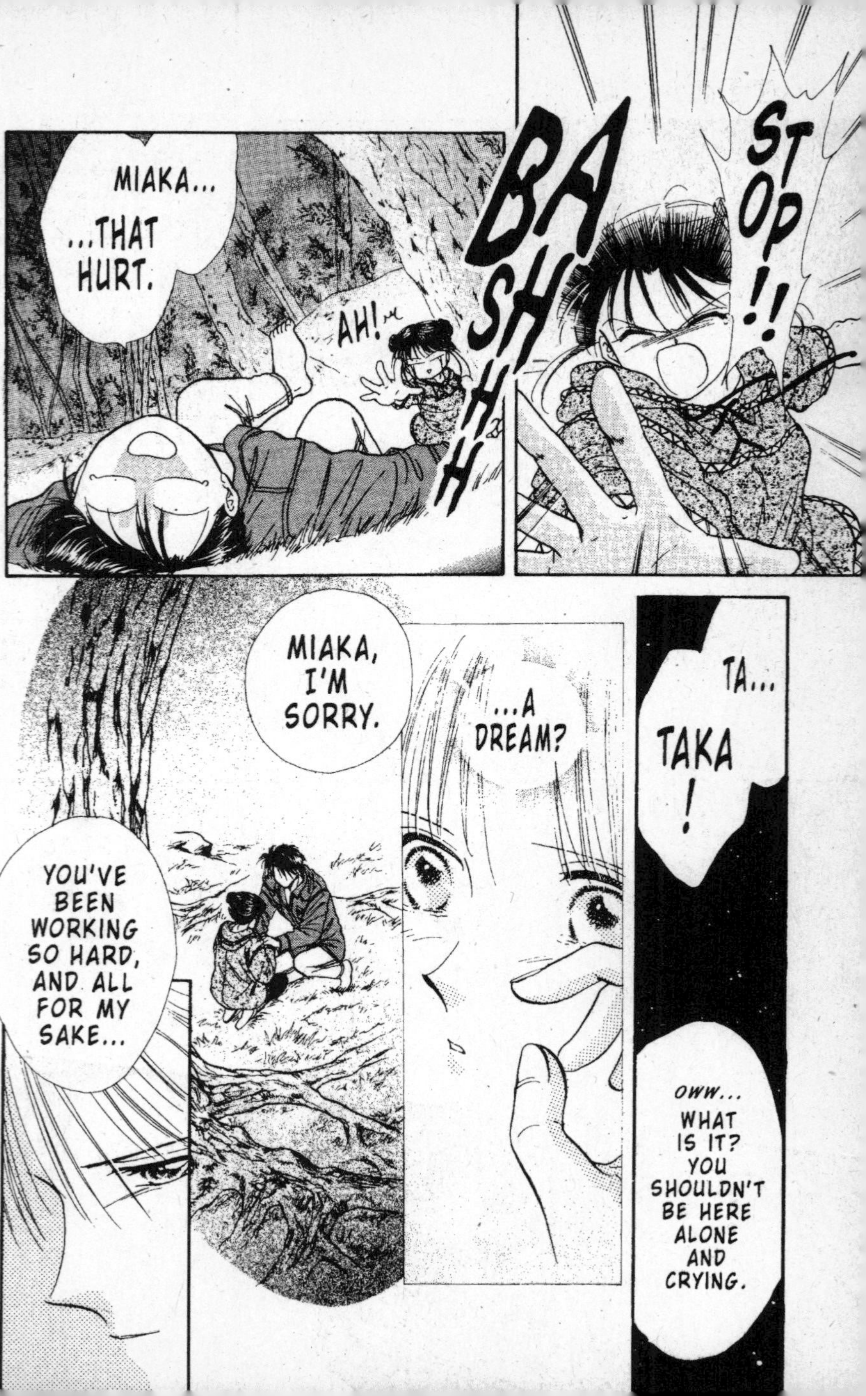
STOP!!
BASHHHH
AH!
MIAKA...
...THAT HURT.
TA...
TAKA!
OWW... WHAT IS IT? YOU SHOULDN'T BE HERE ALONE AND CRYING.
...A DREAM?
MIAKA, I'M SORRY.
YOU'VE BEEN WORKING SO HARD, AND ALL FOR MY SAKE...

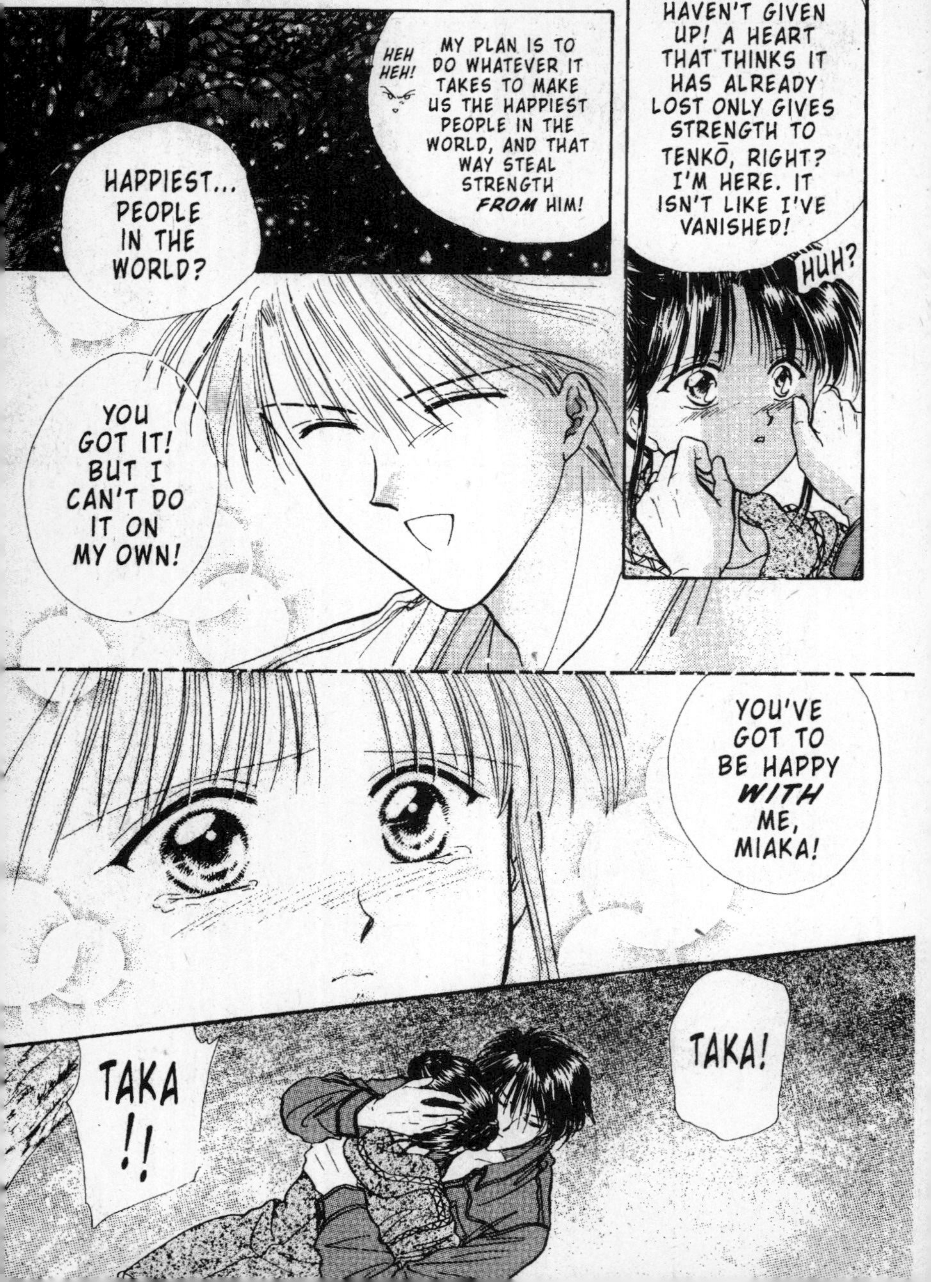
BUT I HAVEN'T GIVEN UP! A HEART THAT THINKS IT HAS ALREADY LOST ONLY GIVES STRENGTH TO TENKŌ, RIGHT? I'M HERE. IT ISN'T LIKE I'VE VANISHED!
HUH?
MY PLAN IS TO DO WHATEVER IT TAKES TO MAKE US THE HAPPIEST PEOPLE IN THE WORLD, AND THAT WAY STEAL STRENGTH *FROM* HIM!
HEH HEH!
HAPPIEST... PEOPLE IN THE WORLD?
YOU GOT IT! BUT I CAN'T DO IT ON MY OWN!
YOU'VE GOT TO BE HAPPY *WITH* ME, MIAKA!
TAKA!
TAKA !!

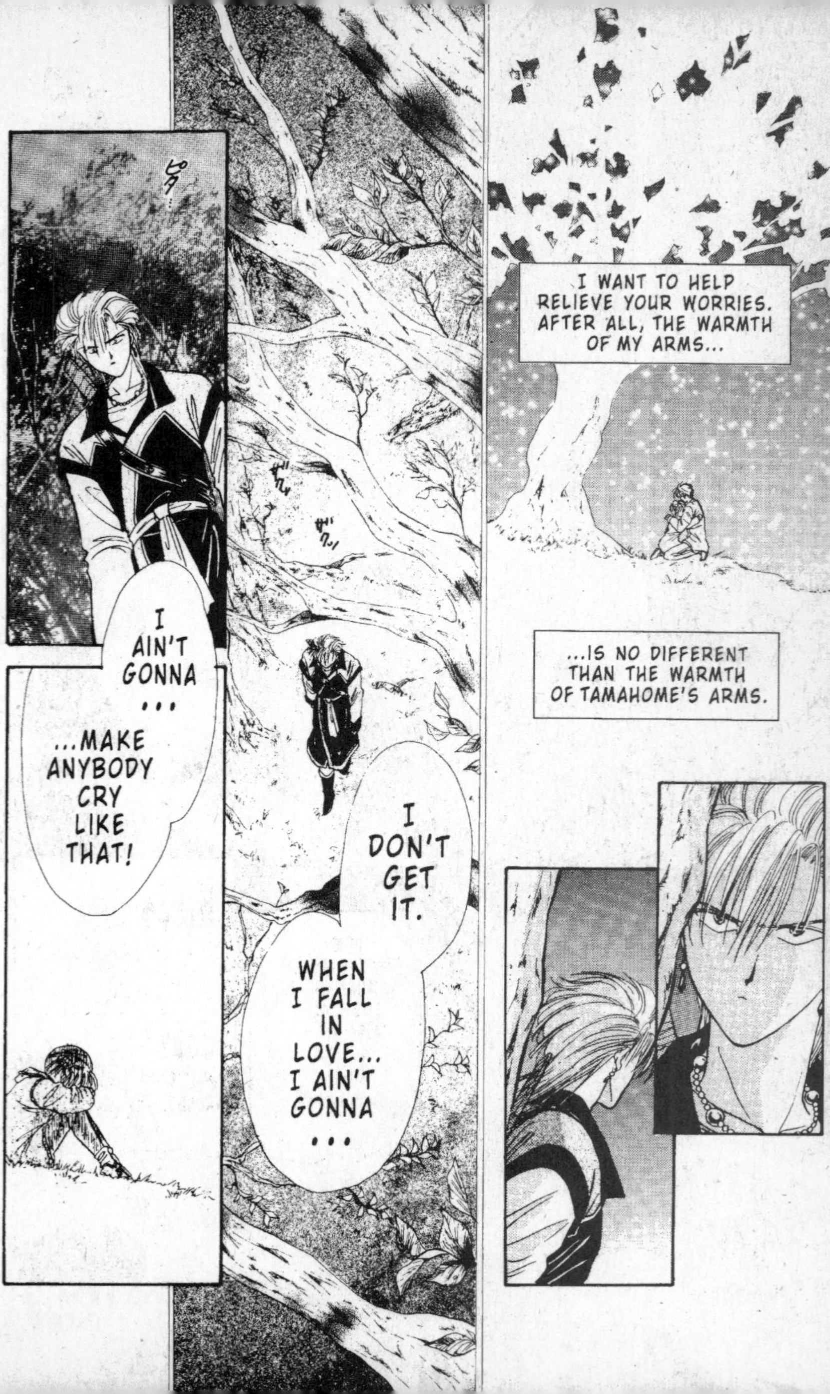
I WANT TO HELP RELIEVE YOUR WORRIES. AFTER ALL, THE WARMTH OF MY ARMS...
...IS NO DIFFERENT THAN THE WARMTH OF TAMAHOME'S ARMS.
I DON'T GET IT.
WHEN I FALL IN LOVE... I AIN'T GONNA ...
I AIN'T GONNA ...
...MAKE ANYBODY CRY LIKE THAT!

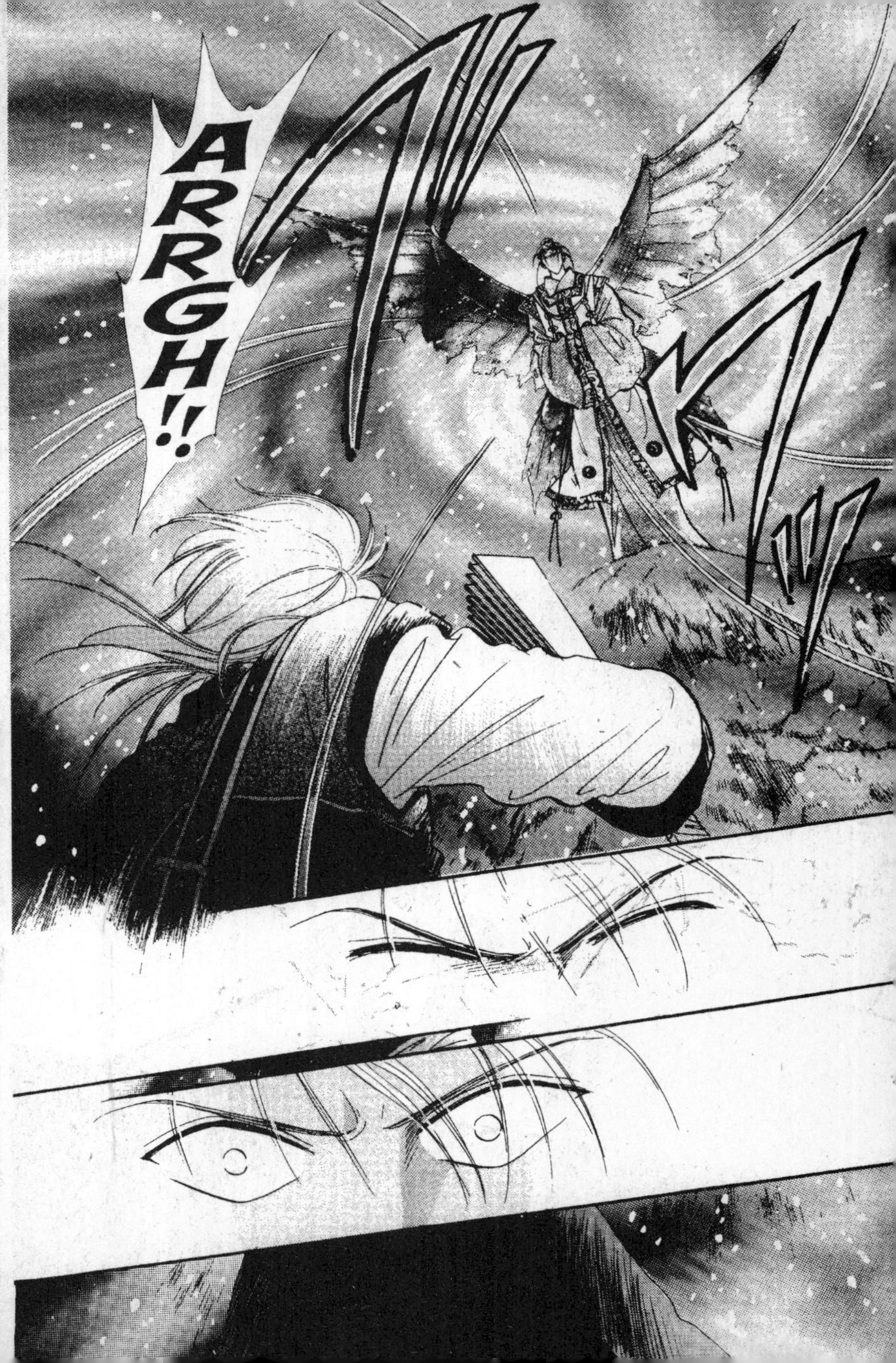
ARRGH!!

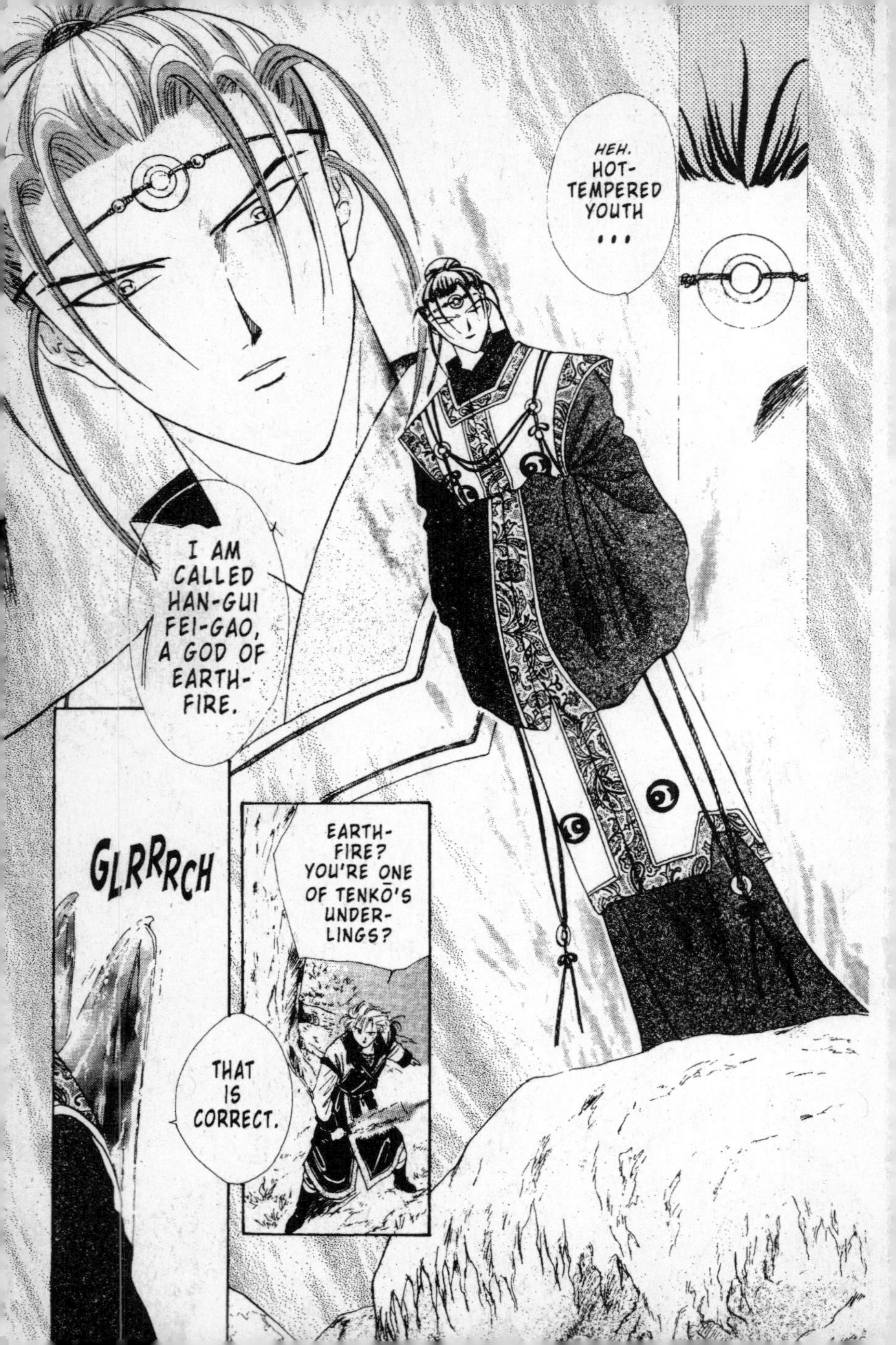
HEH. HOT-TEMPERED YOUTH ...
I AM CALLED HAN-GUI FEI-GAO, A GOD OF EARTH-FIRE.
EARTH-FIRE? YOU'RE ONE OF TENKŌ'S UNDER-LINGS?
THAT IS CORRECT.
GLRRRCH

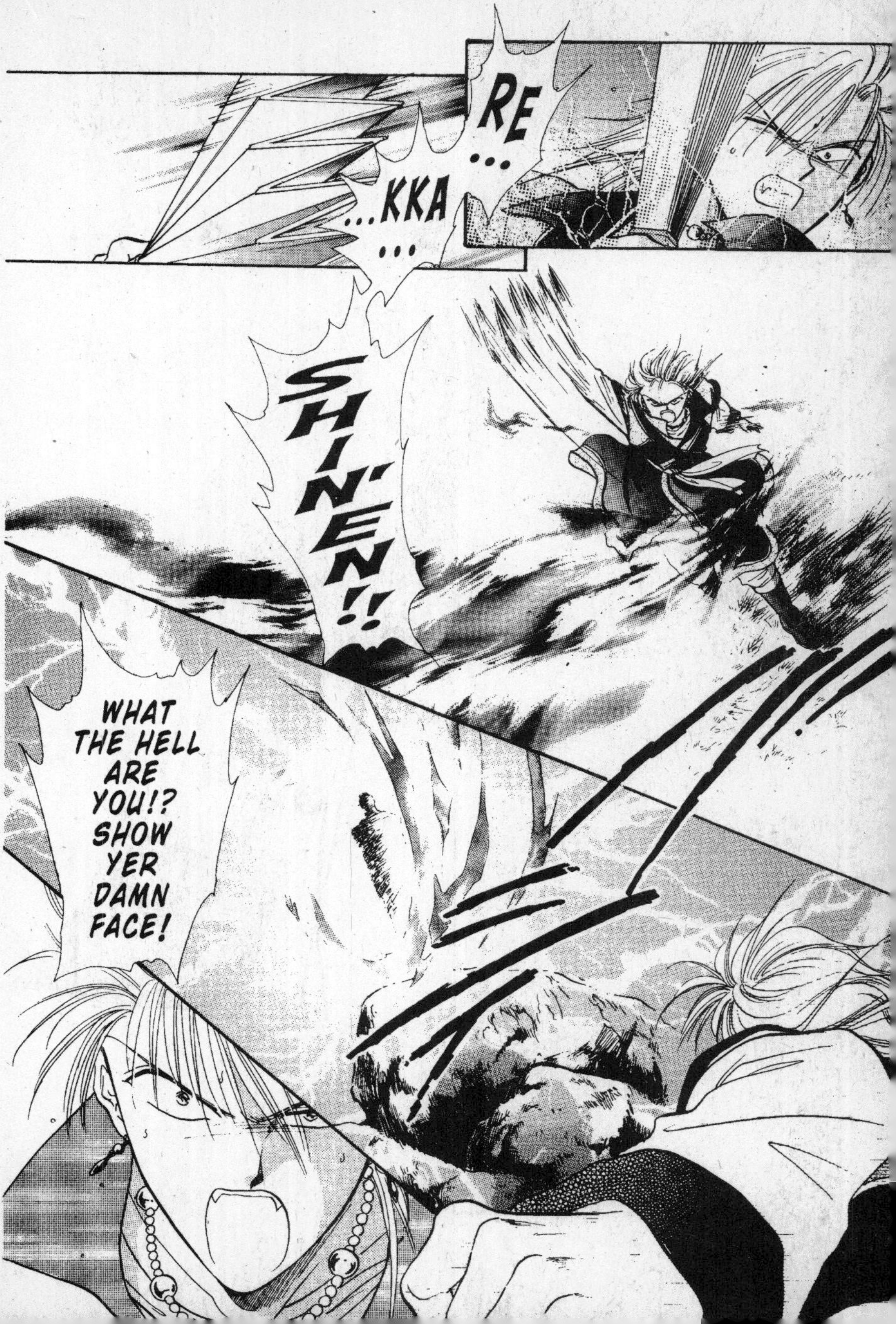
RE...
...KKA...
SHIN'EN!!
WHAT THE HELL ARE YOU!? SHOW YER DAMN FACE!

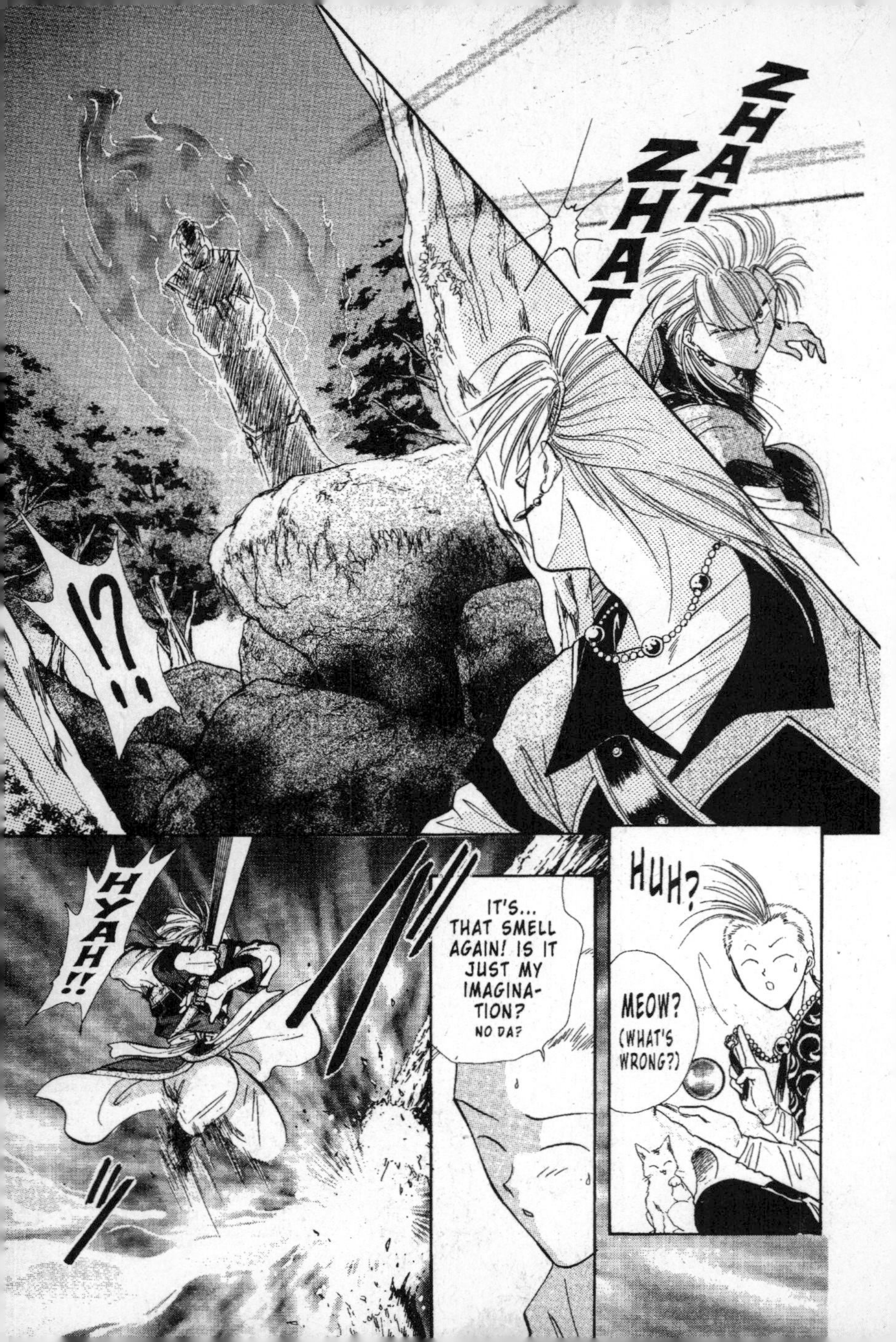
ZHAT
ZHAT
!?!!
HUH?
MEOW? (WHAT'S WRONG?)
IT'S... THAT SMELL AGAIN! IS IT JUST MY IMAGINATION? NO DA?
HYAH!!

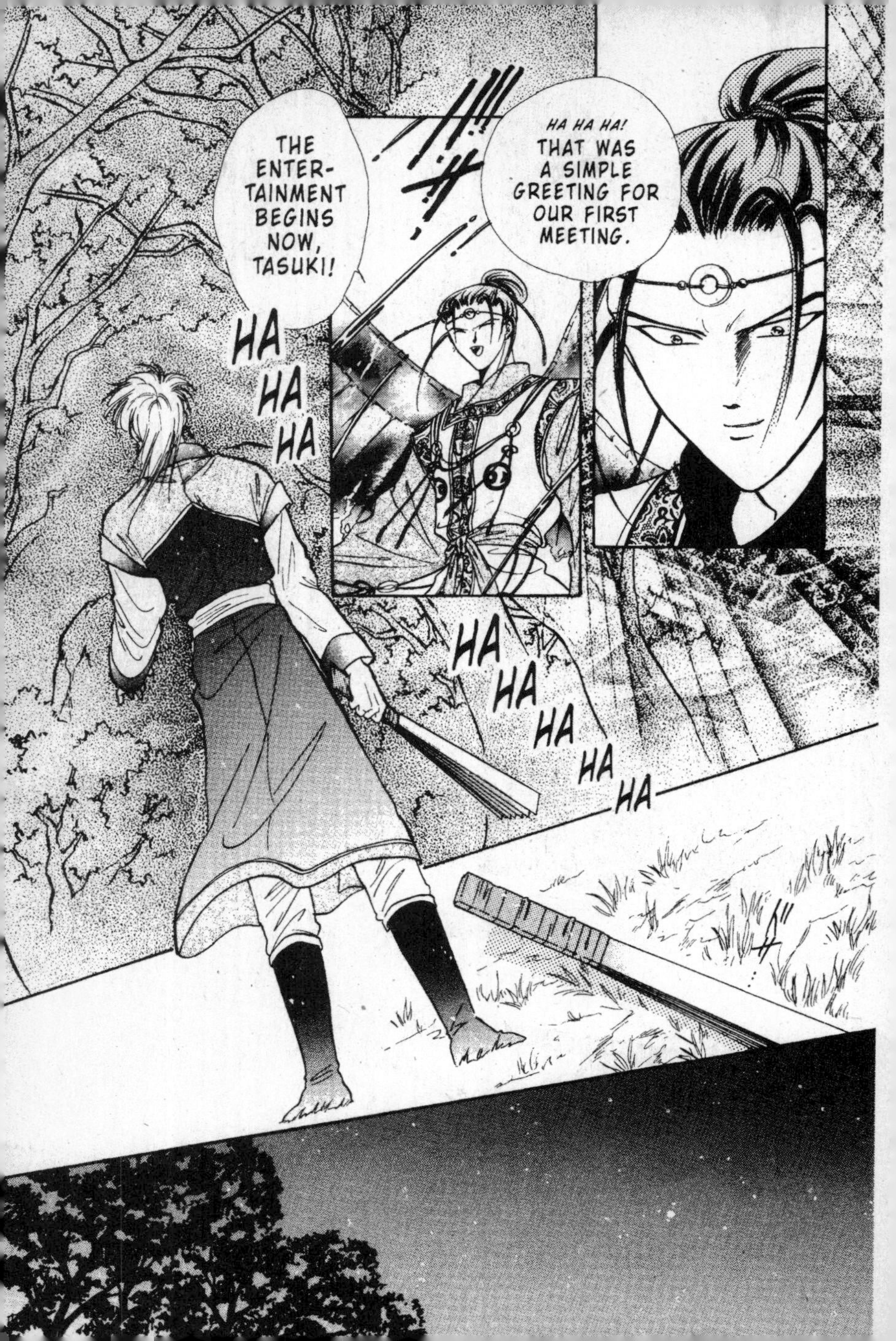
HA HA HA! THAT WAS A SIMPLE GREETING FOR OUR FIRST MEETING.
THE ENTER-TAINMENT BEGINS NOW, TASUKI!
HA HA HA
HA HA HA HA HA

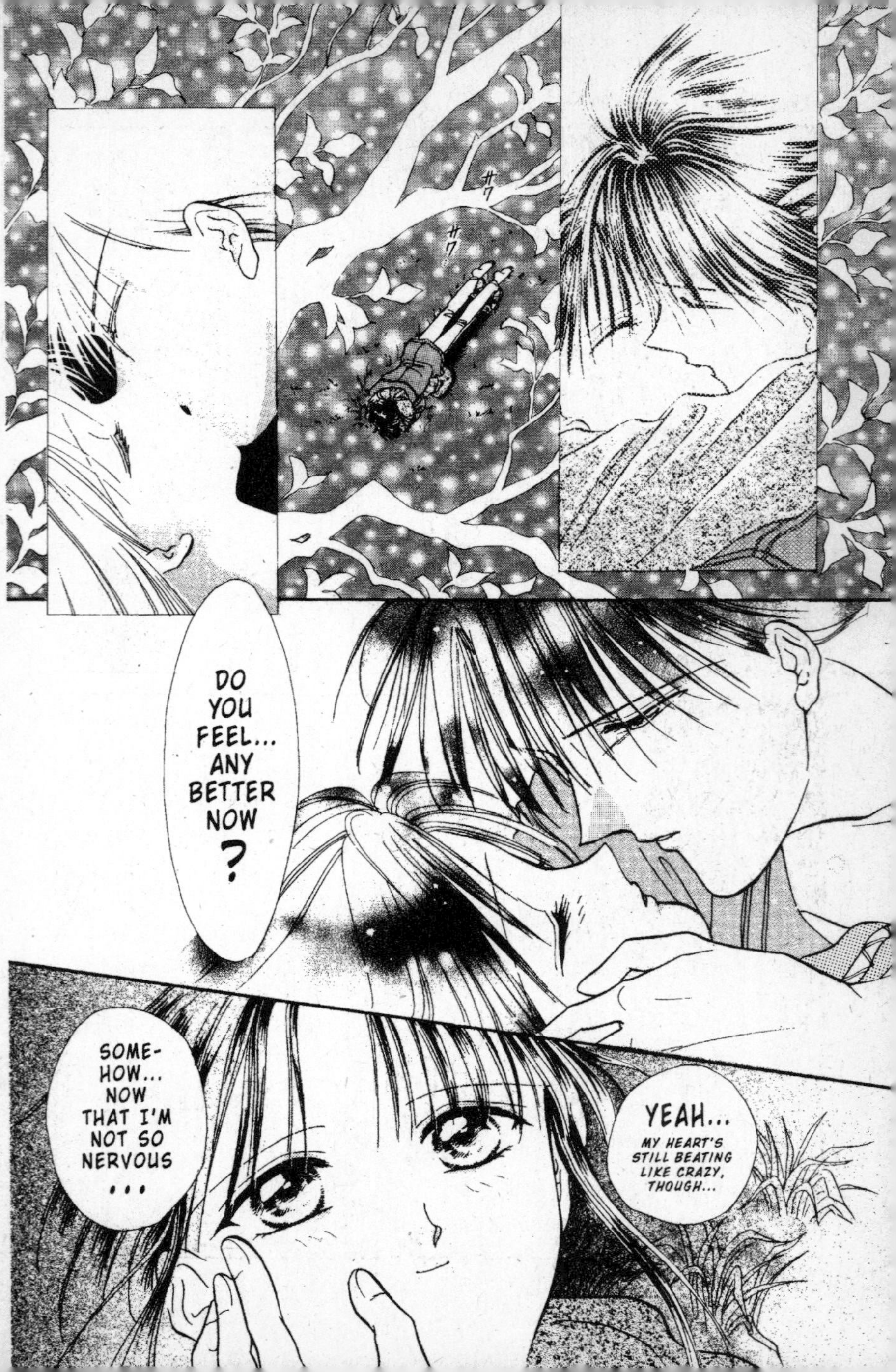
DO YOU FEEL... ANY BETTER NOW?
YEAH... MY HEART'S STILL BEATING LIKE CRAZY, THOUGH...
SOME-HOW... NOW THAT I'M NOT SO NERVOUS...

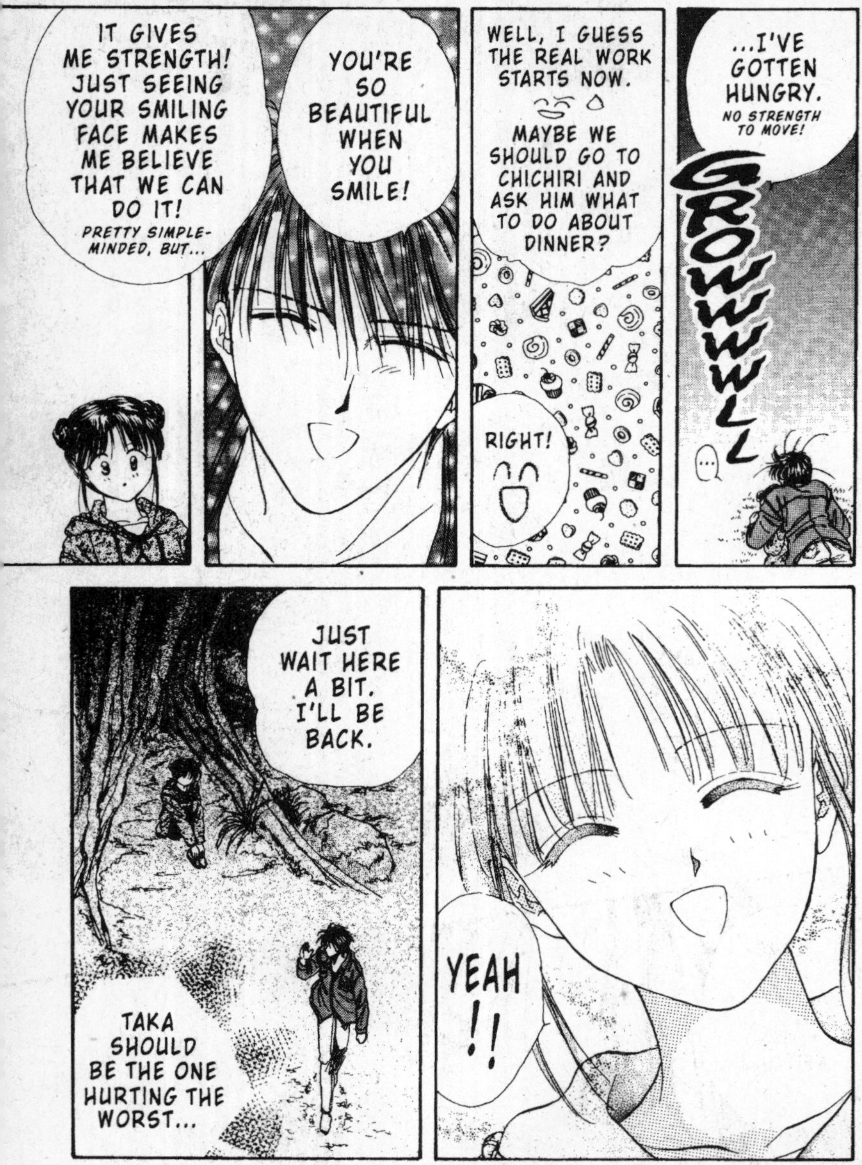
...I'VE GOTTEN HUNGRY.
NO STRENGTH TO MOVE!
GROWWWWLL
...
WELL, I GUESS THE REAL WORK STARTS NOW.
MAYBE WE SHOULD GO TO CHICHIRI AND ASK HIM WHAT TO DO ABOUT DINNER?
RIGHT!
YOU'RE SO BEAUTIFUL WHEN YOU SMILE!
IT GIVES ME STRENGTH! JUST SEEING YOUR SMILING FACE MAKES ME BELIEVE THAT WE CAN DO IT!
PRETTY SIMPLE-MINDED, BUT...
YEAH!!
JUST WAIT HERE A BIT. I'LL BE BACK.
TAKA SHOULD BE THE ONE HURTING THE WORST...

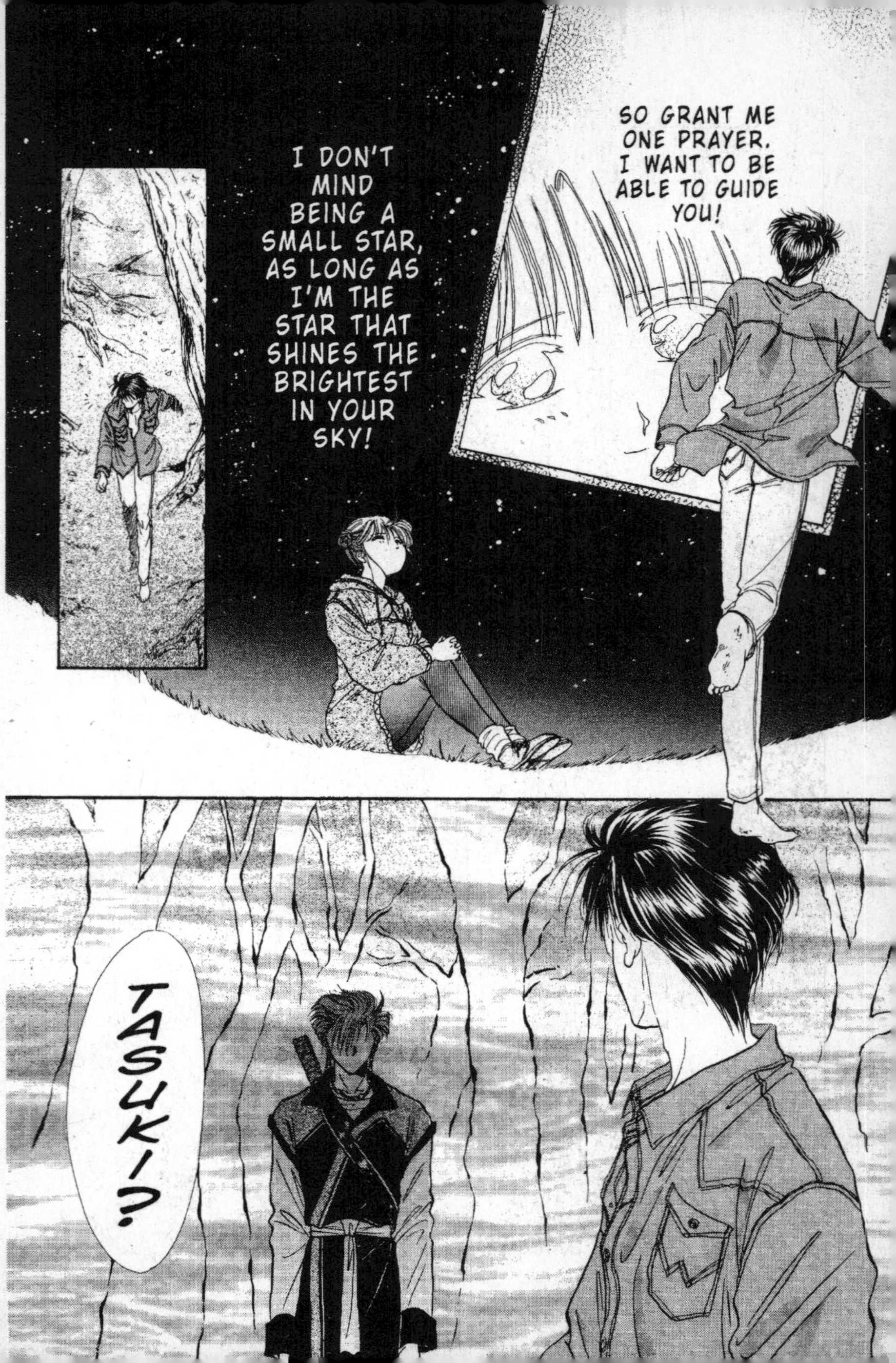
SO GRANT ME ONE PRAYER. I WANT TO BE ABLE TO GUIDE YOU!
I DON'T MIND BEING A SMALL STAR, AS LONG AS I'M THE STAR THAT SHINES THE BRIGHTEST IN YOUR SKY!
TASUKI?

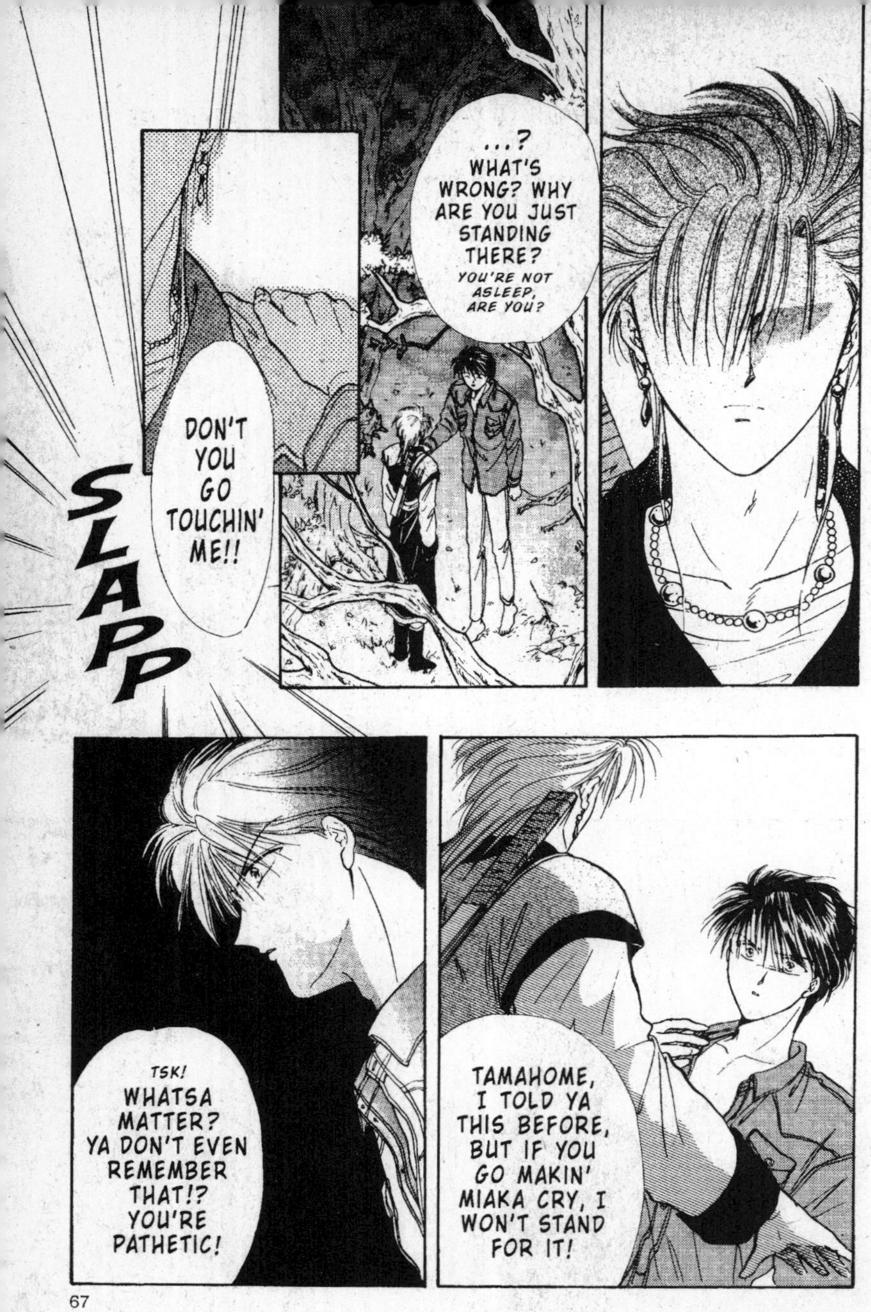
...?
WHAT'S WRONG? WHY ARE YOU JUST STANDING THERE?
YOU'RE NOT ASLEEP, ARE YOU?
DON'T YOU GO TOUCHIN' ME!!
SLAPP
TAMAHOME, I TOLD YA THIS BEFORE, BUT IF YOU GO MAKIN' MIAKA CRY, I WON'T STAND FOR IT!
TSK!
WHATSA MATTER? YA DON'T EVEN REMEMBER THAT!? YOU'RE PATHETIC!

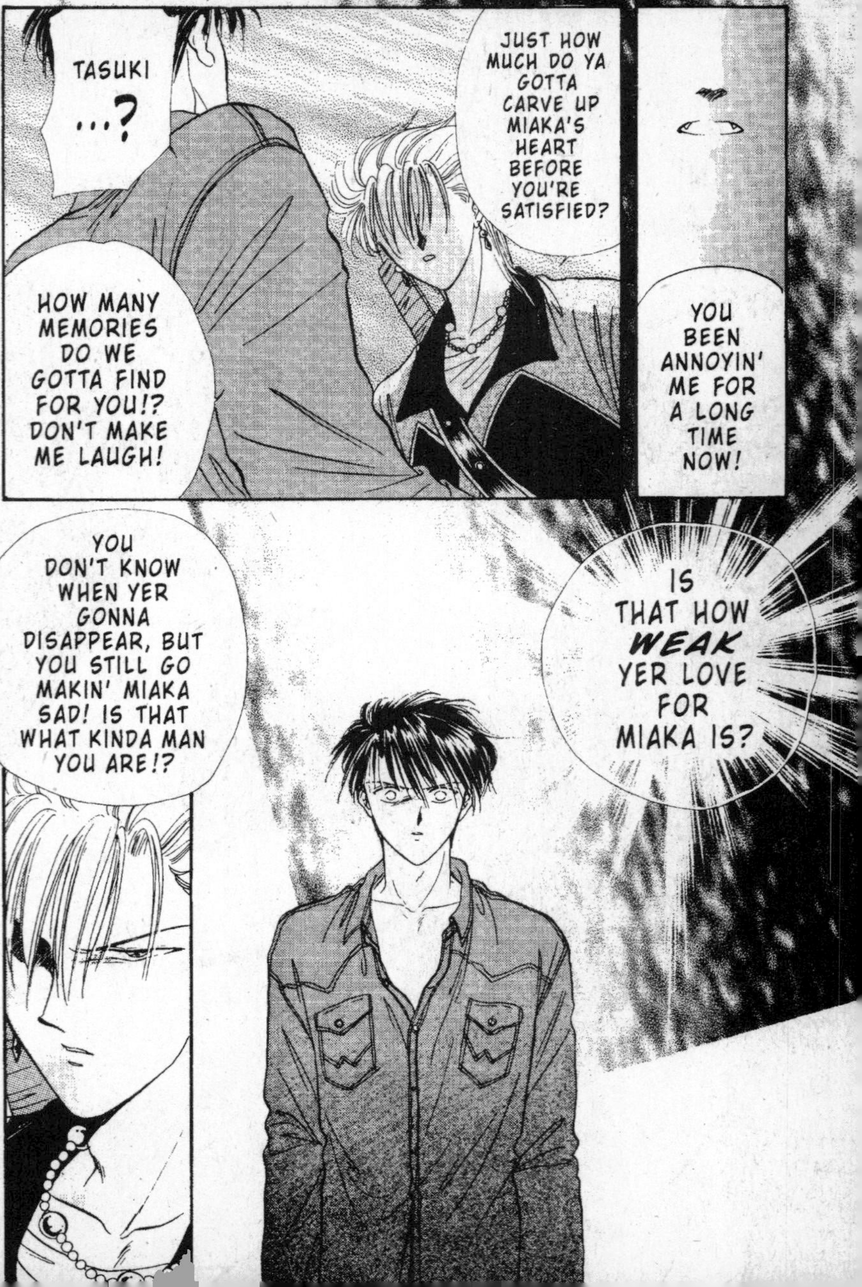
YOU BEEN ANNOYIN' ME FOR A LONG TIME NOW!
JUST HOW MUCH DO YA GOTTA CARVE UP MIAKA'S HEART BEFORE YOU'RE SATISFIED?
TASUKI ...?
HOW MANY MEMORIES DO WE GOTTA FIND FOR YOU!? DON'T MAKE ME LAUGH!
IS THAT HOW ***WEAK*** YER LOVE FOR MIAKA IS?
YOU DON'T KNOW WHEN YER GONNA DISAPPEAR, BUT YOU STILL GO MAKIN' MIAKA SAD! IS THAT WHAT KINDA MAN YOU ARE!?

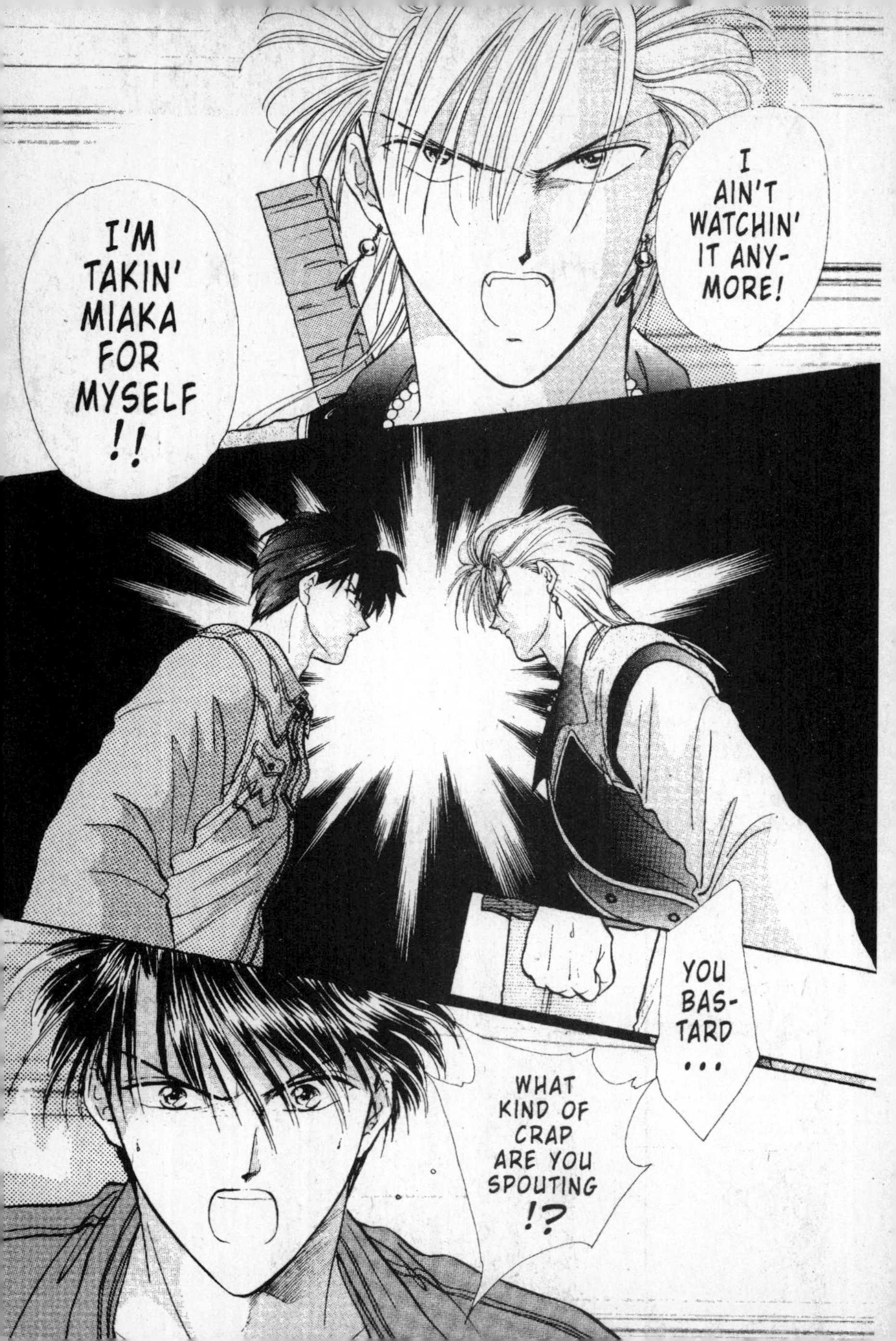
I AIN'T WATCHIN' IT ANYMORE!
I'M TAKIN' MIAKA FOR MYSELF!!
YOU BASTARD...
WHAT KIND OF CRAP ARE YOU SPOUTING!?

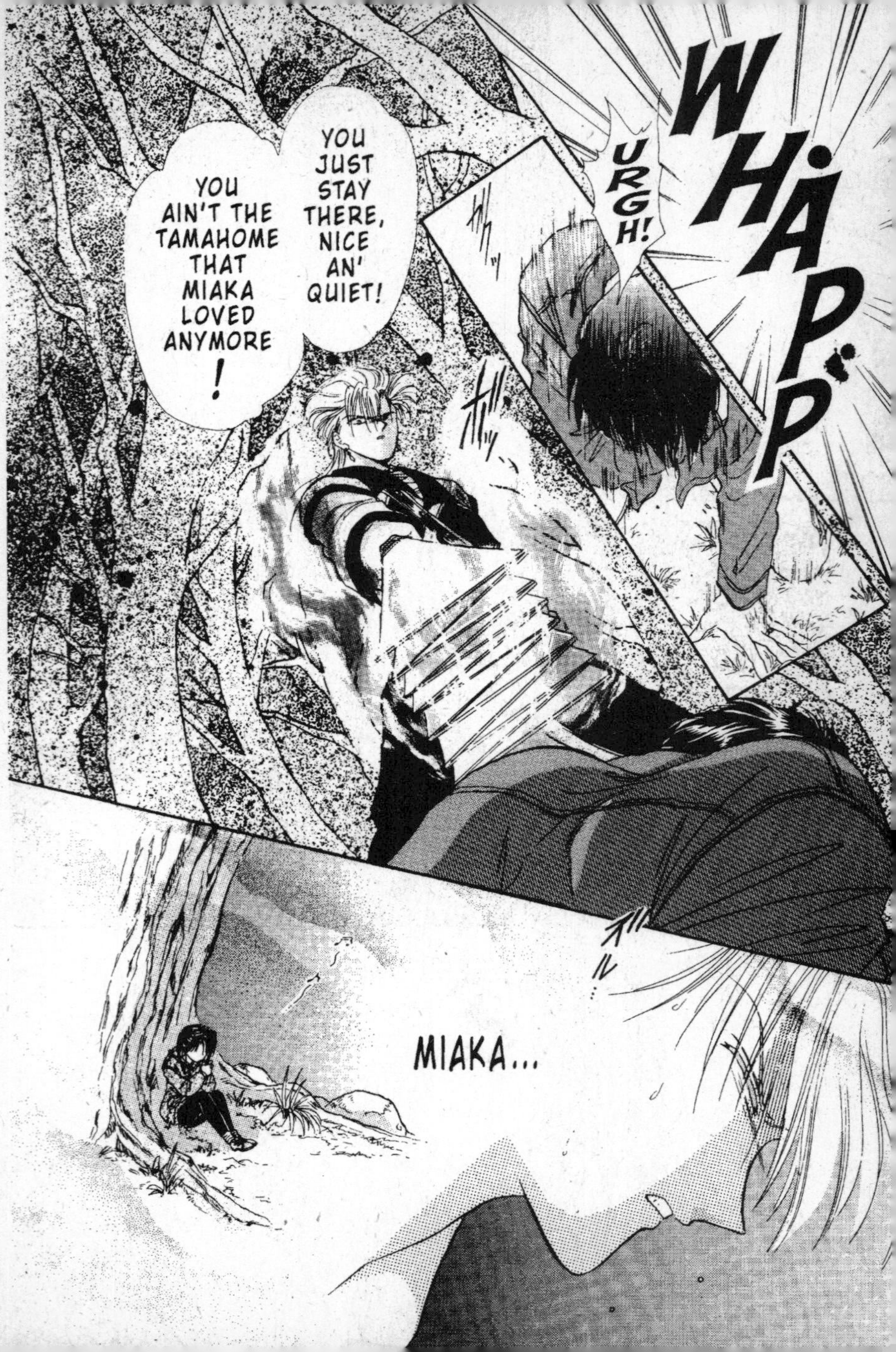
WHAPP
URGH!
YOU JUST STAY THERE, NICE AN' QUIET!
YOU AIN'T THE TAMAHOME THAT MIAKA LOVED ANYMORE!
MIAKA...

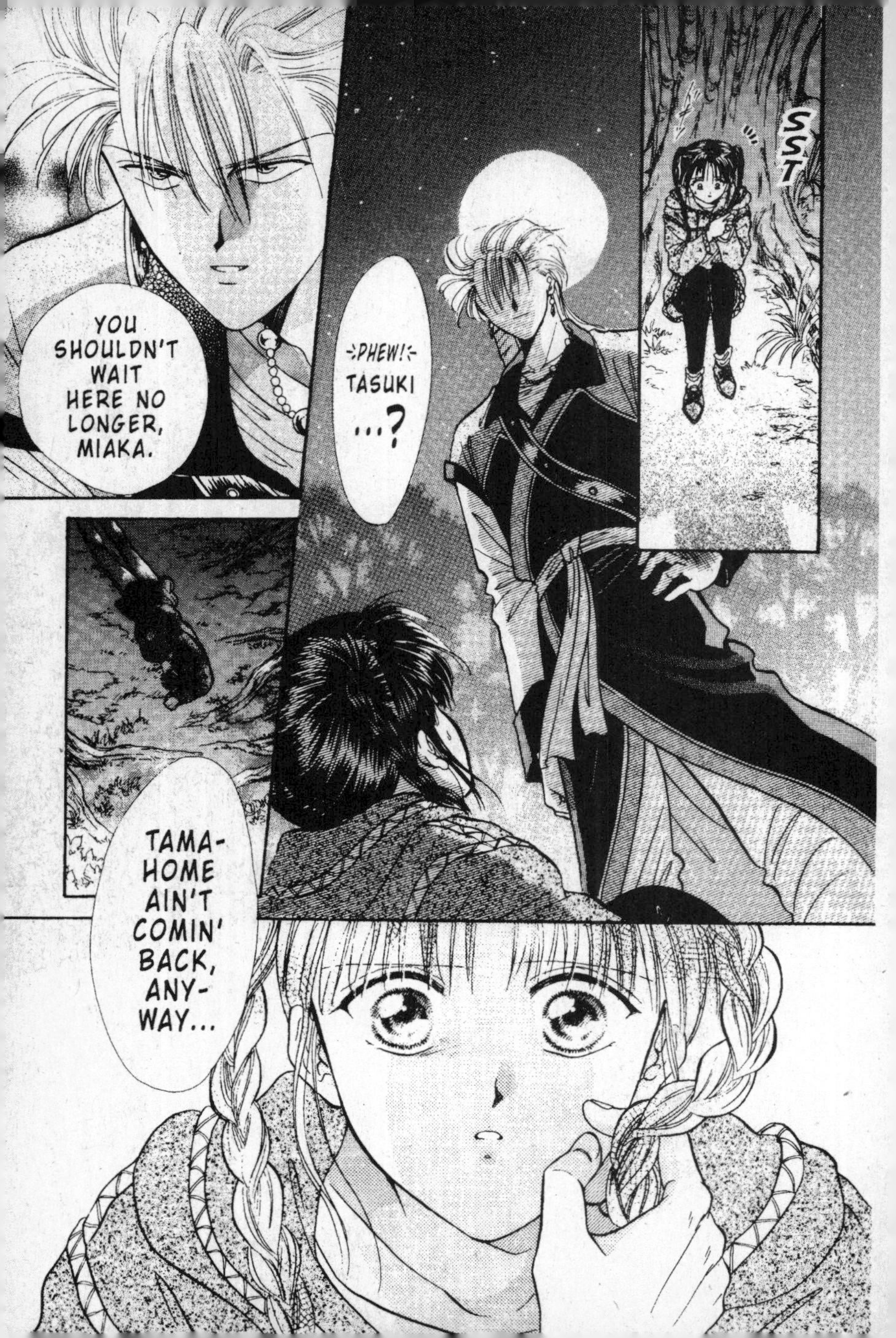
SST
PHEW! TASUKI ...?
YOU SHOULDN'T WAIT HERE NO LONGER, MIAKA.
TAMA-HOME AIN'T COMIN' BACK, ANY-WAY...

QUESTION FOR THIS TIME: "WHAT'S GOING ON!?"

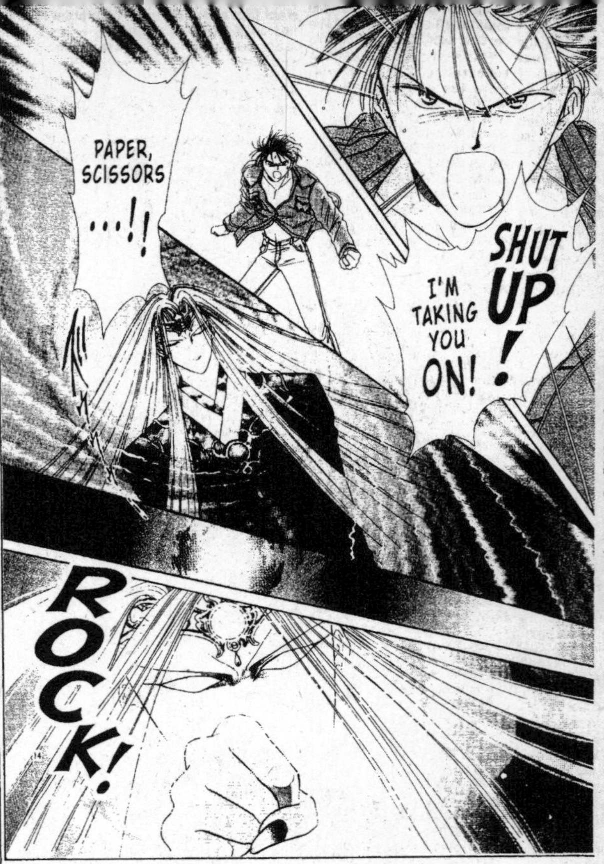
SHUT UP!
I'M TAKING YOU ON!
PAPER, SCISSORS
...!!
ROCK!

ふしぎ悪戯

FUSHIGI AKUGI

THE MALICIOUS PLAY

IDEA BY: MY ASSISTANT H. ☺

14

HERE'S SOME INFORMATION!

The CD Books are coming out again! For Part 2!! "I can't believe it!" is what I thought, but they're actually coming out... sometime around June (1996)! And... they're pulling the songs by the voice actors on the previous five volumes and gathering them into their own CD Book, "Best of Fushigi Yûgi"! (I think that's what it's called.) Yes, they're really all together in one place, and for only 1800 yen! What a bargain!! So for all those people who think that five volumes is a little much, this is for you!! ♥ Anyway, I'll be creating original art for the cover and the liner notes. There'll be 17 songs in all (including one from the phantom Zen-Play CD. ☺

Thanks to everyone for the Valentine's Day gifts this year (1996)!!

I wasn't able to make the White Day (3/14) deadline, but I did get replies out to everybody! I thought I was gonna die! ፀፀ I mean... I GOT THEM FROM 184 PEOPLE!!! I'm sorry! As I expected, I couldn't eat them all myself. My editor said to me, "Don't eat all those! If you try, you'll wind up in the hospital!" and he stopped me. ፀፀ But if I had even one bite of each, it means I accept!! I thank you all for your gifts of love! Most of them (2/3rds?) were made by hand! Inside there were cookies, those senbei crackers I really like, Nakago dolls, scarves...they all made me very happy! (But about the hand-made foods... I'm happy for the thought, but there were some I wasn't able to taste before they spoiled! ፀፀፀ)

A TRUE STORY!

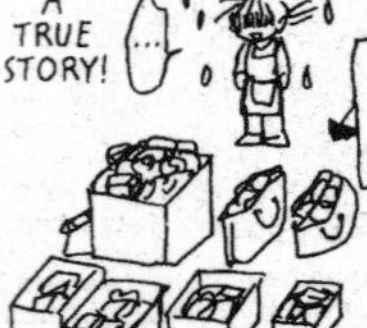
...

THERE WERE 410 ITEMS DELIVERED TO THE CHARACTERS!!

BEST 10!!

NUMBER 1!! TASUKI!! (76 ITEMS) IT'S ONLY NATURAL!

NUMBER 2 NURIKO! (62 ITEMS) THANK YOU!

NUMBER 3 CHICHIRI! (56 ITEMS) NO DA? JUST BARELY MADE A NEW RECORD FOR HIM! CONGRATULATIONS!

NO. 4! TAKA (41 ITEMS) DAMMIT!!

NO. 5! CHIRIKO (32 ITEMS)

NO. 6! HOTOHORI (30 ITEMS)

NO. 7! MITSUKAKE (25 ITEMS)

ON FEBRUARY 14, 15, 16th... I STANK OF MY TREASURE TROVE OF CHOCOLATES! Burp...

AND THE REST...

NO. 8 WATASE (18 ITEMS)

NO. 9 AMIBOSHI (14 ITEMS)

NO. 10 SUBOSHI (7 ITEMS)

NO. 11 NAKAGO (6 ITEMS)

NO. 12 MIAKA (5 ITEMS)

NO. 13 TOKAKI KNEI-GONG (KÔJI) TOMO (3 ITEMS)

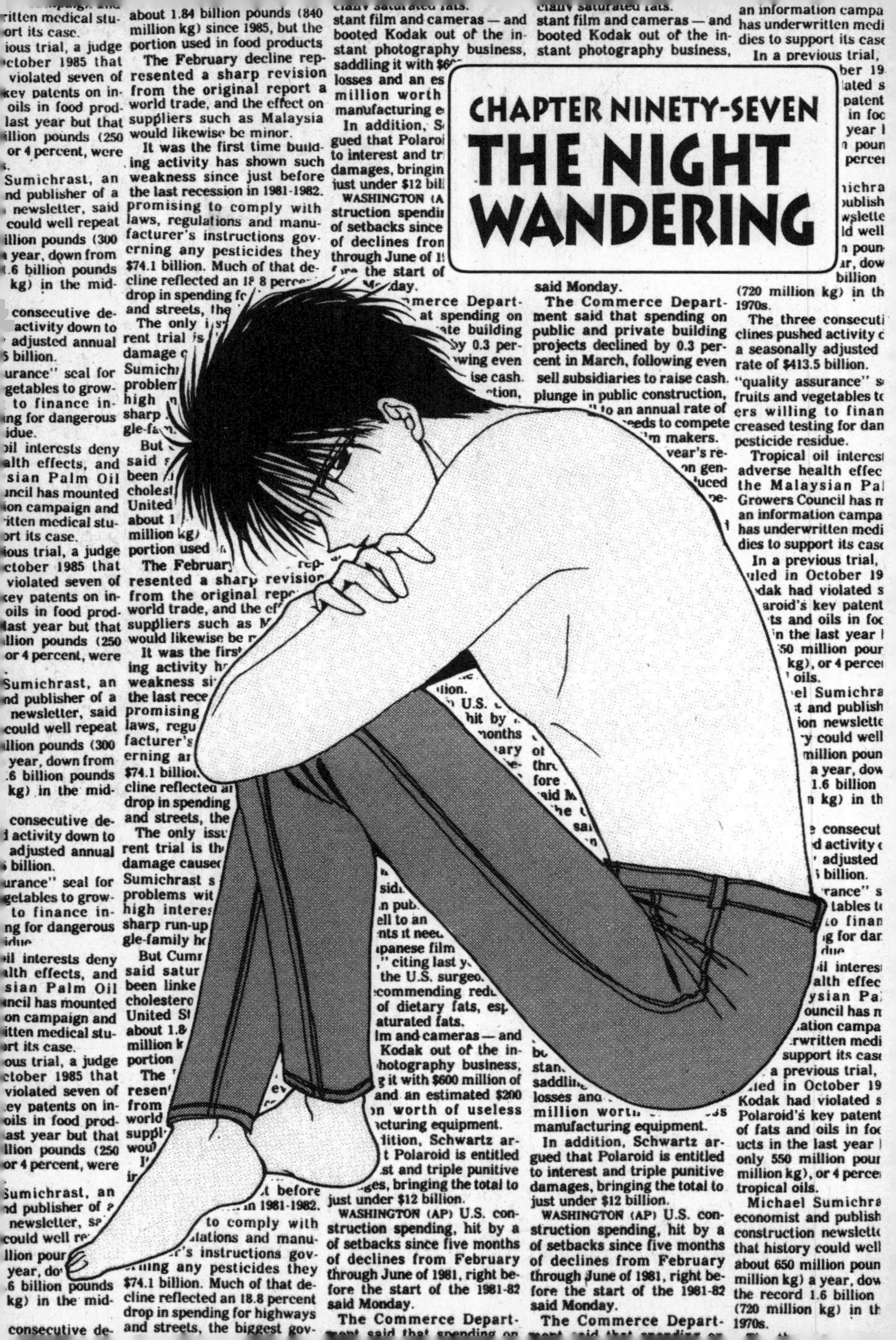
CHAPTER NINETY-SEVEN
THE NIGHT WANDERING

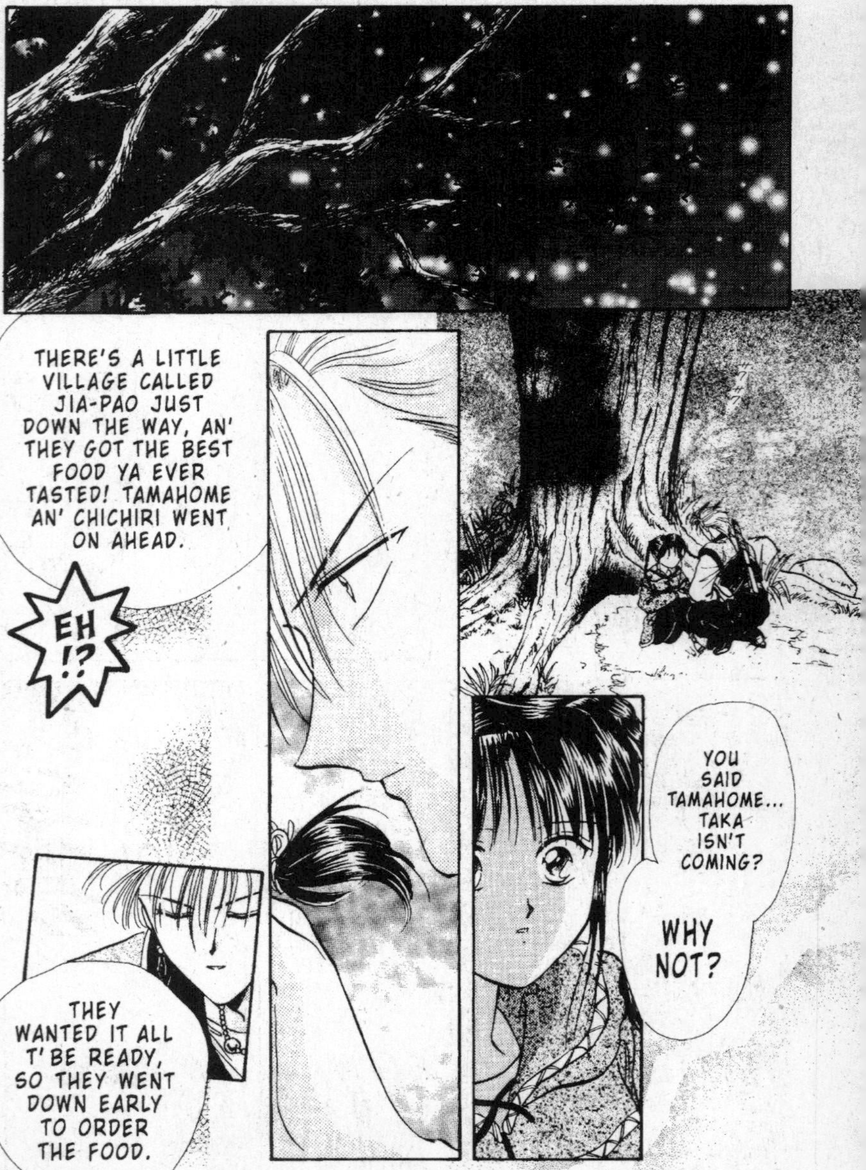
THERE'S A LITTLE VILLAGE CALLED JIA-PAO JUST DOWN THE WAY, AN' THEY GOT THE BEST FOOD YA EVER TASTED! TAMAHOME AN' CHICHIRI WENT ON AHEAD.
EH!?
YOU SAID TAMAHOME... TAKA ISN'T COMING?
WHY NOT?
THEY WANTED IT ALL T' BE READY, SO THEY WENT DOWN EARLY TO ORDER THE FOOD.

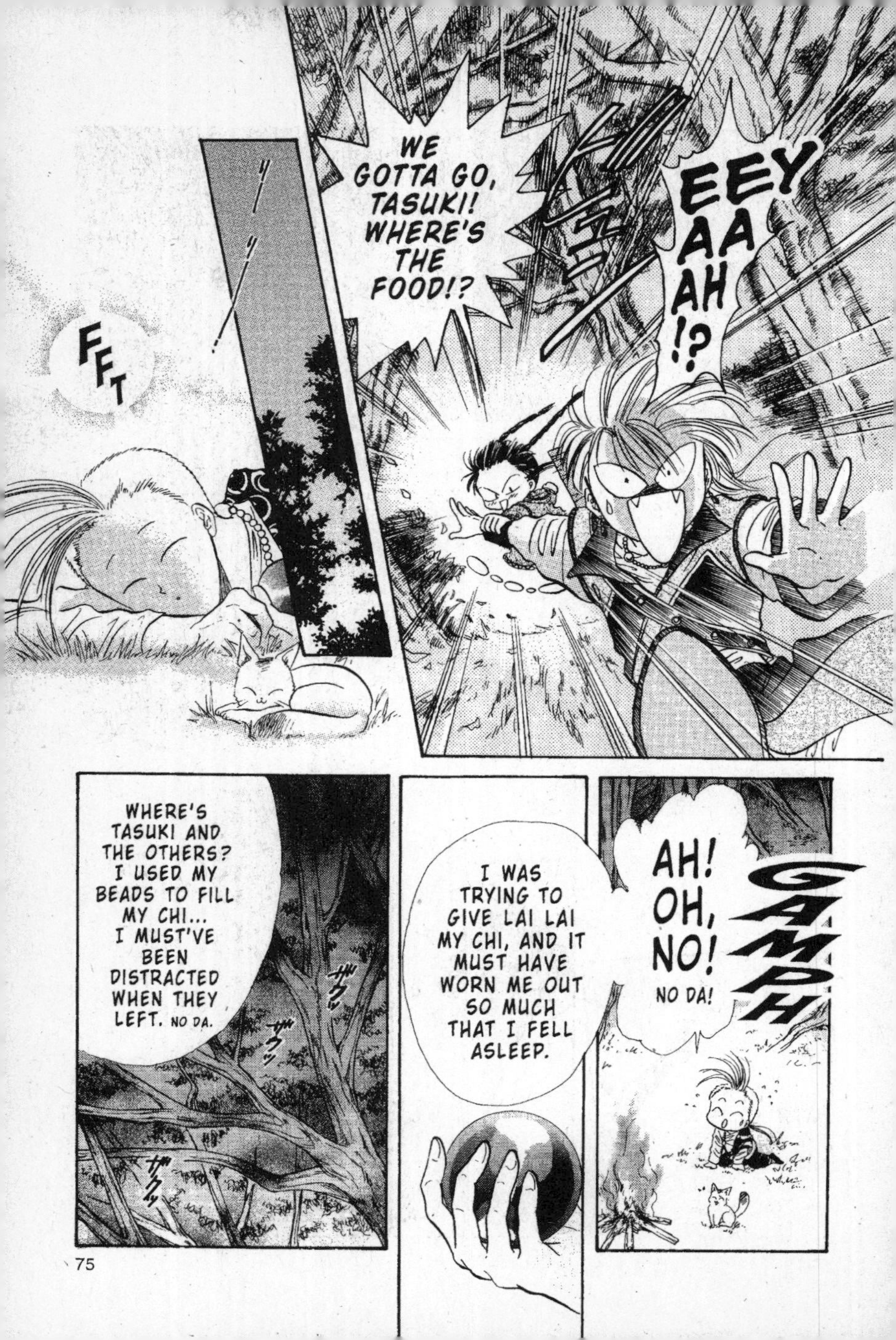
EEYAAAH!?
WE GOTTA GO, TASUKI! WHERE'S THE FOOD!?
FFFT
AH! OH, NO! NO DA!
GAMPH
I WAS TRYING TO GIVE LAI LAI MY CHI, AND IT MUST HAVE WORN ME OUT SO MUCH THAT I FELL ASLEEP.
WHERE'S TASUKI AND THE OTHERS? I USED MY BEADS TO FILL MY CHI... I MUST'VE BEEN DISTRACTED WHEN THEY LEFT. NO DA.

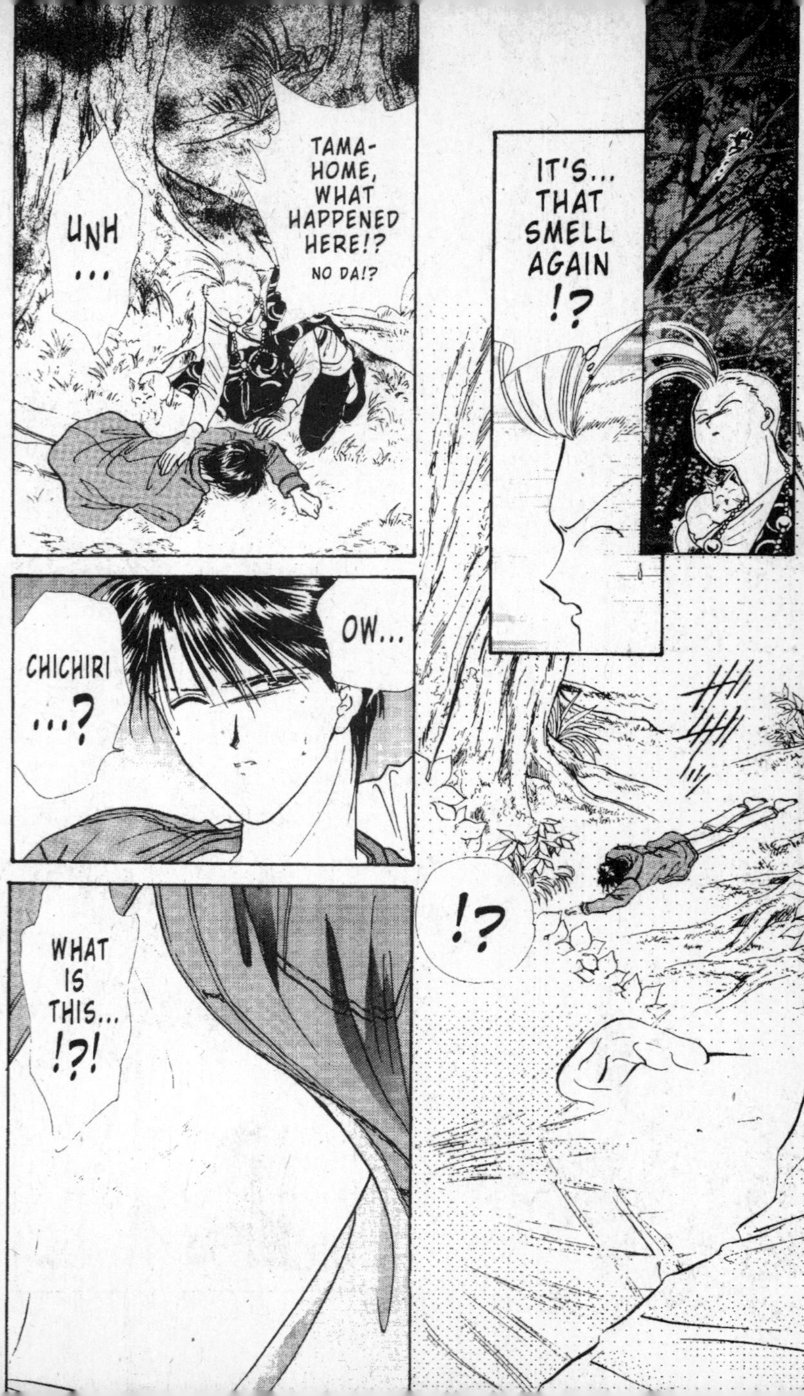
IT'S... THAT SMELL AGAIN !?
!?
TAMA-HOME, WHAT HAPPENED HERE!? NO DA!?
UNH ...
OW...
CHICHIRI ...?
WHAT IS THIS... !?!

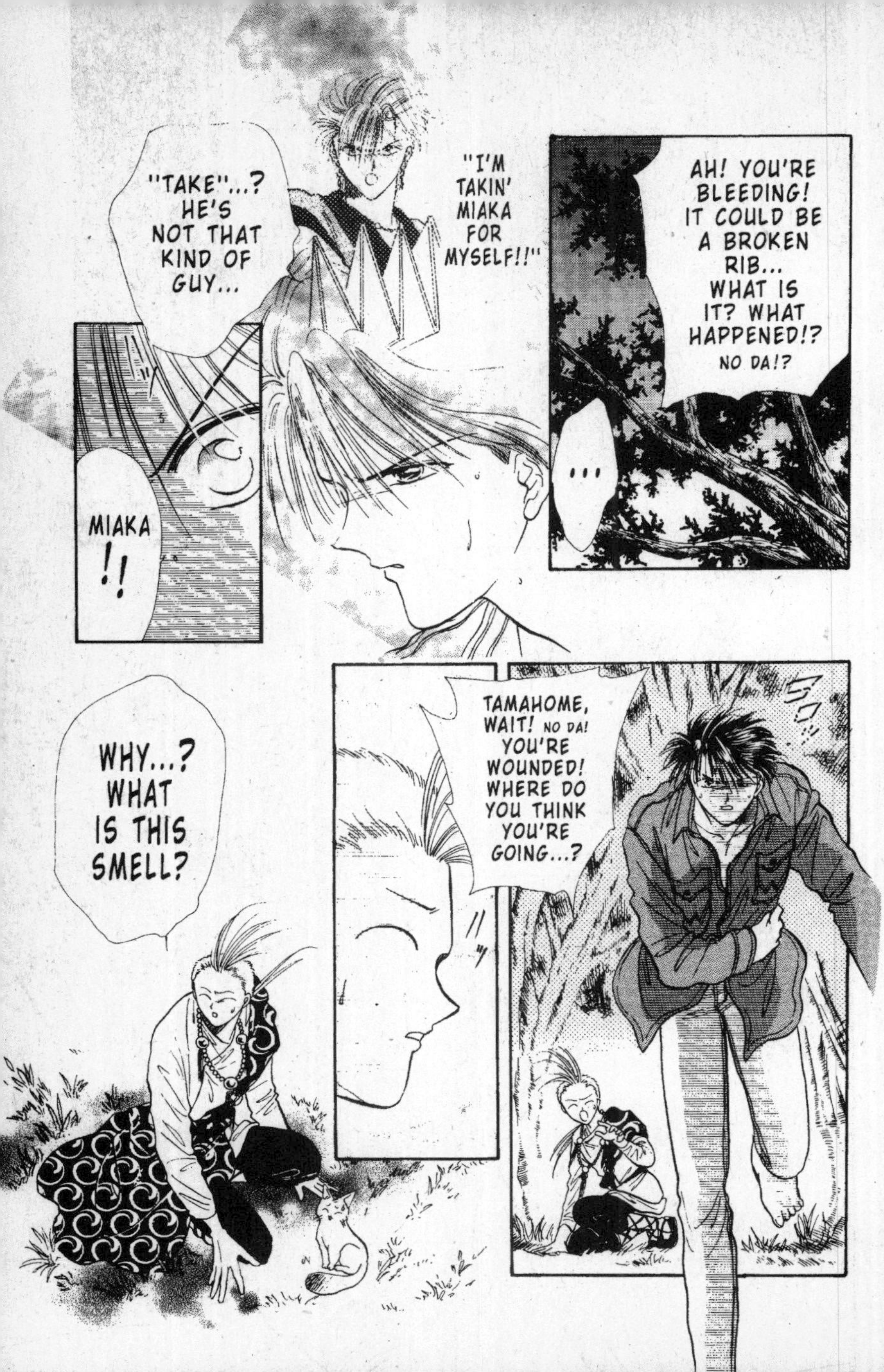
AH! YOU'RE BLEEDING! IT COULD BE A BROKEN RIB... WHAT IS IT? WHAT HAPPENED!? NO DA!?
...
"I'M TAKIN' MIAKA FOR MYSELF!!"
"TAKE"...? HE'S NOT THAT KIND OF GUY...
MIAKA !!
TAMAHOME, WAIT! NO DA! YOU'RE WOUNDED! WHERE DO YOU THINK YOU'RE GOING...?
WHY...? WHAT IS THIS SMELL?

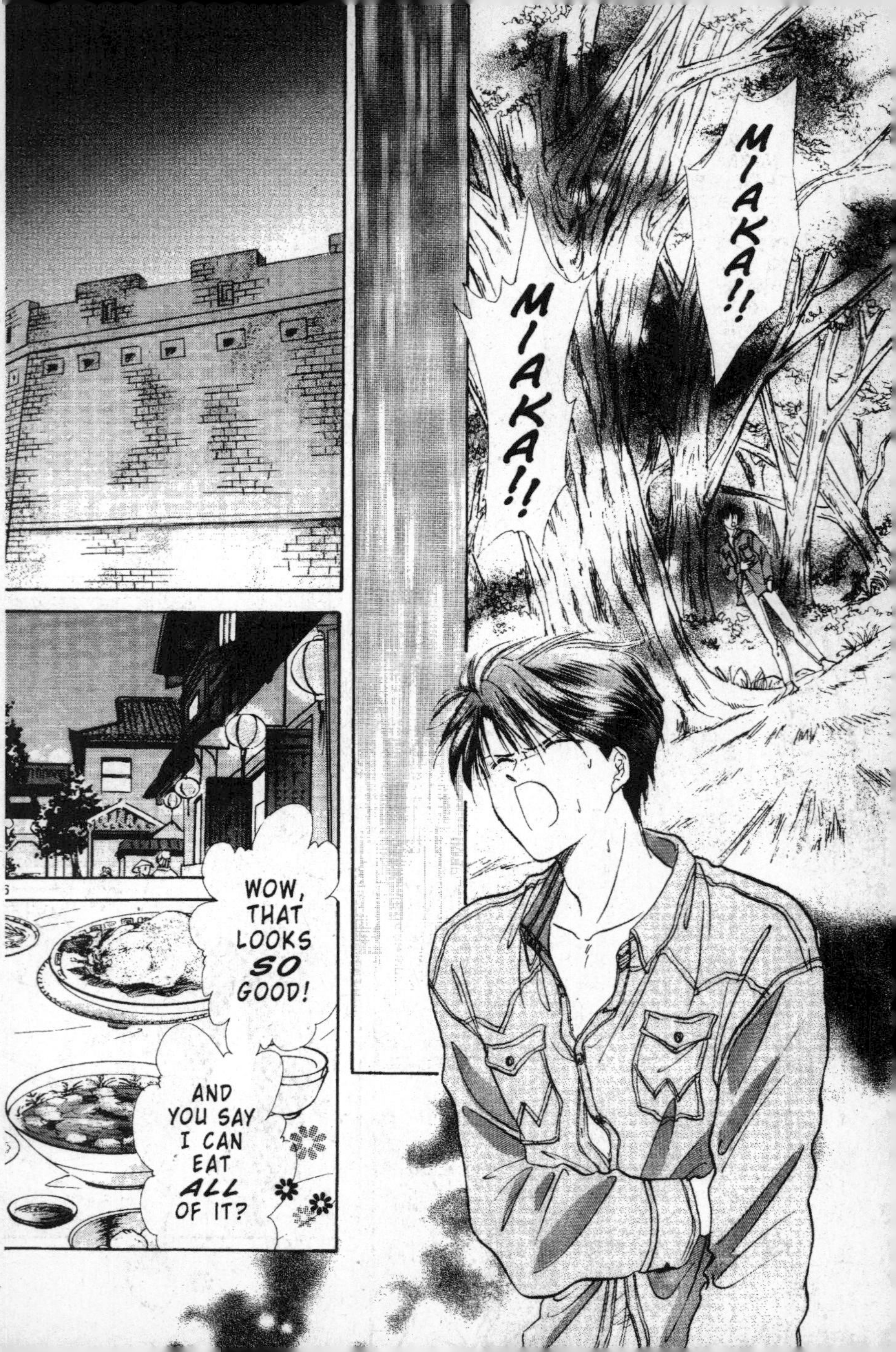
MIAKA!!
MIAKA!!
WOW, THAT LOOKS *SO* GOOD!
AND YOU SAY I CAN EAT *ALL* OF IT?

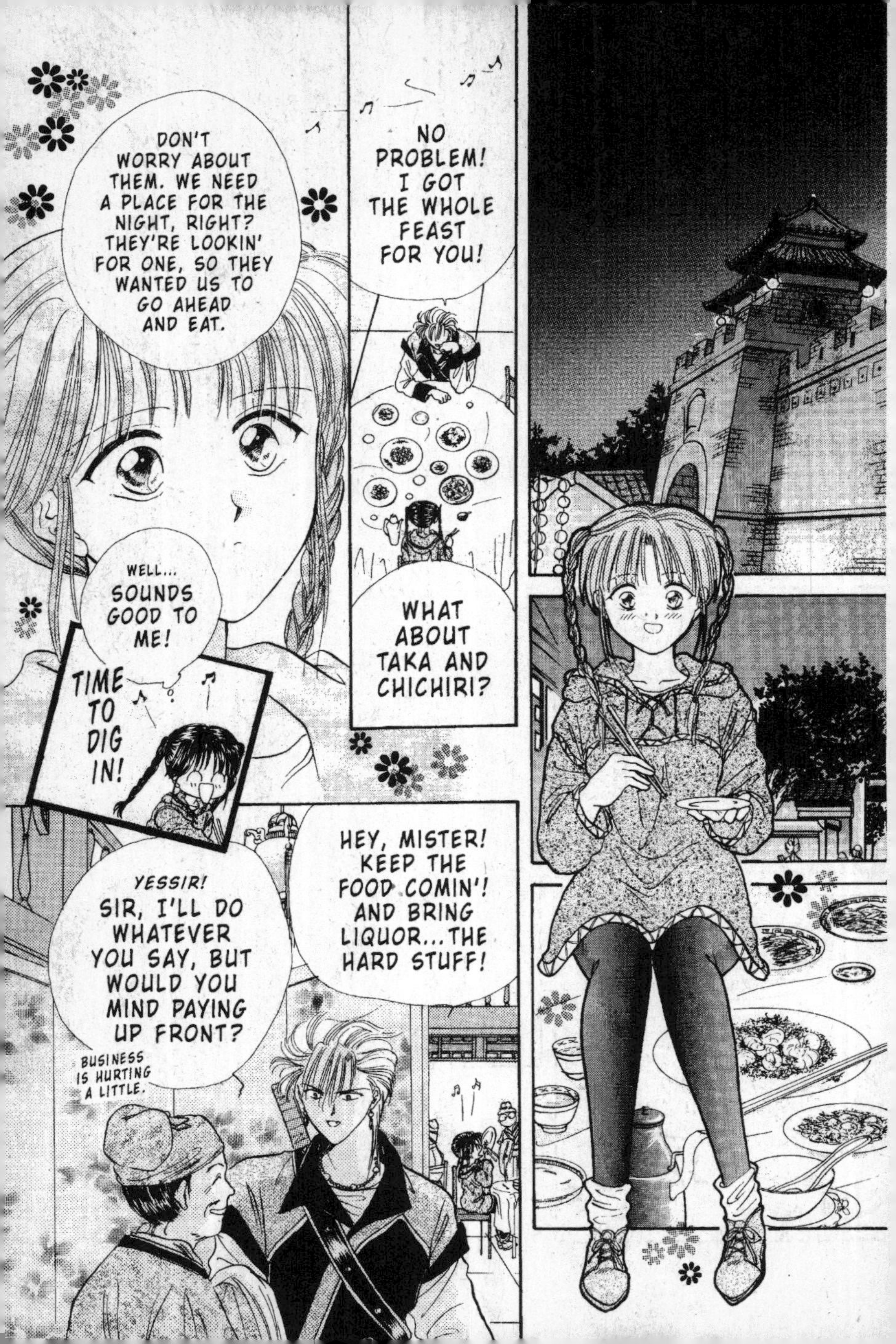
NO PROBLEM! I GOT THE WHOLE FEAST FOR YOU!
WHAT ABOUT TAKA AND CHICHIRI?
DON'T WORRY ABOUT THEM. WE NEED A PLACE FOR THE NIGHT, RIGHT? THEY'RE LOOKIN' FOR ONE, SO THEY WANTED US TO GO AHEAD AND EAT.
WELL... SOUNDS GOOD TO ME!
TIME TO DIG IN!
HEY, MISTER! KEEP THE FOOD COMIN'! AND BRING LIQUOR... THE HARD STUFF!
YESSIR! SIR, I'LL DO WHATEVER YOU SAY, BUT WOULD YOU MIND PAYING UP FRONT?
BUSINESS IS HURTING A LITTLE.

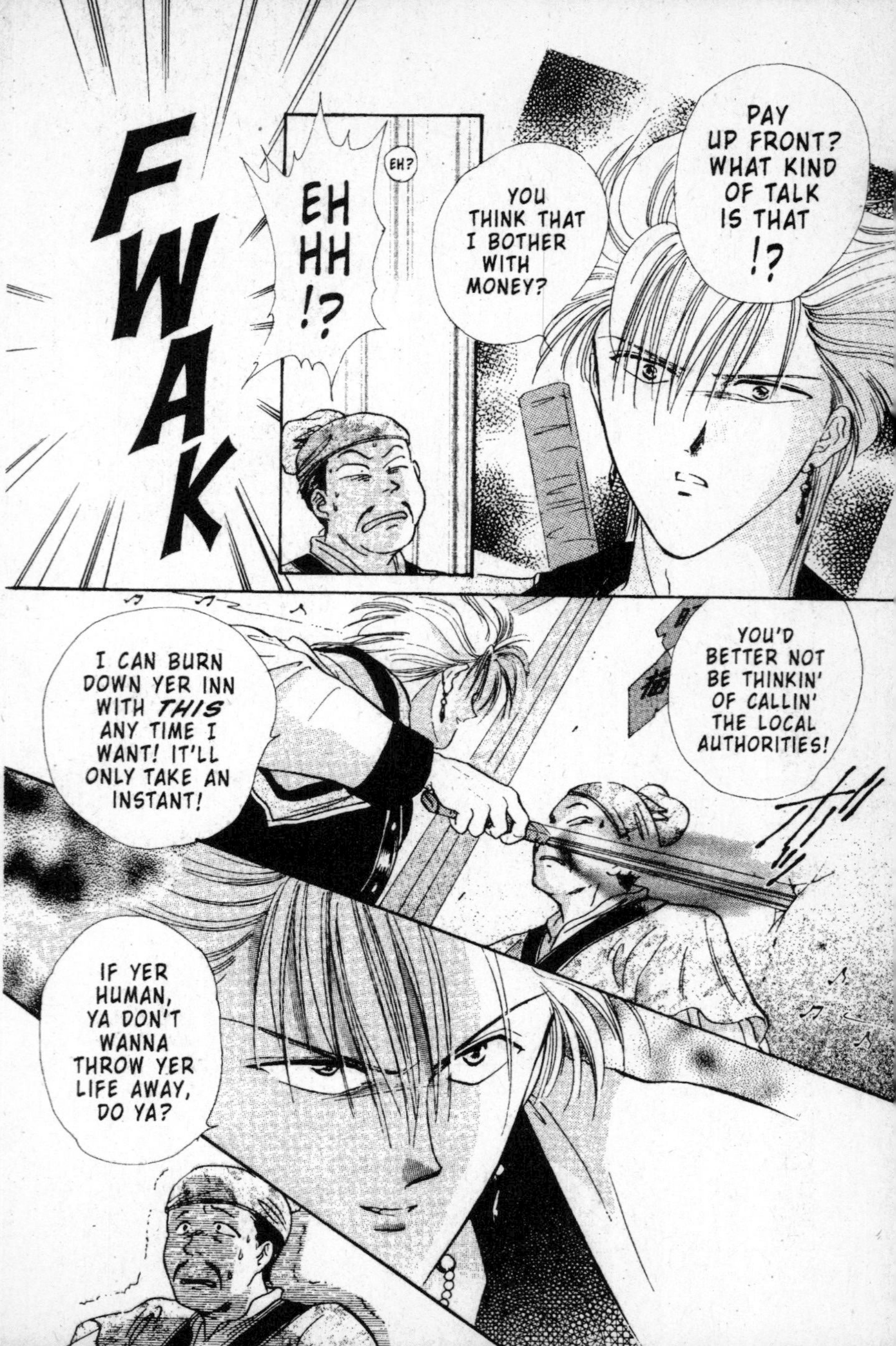
PAY UP FRONT? WHAT KIND OF TALK IS THAT !?
YOU THINK THAT I BOTHER WITH MONEY?
EH?
EH HH !?
FWAK
YOU'D BETTER NOT BE THINKIN' OF CALLIN' THE LOCAL AUTHORITIES!
I CAN BURN DOWN YER INN WITH *THIS* ANY TIME I WANT! IT'LL ONLY TAKE AN INSTANT!
IF YER HUMAN, YA DON'T WANNA THROW YER LIFE AWAY, DO YA?

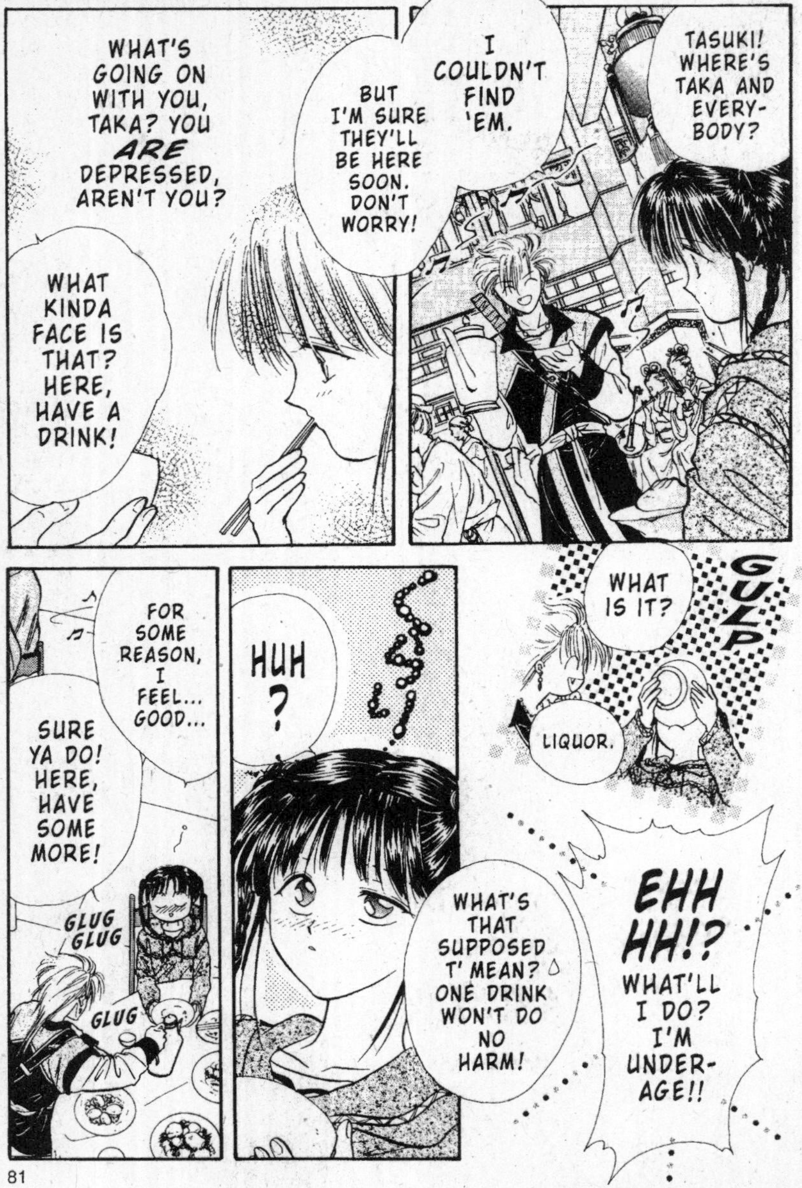
TASUKI! WHERE'S TAKA AND EVERY-BODY?
I COULDN'T FIND 'EM.
BUT I'M SURE THEY'LL BE HERE SOON. DON'T WORRY!
WHAT'S GOING ON WITH YOU, TAKA? YOU ARE DEPRESSED, AREN'T YOU?
WHAT KINDA FACE IS THAT? HERE, HAVE A DRINK!
WHAT IS IT?
GULP
LIQUOR.
EHHHH!? WHAT'LL I DO? I'M UNDER-AGE!!
HUH?
WHAT'S THAT SUPPOSED T' MEAN? ONE DRINK WON'T DO NO HARM!
FOR SOME REASON, I FEEL... GOOD...
SURE YA DO! HERE, HAVE SOME MORE!
GLUG GLUG
GLUG

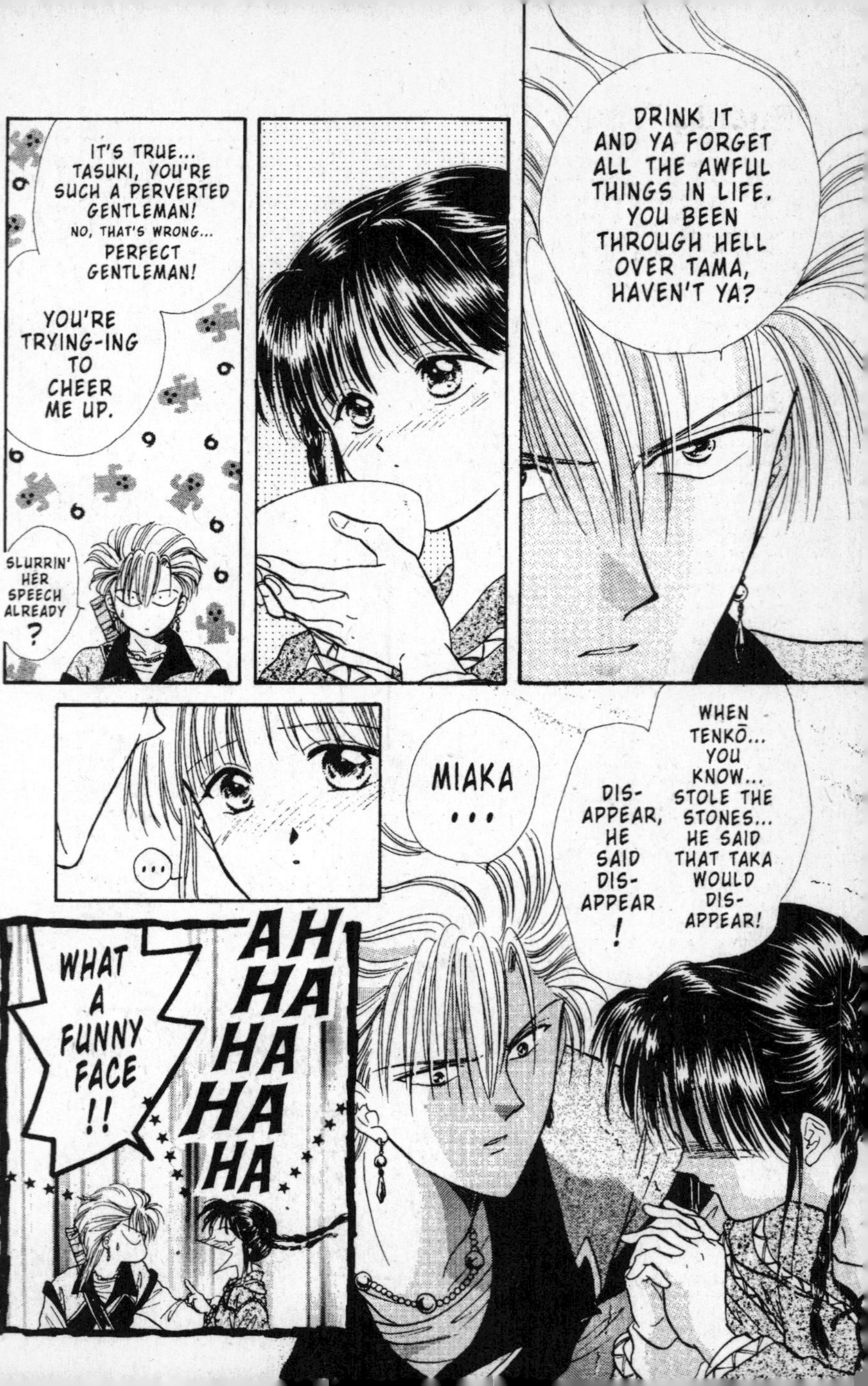
DRINK IT AND YA FORGET ALL THE AWFUL THINGS IN LIFE. YOU BEEN THROUGH HELL OVER TAMA, HAVEN'T YA?
IT'S TRUE... TASUKI, YOU'RE SUCH A PERVERTED GENTLEMAN! NO, THAT'S WRONG... PERFECT GENTLEMAN!
YOU'RE TRYING-ING TO CHEER ME UP.
SLURRIN' HER SPEECH ALREADY ?
WHEN TENKŌ... YOU KNOW... STOLE THE STONES... HE SAID THAT TAKA WOULD DIS-APPEAR! DIS-APPEAR, HE SAID DIS-APPEAR !
MIAKA ...
...
AH HA HA HA HA HA
WHAT A FUNNY FACE !!

Once Part 2 started, Tasuki's popularity went up and up! And it looks like it happened when he gained some sex appeal. It's true that he matured after the end of Part 1, but I didn't try to draw him sexier on purpose. It's just that after we settled on it being two years later, I drew him a little more grown up...just naturally. I did the same for the others, as if they were really alive. *And they are alive! Kind of.* In this story arc, too, another one of those "Don" sound effect scenes popped up. If your question is, "Huh? Why would Tasuki do that sort of thing!?" then all I can say is that it just worked out that way. But we're getting into some impressive territory! Things that Miaka has never done up to this point! Is this really revealing true feelings? And if it is, then it's a different problem from the "evil Tama" we had before. *By the way, water is a symbol for the subconscious.*

At one point when we finished work early, all the assistants started talking about whether Tasuki was really in love with Miaka. One assistant, H, had the same reaction as me. "Hmm..." But M (a Tasuki fan--oh, and by the way, H is a very vocal fan of Amiboshi and Suboshi) said, "This is the day I've been waiting for! He really DOES love her!"

H said, "... But it always seemed like love for a little sister."

M replied, "No! In Part 1, it was just friendship, but this is Part 2! He didn't realize it before, but after they separated, he finally understood his feelings!"

"Ahh... Now that he sees her so in love with Tama..."

"Right! Now she's shown up again, and more than that, Miaka's constantly unhappy!"

"To do that to a girl who was your friend? That's pathetic!"

"But..." I said. And in my heart, I got the image of a brother who dotes too much on his little sister...then goes too far and attempts rape. *(A scandalous thought!)*

But M answered, "Tasuki isn't so much of a beast to do that with a girl he doesn't even like!" *That's true.* ☺ And after that, they began to digress. "Did he ever get her underwear off?" "Oh, normally they just come off along with the pants." Or maybe she's been wandering around all this time with no panties at all! "Would anybody do that!? *Miaka would be crying...!*

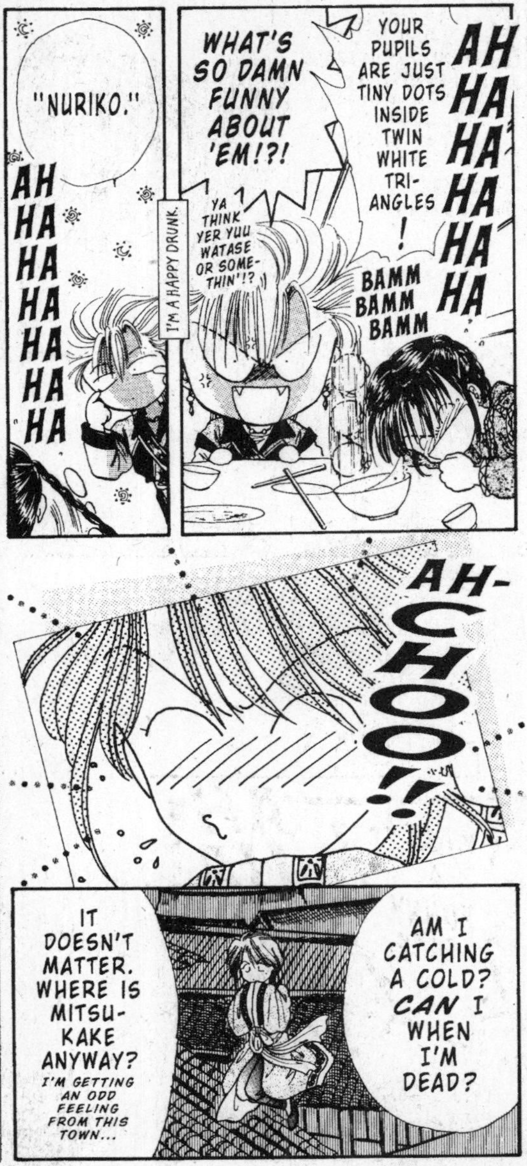
AH HA HA HA HA HA HA HA
YOUR PUPILS ARE JUST TINY DOTS INSIDE TWIN WHITE TRI-ANGLES!
WHAT'S SO DAMN FUNNY ABOUT 'EM!?!
YA THINK YER YUU WATASE OR SOME-THIN'!?
BAMM BAMM BAMM
I'M A HAPPY DRUNK.
"NURIKO."
AH HA HA HA HA HA HA HA
AH-CHOO!!
AM I CATCHING A COLD? CAN I WHEN I'M DEAD?
IT DOESN'T MATTER. WHERE IS MITSU-KAKE ANYWAY?
I'M GETTING AN ODD FEELING FROM THIS TOWN...

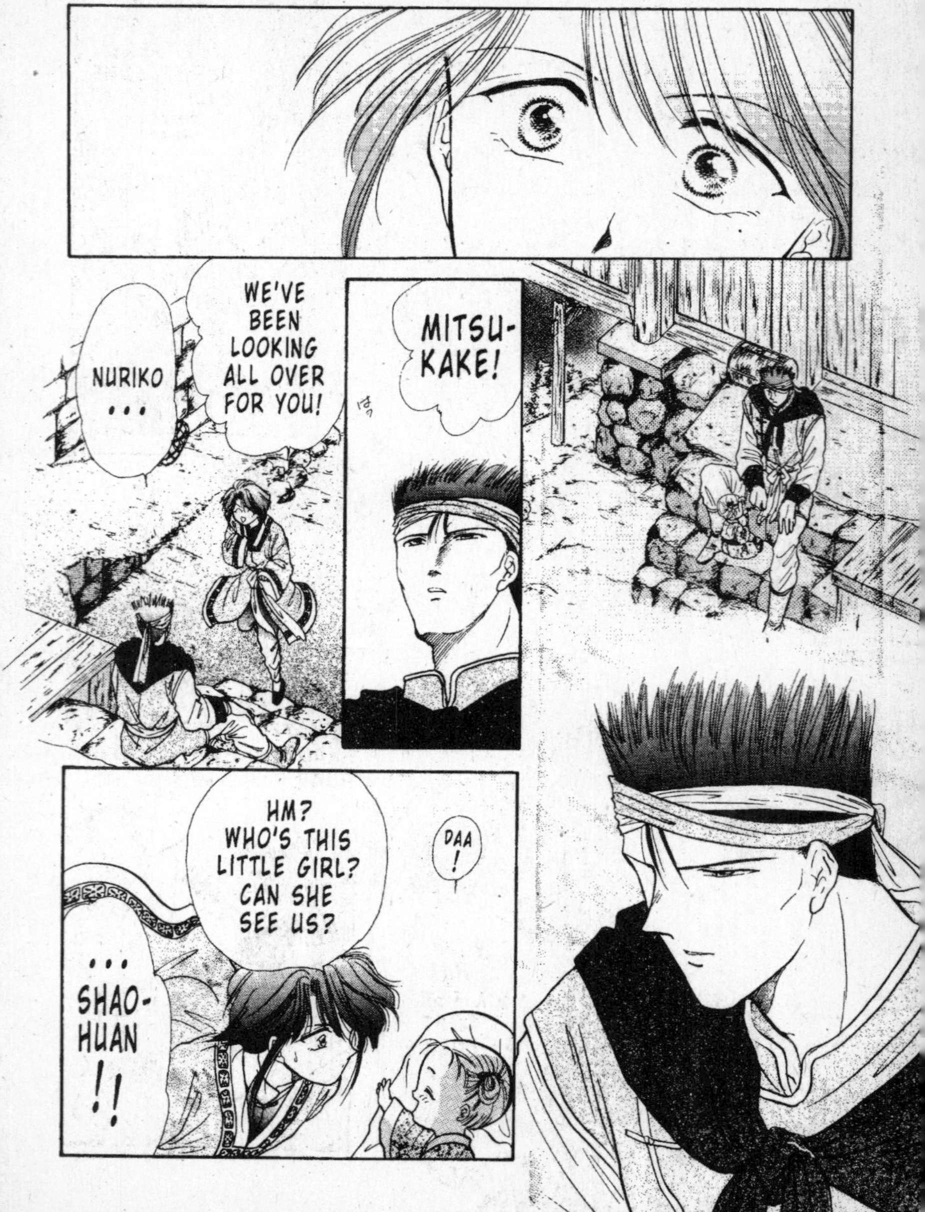

MITSU-KAKE!
はっ
WE'VE BEEN LOOKING ALL OVER FOR YOU!
NURIKO ...
HM? WHO'S THIS LITTLE GIRL? CAN SHE SEE US?
DAA!
... SHAO-HUAN!!

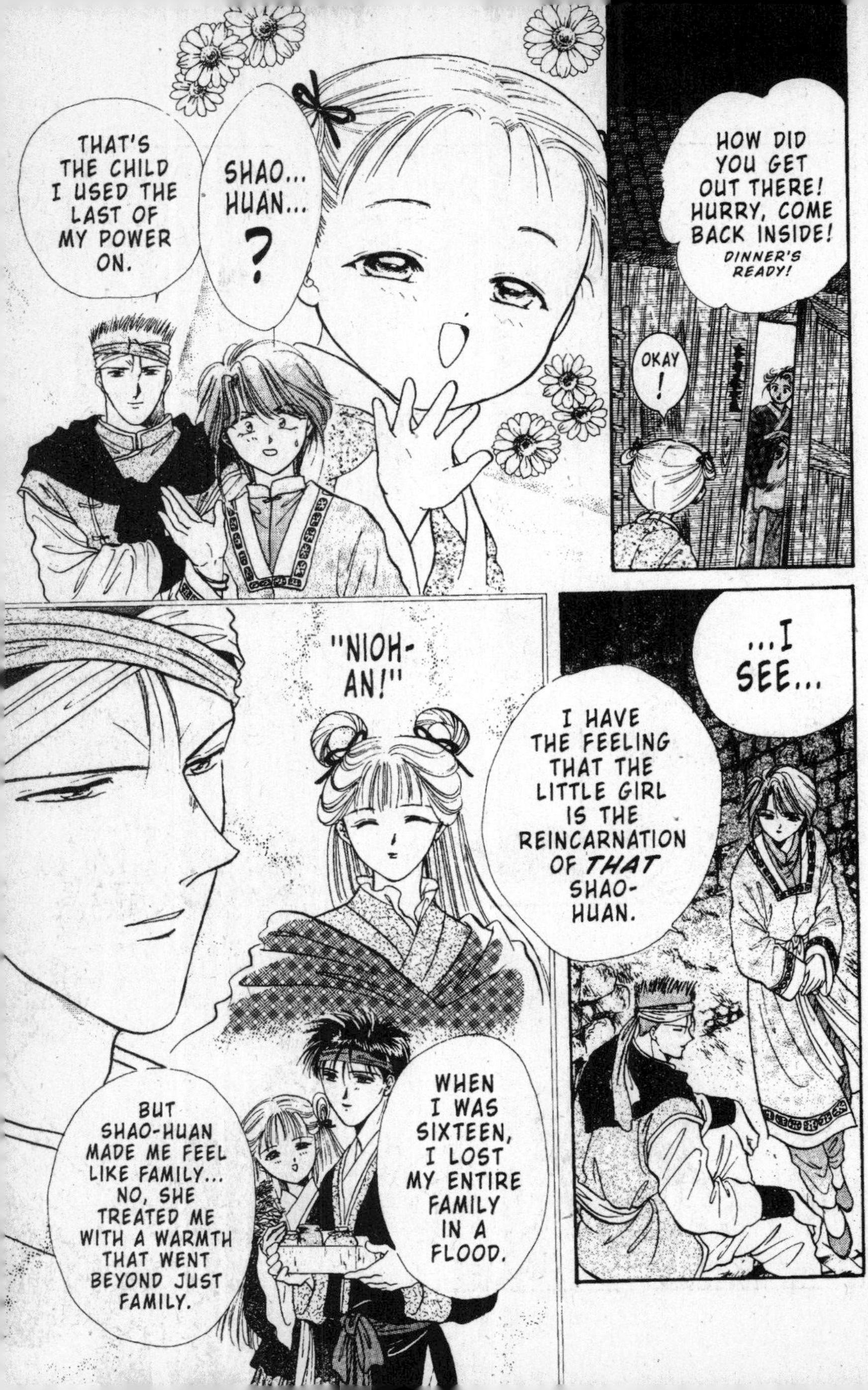
HOW DID YOU GET OUT THERE! HURRY, COME BACK INSIDE! DINNER'S READY!
OKAY!
SHAO... HUAN... ?
THAT'S THE CHILD I USED THE LAST OF MY POWER ON.
...I SEE...
I HAVE THE FEELING THAT THE LITTLE GIRL IS THE REINCARNATION OF *THAT* SHAO-HUAN.
"NIOH-AN!"
WHEN I WAS SIXTEEN, I LOST MY ENTIRE FAMILY IN A FLOOD.
BUT SHAO-HUAN MADE ME FEEL LIKE FAMILY... NO, SHE TREATED ME WITH A WARMTH THAT WENT BEYOND JUST FAMILY.

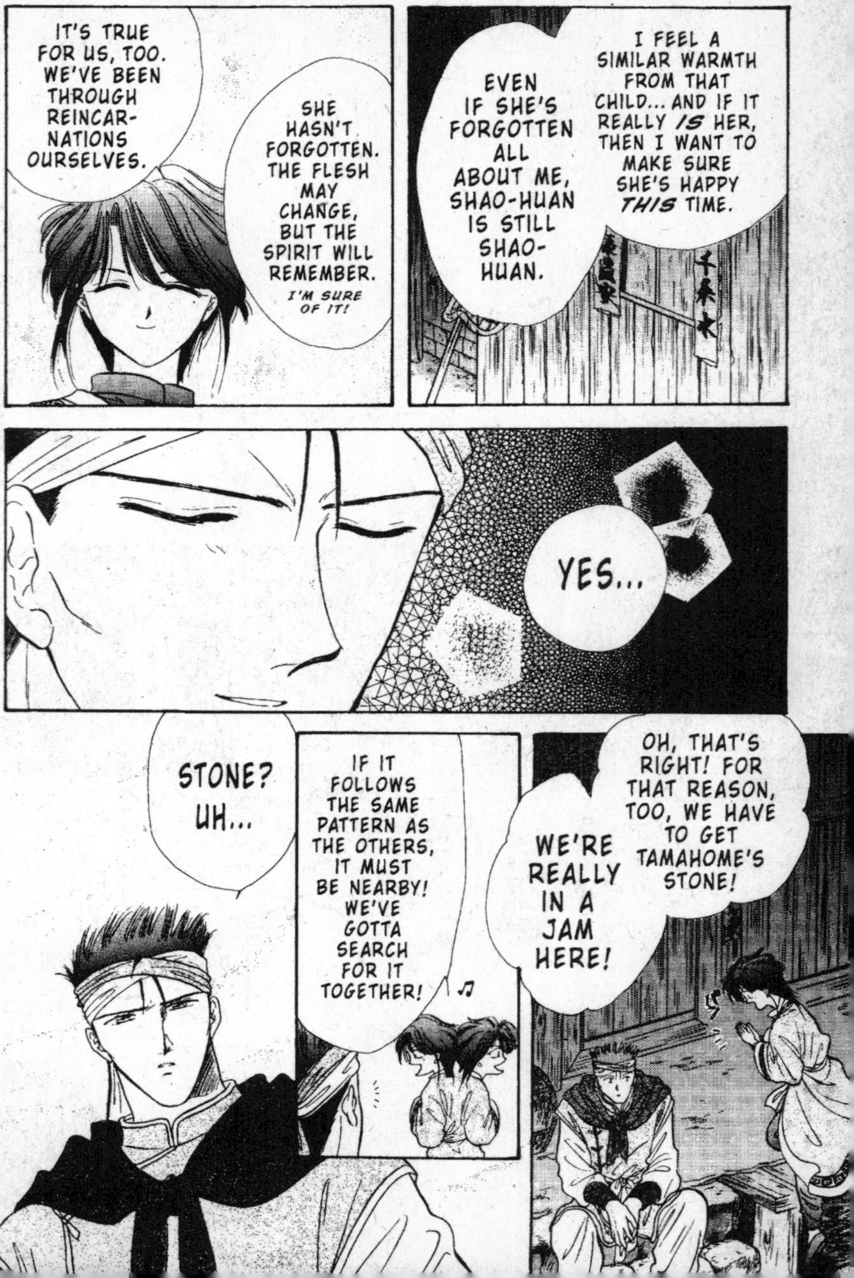
I FEEL A SIMILAR WARMTH FROM THAT CHILD... AND IF IT REALLY *IS* HER, THEN I WANT TO MAKE SURE SHE'S HAPPY *THIS* TIME.
EVEN IF SHE'S FORGOTTEN ALL ABOUT ME, SHAO-HUAN IS STILL SHAO-HUAN.
IT'S TRUE FOR US, TOO. WE'VE BEEN THROUGH REINCAR-NATIONS OURSELVES.
SHE HASN'T FORGOTTEN. THE FLESH MAY CHANGE, BUT THE SPIRIT WILL REMEMBER.
I'M SURE OF IT!
YES...
OH, THAT'S RIGHT! FOR THAT REASON, TOO, WE HAVE TO GET TAMAHOME'S STONE!
WE'RE REALLY IN A JAM HERE!
IF IT FOLLOWS THE SAME PATTERN AS THE OTHERS, IT MUST BE NEARBY! WE'VE GOTTA SEARCH FOR IT TOGETHER! ♫
STONE? UH...

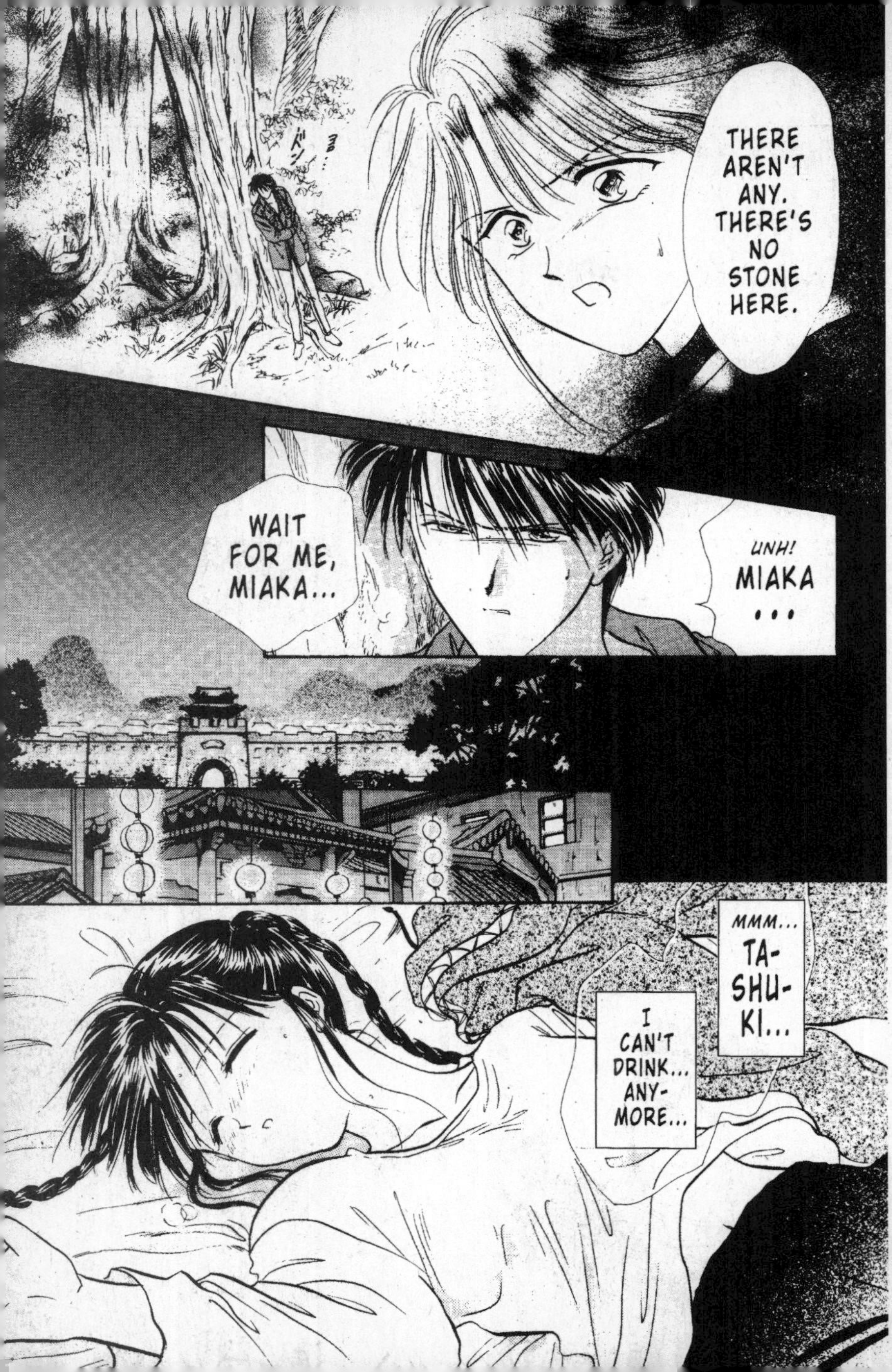
THERE AREN'T ANY. THERE'S NO STONE HERE.
UNH! MIAKA...
WAIT FOR ME, MIAKA...
MMM... TA-SHU-KI...
I CAN'T DRINK... ANY-MORE...

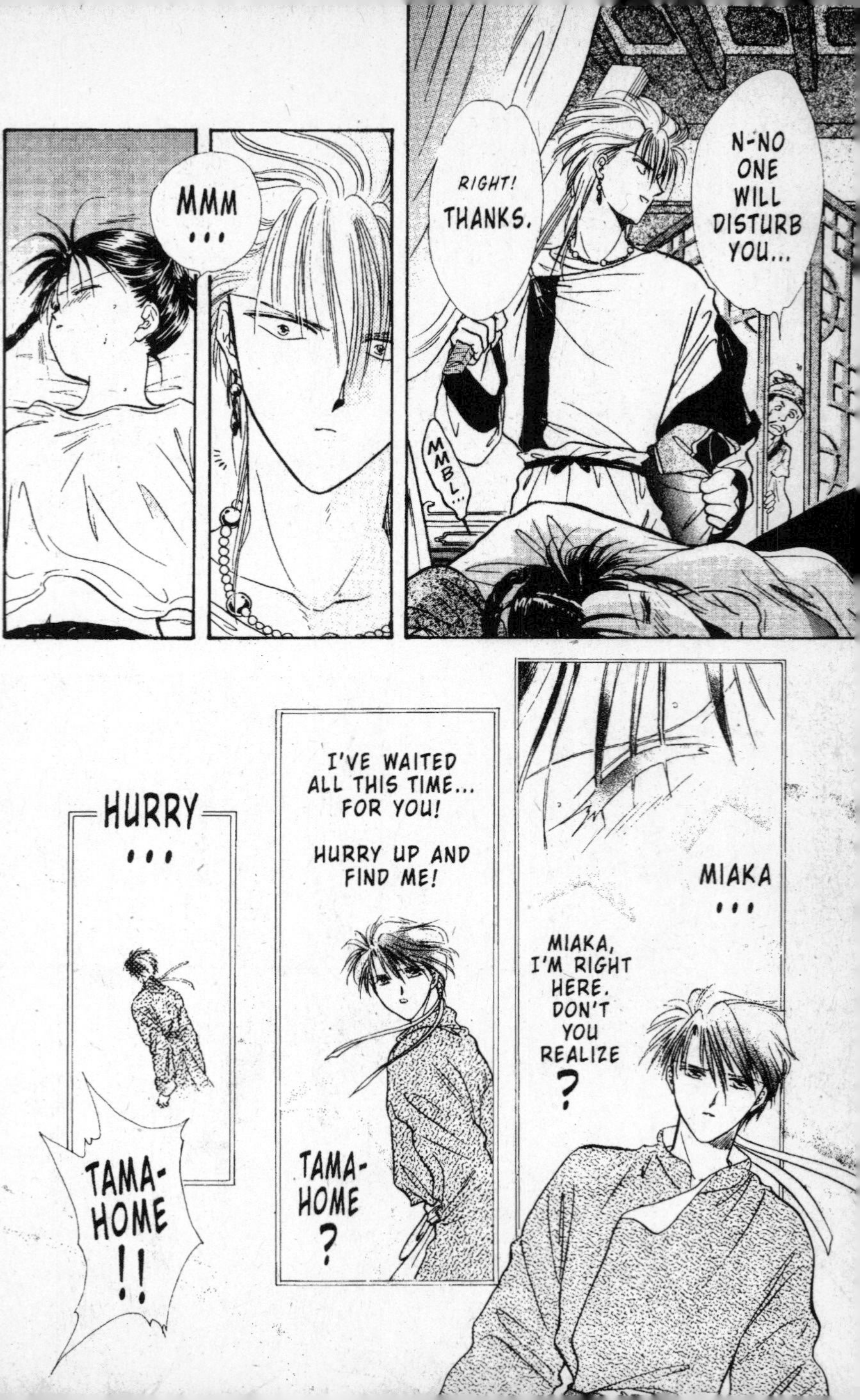
N-NO ONE WILL DISTURB YOU...
RIGHT! THANKS.
MMBL...
MMM ...
MIAKA ...
MIAKA, I'M RIGHT HERE. DON'T YOU REALIZE ?
I'VE WAITED ALL THIS TIME... FOR YOU!
HURRY UP AND FIND ME!
TAMA-HOME ?
HURRY ...
TAMA-HOME !!

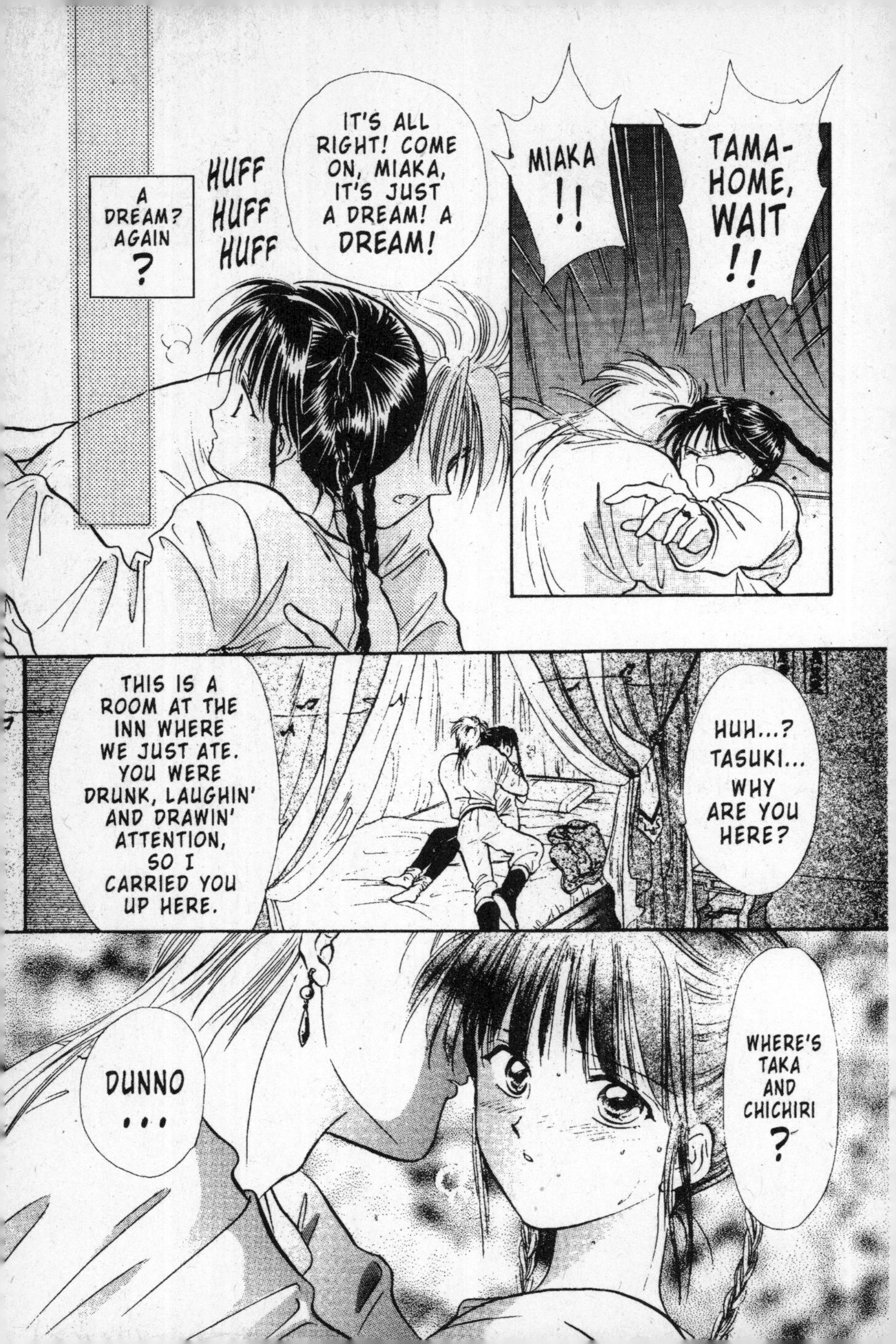
TAMA-HOME, WAIT!!
MIAKA!!
IT'S ALL RIGHT! COME ON, MIAKA, IT'S JUST A DREAM! A DREAM!
HUFF HUFF HUFF
A DREAM? AGAIN?
HUH...? TASUKI... WHY ARE YOU HERE?
THIS IS A ROOM AT THE INN WHERE WE JUST ATE. YOU WERE DRUNK, LAUGHIN' AND DRAWIN' ATTENTION, SO I CARRIED YOU UP HERE.
WHERE'S TAKA AND CHICHIRI?
DUNNO...

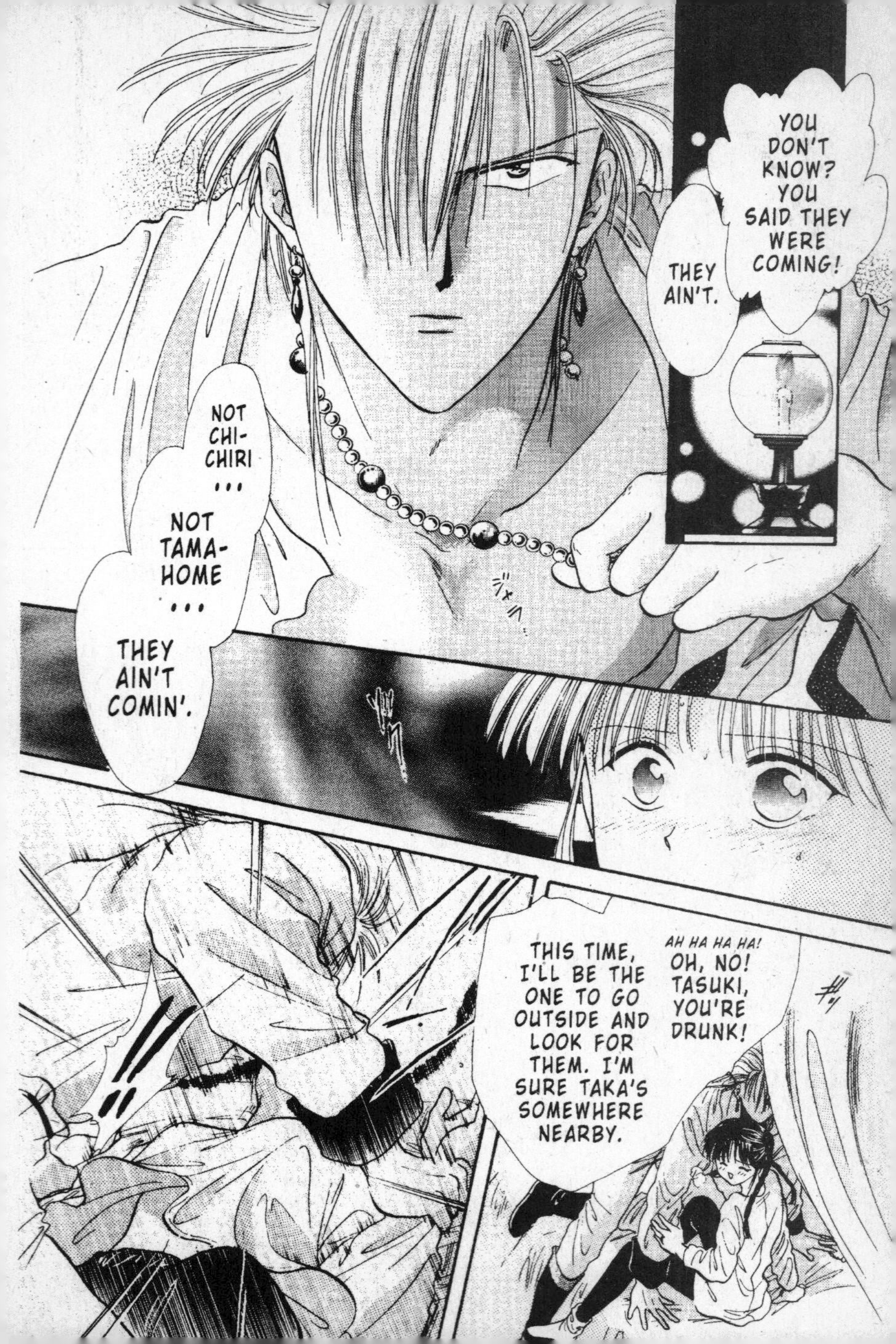
YOU DON'T KNOW? YOU SAID THEY WERE COMING!
THEY AIN'T.
NOT CHI-CHIRI...
NOT TAMA-HOME...
THEY AIN'T COMIN'.
AH HA HA HA! OH, NO! TASUKI, YOU'RE DRUNK!
THIS TIME, I'LL BE THE ONE TO GO OUTSIDE AND LOOK FOR THEM. I'M SURE TAKA'S SOMEWHERE NEARBY.

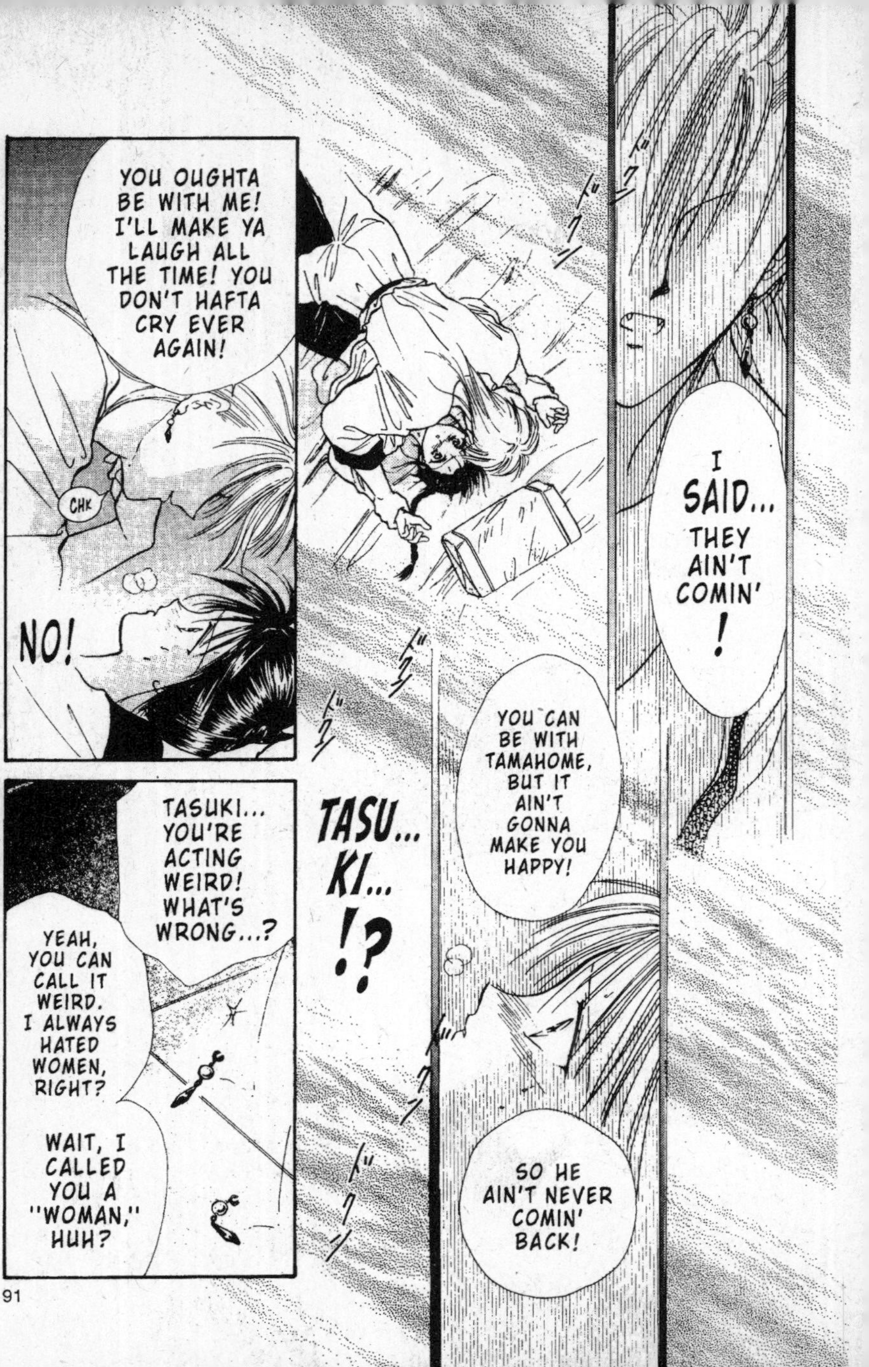
I SAID... THEY AIN'T COMIN'!
YOU CAN BE WITH TAMAHOME, BUT IT AIN'T GONNA MAKE YOU HAPPY!
SO HE AIN'T NEVER COMIN' BACK!
TASU... KI...!?
YOU OUGHTA BE WITH ME! I'LL MAKE YA LAUGH ALL THE TIME! YOU DON'T HAFTA CRY EVER AGAIN!
CHK
NO!
TASUKI... YOU'RE ACTING WEIRD! WHAT'S WRONG...?
YEAH, YOU CAN CALL IT WEIRD. I ALWAYS HATED WOMEN, RIGHT?
WAIT, I CALLED YOU A "WOMAN," HUH?

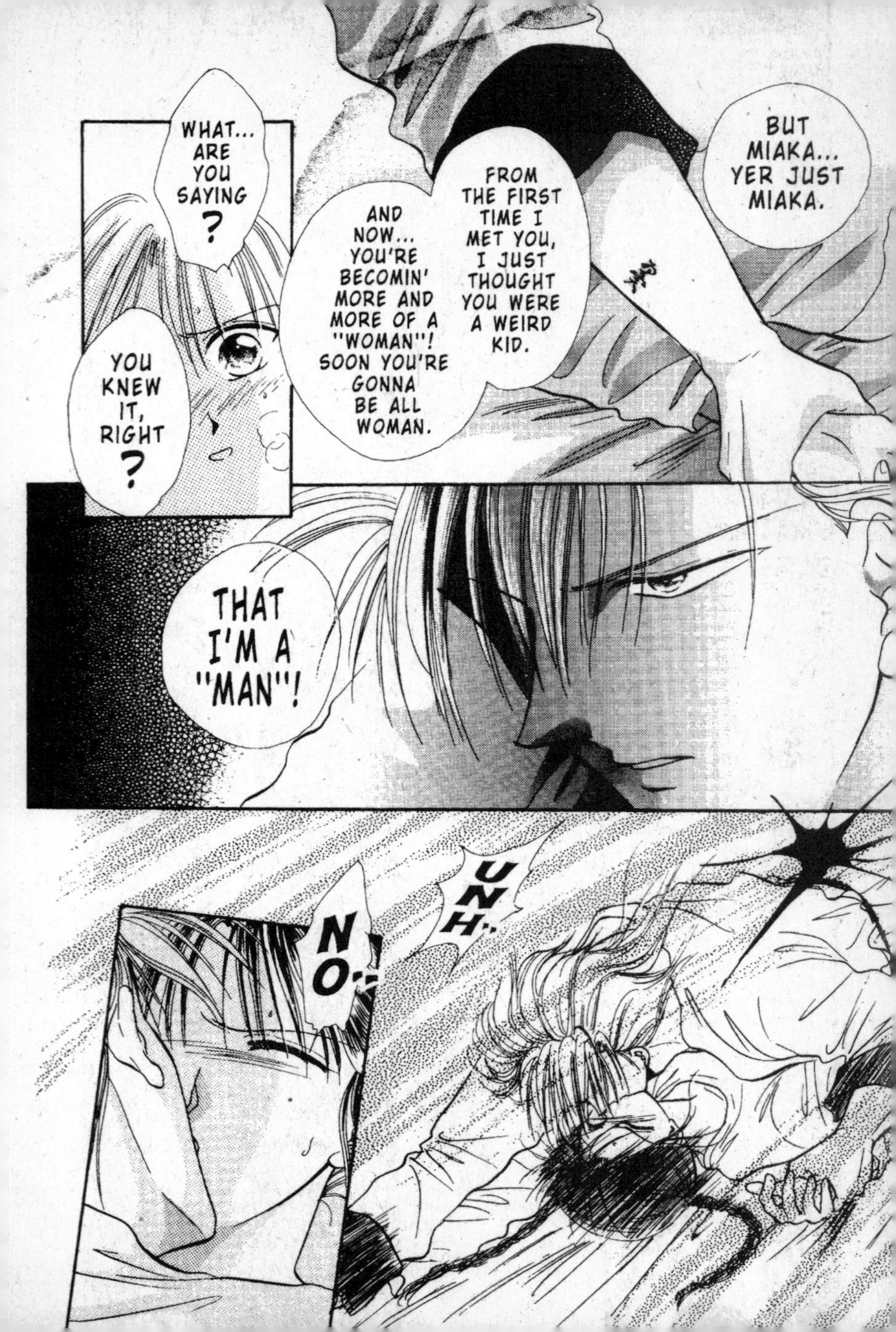
BUT MIAKA... YER JUST MIAKA.
FROM THE FIRST TIME I MET YOU, I JUST THOUGHT YOU WERE A WEIRD KID.
AND NOW... YOU'RE BECOMIN' MORE AND MORE OF A "WOMAN"! SOON YOU'RE GONNA BE ALL WOMAN.
WHAT... ARE YOU SAYING?
YOU KNEW IT, RIGHT?
THAT I'M A "MAN"!
UNH..
NO..

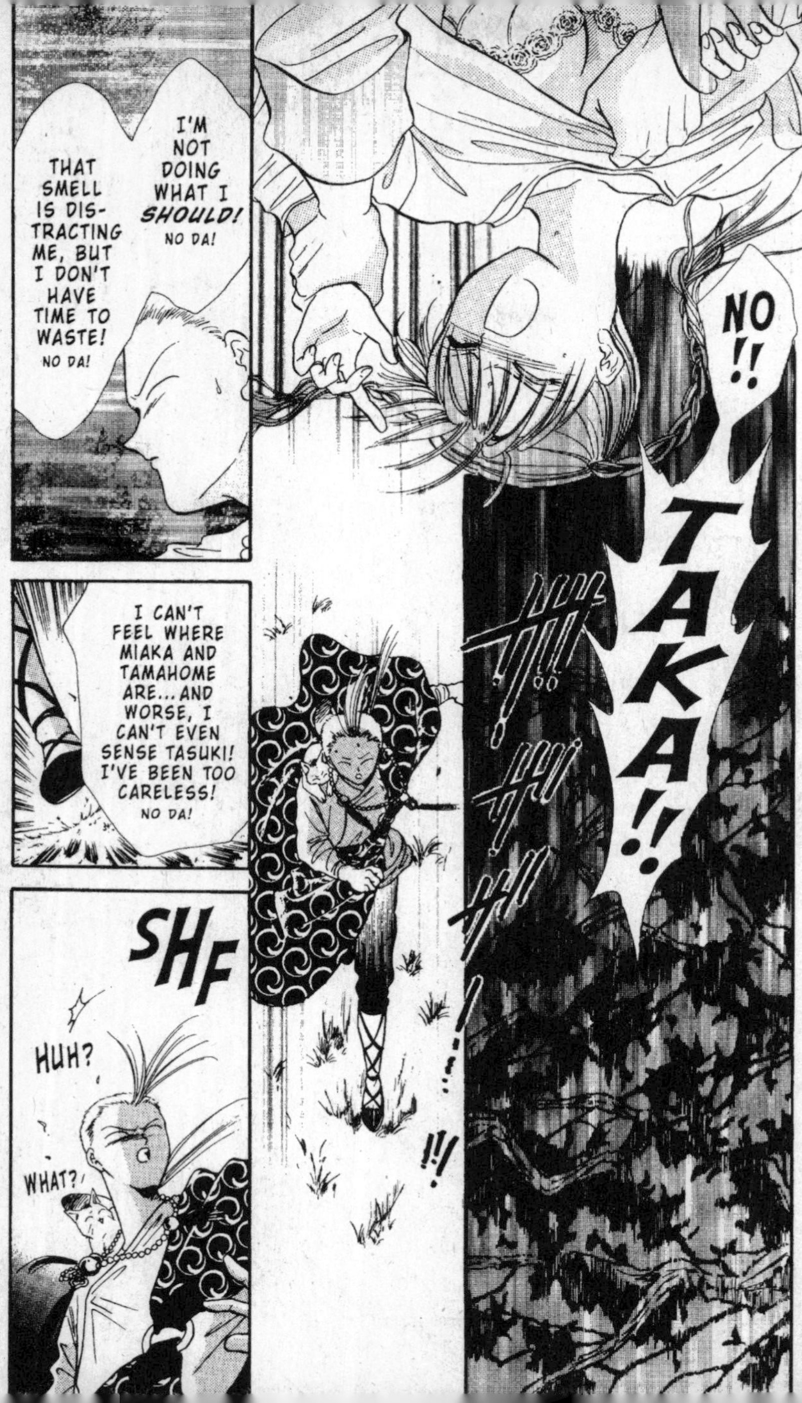
NO!!
TAKA!!
!!!
I'M NOT DOING WHAT I SHOULD! NO DA!
THAT SMELL IS DIS-TRACTING ME, BUT I DON'T HAVE TIME TO WASTE! NO DA!
I CAN'T FEEL WHERE MIAKA AND TAMAHOME ARE... AND WORSE, I CAN'T EVEN SENSE TASUKI! I'VE BEEN TOO CARELESS! NO DA!
SHF
HUH?
WHAT?

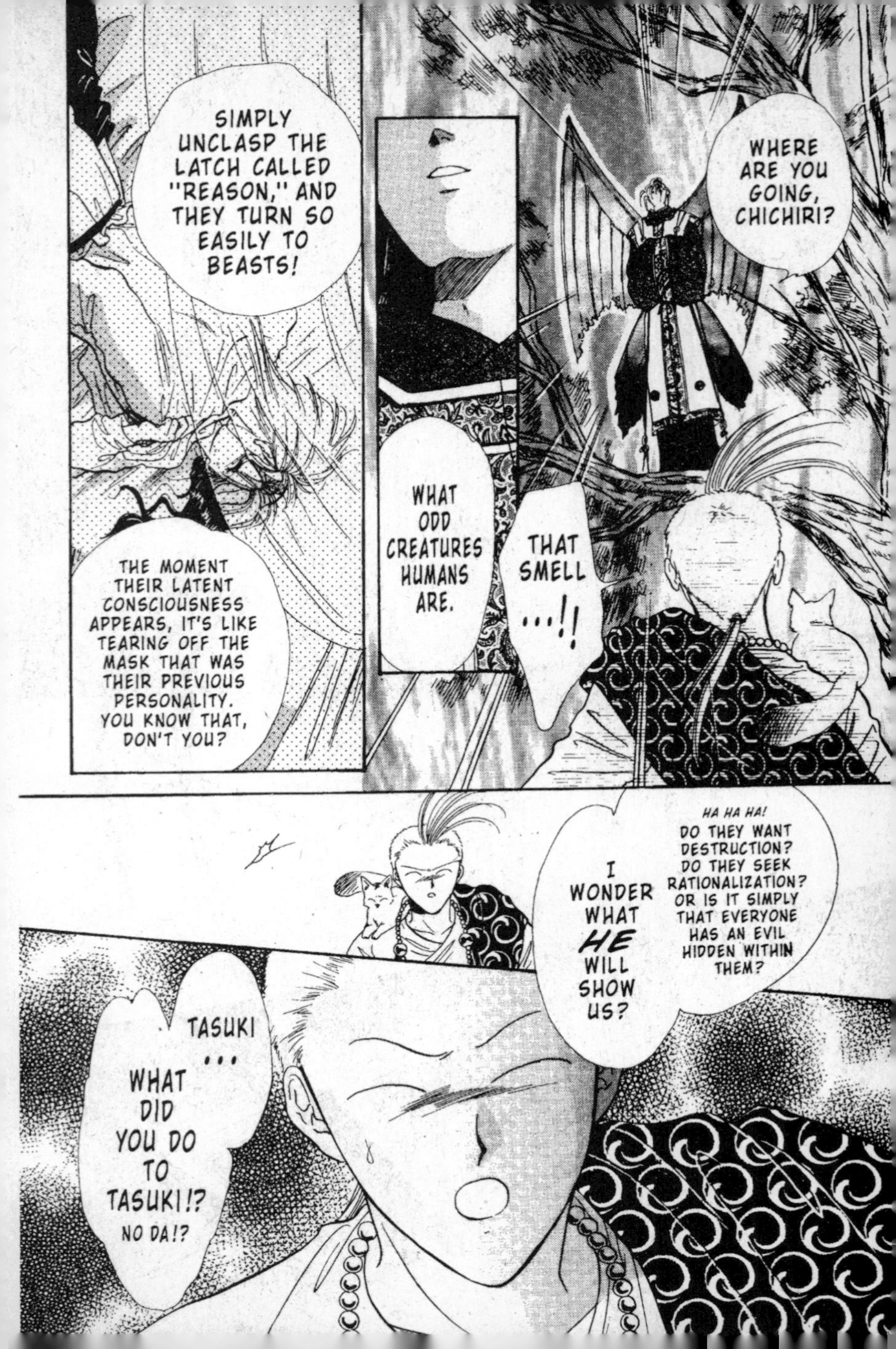
WHERE ARE YOU GOING, CHICHIRI?
THAT SMELL ...!!
WHAT ODD CREATURES HUMANS ARE.
SIMPLY UNCLASP THE LATCH CALLED "REASON," AND THEY TURN SO EASILY TO BEASTS!
THE MOMENT THEIR LATENT CONSCIOUSNESS APPEARS, IT'S LIKE TEARING OFF THE MASK THAT WAS THEIR PREVIOUS PERSONALITY. YOU KNOW THAT, DON'T YOU?
HA HA HA! DO THEY WANT DESTRUCTION? DO THEY SEEK RATIONALIZATION? OR IS IT SIMPLY THAT EVERYONE HAS AN EVIL HIDDEN WITHIN THEM?
I WONDER WHAT HE WILL SHOW US?
TASUKI ... WHAT DID YOU DO TO TASUKI!? NO DA!?

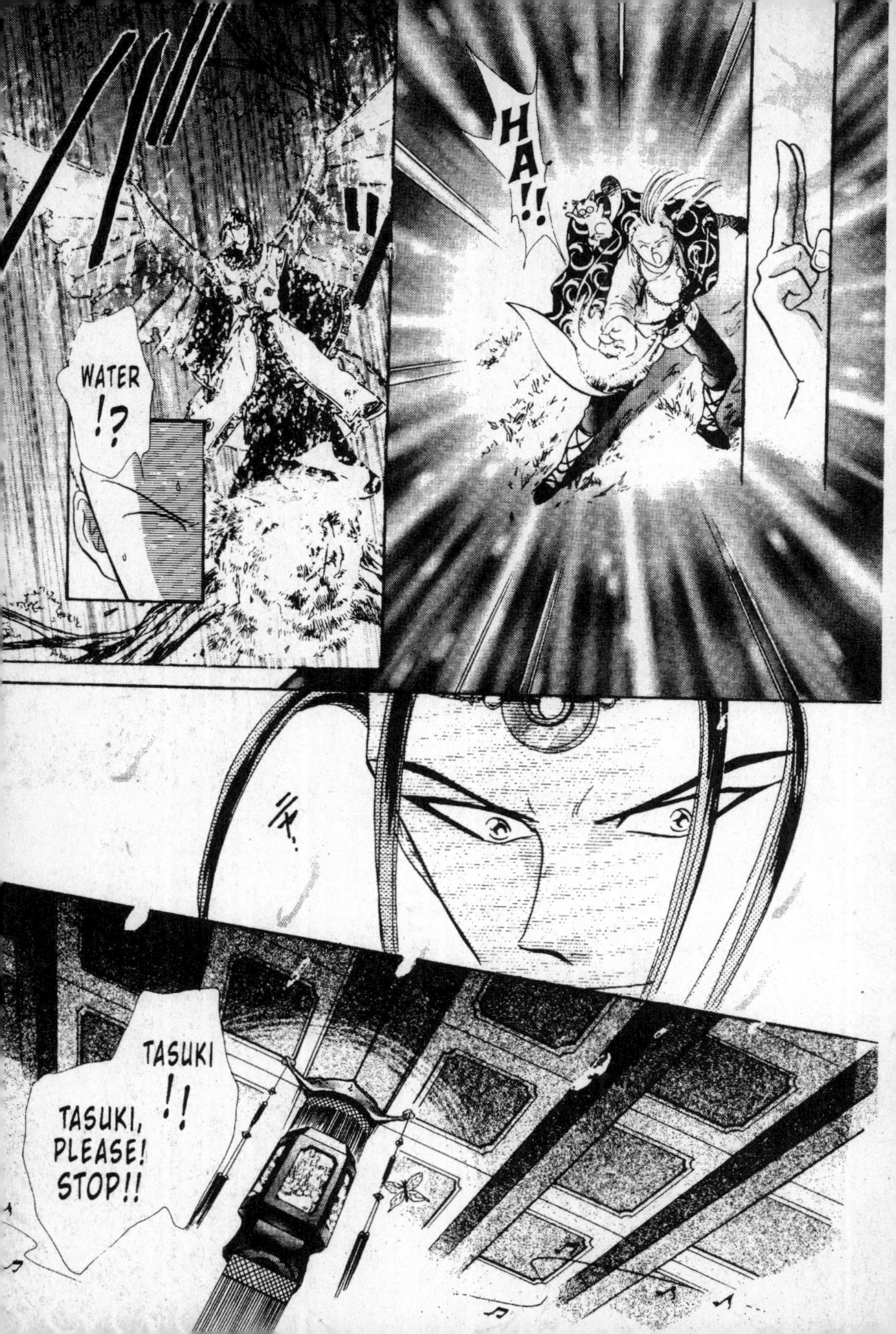
HA!!
!!
WATER !?
TASUKI!!
TASUKI, PLEASE! STOP!!

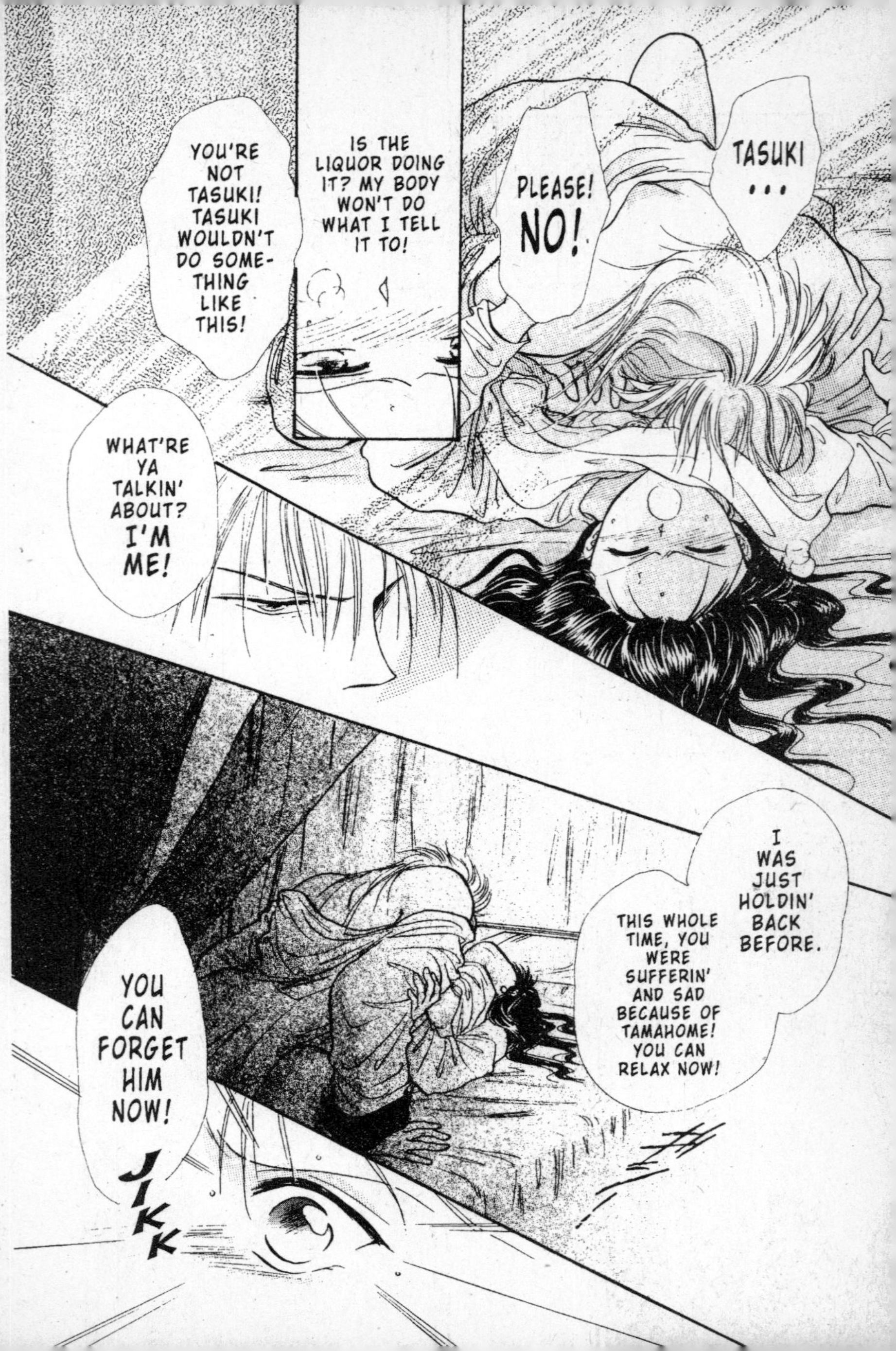
TASUKI...
PLEASE! NO!
IS THE LIQUOR DOING IT? MY BODY WON'T DO WHAT I TELL IT TO!
YOU'RE NOT TASUKI! TASUKI WOULDN'T DO SOME-THING LIKE THIS!
WHAT'RE YA TALKIN' ABOUT? I'M ME!
I WAS JUST HOLDIN' BACK BEFORE.
THIS WHOLE TIME, YOU WERE SUFFERIN' AND SAD BECAUSE OF TAMAHOME! YOU CAN RELAX NOW!
YOU CAN FORGET HIM NOW!
JIKK

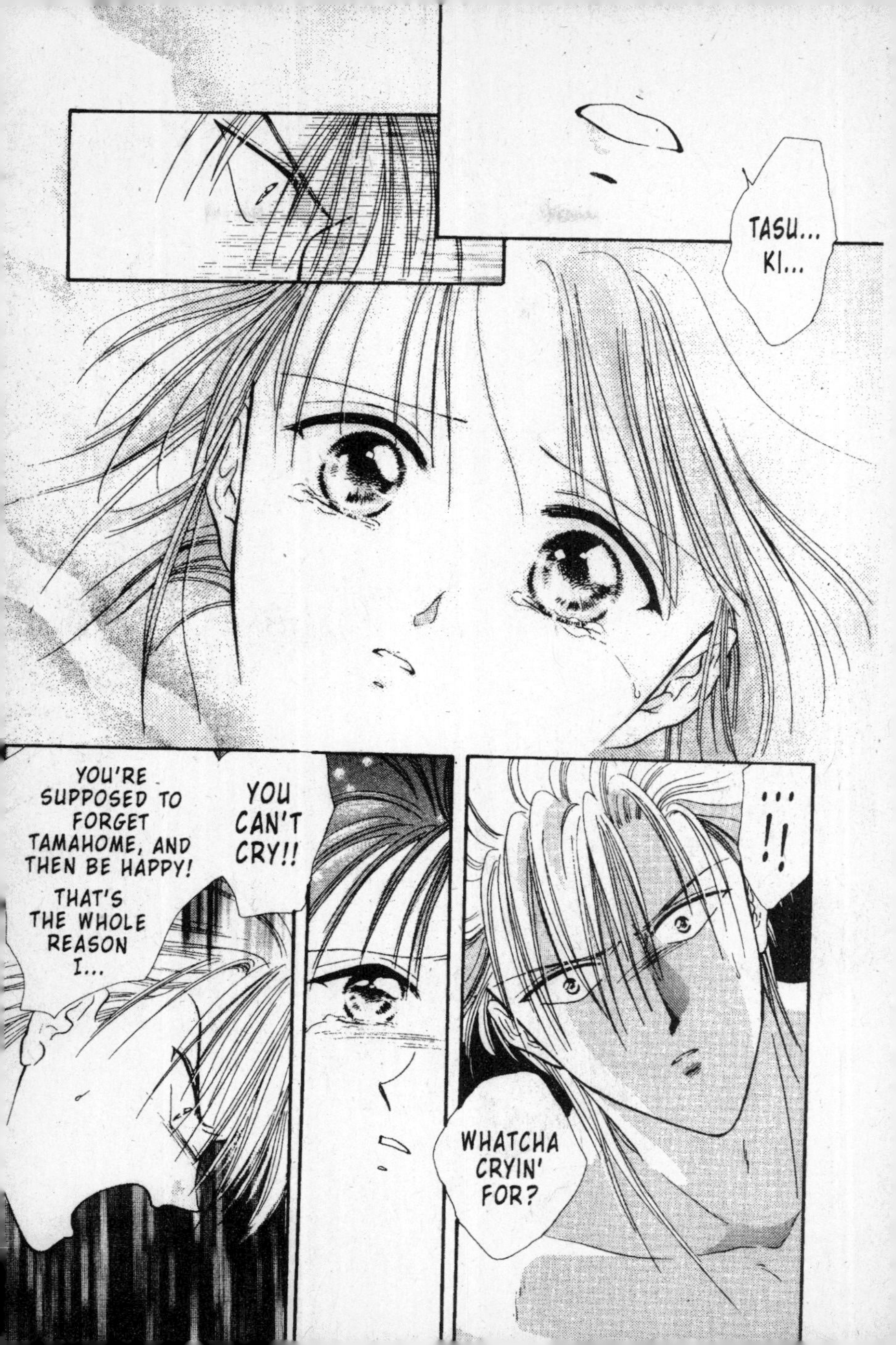
TASU... KI...
...!!
WHATCHA CRYIN' FOR?
YOU CAN'T CRY!!
YOU'RE SUPPOSED TO FORGET TAMAHOME, AND THEN BE HAPPY!
THAT'S THE WHOLE REASON I...

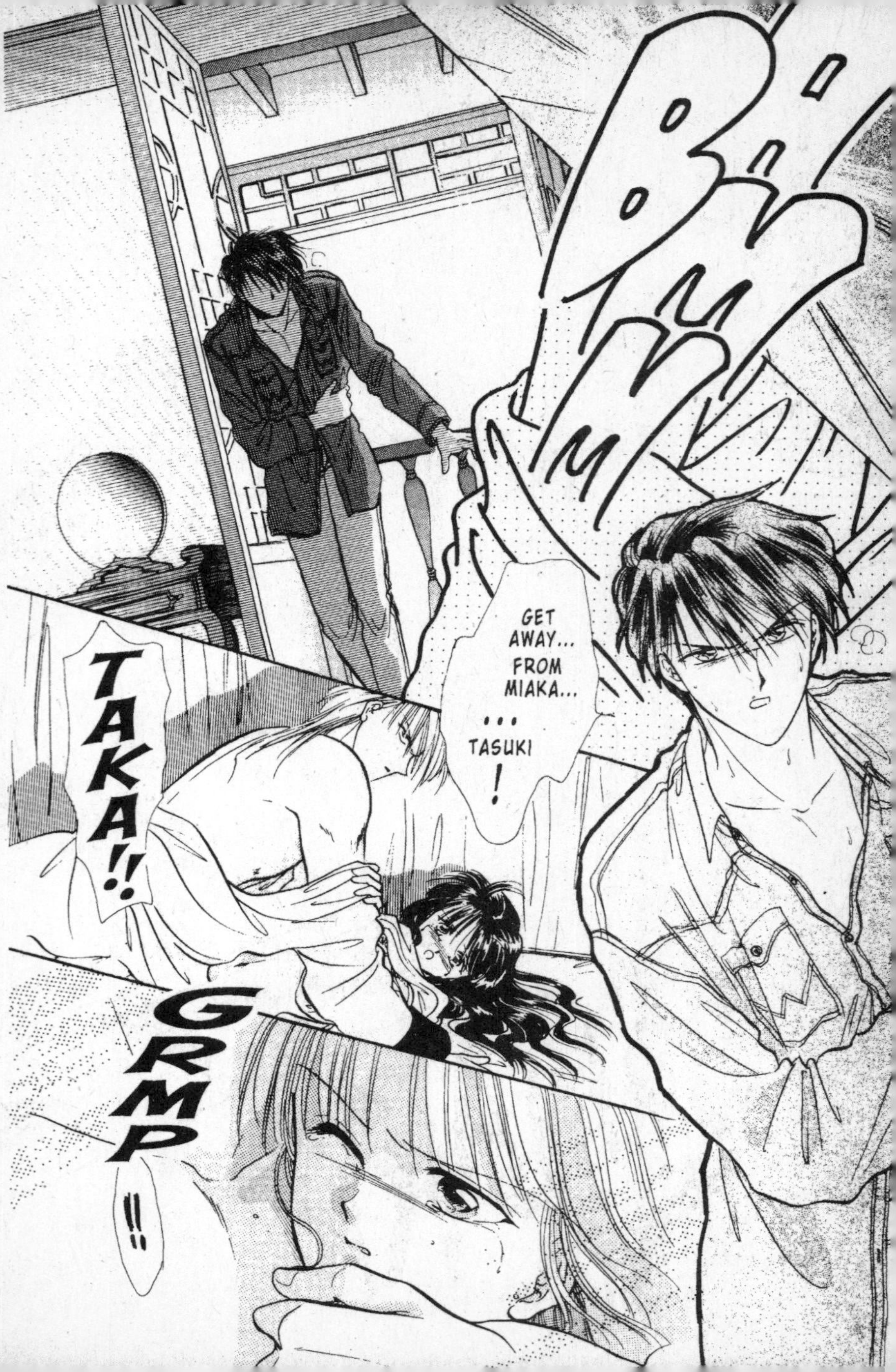
GET AWAY... FROM MIAKA...
...TASUKI!
TAKA!!
GRMP!!!

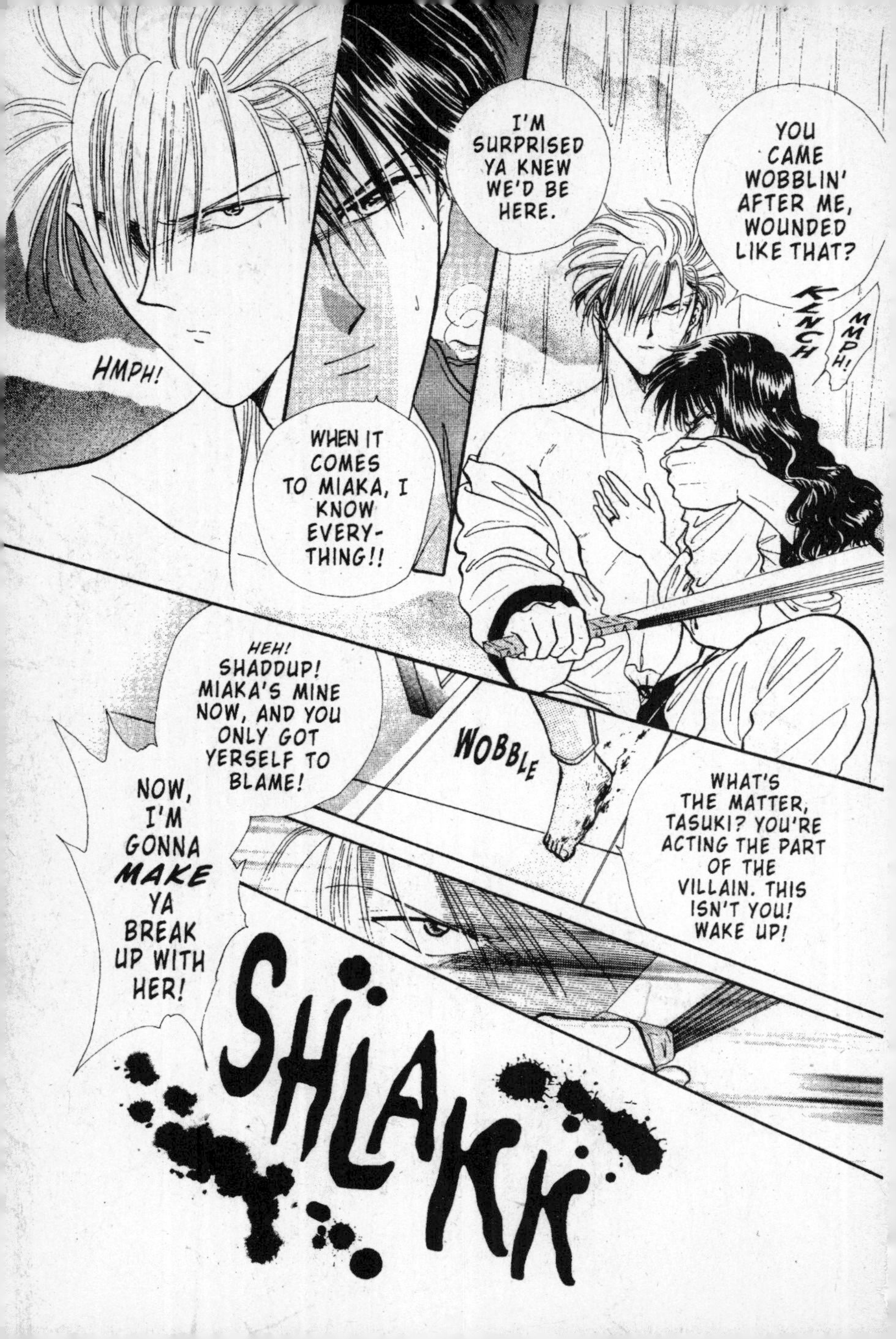
YOU CAME WOBBLIN' AFTER ME, WOUNDED LIKE THAT?
MMPH!
I'M SURPRISED YA KNEW WE'D BE HERE.
HMPH!
WHEN IT COMES TO MIAKA, I KNOW EVERY-THING!!
WHAT'S THE MATTER, TASUKI? YOU'RE ACTING THE PART OF THE VILLAIN. THIS ISN'T YOU! WAKE UP!
WOBBLE
HEH! SHADDUP! MIAKA'S MINE NOW, AND YOU ONLY GOT YERSELF TO BLAME!
NOW, I'M GONNA *MAKE* YA BREAK UP WITH HER!
SHLAKK

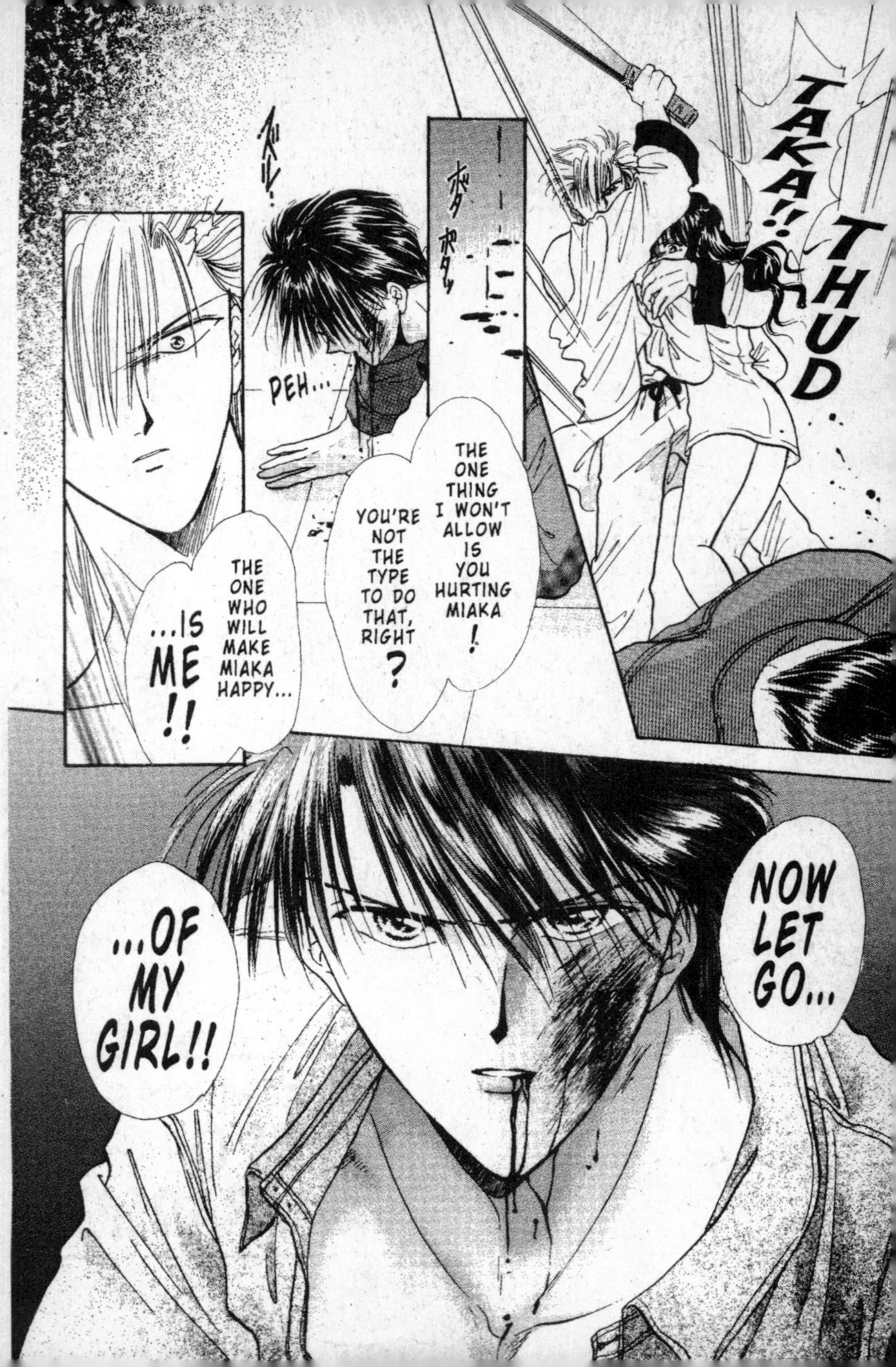
TAKA!!
THUD
PEH...
THE ONE THING I WON'T ALLOW IS YOU HURTING MIAKA!
YOU'RE NOT THE TYPE TO DO THAT, RIGHT?
THE ONE WHO WILL MAKE MIAKA HAPPY...
...IS ME!!
NOW LET GO...
...OF MY GIRL!!

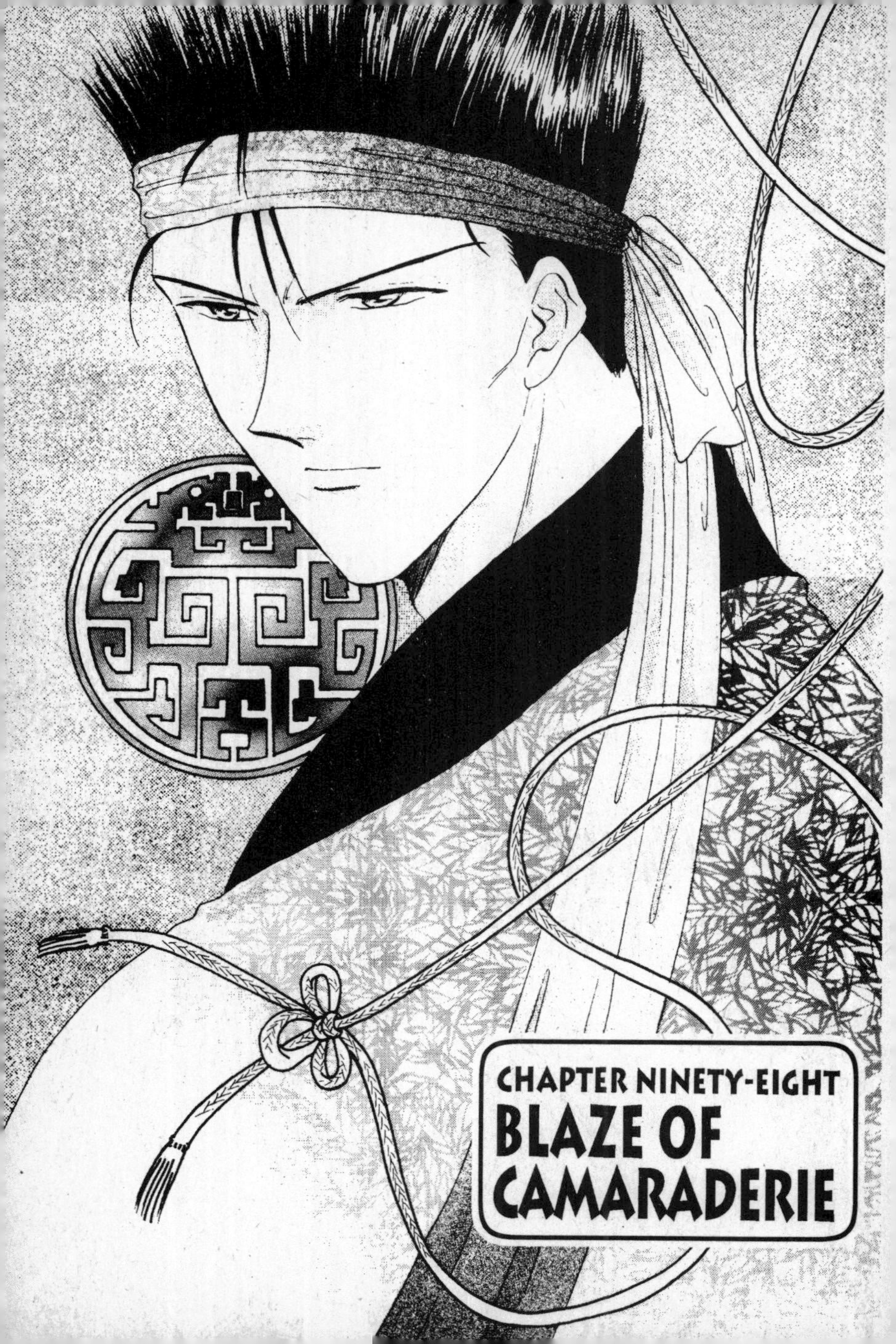

CHAPTER NINETY-EIGHT
BLAZE OF CAMARADERIE

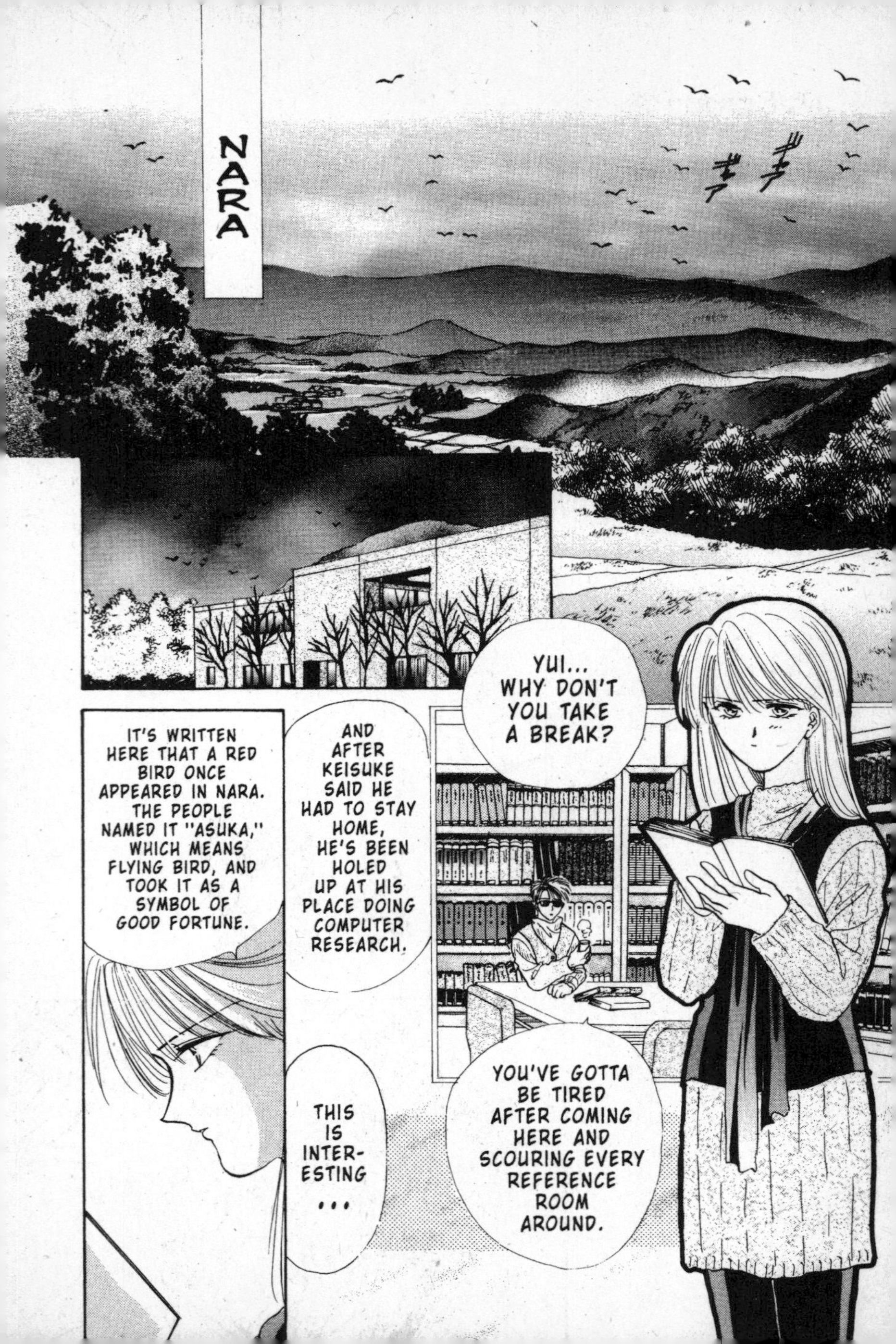
NARA
YUI... WHY DON'T YOU TAKE A BREAK?
YOU'VE GOTTA BE TIRED AFTER COMING HERE AND SCOURING EVERY REFERENCE ROOM AROUND.
AND AFTER KEISUKE SAID HE HAD TO STAY HOME, HE'S BEEN HOLED UP AT HIS PLACE DOING COMPUTER RESEARCH.
THIS IS INTER-ESTING...
IT'S WRITTEN HERE THAT A RED BIRD ONCE APPEARED IN NARA. THE PEOPLE NAMED IT "ASUKA," WHICH MEANS FLYING BIRD, AND TOOK IT AS A SYMBOL OF GOOD FORTUNE.

Demon

CONTINUED... "I agree that he loves her -- a friendship turned into something more."
"Upon receiving artificial respiration, he suddenly becomes aware of women."
"It isn't as if Tasuki's aversion to girls makes him completely uninterested in women from a physical standpoint. ☺"
Yeah, his basic male urges coming to the fore has a pretty deep meaning, and that is: Just because he's a friend, it doesn't mean that you should let your guard down! *Scary!*
"This is terrible for Miaka! The worst! Quite a shock! He's her friend. She probably thought of him as an older brother, and he tries to rape her!"
That's pretty frightening, right? But the thing that made me laugh the most was one assistant had seen on TV "Kare no Iru Onna wo Kukoku Hō" ("How He Seduces His Girl"), and she said that Tasuki tried every method mentioned in the show! ☺ The last method on the program was holding her down and having his way. For a drinker like Tasuki to spend the night not drinking means that it was all planned. In the future, he might become good at picking up the girls.
... But actually, all I wanted to do was wound Tasuki a little. He makes me mad sometimes! ☺ It means that he gets very hurt and loses his friends... but he's the only character who hadn't hurt himself yet.
But in growing up, you have to risk getting wounded. He's displaying his ignorance of love! He has a lot of bad points too, you know! You've all seen how he blurts things out without thinking! ☺ But a side of him that he would never want people to see came out here. A part that he himself didn't know about. I know it's a hard thing, but I think it would have been even worse if Taka hadn't dealt with it like an adult. ☺
And it all ended with that sound effect, "Don." (My assistants were so shocked, they cried.) And in the end, "What's this? So Taka and Tasuki like each other after all!" ☺
Looking at the situation, the way Tasuki shows love is more represented by his repartee with Taka than by what he does with Miaka. He just built up resentment toward Taka without understanding what true "strength" is.
This time, the background music is "Love Fhantom" by B'z!!

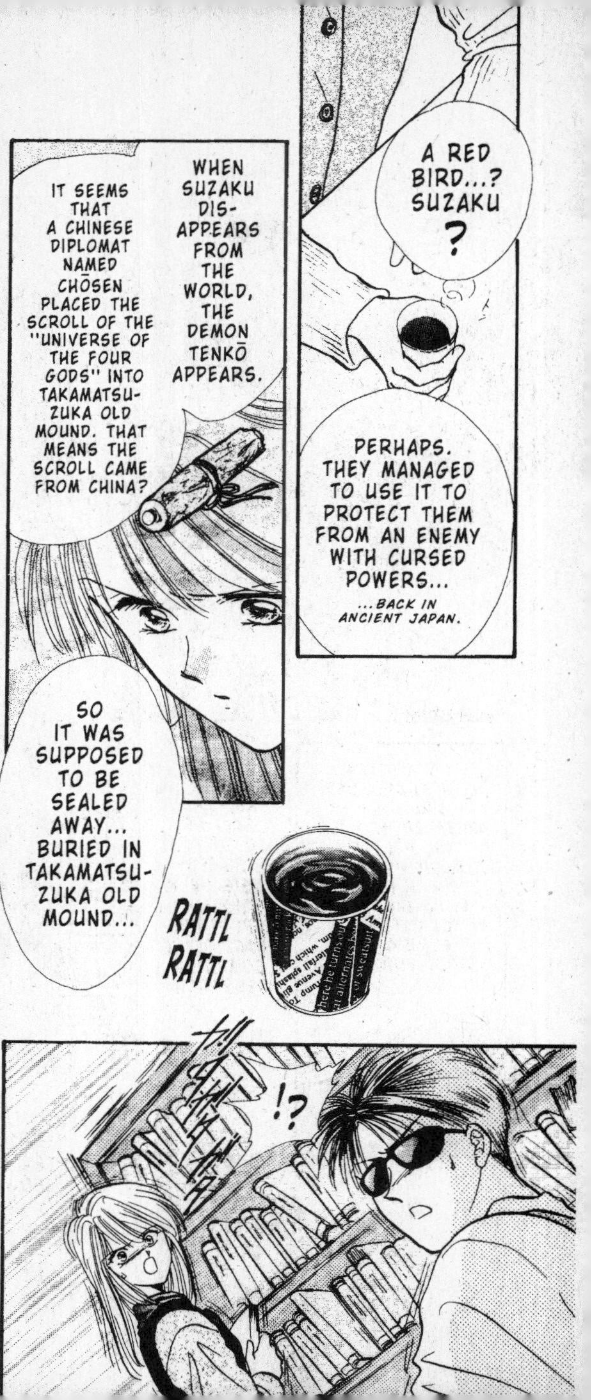
A RED BIRD...? SUZAKU?
PERHAPS. THEY MANAGED TO USE IT TO PROTECT THEM FROM AN ENEMY WITH CURSED POWERS...
...BACK IN ANCIENT JAPAN.
WHEN SUZAKU DISAPPEARS FROM THE WORLD, THE DEMON TENKŌ APPEARS.
IT SEEMS THAT A CHINESE DIPLOMAT NAMED CHŌSEN PLACED THE SCROLL OF THE "UNIVERSE OF THE FOUR GODS" INTO TAKAMATSUZUKA OLD MOUND. THAT MEANS THE SCROLL CAME FROM CHINA?
SO IT WAS SUPPOSED TO BE SEALED AWAY... BURIED IN TAKAMATSUZUKA OLD MOUND...
RATTL RATTL
!?

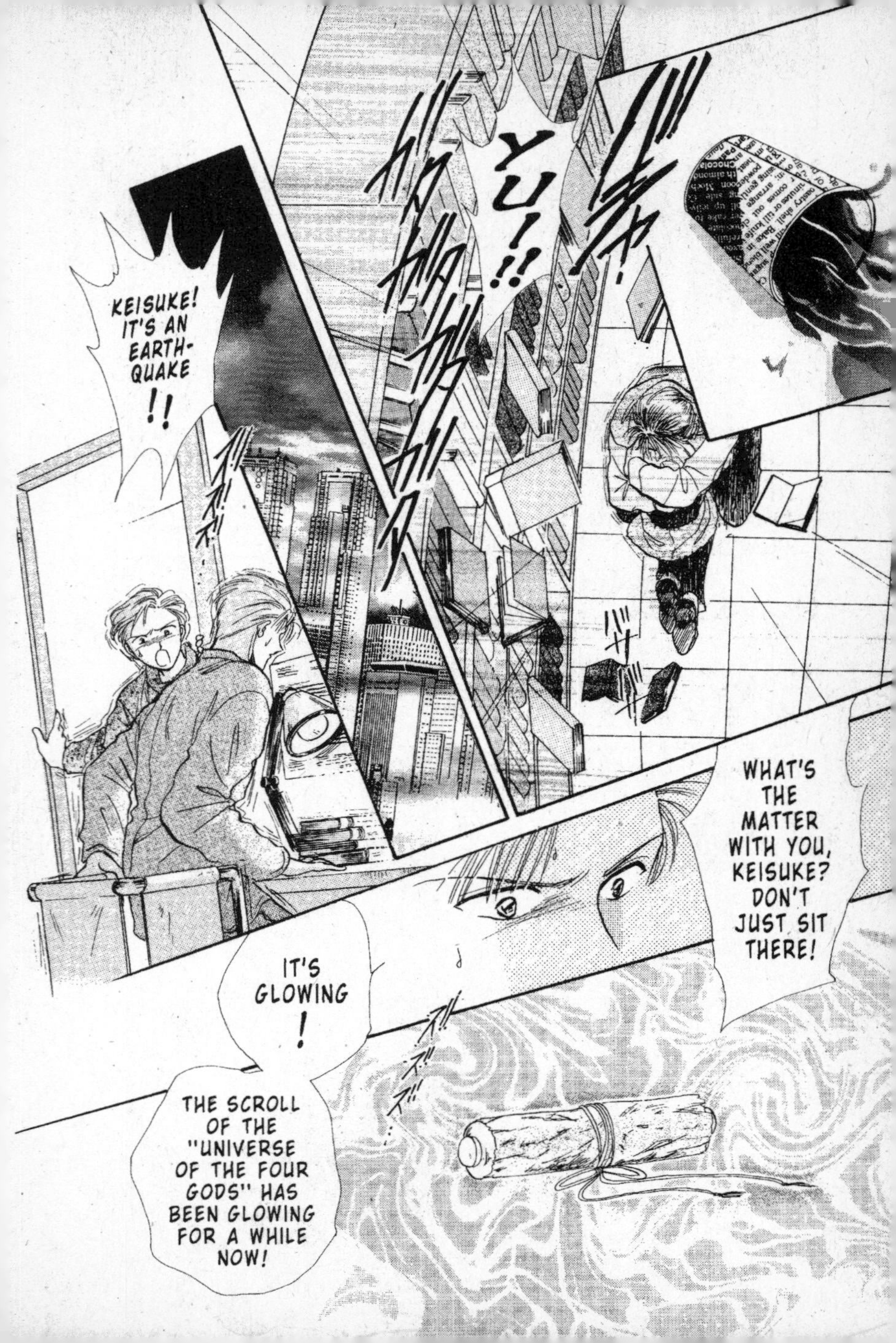
KEISUKE! IT'S AN EARTH-QUAKE!!
WHAT'S THE MATTER WITH YOU, KEISUKE? DON'T JUST SIT THERE!
IT'S GLOWING!
THE SCROLL OF THE "UNIVERSE OF THE FOUR GODS" HAS BEEN GLOWING FOR A WHILE NOW!

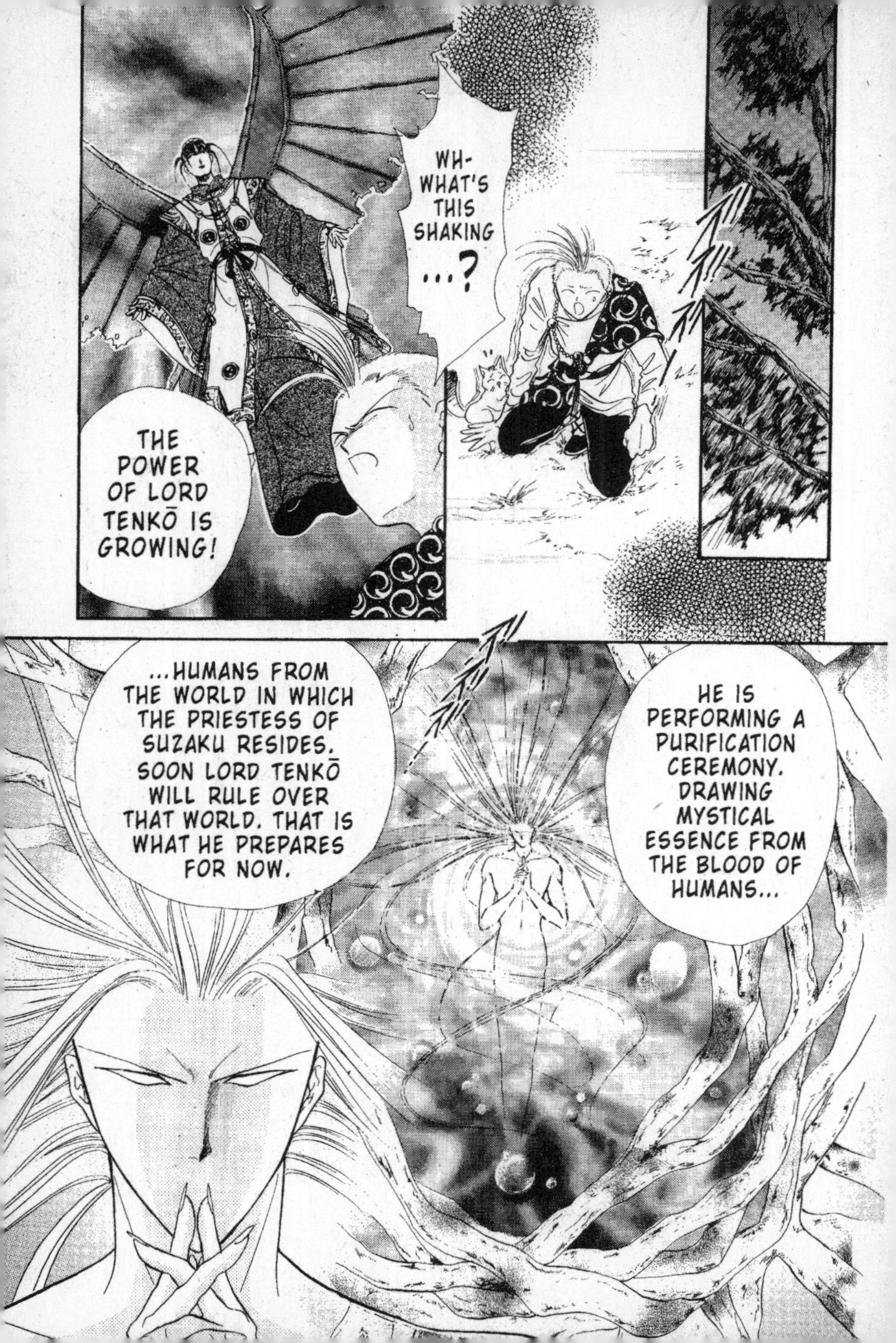
WH- WHAT'S THIS SHAKING ...?
THE POWER OF LORD TENKŌ IS GROWING!
HE IS PERFORMING A PURIFICATION CEREMONY. DRAWING MYSTICAL ESSENCE FROM THE BLOOD OF HUMANS...
...HUMANS FROM THE WORLD IN WHICH THE PRIESTESS OF SUZAKU RESIDES. SOON LORD TENKŌ WILL RULE OVER THAT WORLD. THAT IS WHAT HE PREPARES FOR NOW.

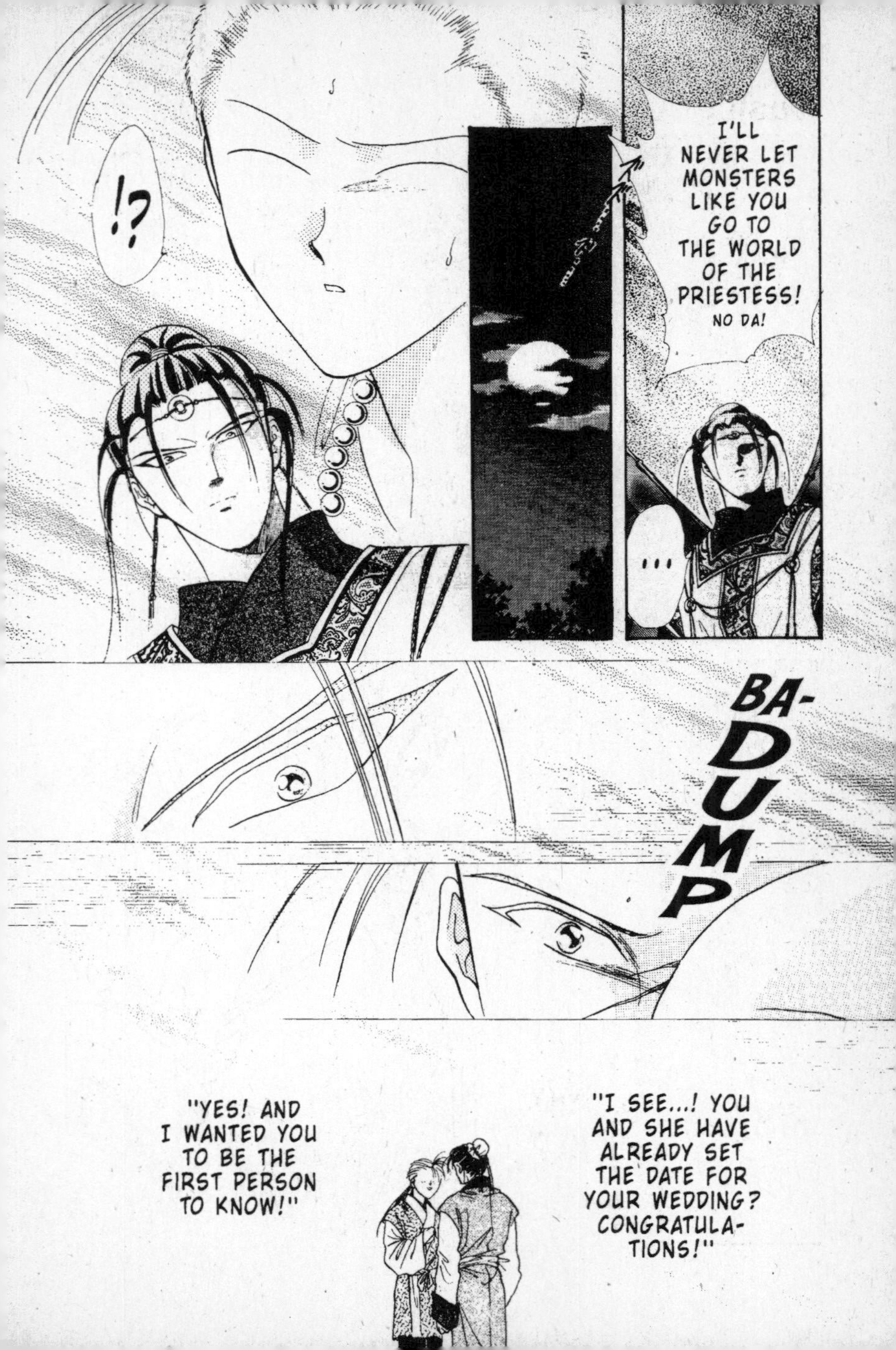
I'LL NEVER LET MONSTERS LIKE YOU GO TO THE WORLD OF THE PRIESTESS! NO DA!
...
!?
BA-DUMP
"I SEE...! YOU AND SHE HAVE ALREADY SET THE DATE FOR YOUR WEDDING? CONGRATULATIONS!"
"YES! AND I WANTED YOU TO BE THE FIRST PERSON TO KNOW!"

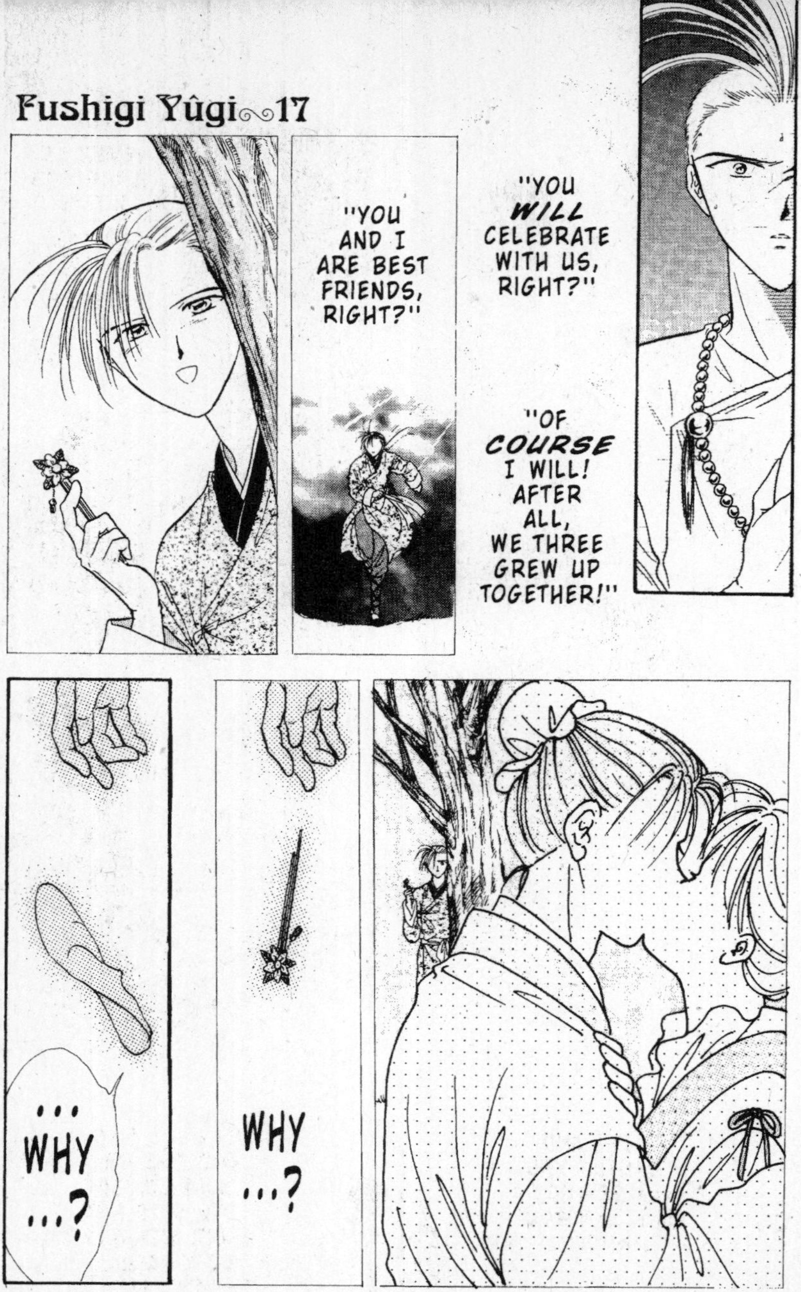
"YOU WILL CELEBRATE WITH US, RIGHT?"
"OF COURSE I WILL! AFTER ALL, WE THREE GREW UP TOGETHER!"
"YOU AND I ARE BEST FRIENDS, RIGHT?"
WHY ...?
... WHY ...?

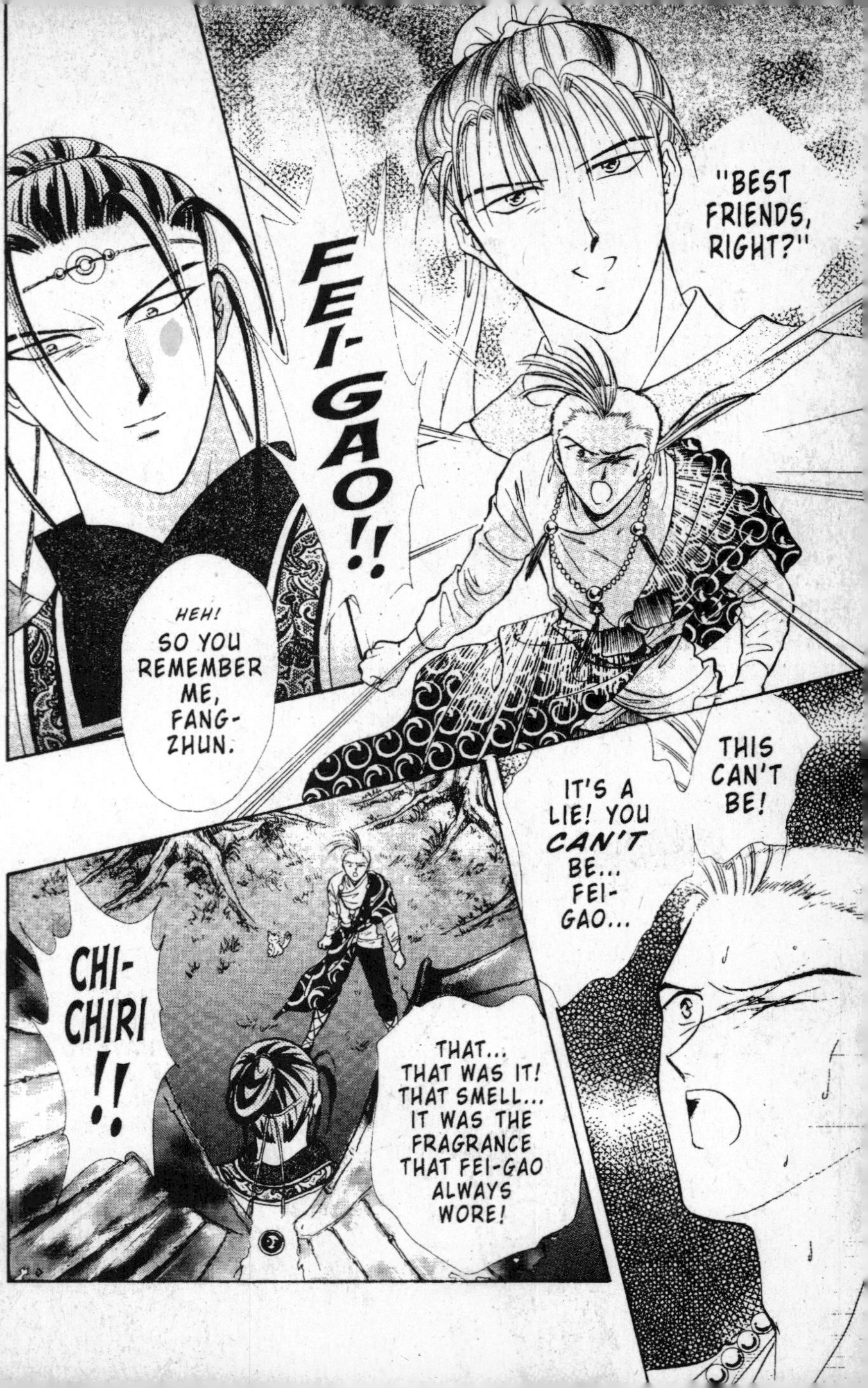
"BEST FRIENDS, RIGHT?"
FEI-GAO!!
HEH! SO YOU REMEMBER ME, FANG-ZHUN.
THIS CAN'T BE!
IT'S A LIE! YOU CAN'T BE... FEI-GAO...
CHI-CHIRI!!
THAT... THAT WAS IT! THAT SMELL... IT WAS THE FRAGRANCE THAT FEI-GAO ALWAYS WORE!

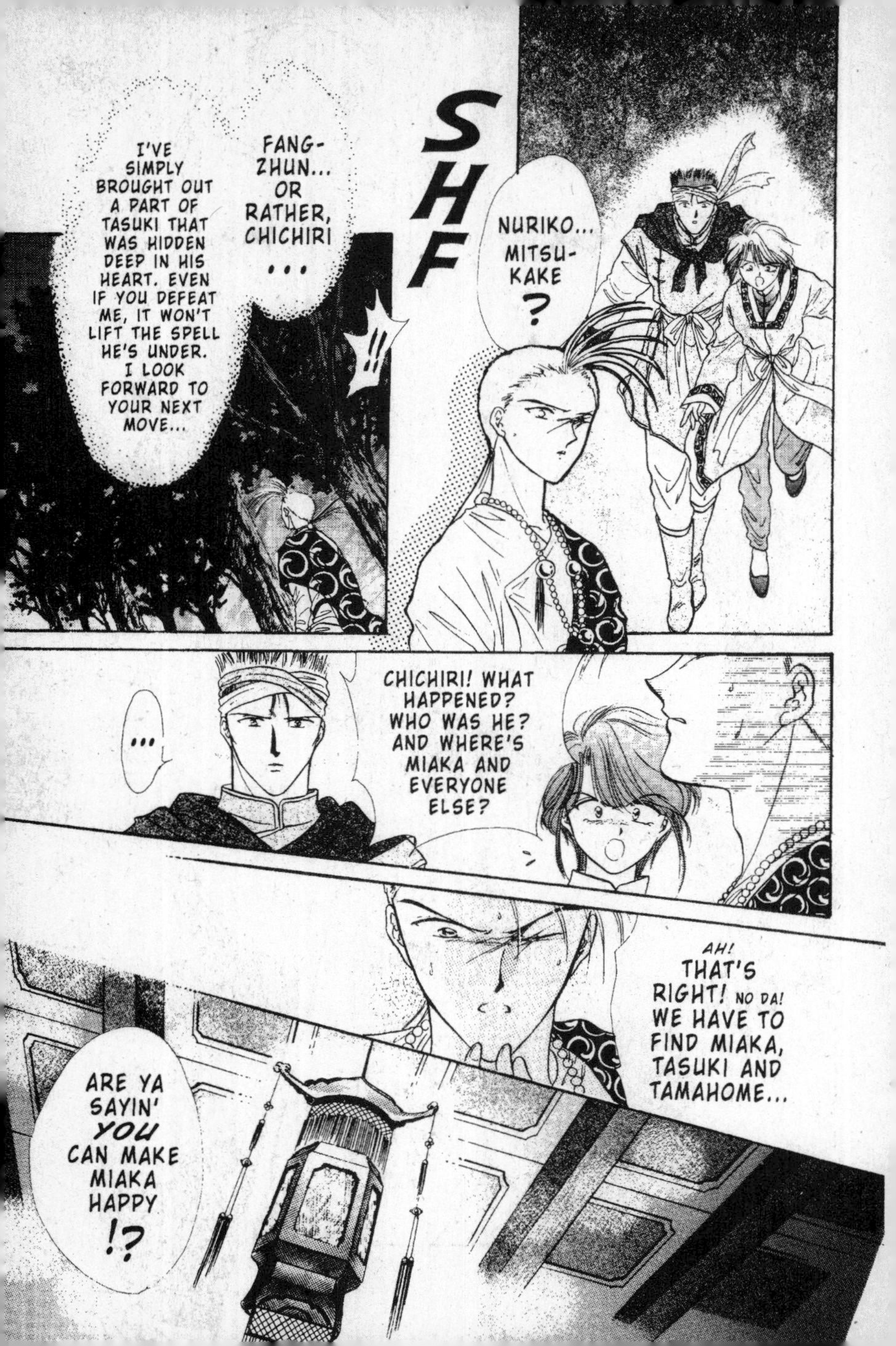
SHF
NURIKO... MITSUKAKE ?
!!
FANG-ZHUN... OR RATHER, CHICHIRI ...
I'VE SIMPLY BROUGHT OUT A PART OF TASUKI THAT WAS HIDDEN DEEP IN HIS HEART. EVEN IF YOU DEFEAT ME, IT WON'T LIFT THE SPELL HE'S UNDER. I LOOK FORWARD TO YOUR NEXT MOVE...
CHICHIRI! WHAT HAPPENED? WHO WAS HE? AND WHERE'S MIAKA AND EVERYONE ELSE?
...
AH! THAT'S RIGHT! NO DA! WE HAVE TO FIND MIAKA, TASUKI AND TAMAHOME...
ARE YA SAYIN' *YOU* CAN MAKE MIAKA HAPPY !?

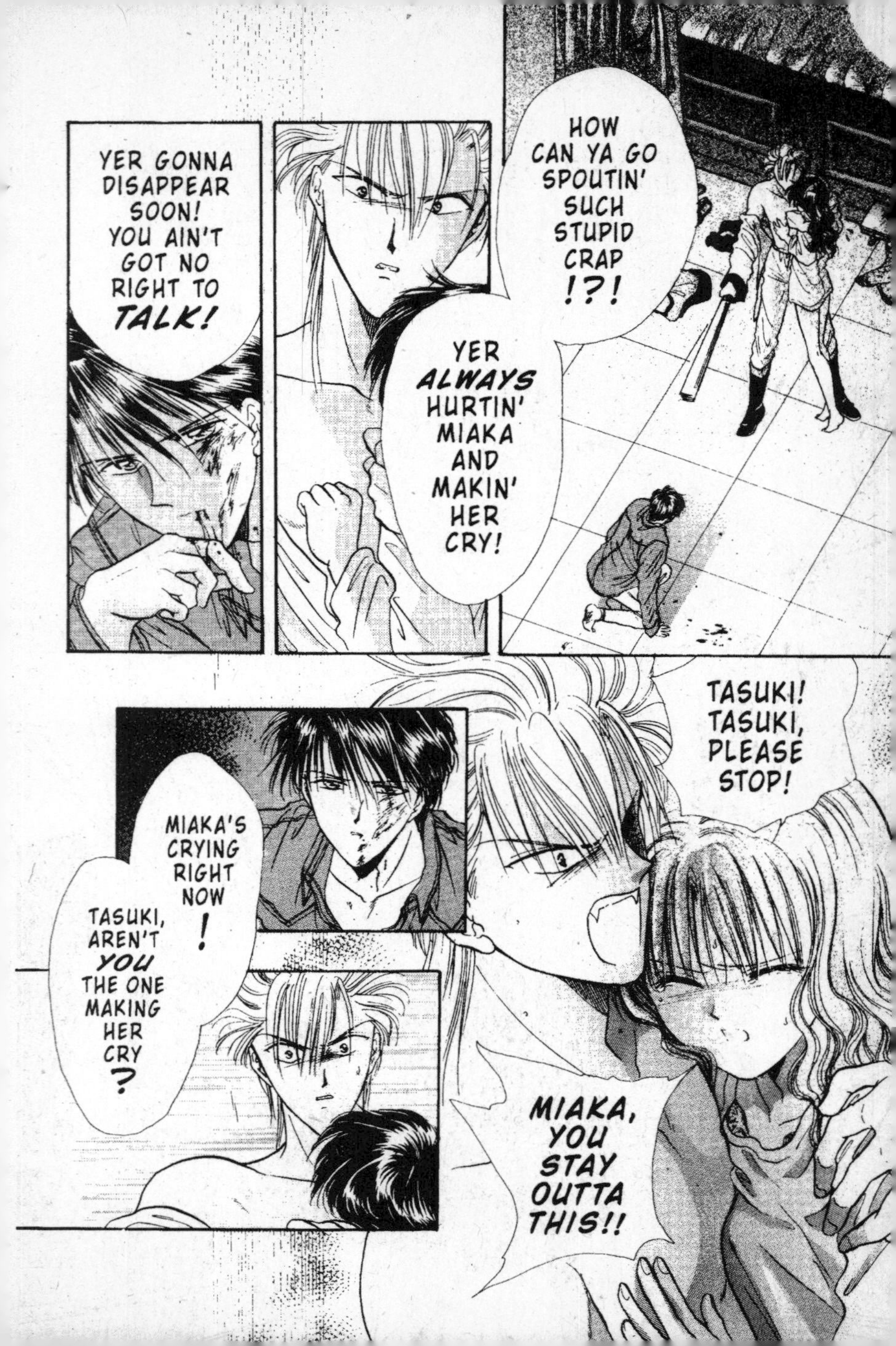
HOW CAN YA GO SPOUTIN' SUCH STUPID CRAP !?!
YER *ALWAYS* HURTIN' MIAKA AND MAKIN' HER CRY!
YER GONNA DISAPPEAR SOON! YOU AIN'T GOT NO RIGHT TO *TALK!*
TASUKI! TASUKI, PLEASE STOP!
MIAKA, YOU STAY OUTTA THIS!!
MIAKA'S CRYING RIGHT NOW!
TASUKI, AREN'T *YOU* THE ONE MAKING HER CRY?

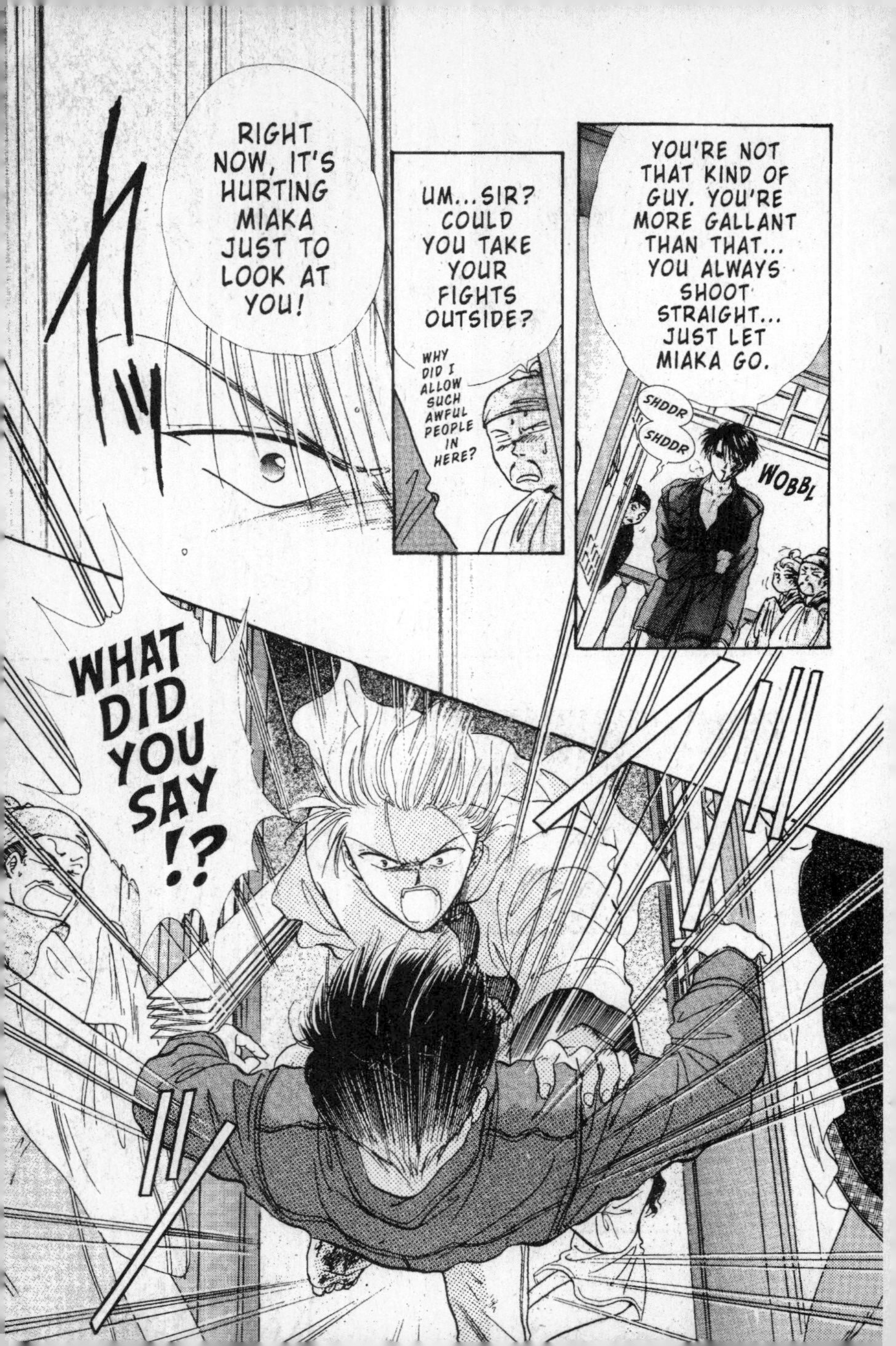
YOU'RE NOT THAT KIND OF GUY. YOU'RE MORE GALLANT THAN THAT... YOU ALWAYS SHOOT STRAIGHT... JUST LET MIAKA GO.
SHDDR
SHDDR
WOBBL
UM...SIR? COULD YOU TAKE YOUR FIGHTS OUTSIDE?
WHY DID I ALLOW SUCH AWFUL PEOPLE IN HERE?
RIGHT NOW, IT'S HURTING MIAKA JUST TO LOOK AT YOU!
WHAT DID YOU SAY !?

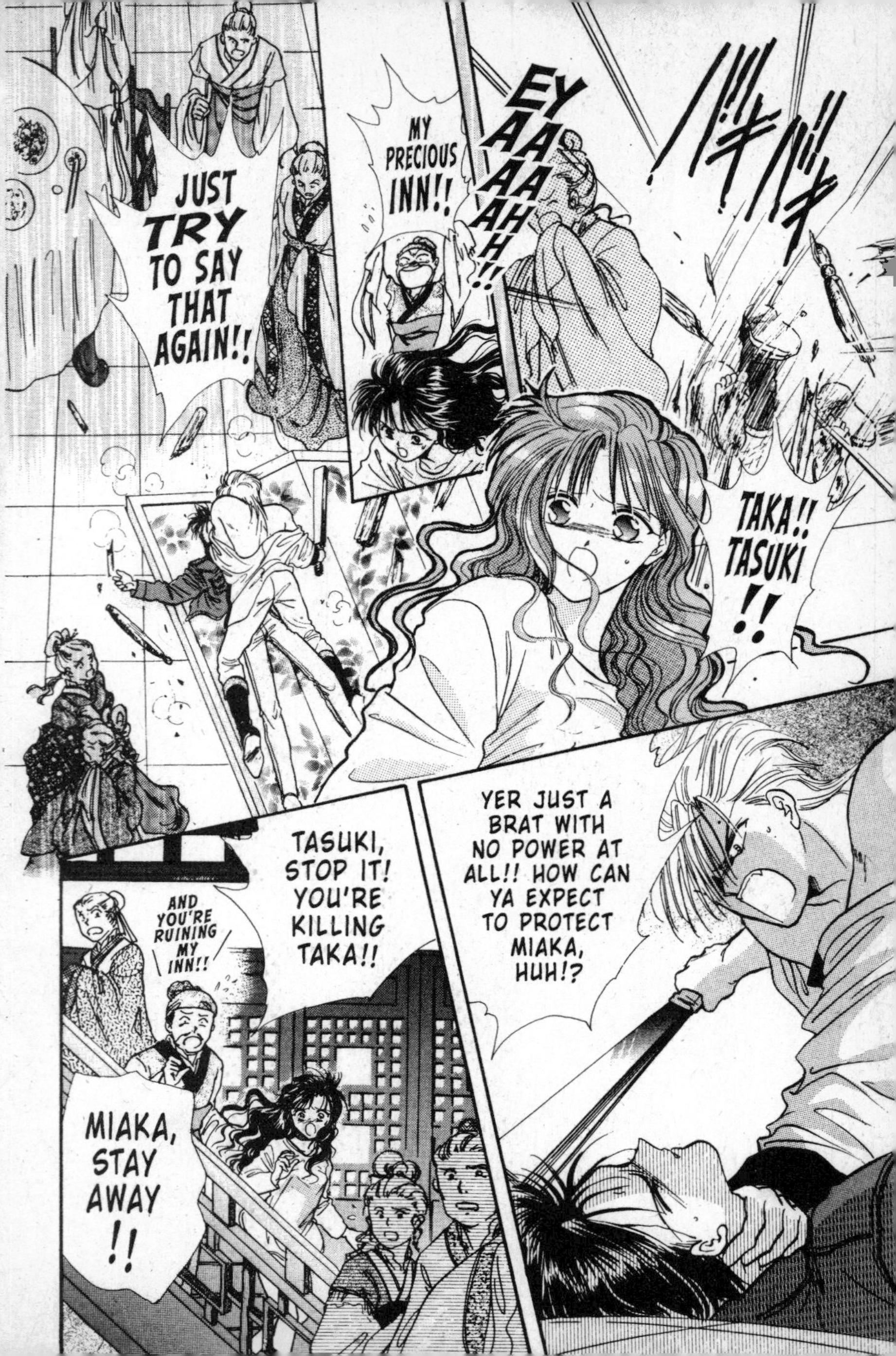

バキバキ
TAKA!! TASUKI!!
EYAAAAAHH!!
MY PRECIOUS INN!!
JUST TRY TO SAY THAT AGAIN!!
YER JUST A BRAT WITH NO POWER AT ALL!! HOW CAN YA EXPECT TO PROTECT MIAKA, HUH!?
TASUKI, STOP IT! YOU'RE KILLING TAKA!!
AND YOU'RE RUINING MY INN!!
MIAKA, STAY AWAY!!

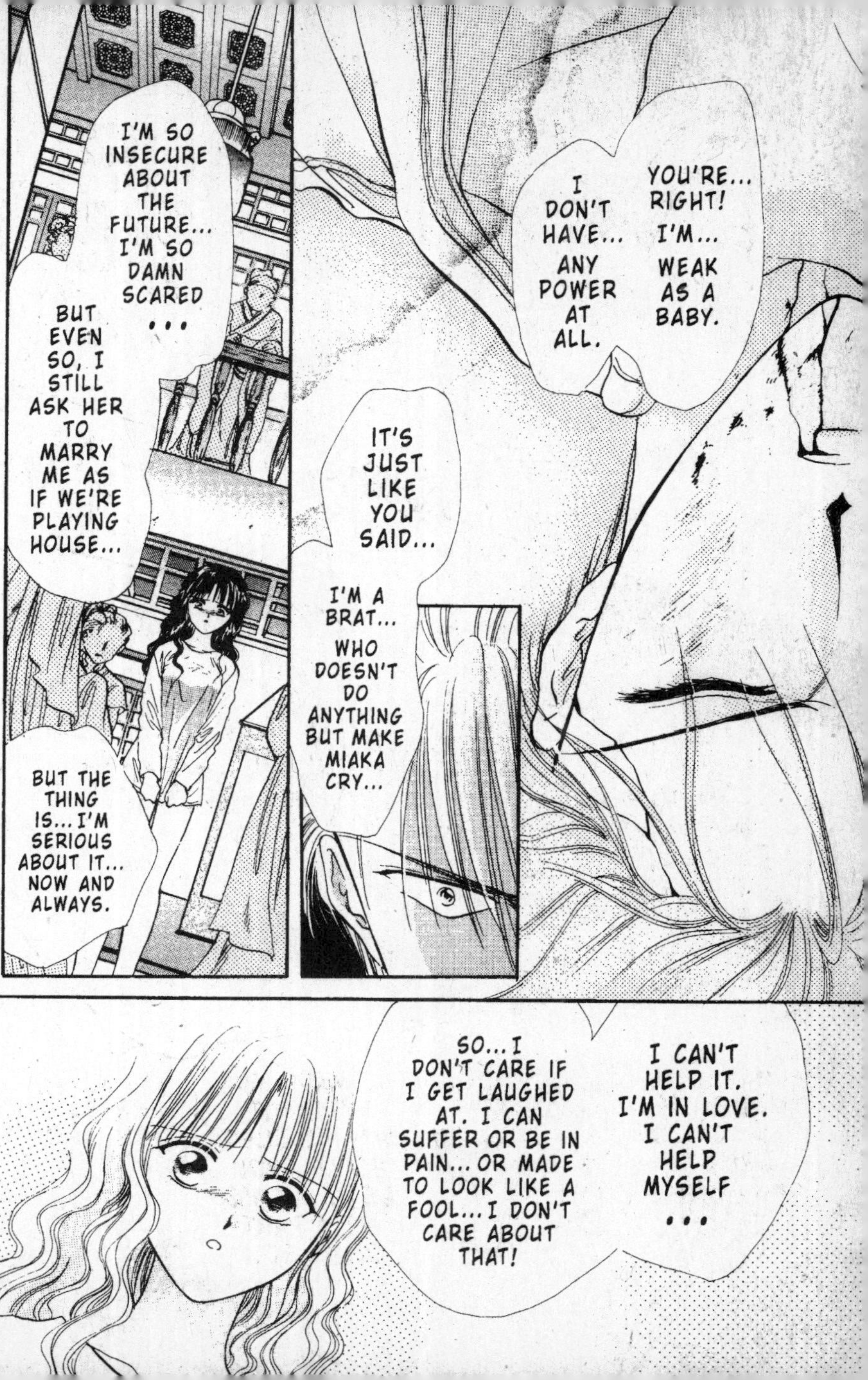

YOU'RE... RIGHT! I'M... WEAK AS A BABY.
I DON'T HAVE... ANY POWER AT ALL.
IT'S JUST LIKE YOU SAID...
I'M A BRAT... WHO DOESN'T DO ANYTHING BUT MAKE MIAKA CRY...
I'M SO INSECURE ABOUT THE FUTURE... I'M SO DAMN SCARED...
BUT EVEN SO, I STILL ASK HER TO MARRY ME AS IF WE'RE PLAYING HOUSE...
BUT THE THING IS... I'M SERIOUS ABOUT IT... NOW AND ALWAYS.
I CAN'T HELP IT. I'M IN LOVE. I CAN'T HELP MYSELF...
SO... I DON'T CARE IF I GET LAUGHED AT. I CAN SUFFER OR BE IN PAIN... OR MADE TO LOOK LIKE A FOOL... I DON'T CARE ABOUT THAT!

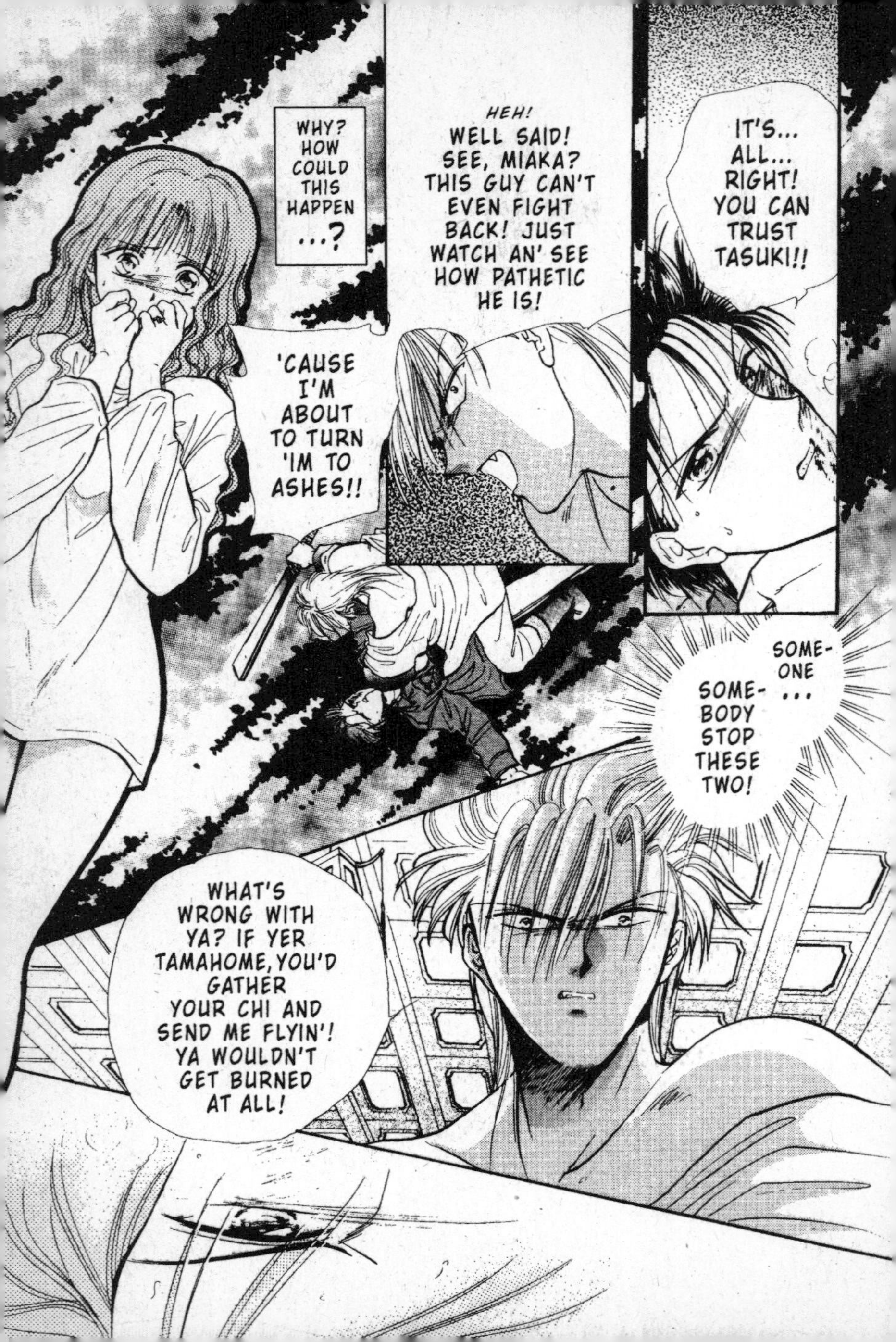
IT'S... ALL... RIGHT! YOU CAN TRUST TASUKI!!
HEH! WELL SAID! SEE, MIAKA? THIS GUY CAN'T EVEN FIGHT BACK! JUST WATCH AN' SEE HOW PATHETIC HE IS!
'CAUSE I'M ABOUT TO TURN 'IM TO ASHES!!
WHY? HOW COULD THIS HAPPEN ...?
SOME-ONE...
SOME-BODY STOP THESE TWO!
WHAT'S WRONG WITH YA? IF YER TAMAHOME, YOU'D GATHER YOUR CHI AND SEND ME FLYIN'! YA WOULDN'T GET BURNED AT ALL!

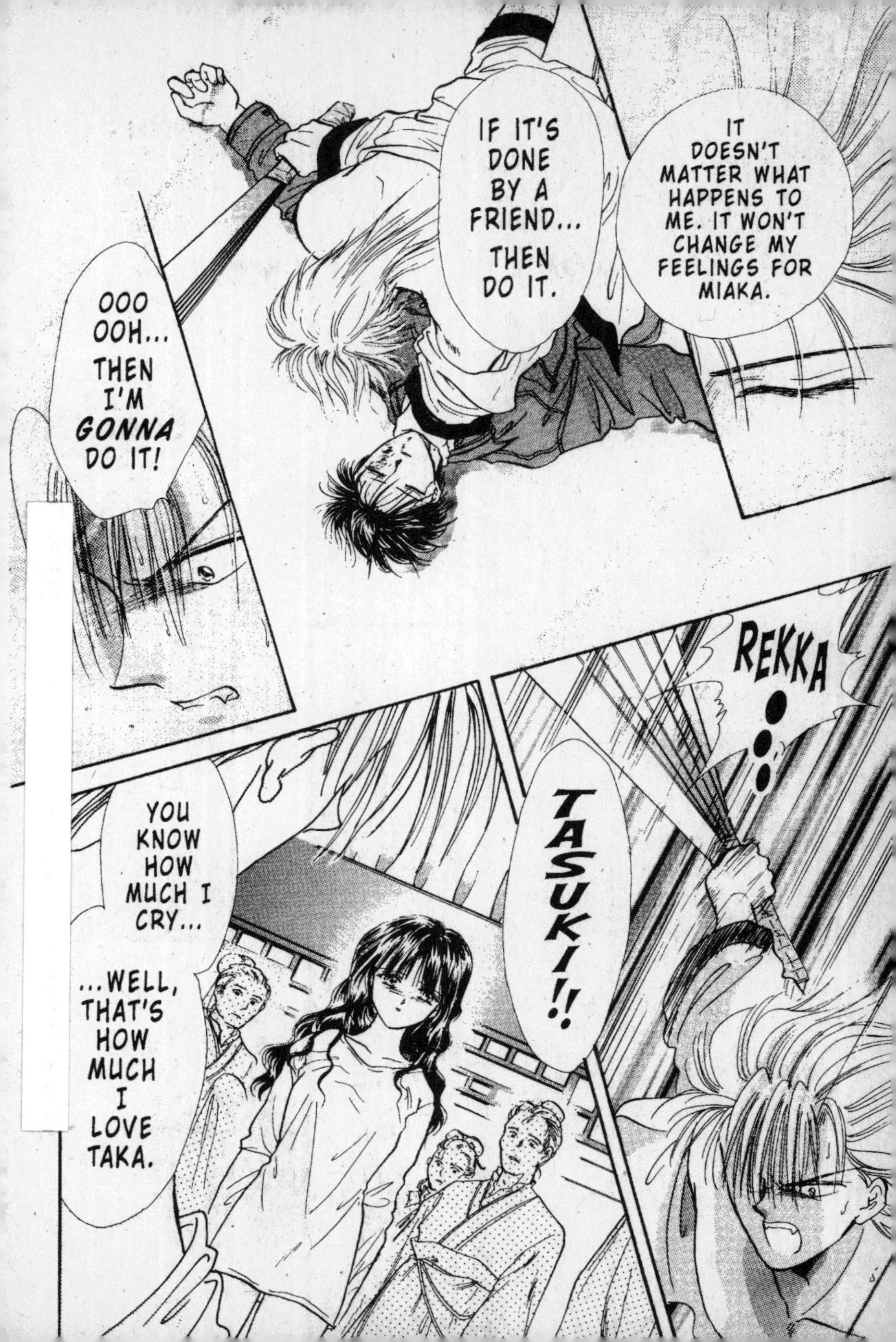
IT DOESN'T MATTER WHAT HAPPENS TO ME. IT WON'T CHANGE MY FEELINGS FOR MIAKA.
IF IT'S DONE BY A FRIEND...
THEN DO IT.
OOOOOH... THEN I'M *GONNA* DO IT!
REKKA...
TASUKI!!
YOU KNOW HOW MUCH I CRY...
...WELL, THAT'S HOW MUCH I LOVE TAKA.

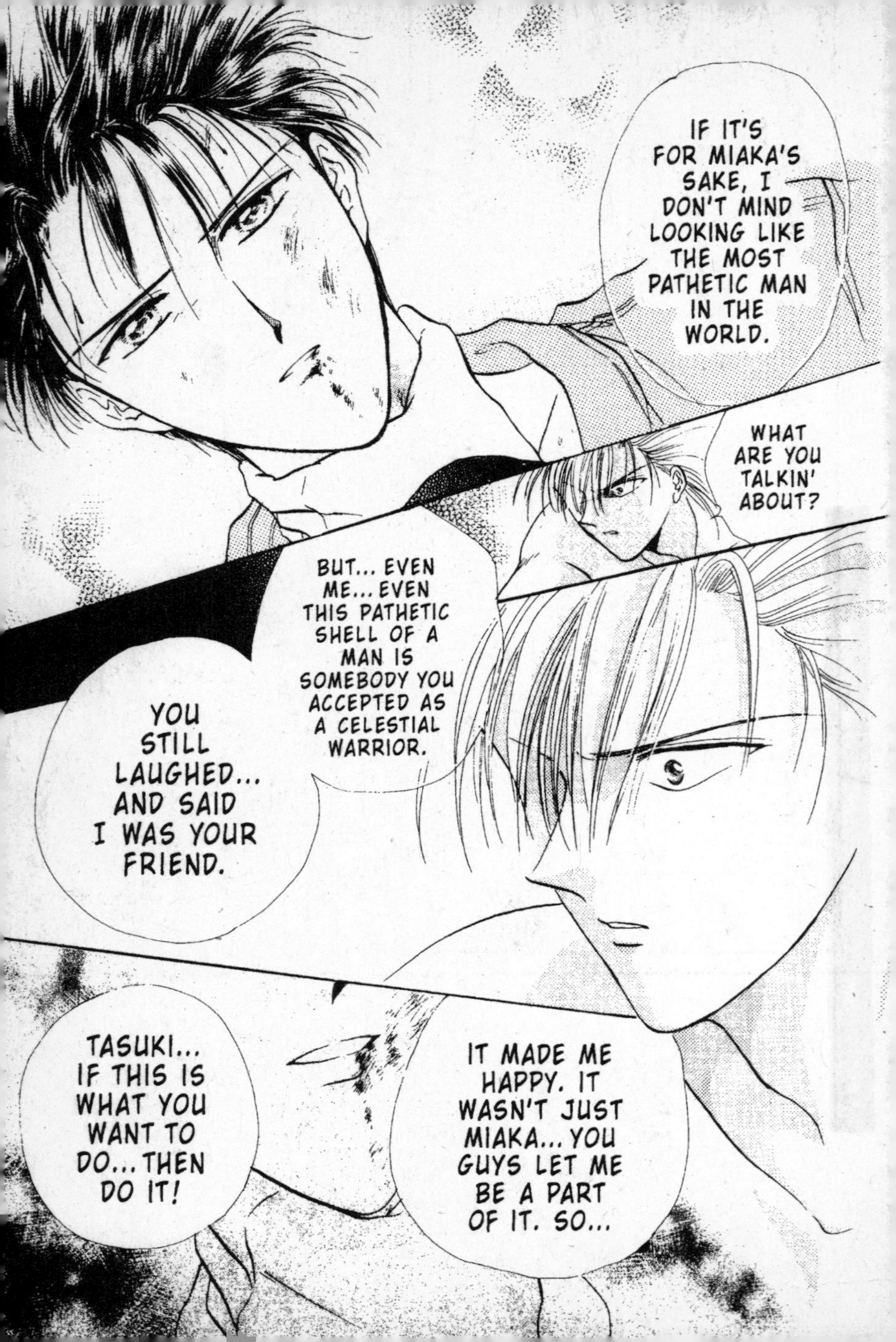
IF IT'S FOR MIAKA'S SAKE, I DON'T MIND LOOKING LIKE THE MOST PATHETIC MAN IN THE WORLD.
WHAT ARE YOU TALKIN' ABOUT?
BUT... EVEN ME... EVEN THIS PATHETIC SHELL OF A MAN IS SOMEBODY YOU ACCEPTED AS A CELESTIAL WARRIOR.
YOU STILL LAUGHED... AND SAID I WAS YOUR FRIEND.
IT MADE ME HAPPY. IT WASN'T JUST MIAKA... YOU GUYS LET ME BE A PART OF IT. SO...
TASUKI... IF THIS IS WHAT YOU WANT TO DO... THEN DO IT!

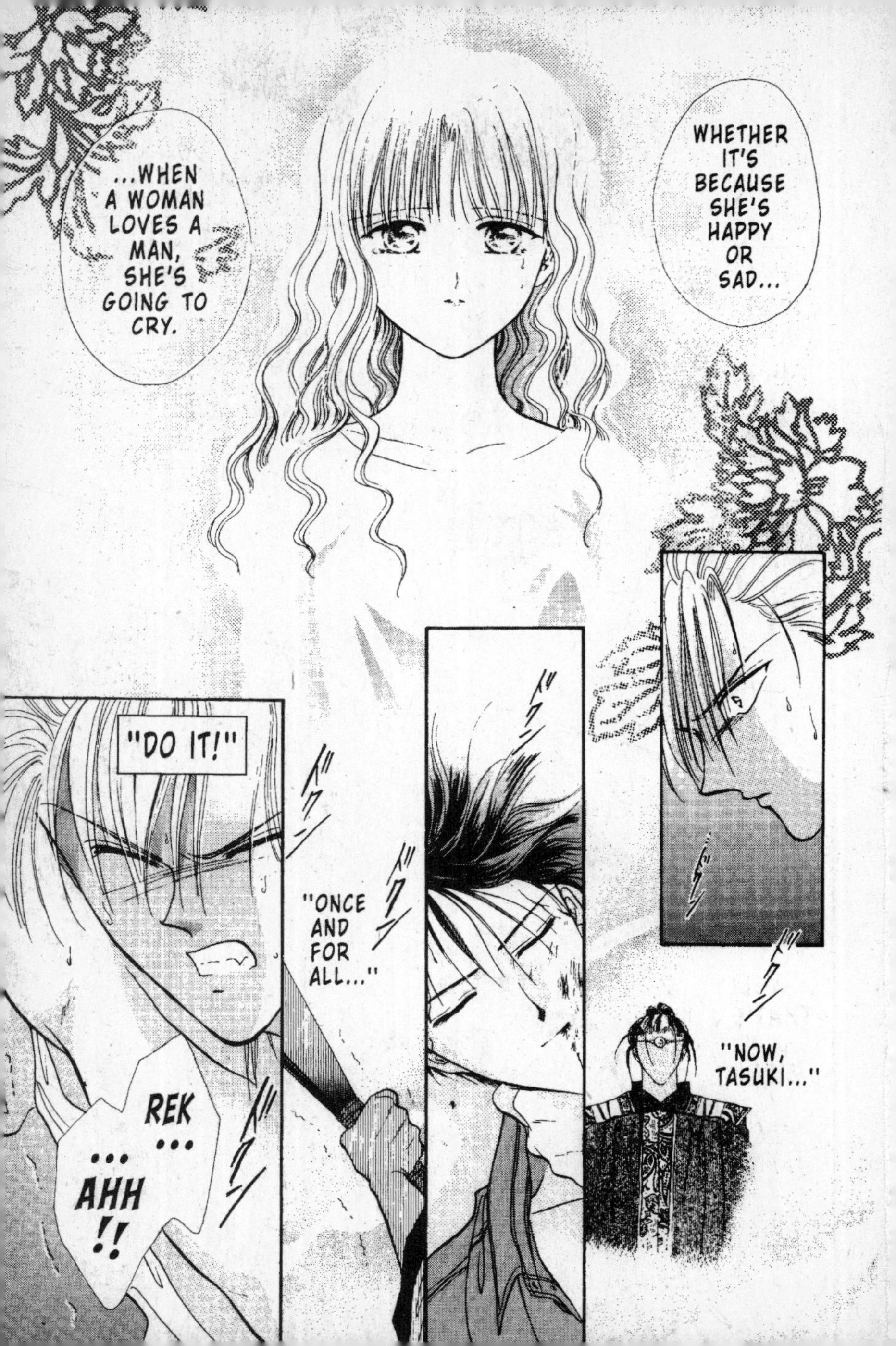
WHETHER IT'S BECAUSE SHE'S HAPPY OR SAD...
...WHEN A WOMAN LOVES A MAN, SHE'S GOING TO CRY.
"NOW, TASUKI..."
"ONCE AND FOR ALL..."
"DO IT!"
REK... ...AHH!!

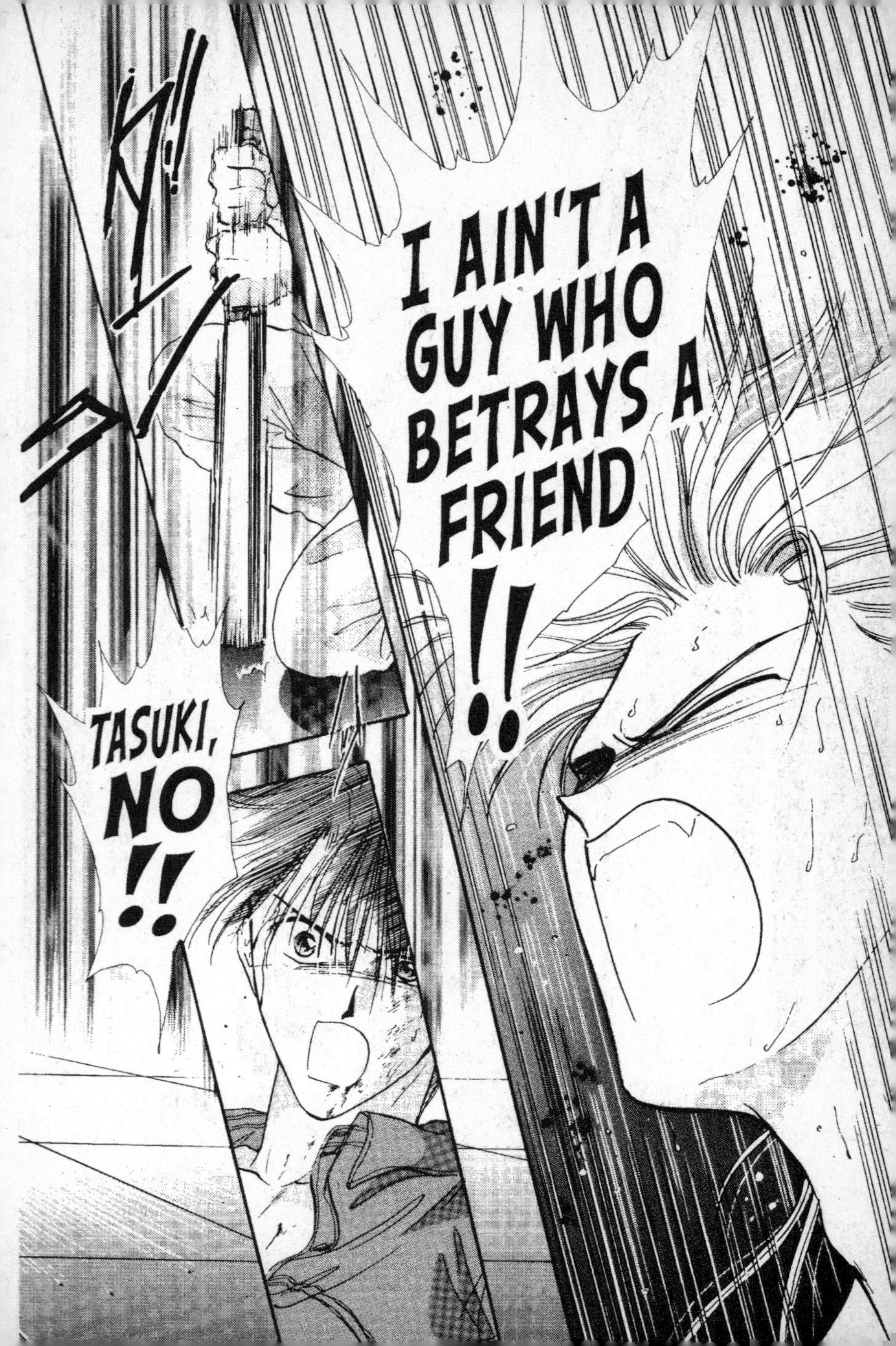
I AIN'T A GUY WHO BETRAYS A FRIEND!!
TASUKI, NO!!

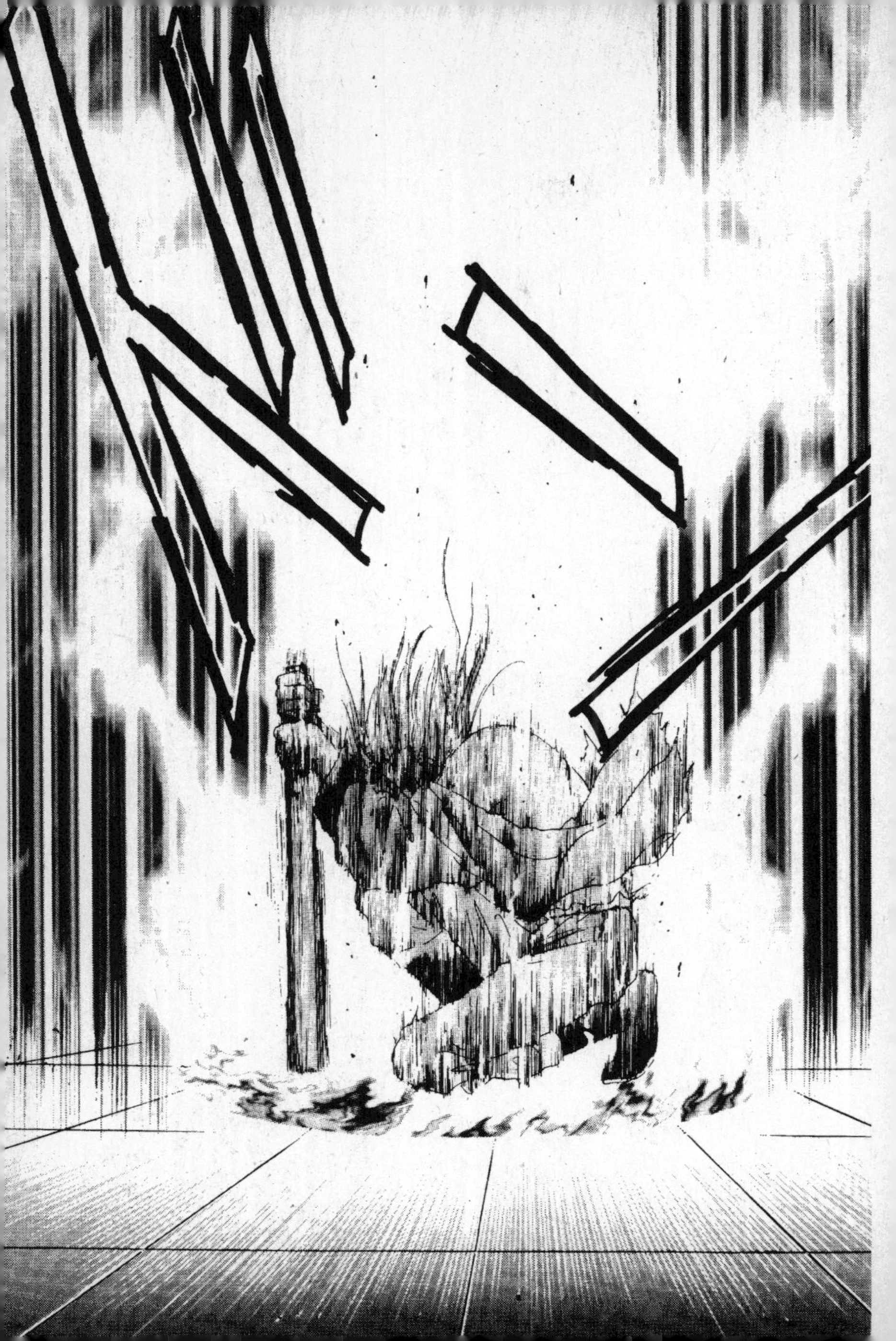

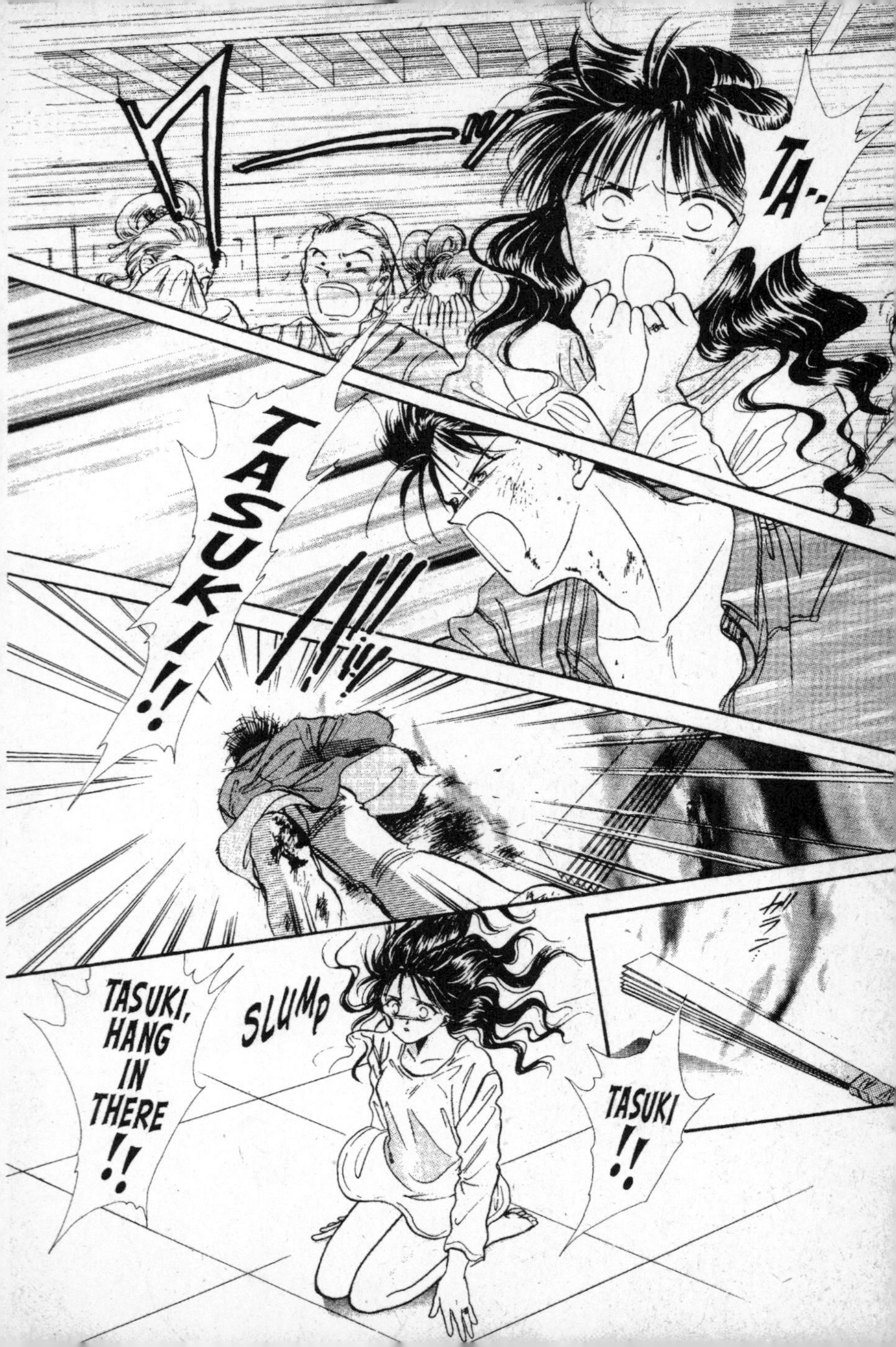
TA--
TASUKI!!
TASUKI!!
SLUMP
TASUKI, HANG IN THERE!!

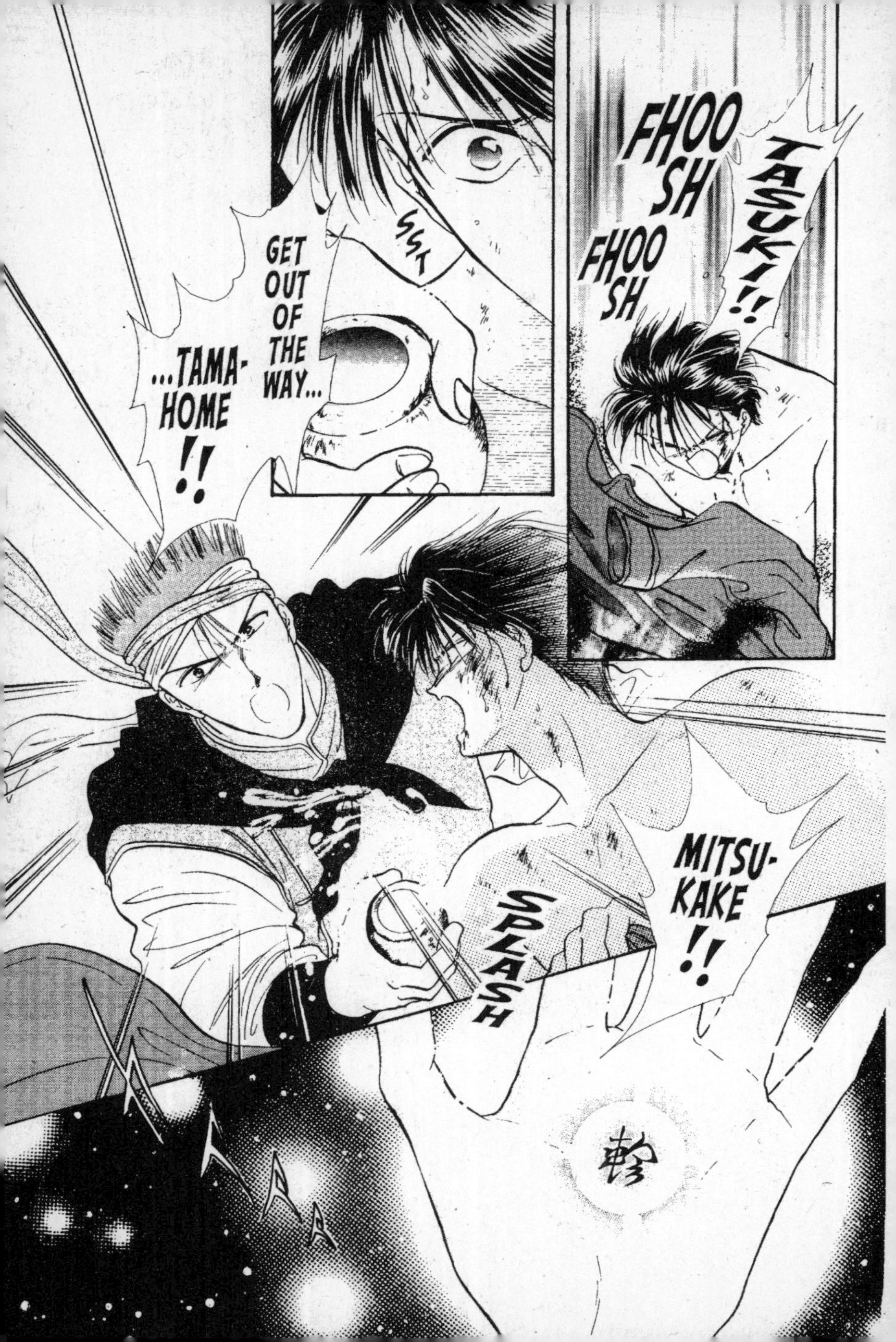
TASUKI!!
FHOOSH
FHOOSH
SSST
GET OUT OF THE WAY...
...TAMAHOME!!
MITSUKAKE!!
SPLASH
軫

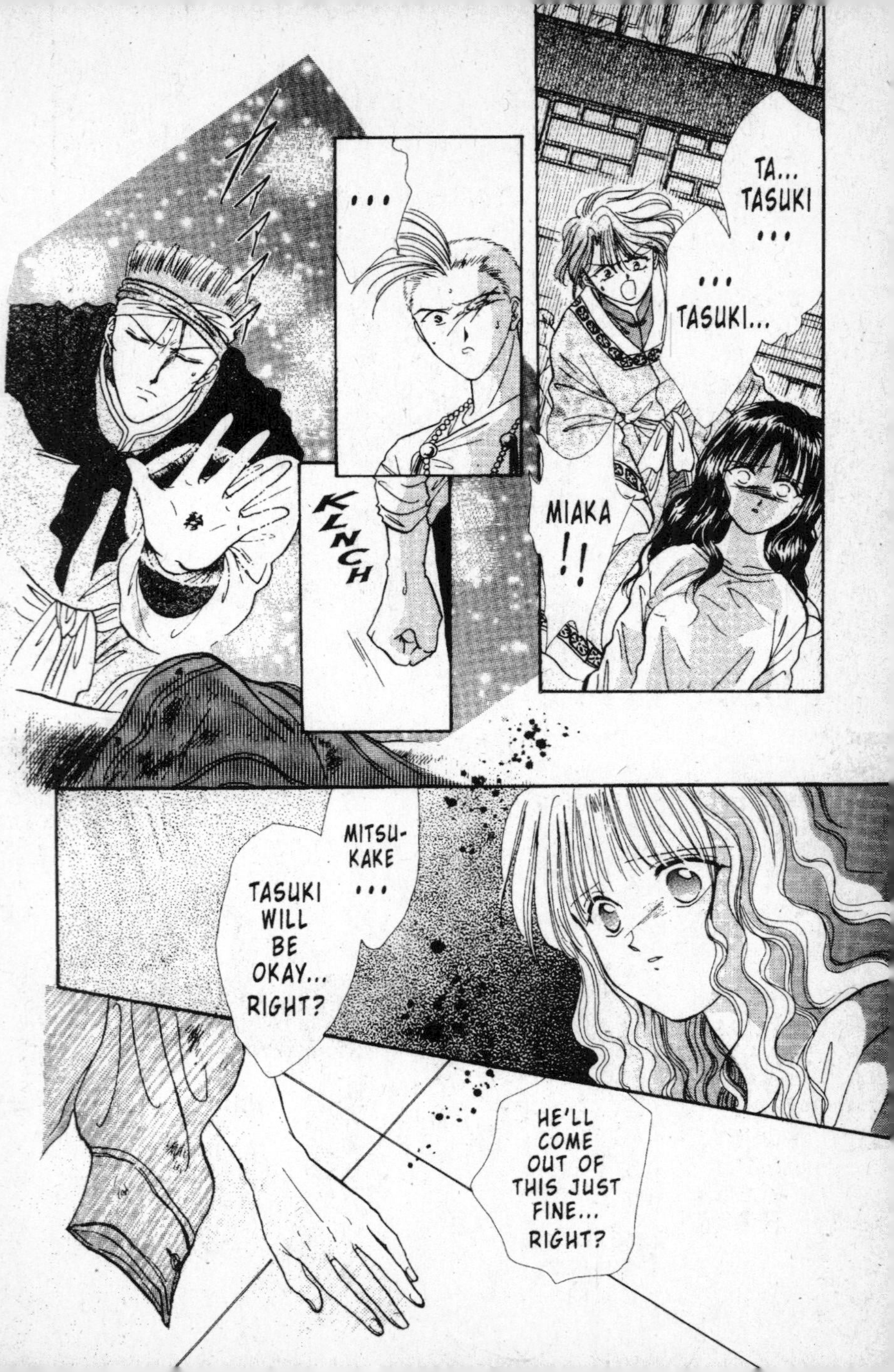
TA... TASUKI ...
... TASUKI...
MIAKA !!
...
KLNCH
MITSUKAKE ...
TASUKI WILL BE OKAY... RIGHT?
HE'LL COME OUT OF THIS JUST FINE... RIGHT?

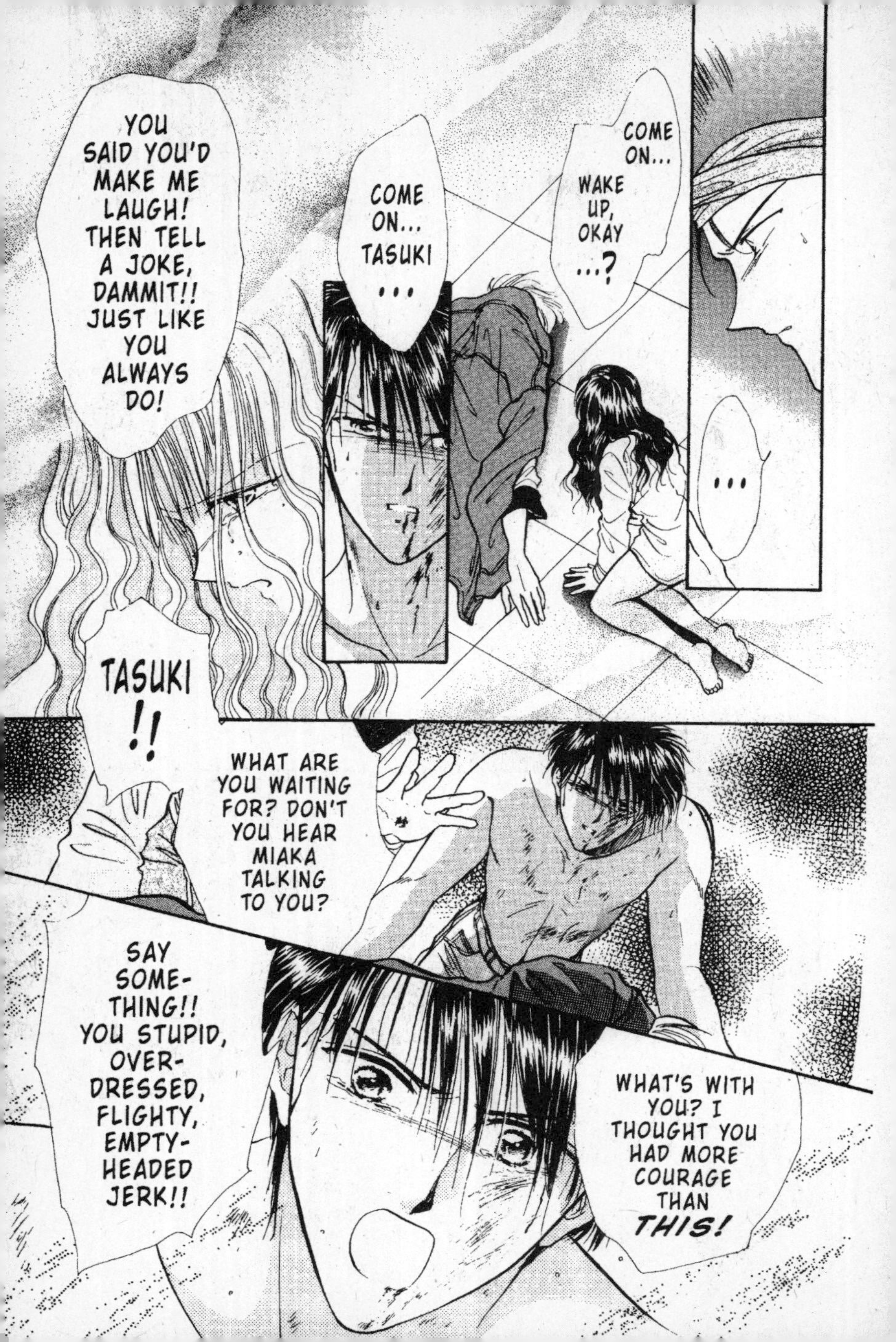
...
COME ON... WAKE UP, OKAY...?
COME ON... TASUKI...
YOU SAID YOU'D MAKE ME LAUGH! THEN TELL A JOKE, DAMMIT!! JUST LIKE YOU ALWAYS DO!
TASUKI!!
WHAT ARE YOU WAITING FOR? DON'T YOU HEAR MIAKA TALKING TO YOU?
WHAT'S WITH YOU? I THOUGHT YOU HAD MORE COURAGE THAN THIS!
SAY SOME-THING!! YOU STUPID, OVER-DRESSED, FLIGHTY, EMPTY-HEADED JERK!!

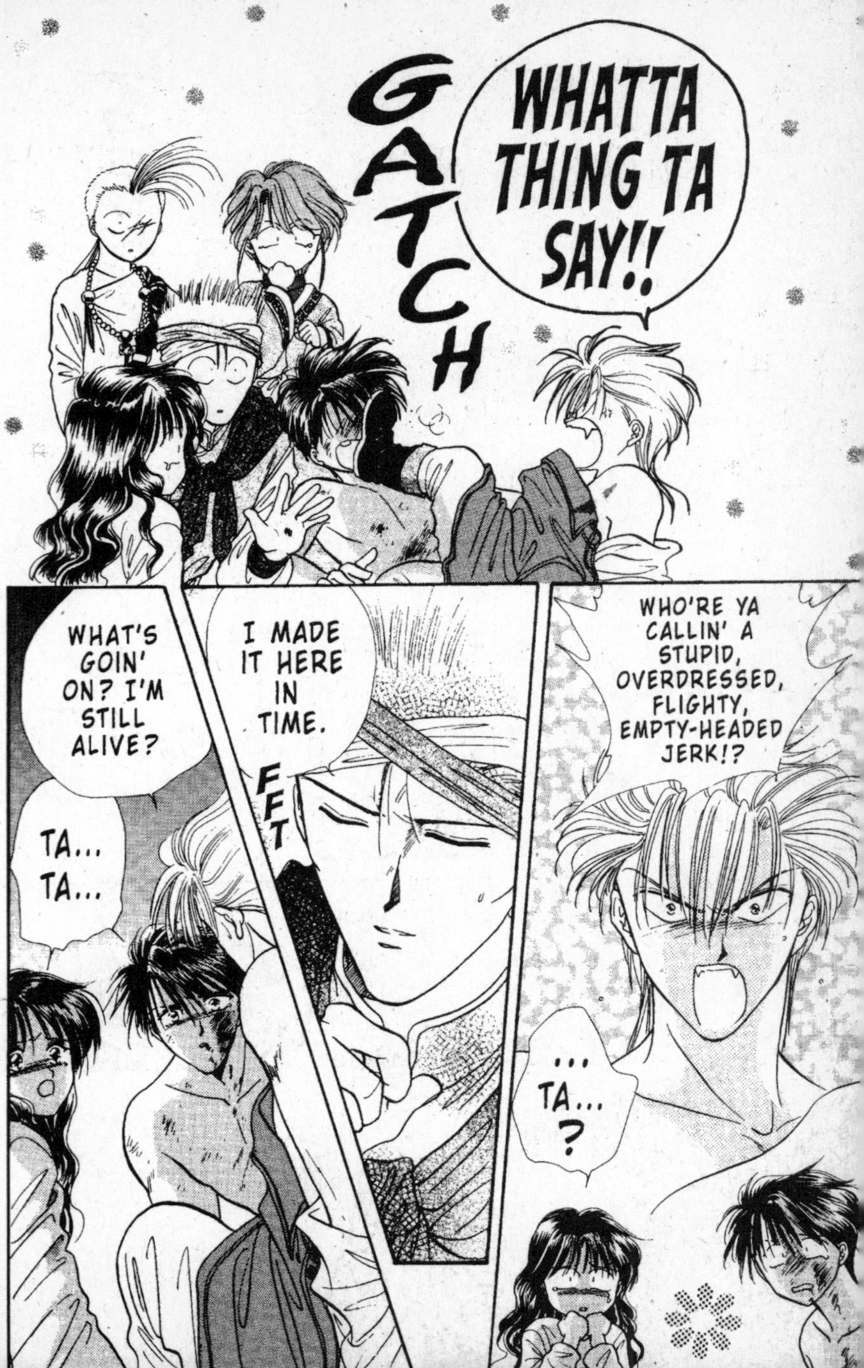
WHATTA THING TA SAY!!
GATCH
WHO'RE YA CALLIN' A STUPID, OVERDRESSED, FLIGHTY, EMPTY-HEADED JERK!?
... TA... ?
I MADE IT HERE IN TIME.
FFT
WHAT'S GOIN' ON? I'M STILL ALIVE?
TA... TA...

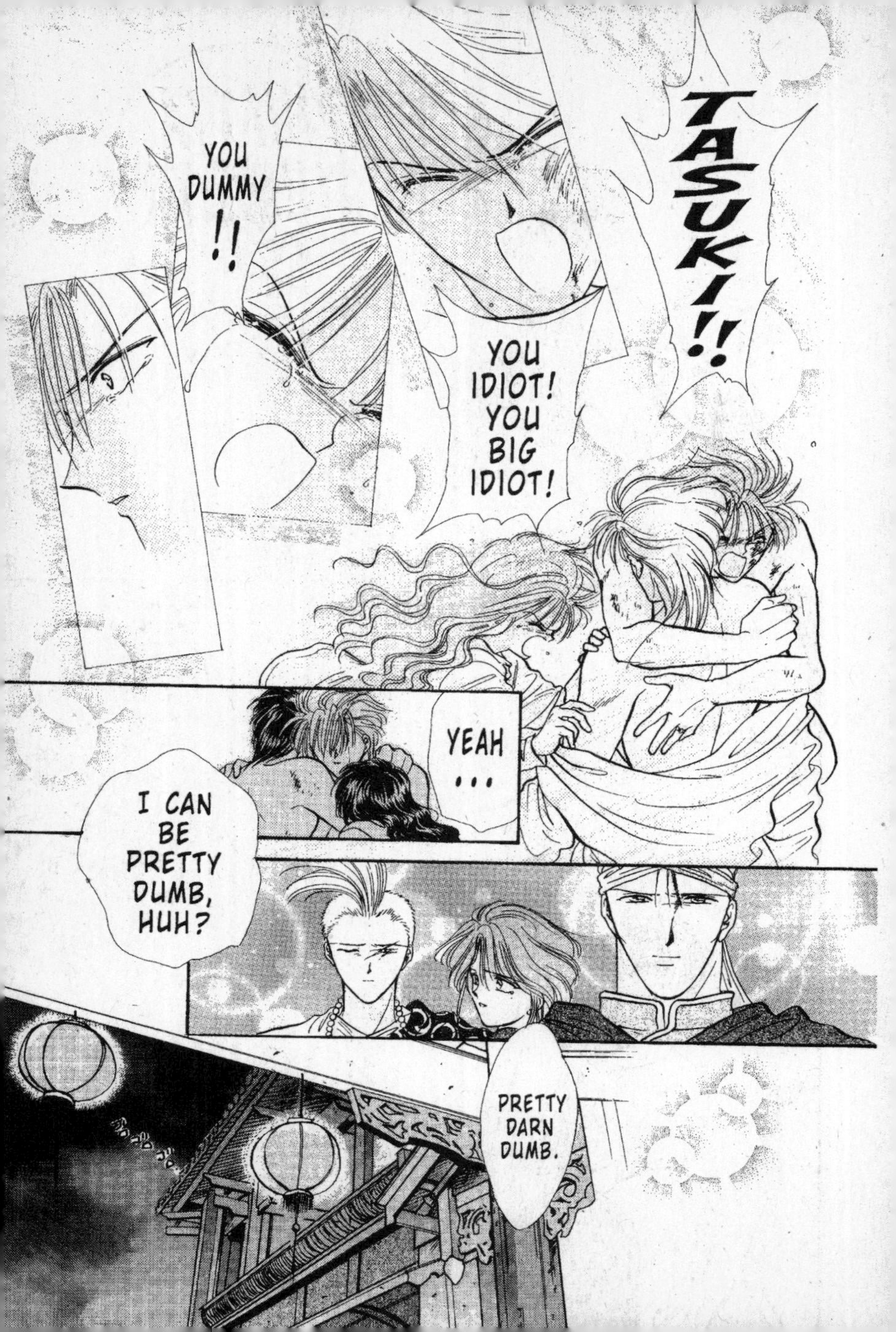
TASUKI!!
YOU IDIOT! YOU BIG IDIOT!
YOU DUMMY!!
YEAH...
I CAN BE PRETTY DUMB, HUH?
PRETTY DARN DUMB.

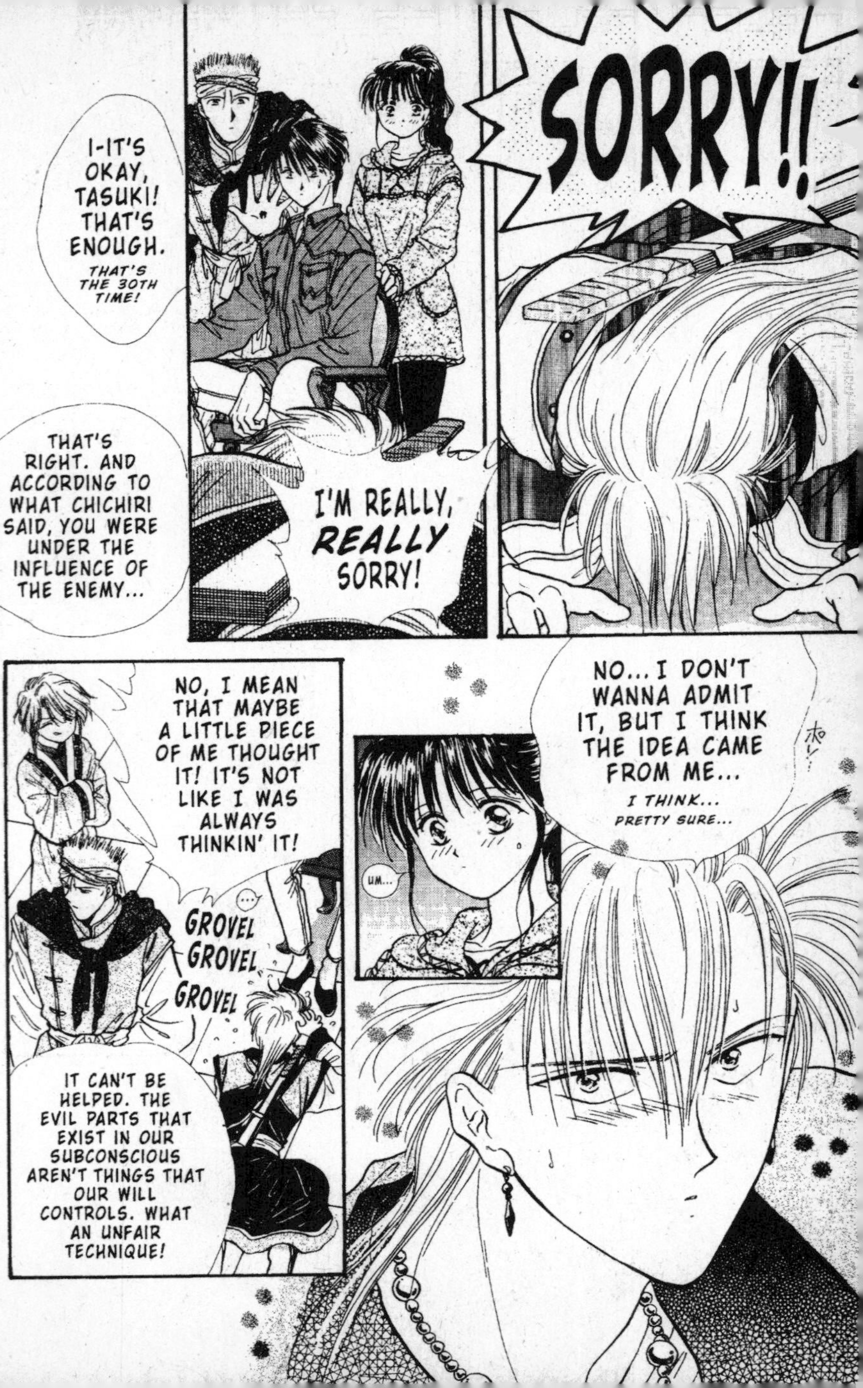

SORRY!!
I-IT'S OKAY, TASUKI! THAT'S ENOUGH.
THAT'S THE 30TH TIME!
I'M REALLY, *REALLY* SORRY!
THAT'S RIGHT. AND ACCORDING TO WHAT CHICHIRI SAID, YOU WERE UNDER THE INFLUENCE OF THE ENEMY...
NO... I DON'T WANNA ADMIT IT, BUT I THINK THE IDEA CAME FROM ME...
I THINK... PRETTY SURE...
UM...
NO, I MEAN THAT MAYBE A LITTLE PIECE OF ME THOUGHT IT! IT'S NOT LIKE I WAS ALWAYS THINKIN' IT!
...
GROVEL
GROVEL
GROVEL
IT CAN'T BE HELPED. THE EVIL PARTS THAT EXIST IN OUR SUBCONSCIOUS AREN'T THINGS THAT OUR WILL CONTROLS. WHAT AN UNFAIR TECHNIQUE!

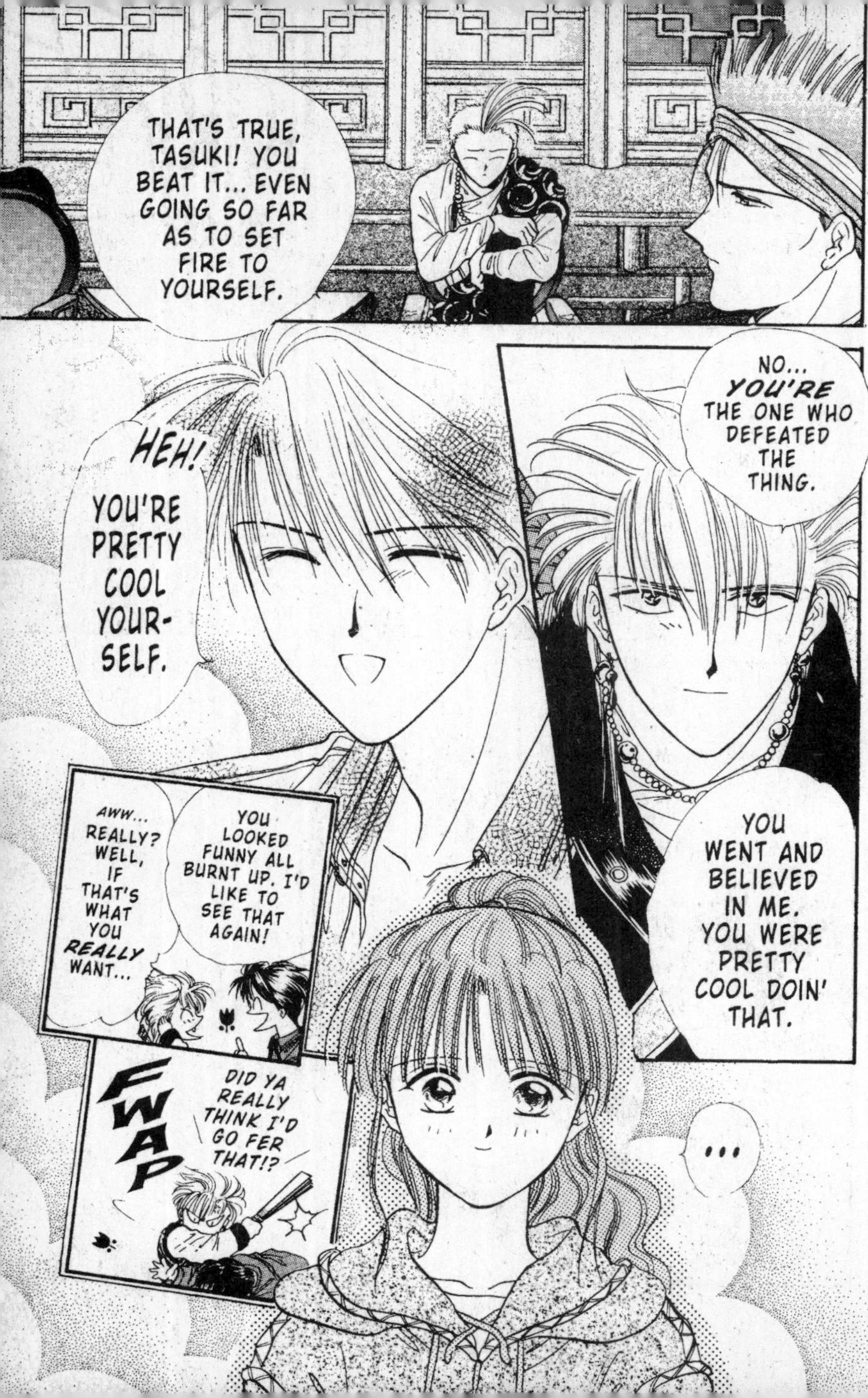
THAT'S TRUE, TASUKI! YOU BEAT IT... EVEN GOING SO FAR AS TO SET FIRE TO YOURSELF.
NO... *YOU'RE* THE ONE WHO DEFEATED THE THING.
YOU WENT AND BELIEVED IN ME. YOU WERE PRETTY COOL DOIN' THAT.
HEH!
YOU'RE PRETTY COOL YOUR-SELF.
YOU LOOKED FUNNY ALL BURNT UP. I'D LIKE TO SEE THAT AGAIN!
AWW... REALLY? WELL, IF THAT'S WHAT YOU *REALLY* WANT...
DID YA REALLY THINK I'D GO FER THAT!?
FWAP
...

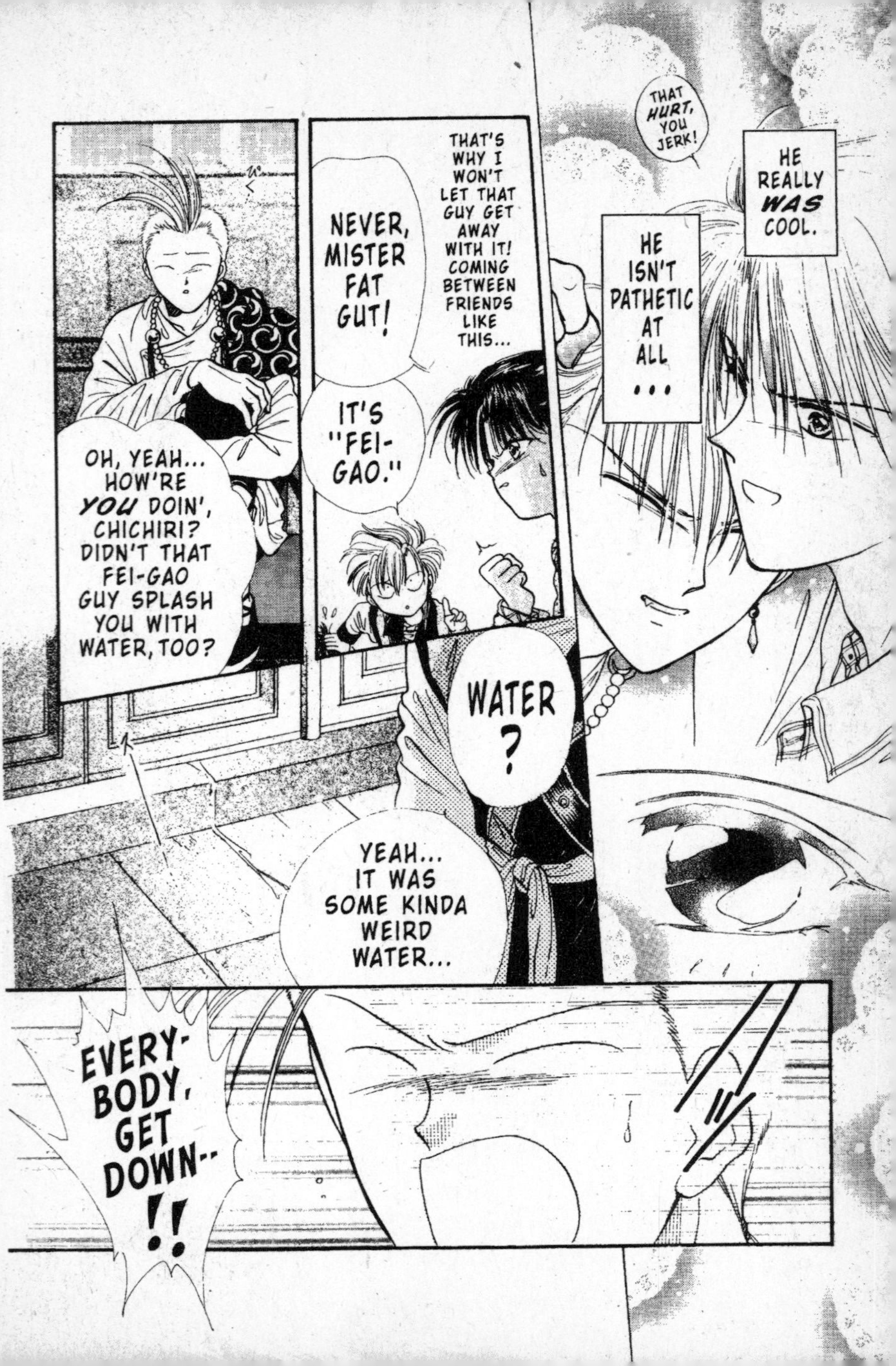
THAT HURT, YOU JERK!
HE REALLY WAS COOL.
HE ISN'T PATHETIC AT ALL...
THAT'S WHY I WON'T LET THAT GUY GET AWAY WITH IT! COMING BETWEEN FRIENDS LIKE THIS...
NEVER, MISTER FAT GUT!
IT'S "FEI-GAO."
OH, YEAH... HOW'RE YOU DOIN', CHICHIRI? DIDN'T THAT FEI-GAO GUY SPLASH YOU WITH WATER, TOO?
WATER?
YEAH... IT WAS SOME KINDA WEIRD WATER...
EVERY-BODY, GET DOWN--!!

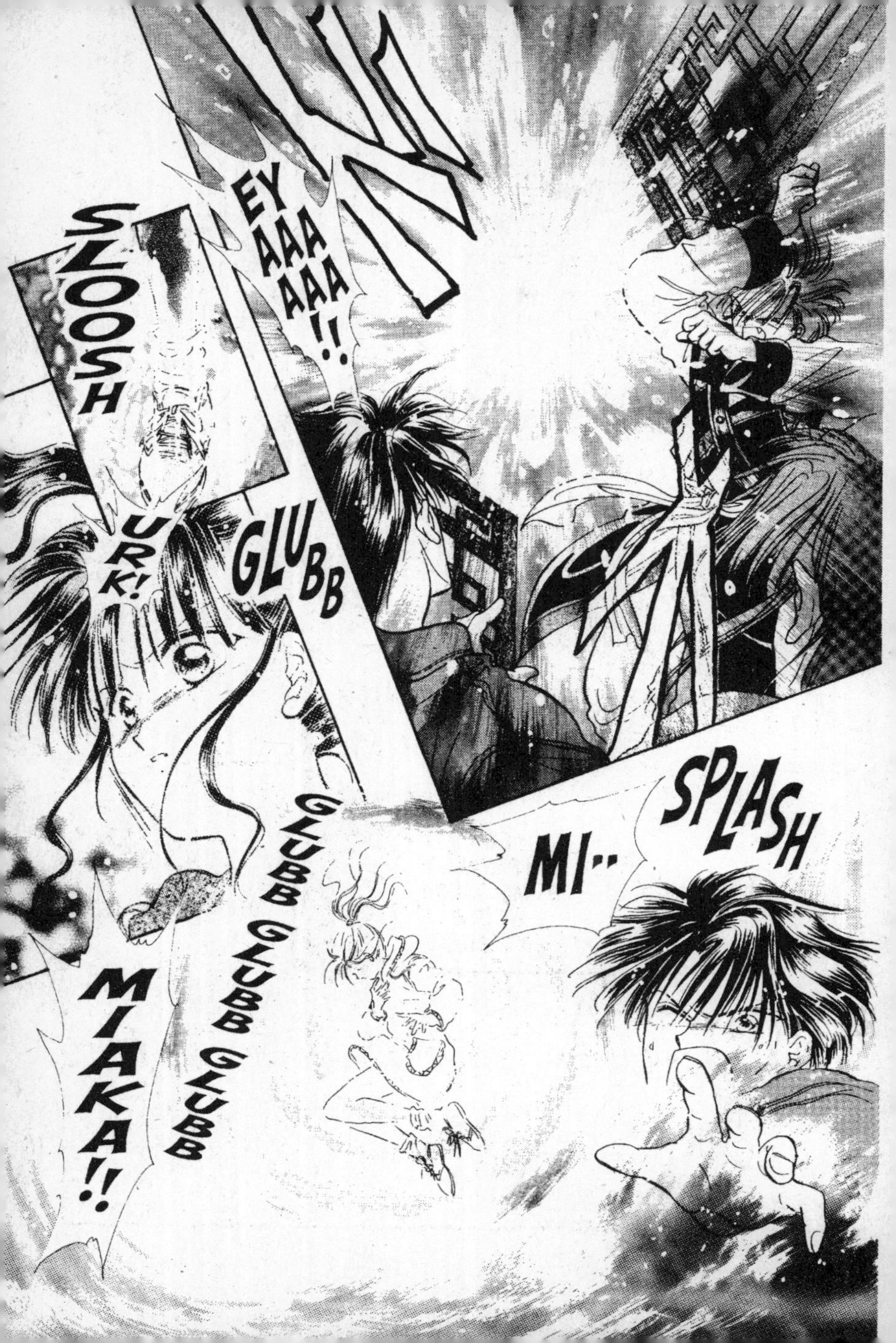
EYAAAAAAA!!
SLOOSH
GLUBB
URK!
SPLASH
MI..
GLUBB GLUBB GLUBB GLUBB
MIAKA!!

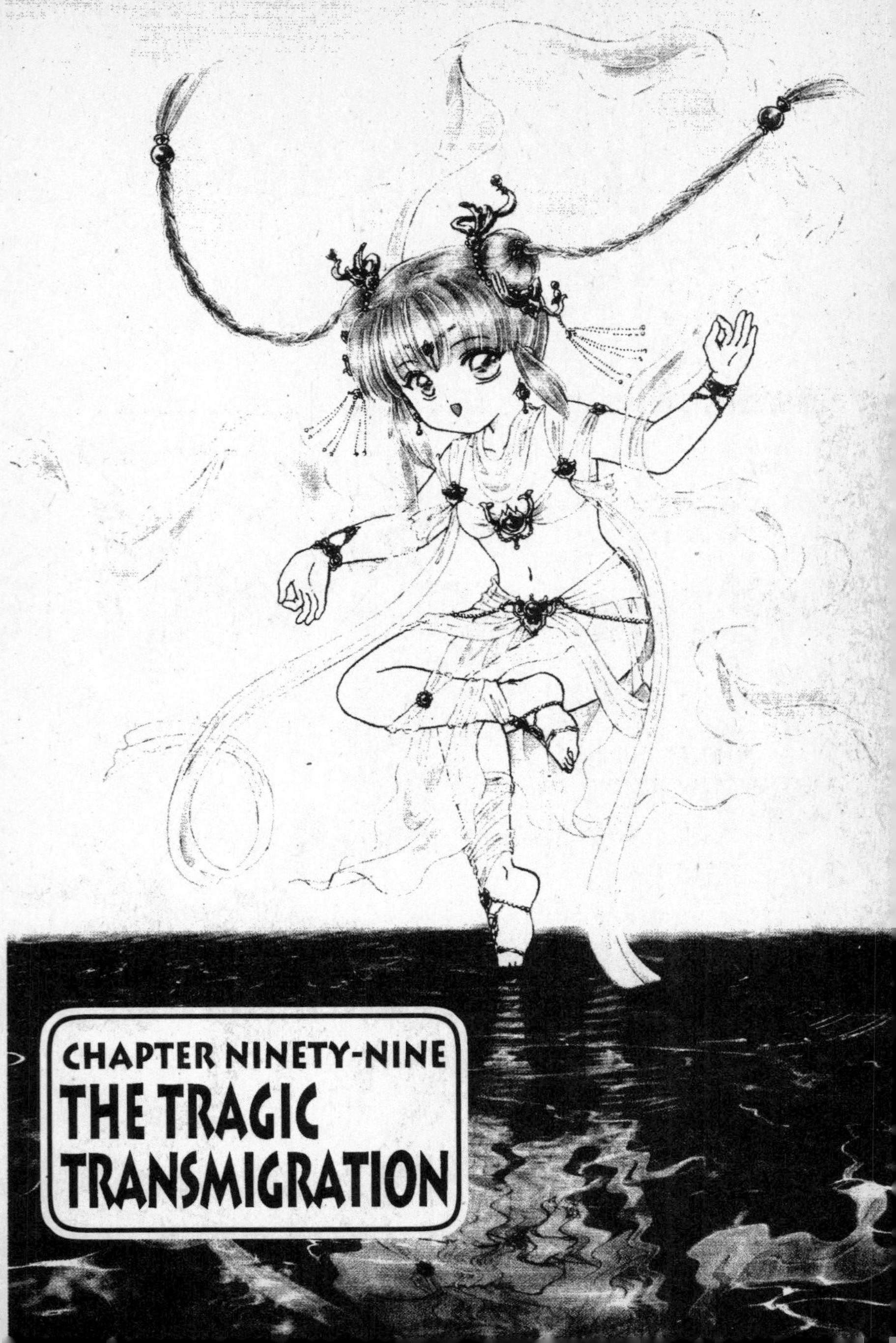
CHAPTER NINETY-NINE
THE TRAGIC TRANSMIGRATION

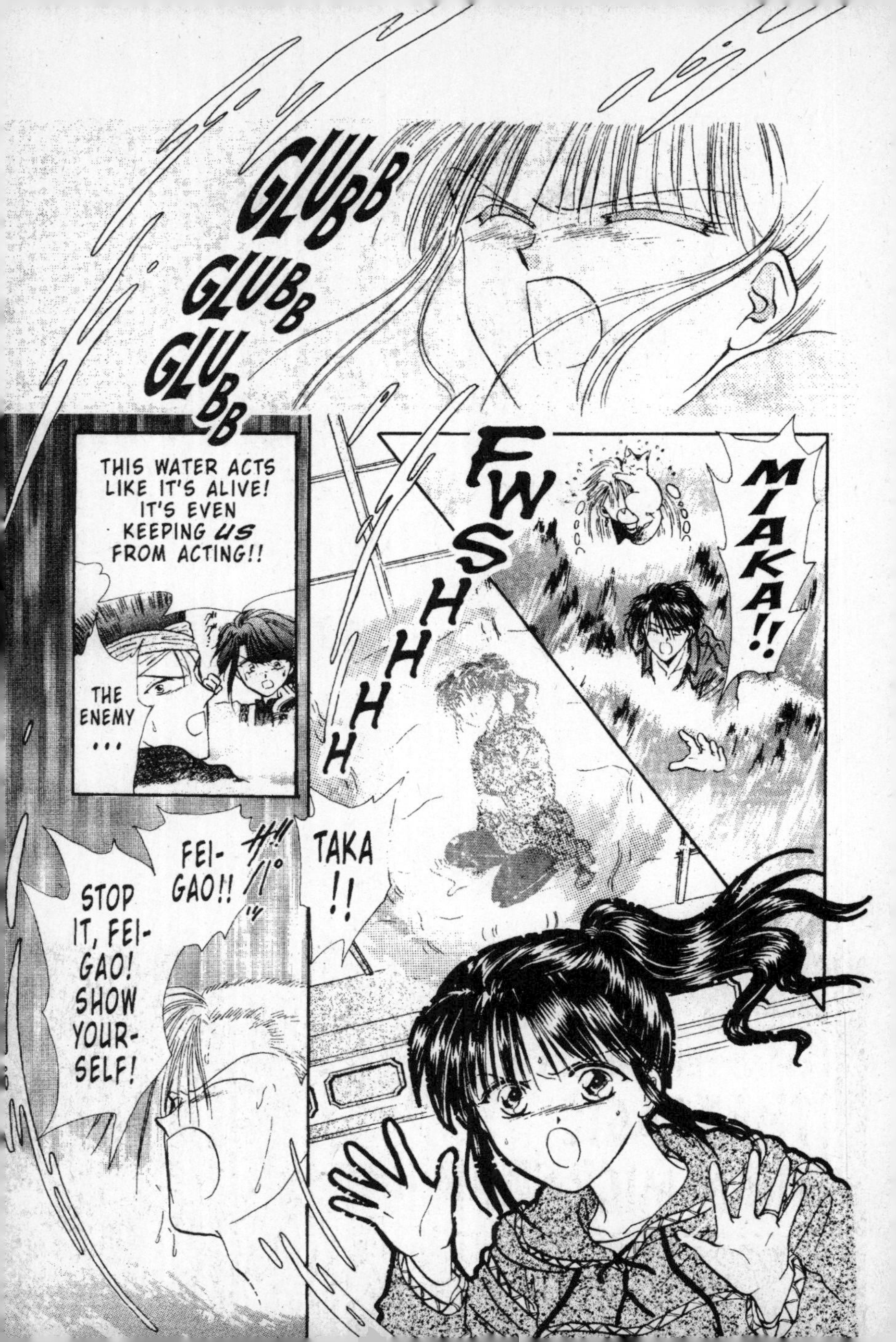
GLUBB
GLUBB
GLUBB
MIAKA!!
FWSHHHHH
THIS WATER ACTS LIKE IT'S ALIVE! IT'S EVEN KEEPING *US* FROM ACTING!!
THE ENEMY...
TAKA!!
FEI-GAO!!
STOP IT, FEI-GAO! SHOW YOURSELF!

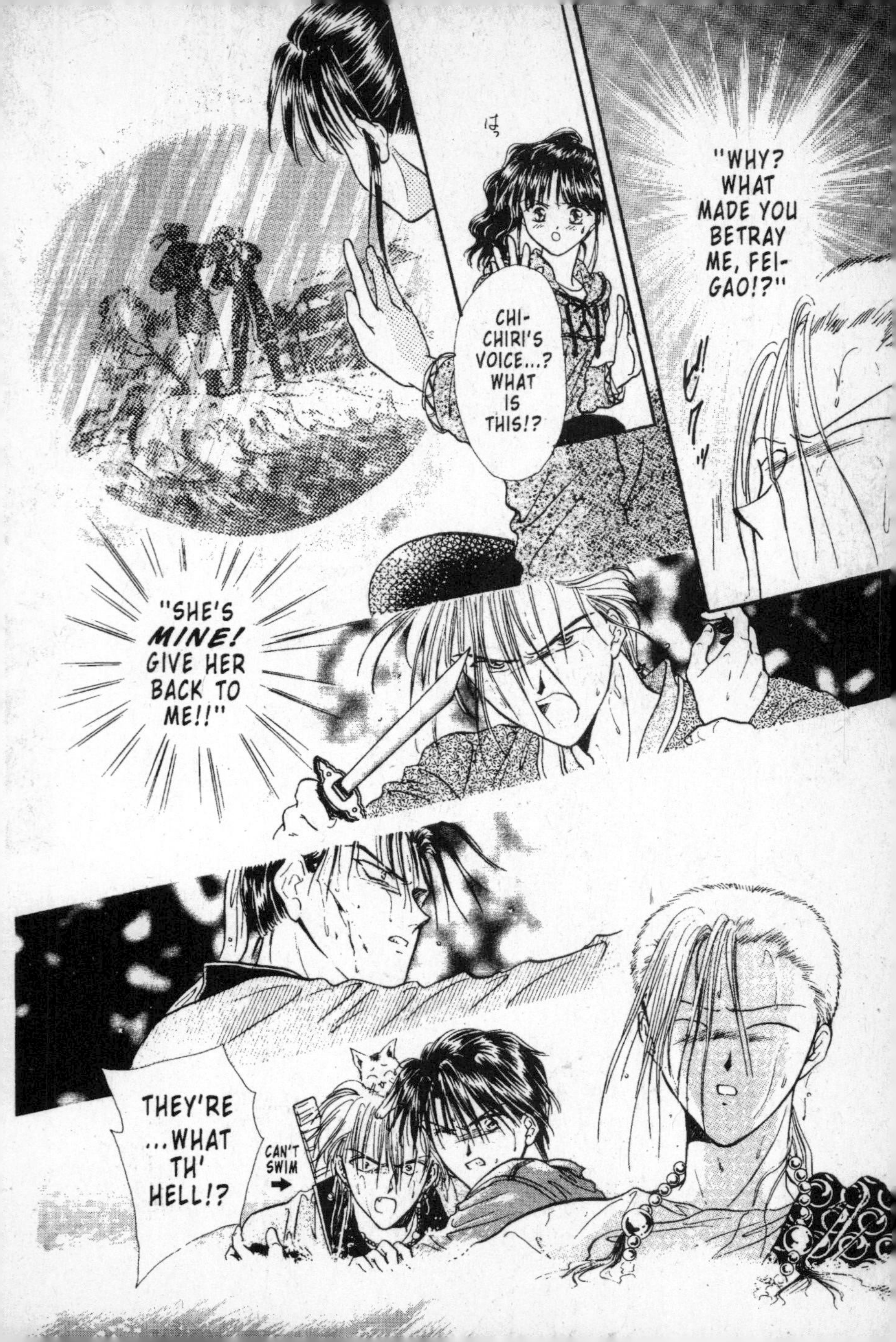
"WHY? WHAT MADE YOU BETRAY ME, FEI-GAO!?"
はっ
CHI-CHIRI'S VOICE...? WHAT IS THIS!?
"SHE'S *MINE!* GIVE HER BACK TO ME!!"
THEY'RE ...WHAT TH' HELL!?
CAN'T SWIM →

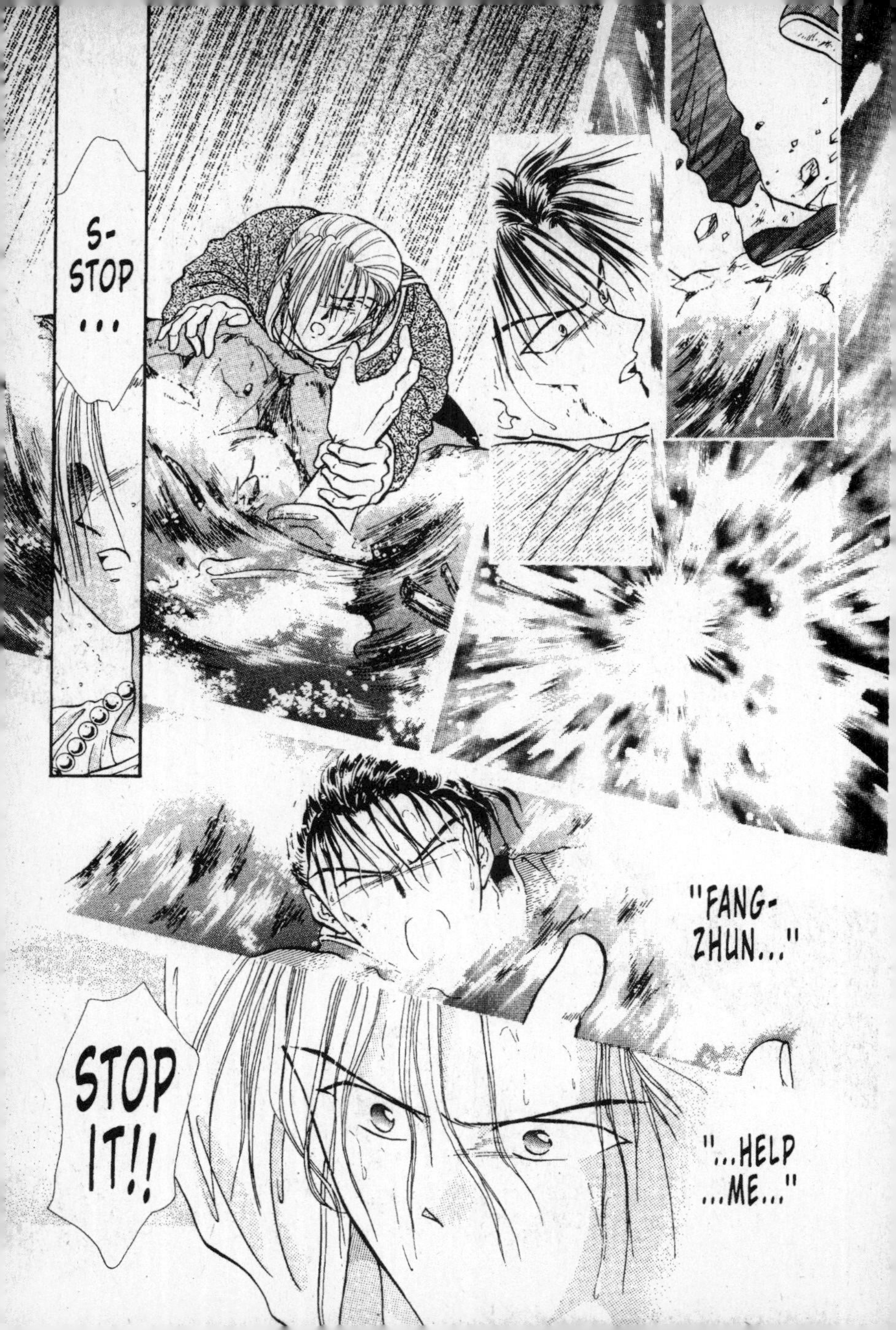
S-STOP...
"FANG-ZHUN..."
"...HELP ...ME..."
STOP IT!!

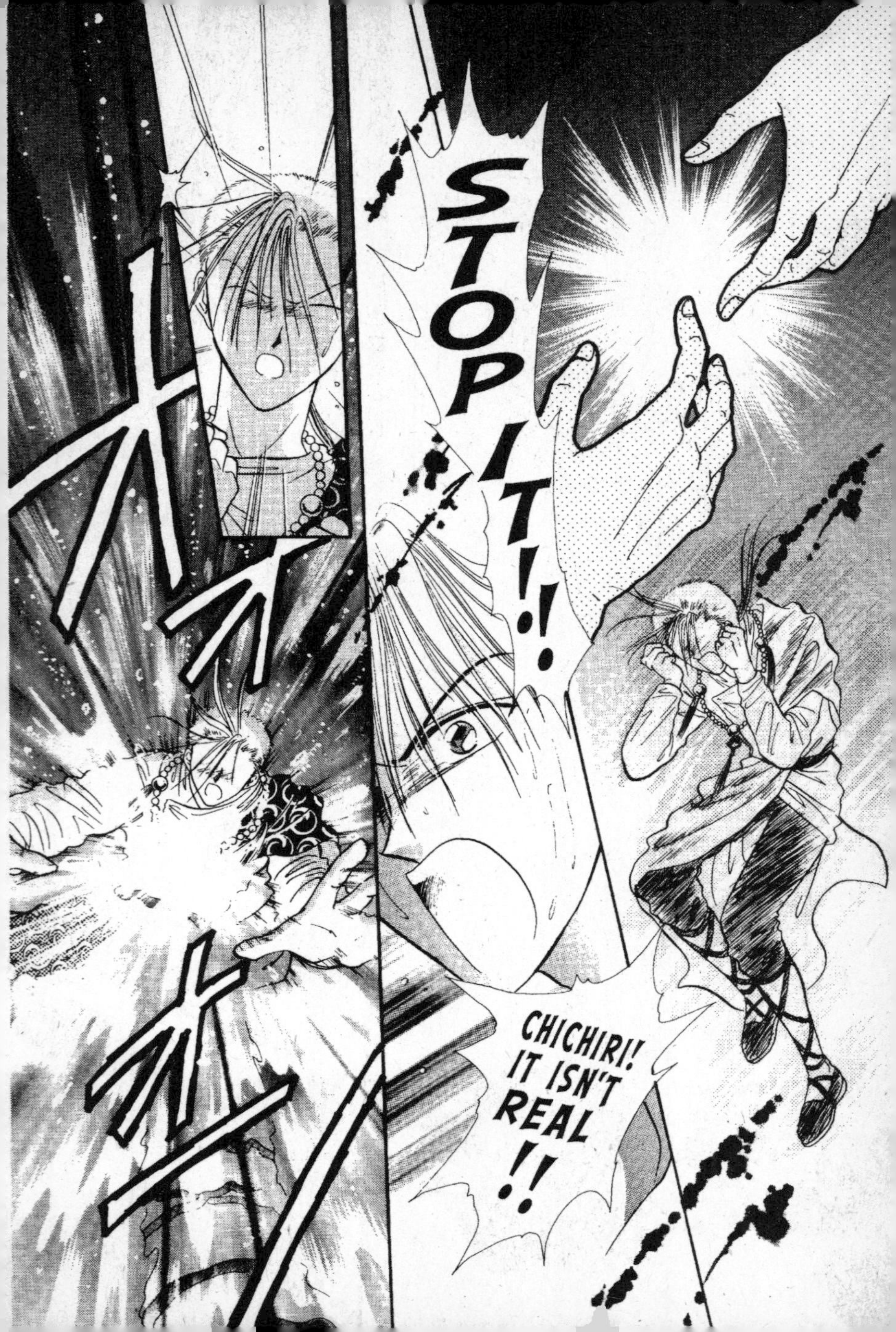
STOP IT!!
CHICHIRI! IT ISN'T REAL!!

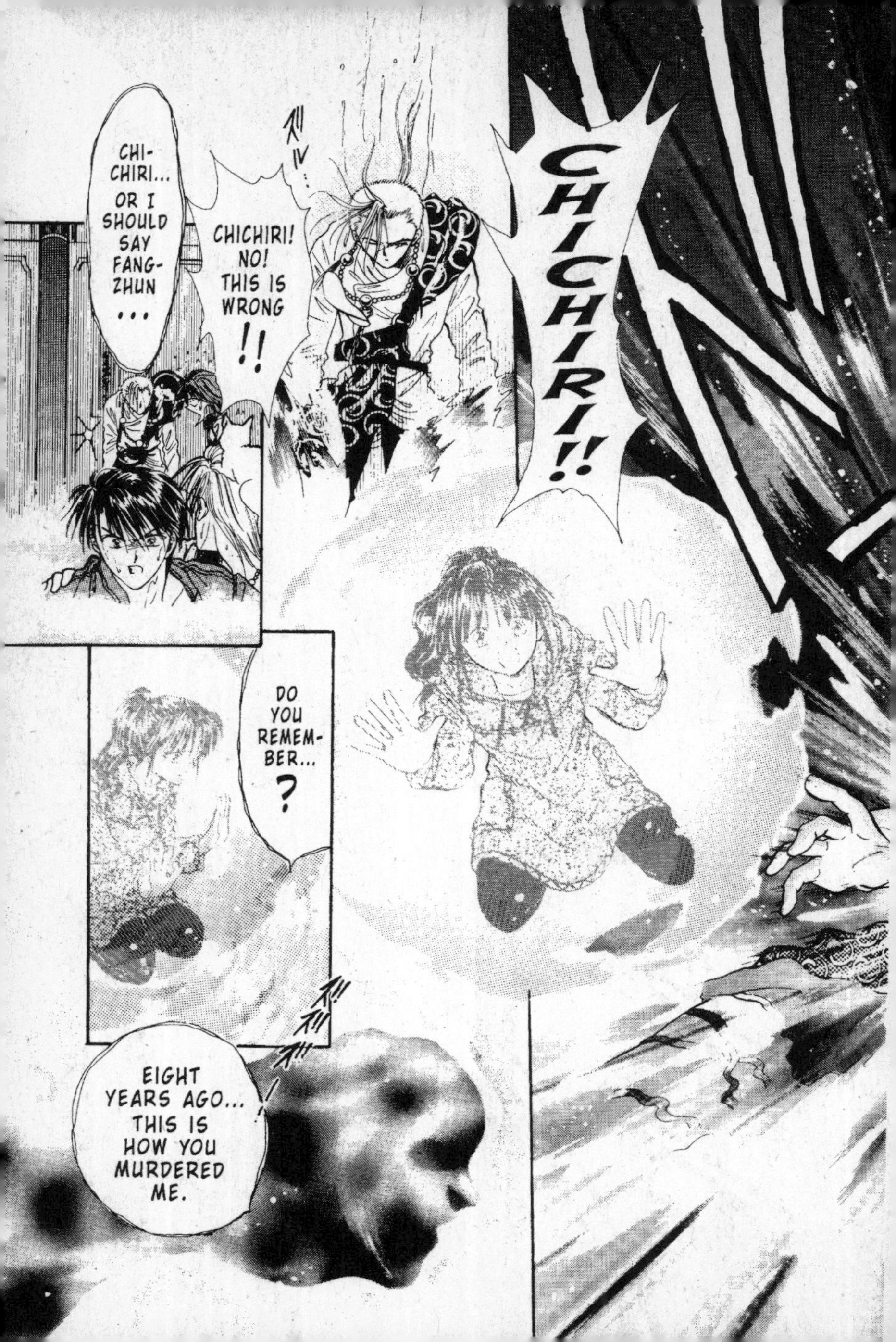
CHICHIRI!!
ズル…
CHICHIRI! NO! THIS IS WRONG!!
CHI-CHIRI... OR I SHOULD SAY FANG-ZHUN...
DO YOU REMEMBER...?
EIGHT YEARS AGO... THIS IS HOW YOU MURDERED ME.

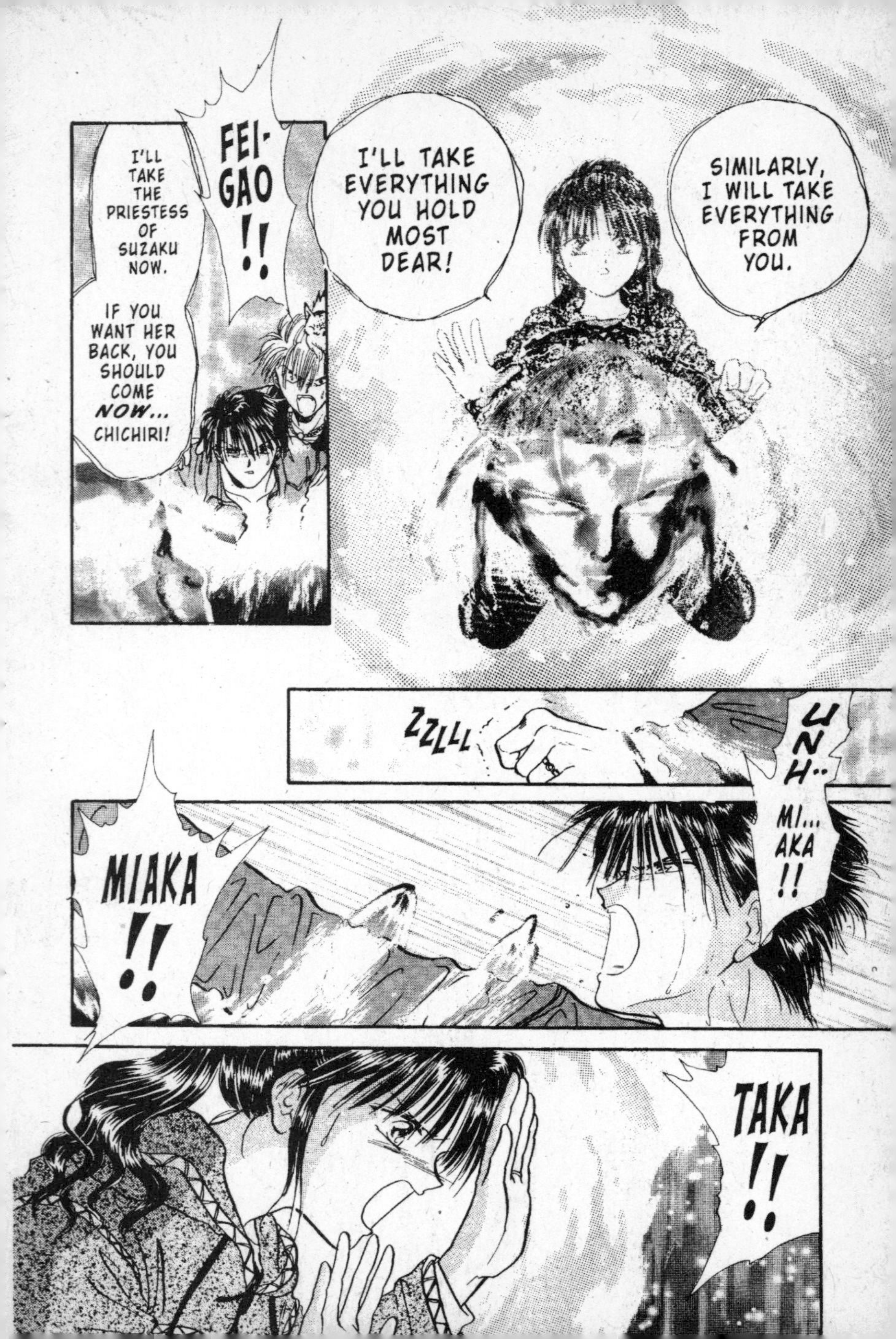
SIMILARLY, I WILL TAKE EVERYTHING FROM YOU.
I'LL TAKE EVERYTHING YOU HOLD MOST DEAR!
FEI-GAO!!
I'LL TAKE THE PRIESTESS OF SUZAKU NOW.
IF YOU WANT HER BACK, YOU SHOULD COME *NOW*... CHICHIRI!
UNH..
ZZLLL
MI... AKA!!
MIAKA!!
TAKA!!

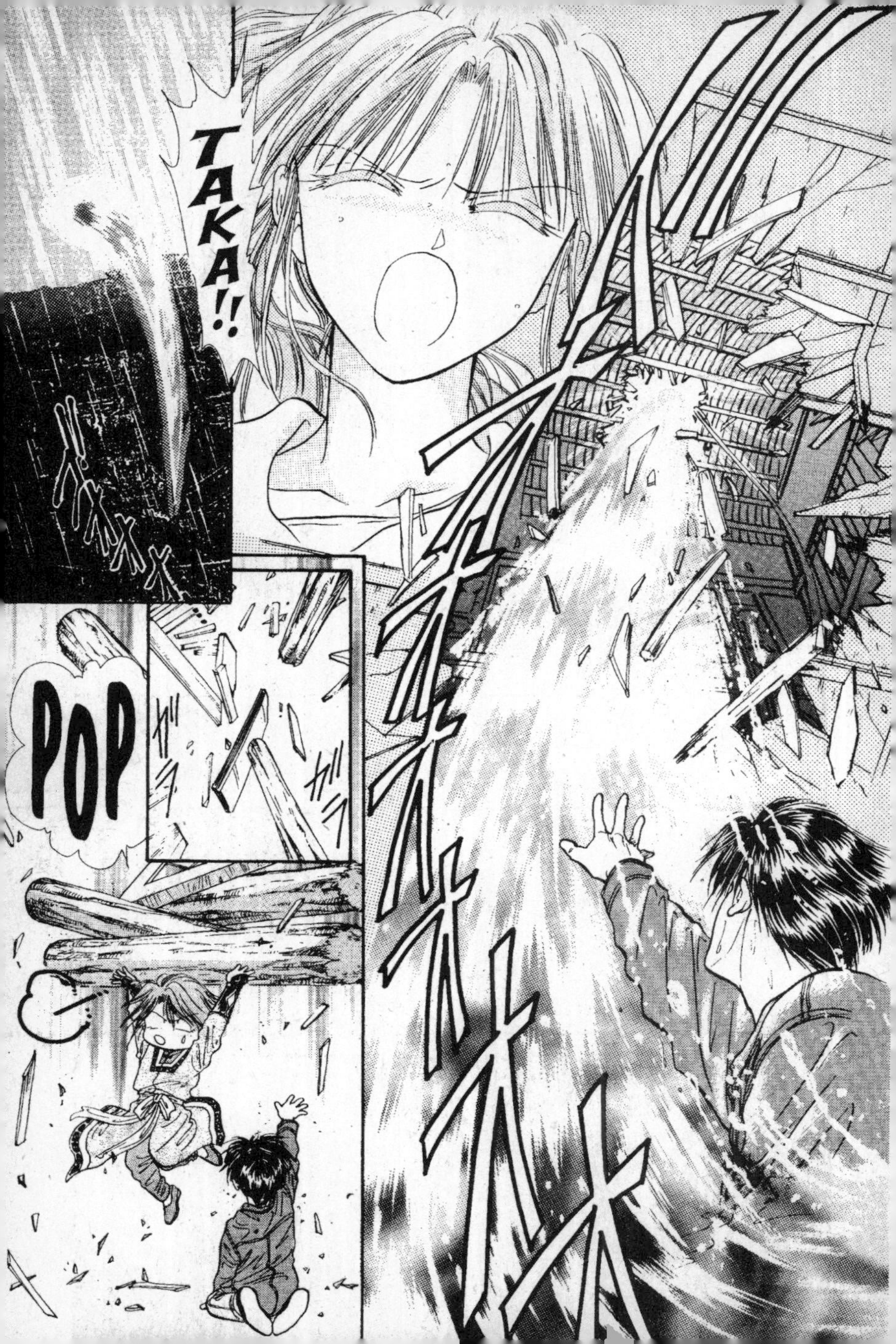
TAKA!!
POP

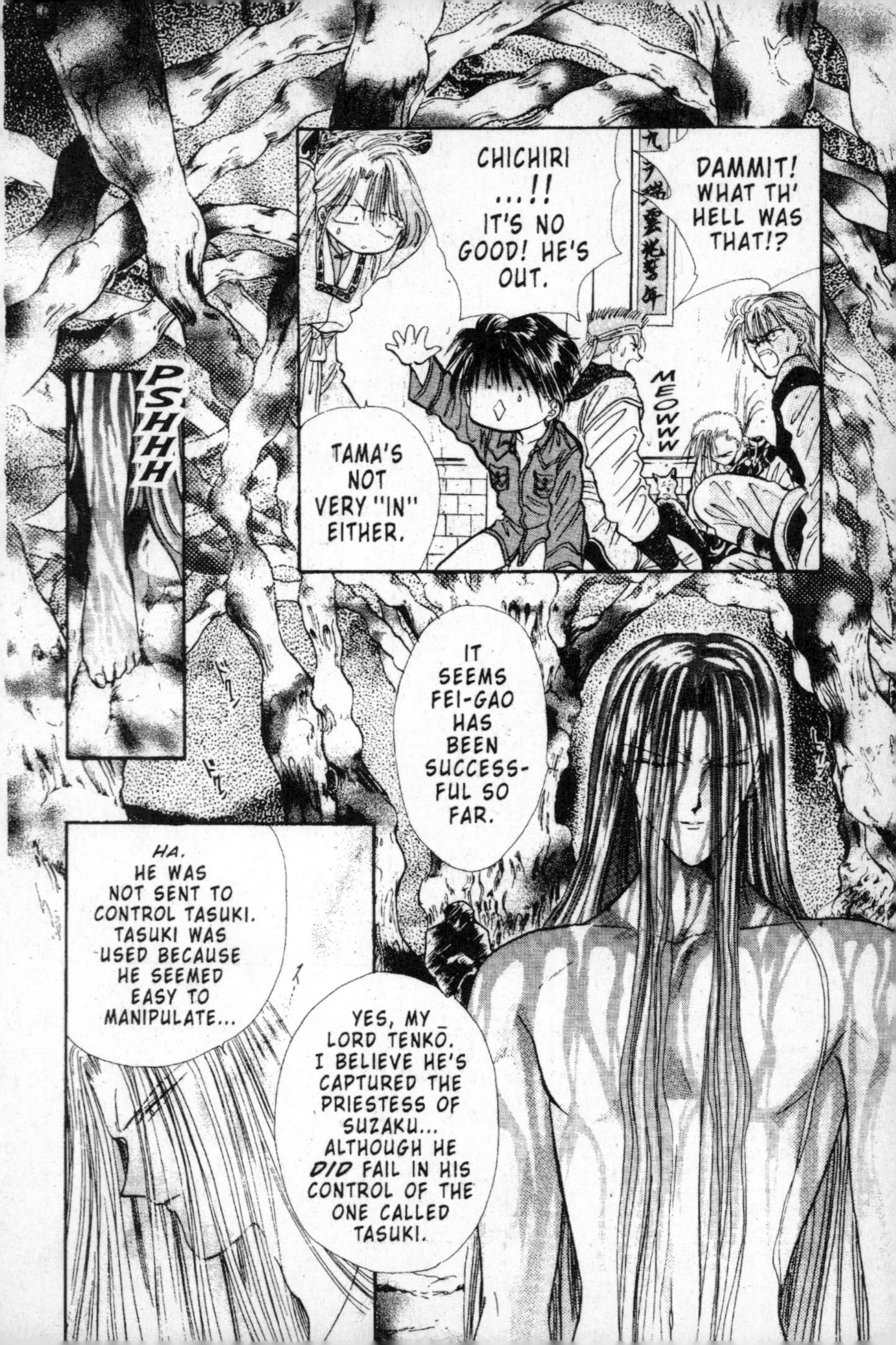
DAMMIT! WHAT TH' HELL WAS THAT!?
CHICHIRI ...!! IT'S NO GOOD! HE'S OUT.
MEOWWW
TAMA'S NOT VERY "IN" EITHER.
PSHHH
IT SEEMS FEI-GAO HAS BEEN SUCCESS-FUL SO FAR.
YES, MY LORD TENKŌ. I BELIEVE HE'S CAPTURED THE PRIESTESS OF SUZAKU... ALTHOUGH HE *DID* FAIL IN HIS CONTROL OF THE ONE CALLED TASUKI.
HA. HE WAS NOT SENT TO CONTROL TASUKI. TASUKI WAS USED BECAUSE HE SEEMED EASY TO MANIPULATE...

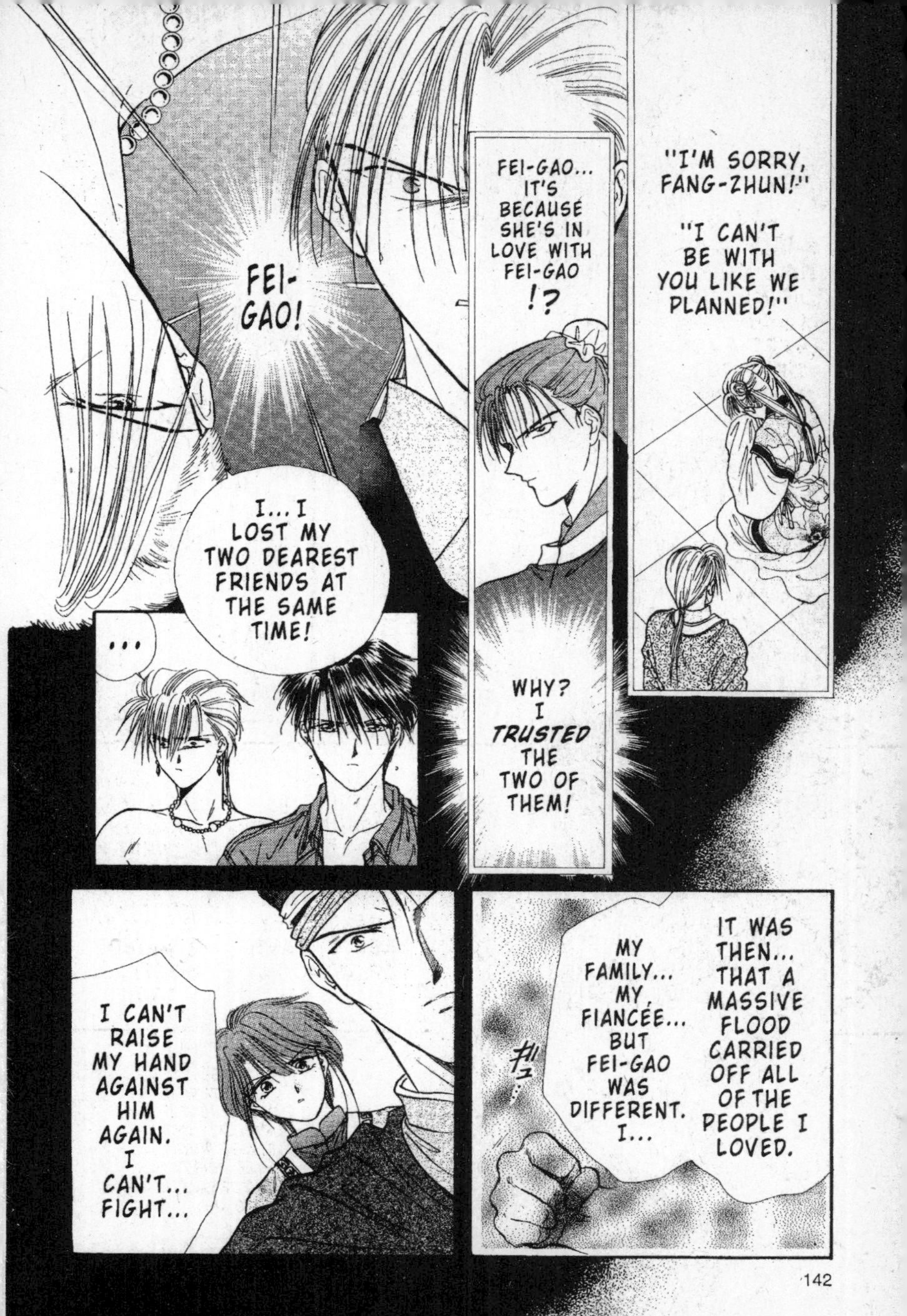
"I'M SORRY, FANG-ZHUN!"
"I CAN'T BE WITH YOU LIKE WE PLANNED!"
FEI-GAO... IT'S BECAUSE SHE'S IN LOVE WITH FEI-GAO !?
WHY? I *TRUSTED* THE TWO OF THEM!
FEI-GAO!
I... I LOST MY TWO DEAREST FRIENDS AT THE SAME TIME!
...
IT WAS THEN... THAT A MASSIVE FLOOD CARRIED OFF ALL OF THE PEOPLE I LOVED.
MY FAMILY... MY FIANCÉE... BUT FEI-GAO WAS DIFFERENT. I...
I CAN'T RAISE MY HAND AGAINST HIM AGAIN. I CAN'T... FIGHT...

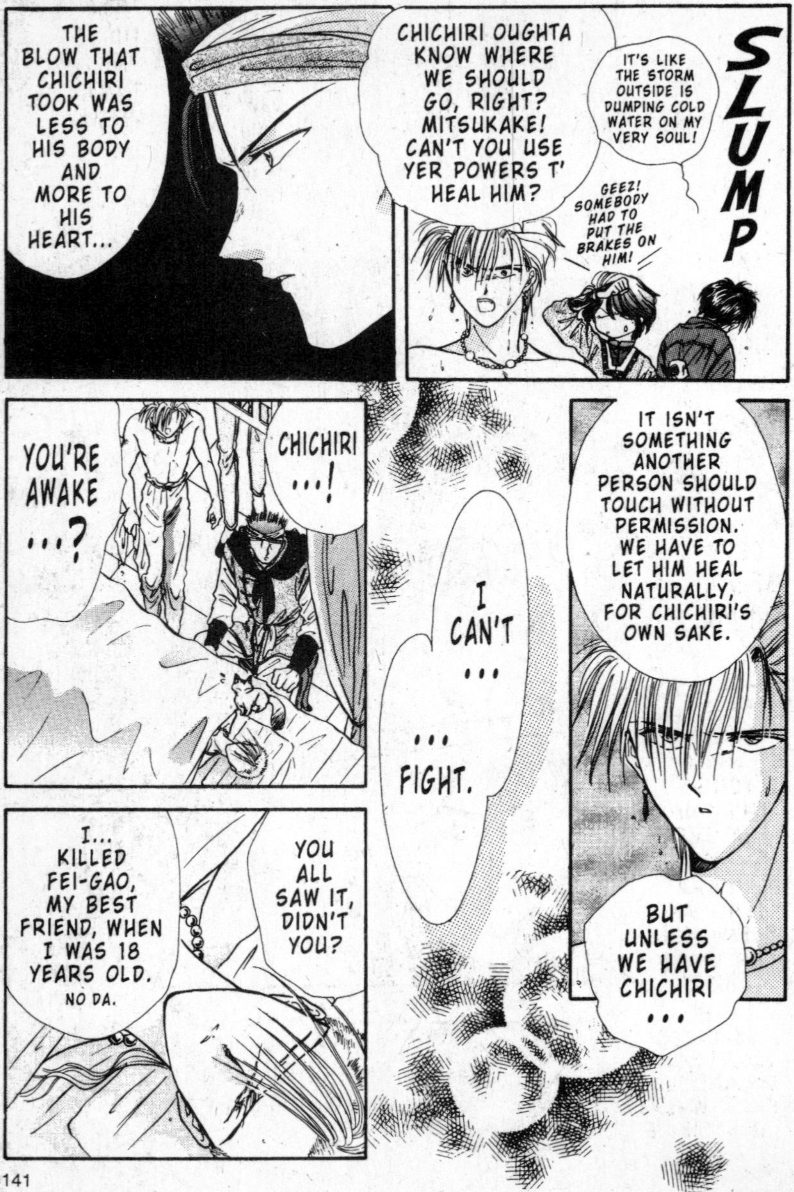
CHICHIRI OUGHTA KNOW WHERE WE SHOULD GO, RIGHT? MITSUKAKE! CAN'T YOU USE YER POWERS T' HEAL HIM?
SLUMP
IT'S LIKE THE STORM OUTSIDE IS DUMPING COLD WATER ON MY VERY SOUL!
GEEZ! SOMEBODY HAD TO PUT THE BRAKES ON HIM!
THE BLOW THAT CHICHIRI TOOK WAS LESS TO HIS BODY AND MORE TO HIS HEART...
IT ISN'T SOMETHING ANOTHER PERSON SHOULD TOUCH WITHOUT PERMISSION. WE HAVE TO LET HIM HEAL NATURALLY, FOR CHICHIRI'S OWN SAKE.
BUT UNLESS WE HAVE CHICHIRI...
I CAN'T...
...FIGHT.
CHICHIRI...!
YOU'RE AWAKE...?
YOU ALL SAW IT, DIDN'T YOU?
I... KILLED FEI-GAO, MY BEST FRIEND, WHEN I WAS 18 YEARS OLD.
NO DA.

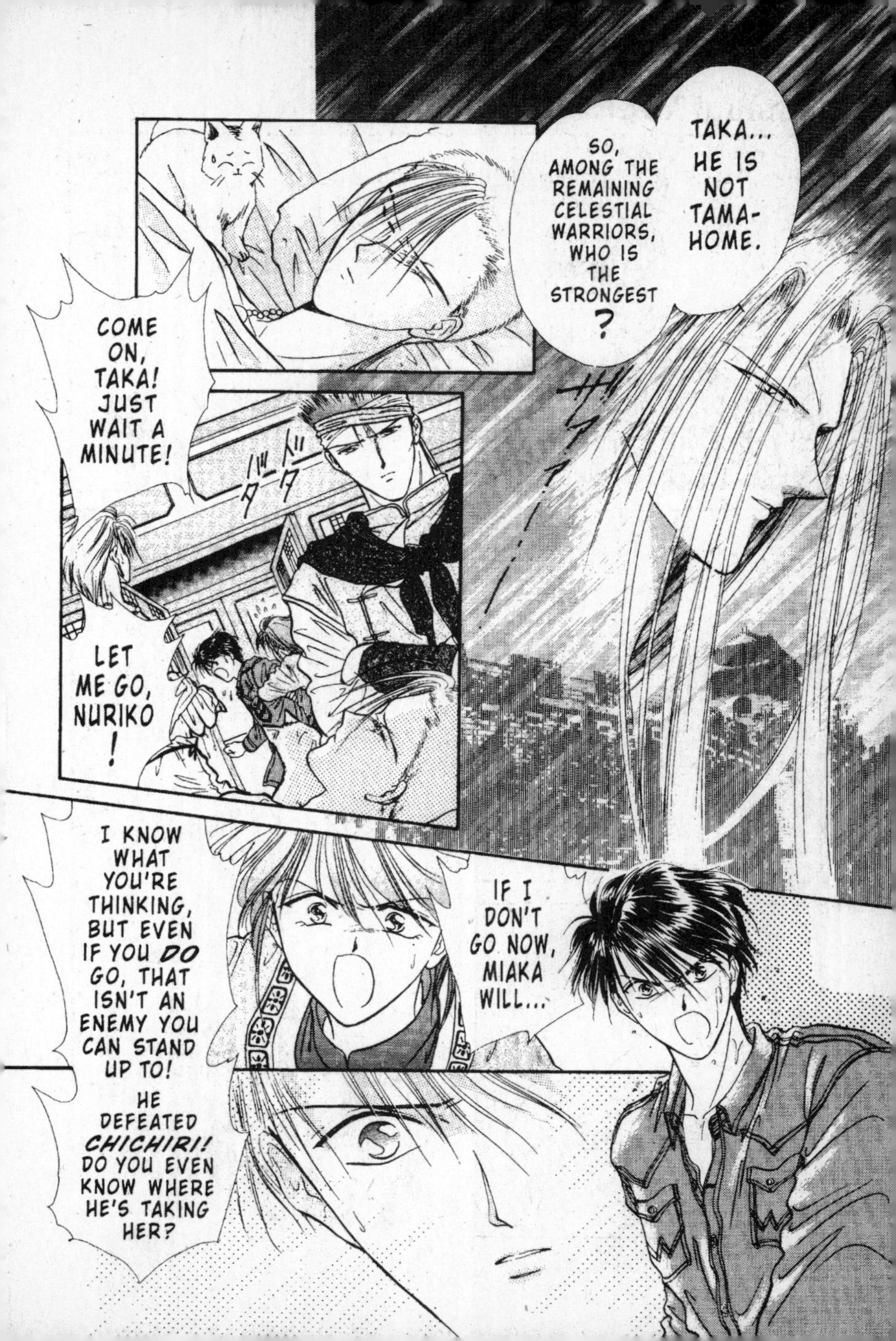
TAKA... HE IS NOT TAMA-HOME.
SO, AMONG THE REMAINING CELESTIAL WARRIORS, WHO IS THE STRONGEST?
COME ON, TAKA! JUST WAIT A MINUTE!
LET ME GO, NURIKO!
IF I DON'T GO NOW, MIAKA WILL...
I KNOW WHAT YOU'RE THINKING, BUT EVEN IF YOU *DO* GO, THAT ISN'T AN ENEMY YOU CAN STAND UP TO!
HE DEFEATED *CHICHIRI!* DO YOU EVEN KNOW WHERE HE'S TAKING HER?

Demon

CON-TINUED... But according to my assistants, "Tasuki isn't so much after sex as wanting to give himself to someone else." Hm. That's deep. Good luck growing up, Tasuki! If I were Miaka, you'd be my number one guy! (But actually, I love Taka.)
The big break was Chichiri! The shadowy man who was putting pressure on the celestial warriors had pressure put on him by Chichiri fans throughout the entire country. (How many artists have the ego to say a thing like that!?) Sorry for keeping you waiting! Chichiri is a very strong and able warrior, but he's been living his life punishing himself for the wounds he's inflicted on others. The charms of a man who can pierce through his own defenses has really caught the eye of women everywhere (including housewives!). But, to be fair, Tasuki also has a large group of manic housewives as fans. *Tama does too.* Countless numbers! *That's such an exaggeration!*☺
And... there is a faction that's been clamoring to hear about Chichiri's past, so they should be happy...but I'll bet that soon I'll hear from a group that DIDN'T want to know! I didn't do it to please the fans, but to show his past to the other celestial warriors. Chichiri is the type to pierce through the shadows, but with the pain of this one part of his past, he probably felt that he wasn't good enough to become a Celestial Warrior. It could be that if he allowed himself to be swayed just a little more by self-doubt, he might never have joined the others. So from Chichiri's point of view, he might have done something terrible (Tasuki, too), but even so, the others just take the information in without a trace of blame. Isn't that what being a friend means? (He did tell Miaka once, but it must have been a painful revelation for him. Still, he was doing it to cheer her up.)
All people, no matter who they are, have their bad sides and weaknesses. In the end, Nuriko and Chiriko beat theirs. Tamahome is fighting his inner demons even now. And since Chichiri is human too, he had to face his pain... not by fighting it, but by realizing nothing can be done about it and accepting it. That point might have been the awakening of his powers... in the midst of his sadness. But it's probably his understanding of how evil people can be that made him want to become the kind of person whom other people could depend on for protection. He's a nice guy after all.

BACKGROUND MUSIC: "SHA•RION" BY ERI. THE FIGHT SCENES ARE THE THIRD SONG FROM PANZER DRAGOON.

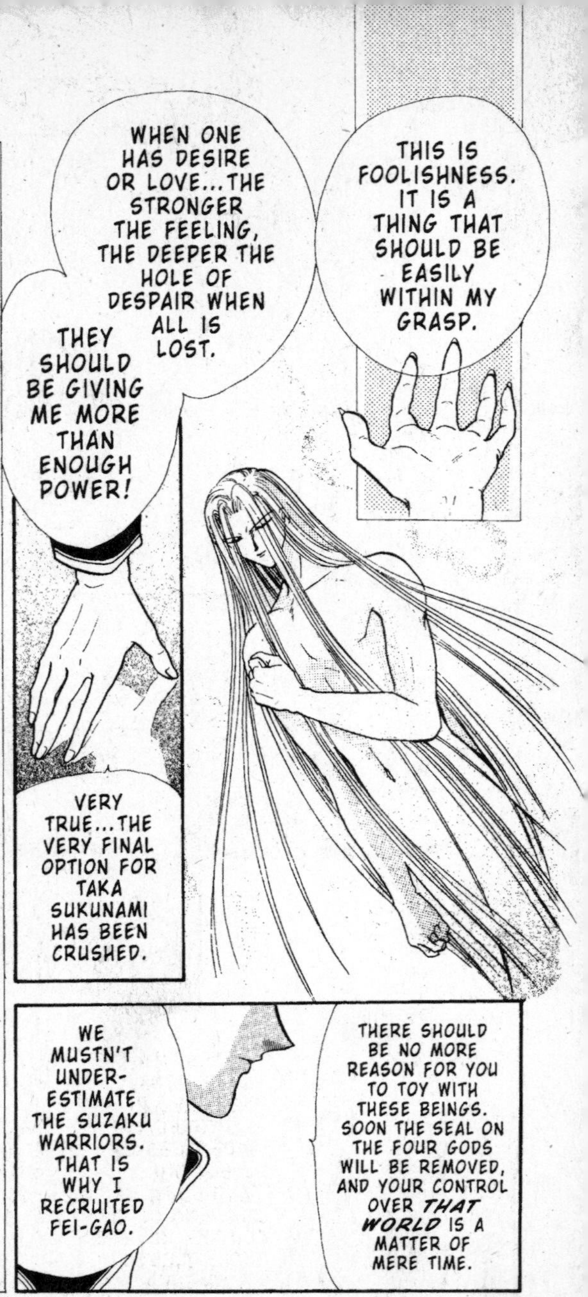

THIS IS FOOLISHNESS. IT IS A THING THAT SHOULD BE EASILY WITHIN MY GRASP.
WHEN ONE HAS DESIRE OR LOVE...THE STRONGER THE FEELING, THE DEEPER THE HOLE OF DESPAIR WHEN ALL IS LOST.
THEY SHOULD BE GIVING ME MORE THAN ENOUGH POWER!
VERY TRUE...THE VERY FINAL OPTION FOR TAKA SUKUNAMI HAS BEEN CRUSHED.
THERE SHOULD BE NO MORE REASON FOR YOU TO TOY WITH THESE BEINGS. SOON THE SEAL ON THE FOUR GODS WILL BE REMOVED, AND YOUR CONTROL OVER *THAT WORLD* IS A MATTER OF MERE TIME.
WE MUSTN'T UNDER-ESTIMATE THE SUZAKU WARRIORS. THAT IS WHY I RECRUITED FEI-GAO.

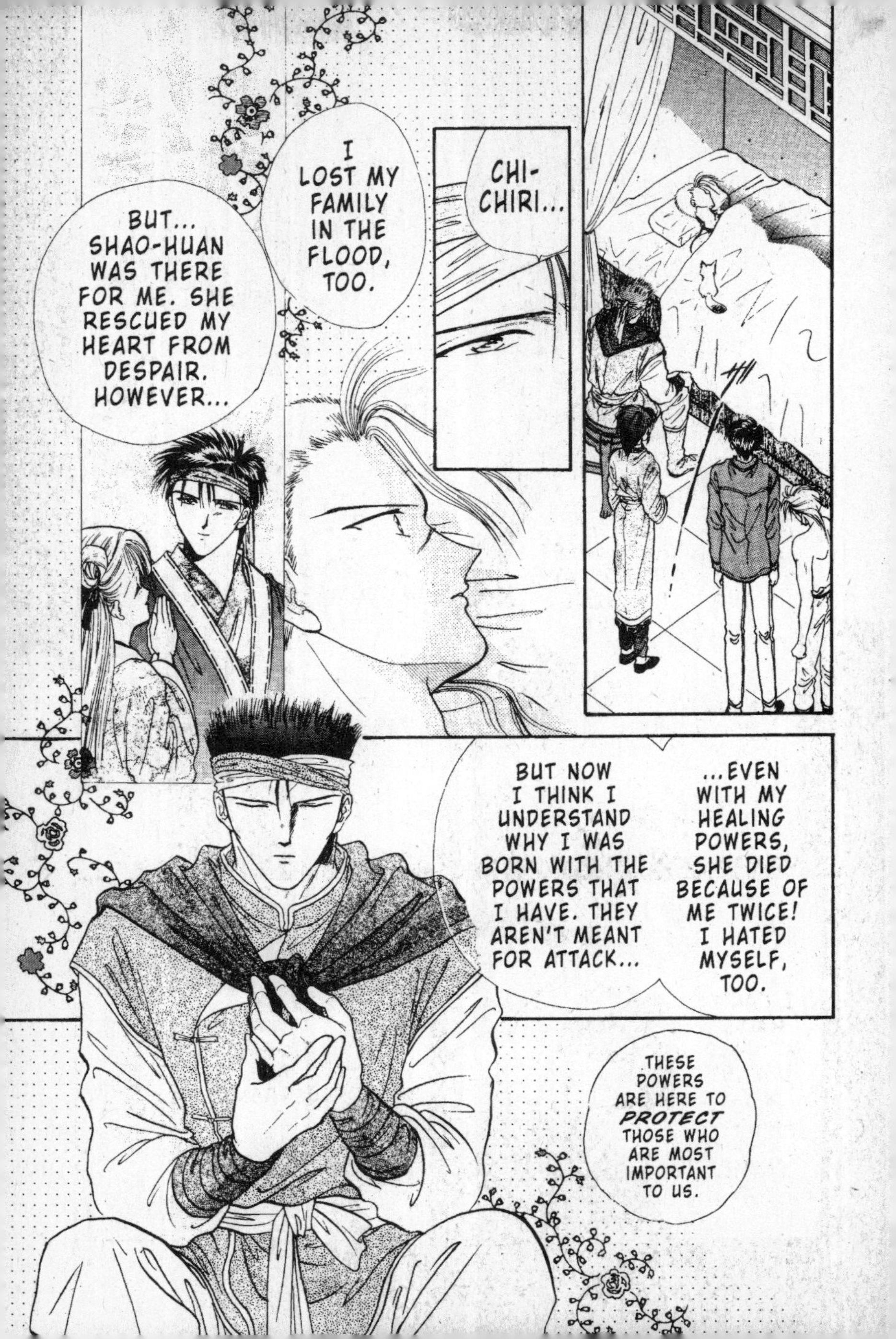
CHI-CHIRI...
I LOST MY FAMILY IN THE FLOOD, TOO.
BUT... SHAO-HUAN WAS THERE FOR ME. SHE RESCUED MY HEART FROM DESPAIR. HOWEVER...
...EVEN WITH MY HEALING POWERS, SHE DIED BECAUSE OF ME TWICE! I HATED MYSELF, TOO.
BUT NOW I THINK I UNDERSTAND WHY I WAS BORN WITH THE POWERS THAT I HAVE. THEY AREN'T MEANT FOR ATTACK...
THESE POWERS ARE HERE TO *PROTECT* THOSE WHO ARE MOST IMPORTANT TO US.

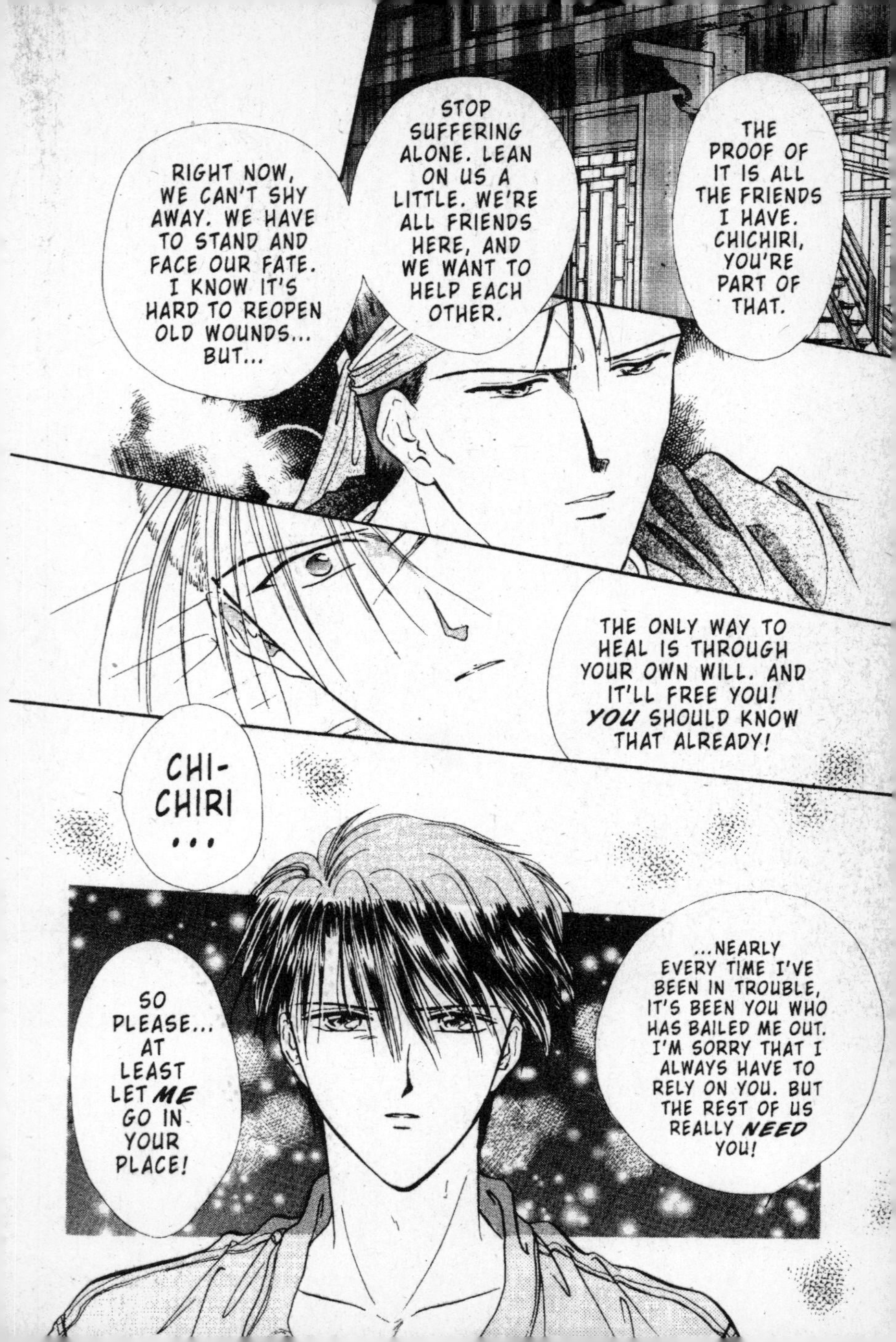
THE PROOF OF IT IS ALL THE FRIENDS I HAVE. CHICHIRI, YOU'RE PART OF THAT.
STOP SUFFERING ALONE. LEAN ON US A LITTLE. WE'RE ALL FRIENDS HERE, AND WE WANT TO HELP EACH OTHER.
RIGHT NOW, WE CAN'T SHY AWAY. WE HAVE TO STAND AND FACE OUR FATE. I KNOW IT'S HARD TO REOPEN OLD WOUNDS... BUT...
THE ONLY WAY TO HEAL IS THROUGH YOUR OWN WILL. AND IT'LL FREE YOU! ***YOU*** SHOULD KNOW THAT ALREADY!
CHI-CHIRI...
...NEARLY EVERY TIME I'VE BEEN IN TROUBLE, IT'S BEEN YOU WHO HAS BAILED ME OUT. I'M SORRY THAT I ALWAYS HAVE TO RELY ON YOU. BUT THE REST OF US REALLY ***NEED*** YOU!
SO PLEASE... AT LEAST LET ***ME*** GO IN YOUR PLACE!

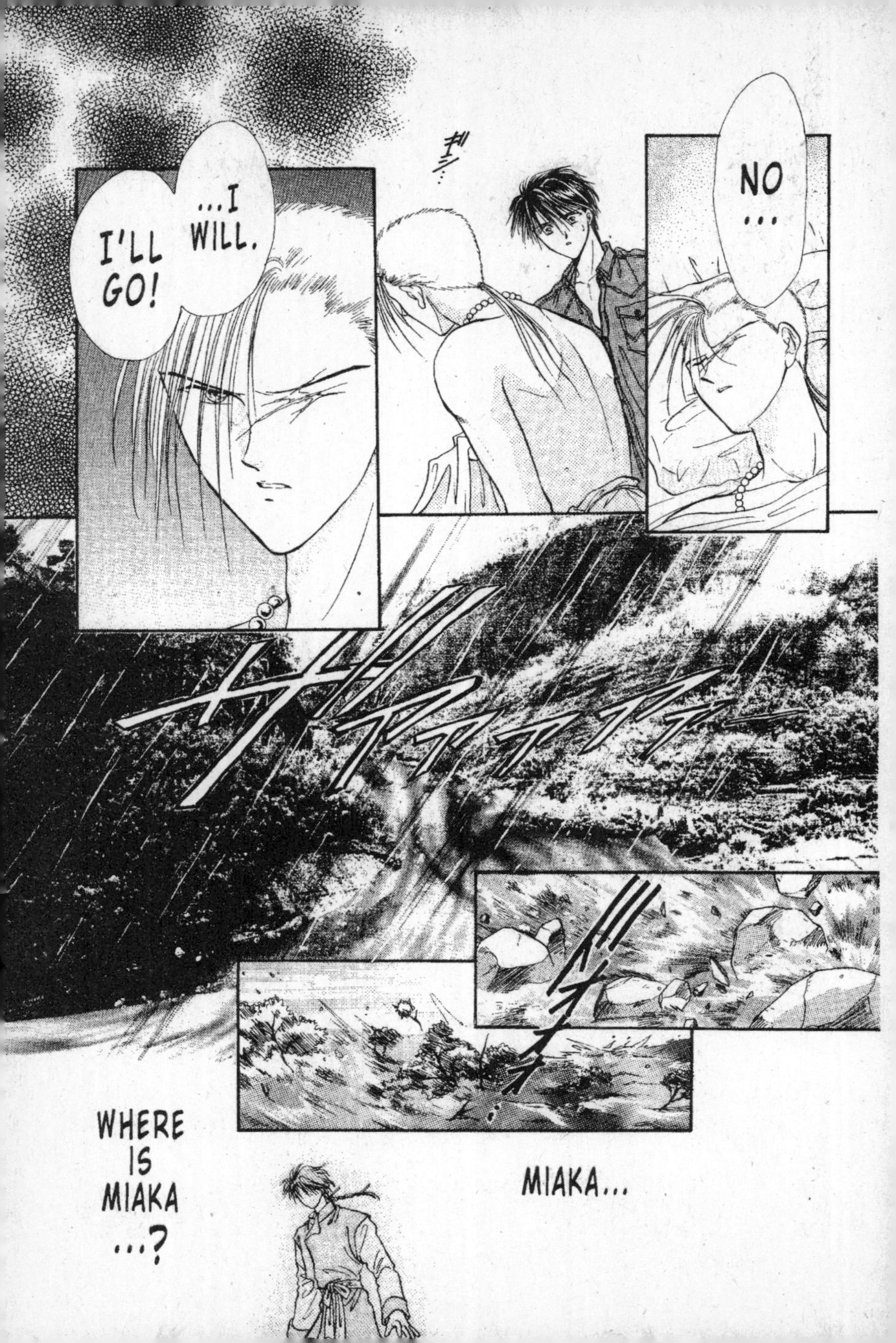
NO ...
...I WILL.
I'LL GO!
MIAKA...
WHERE IS MIAKA ...?

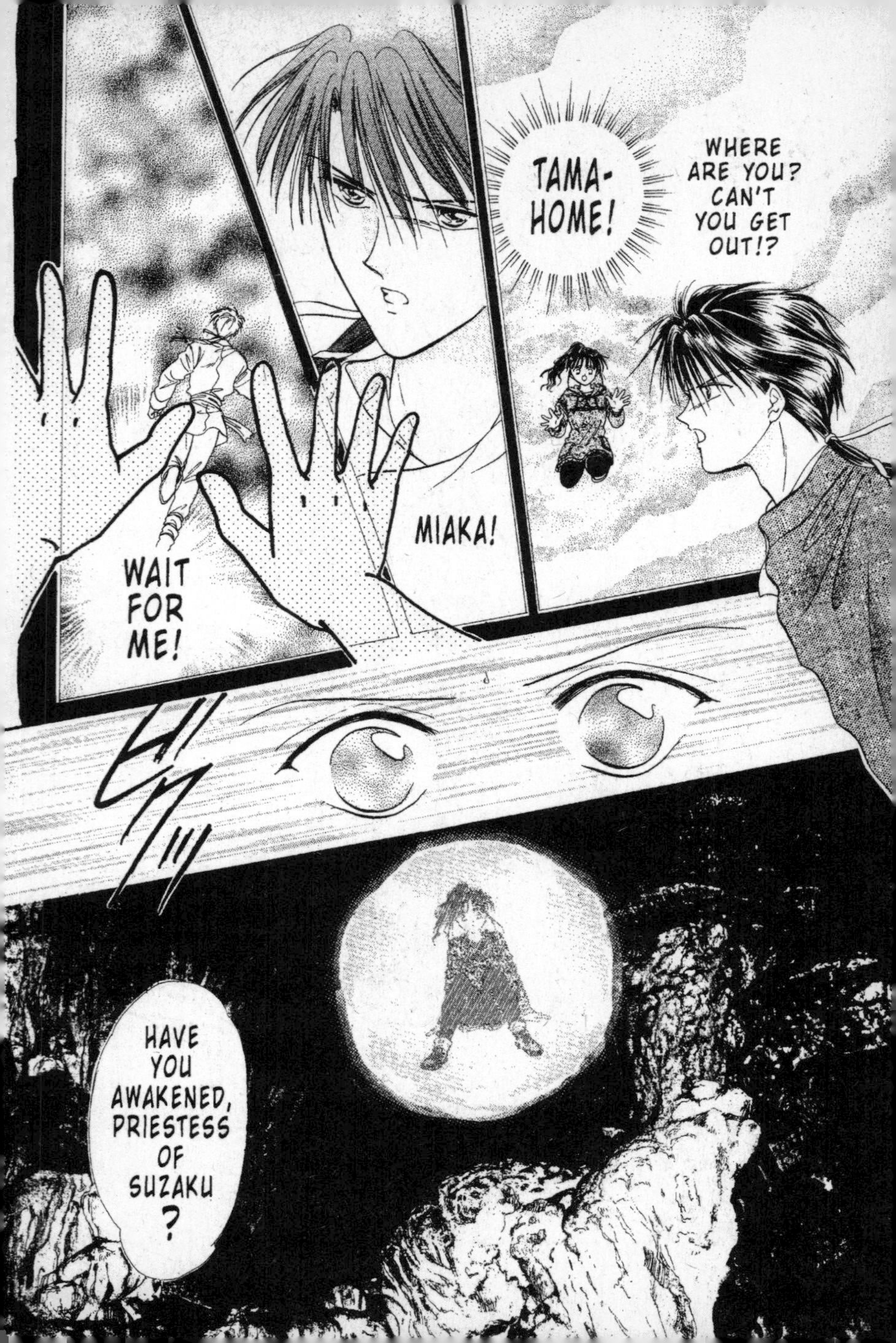
WHERE ARE YOU? CAN'T YOU GET OUT!?
TAMA-HOME!
MIAKA!
WAIT FOR ME!
HAVE YOU AWAKENED, PRIESTESS OF SUZAKU?

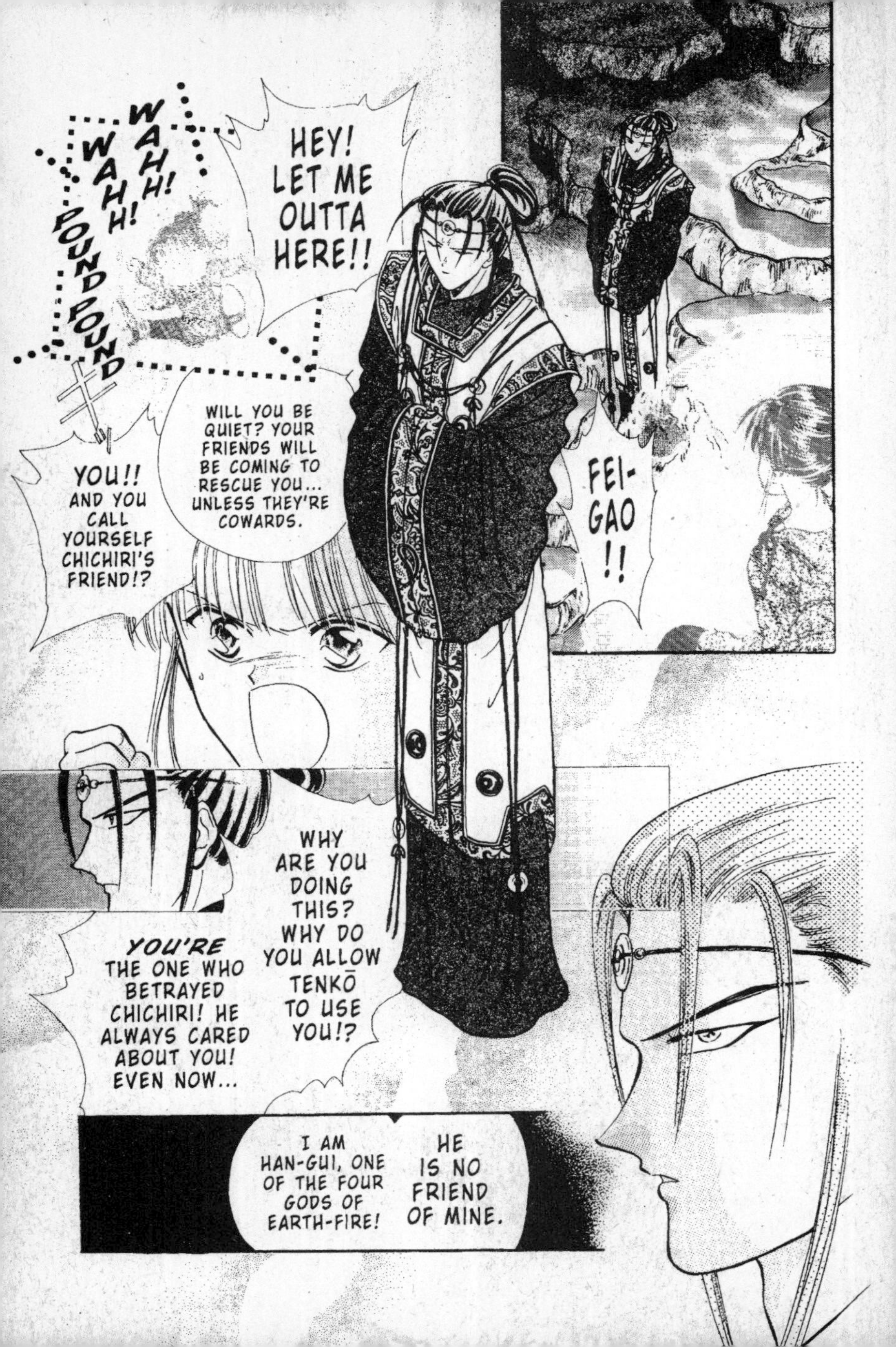
FEI-GAO!!
HEY! LET ME OUTTA HERE!!
WAHH! WAHH!
POUND POUND
WILL YOU BE QUIET? YOUR FRIENDS WILL BE COMING TO RESCUE YOU... UNLESS THEY'RE COWARDS.
YOU!! AND YOU CALL YOURSELF CHICHIRI'S FRIEND!?
WHY ARE YOU DOING THIS? WHY DO YOU ALLOW TENKŌ TO USE YOU!?
YOU'RE THE ONE WHO BETRAYED CHICHIRI! HE ALWAYS CARED ABOUT YOU! EVEN NOW...
HE IS NO FRIEND OF MINE.
I AM HAN-GUI, ONE OF THE FOUR GODS OF EARTH-FIRE!

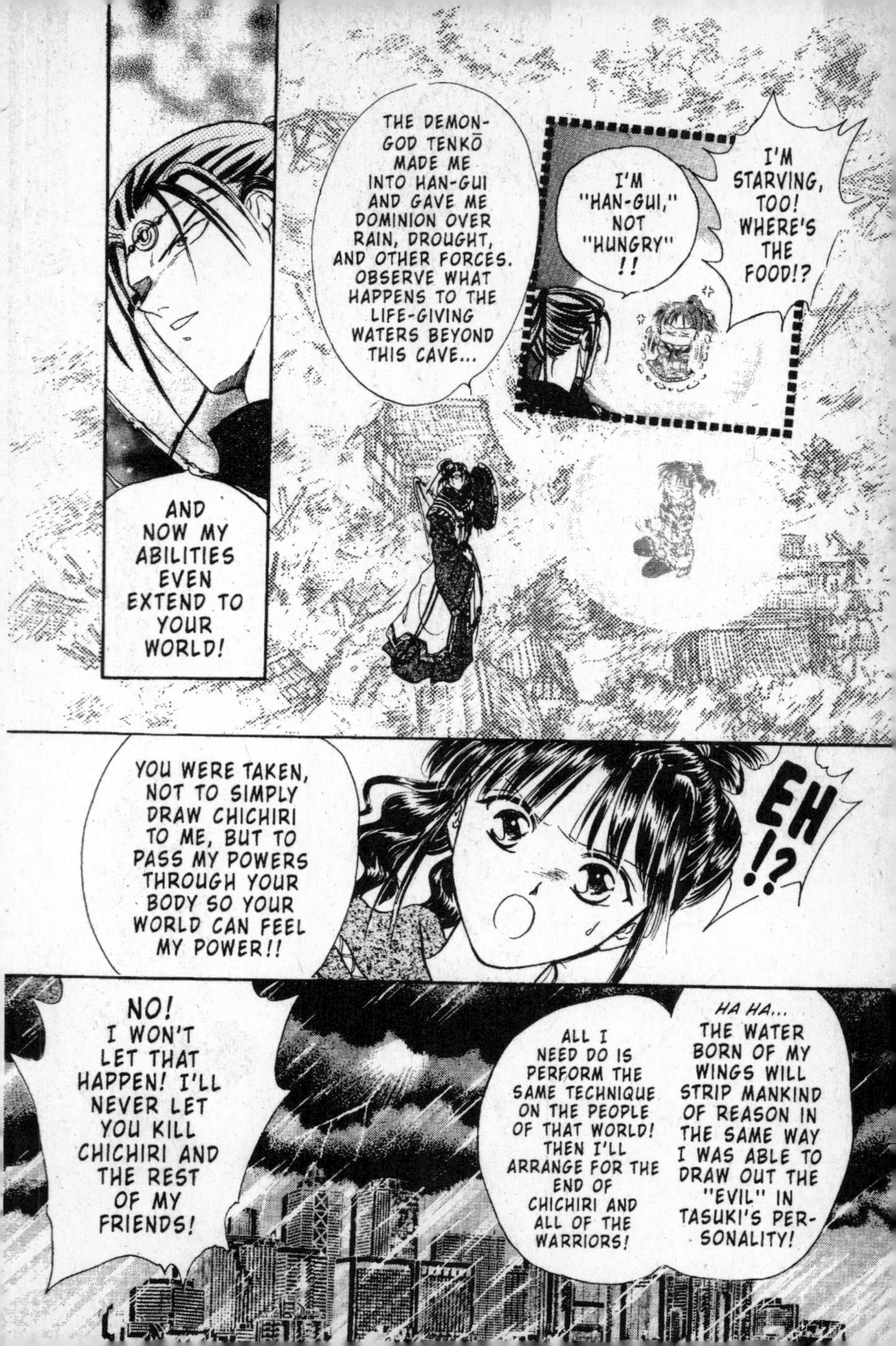
I'M "HAN-GUI," NOT "HUNGRY" !!
I'M STARVING, TOO! WHERE'S THE FOOD!?
THE DEMON-GOD TENKŌ MADE ME INTO HAN-GUI AND GAVE ME DOMINION OVER RAIN, DROUGHT, AND OTHER FORCES. OBSERVE WHAT HAPPENS TO THE LIFE-GIVING WATERS BEYOND THIS CAVE...
AND NOW MY ABILITIES EVEN EXTEND TO YOUR WORLD!
EH!?
YOU WERE TAKEN, NOT TO SIMPLY DRAW CHICHIRI TO ME, BUT TO PASS MY POWERS THROUGH YOUR BODY SO YOUR WORLD CAN FEEL MY POWER!!
HA HA... THE WATER BORN OF MY WINGS WILL STRIP MANKIND OF REASON IN THE SAME WAY I WAS ABLE TO DRAW OUT THE "EVIL" IN TASUKI'S PERSONALITY!
ALL I NEED DO IS PERFORM THE SAME TECHNIQUE ON THE PEOPLE OF THAT WORLD! THEN I'LL ARRANGE FOR THE END OF CHICHIRI AND ALL OF THE WARRIORS!
NO! I WON'T LET THAT HAPPEN! I'LL NEVER LET YOU KILL CHICHIRI AND THE REST OF MY FRIENDS!

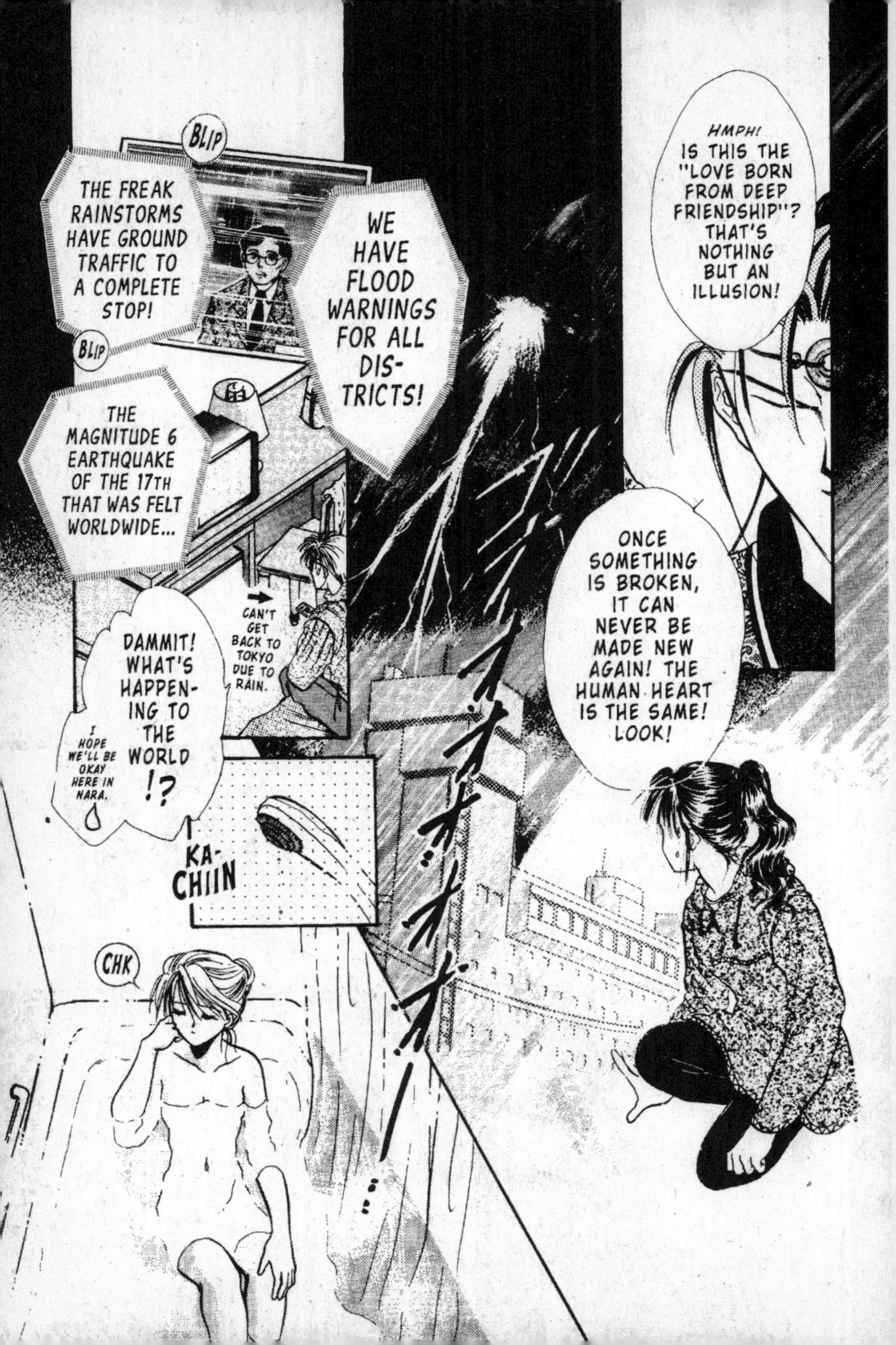
HMPH! IS THIS THE "LOVE BORN FROM DEEP FRIENDSHIP"? THAT'S NOTHING BUT AN ILLUSION!
ONCE SOMETHING IS BROKEN, IT CAN NEVER BE MADE NEW AGAIN! THE HUMAN HEART IS THE SAME! LOOK!
BLIP
WE HAVE FLOOD WARNINGS FOR ALL DIS-TRICTS!
THE FREAK RAINSTORMS HAVE GROUND TRAFFIC TO A COMPLETE STOP!
BLIP
THE MAGNITUDE 6 EARTHQUAKE OF THE 17TH THAT WAS FELT WORLDWIDE...
CAN'T GET BACK TO TOKYO DUE TO RAIN.
DAMMIT! WHAT'S HAPPEN-ING TO THE WORLD !?
I HOPE WE'LL BE OKAY HERE IN NARA.
KA-CHIIN
CHK

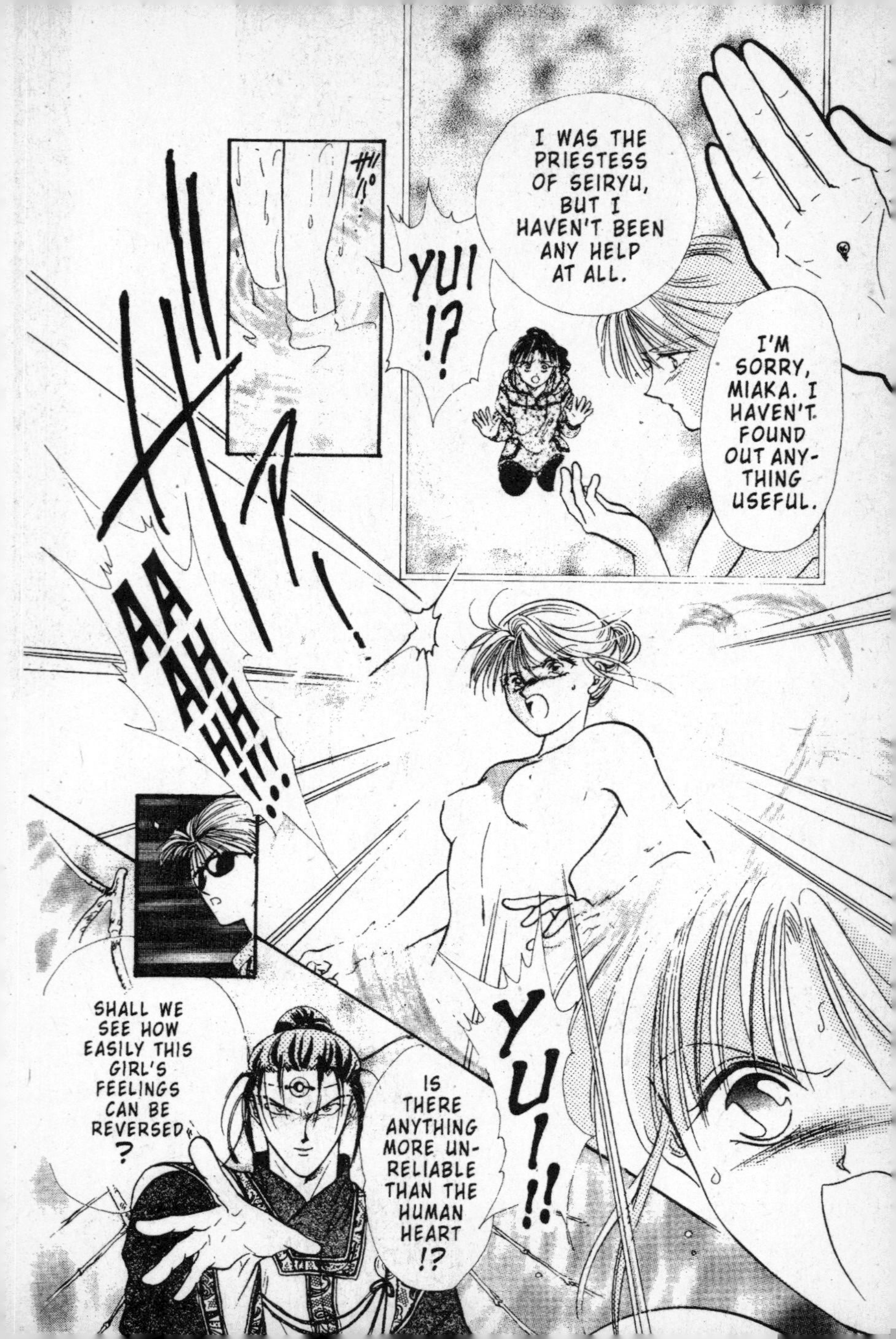
I WAS THE PRIESTESS OF SEIRYU, BUT I HAVEN'T BEEN ANY HELP AT ALL.
I'M SORRY, MIAKA. I HAVEN'T FOUND OUT ANYTHING USEFUL.
YUI !?
AAAHH!!!
YUI!!
IS THERE ANYTHING MORE UNRELIABLE THAN THE HUMAN HEART !?
SHALL WE SEE HOW EASILY THIS GIRL'S FEELINGS CAN BE REVERSED ?

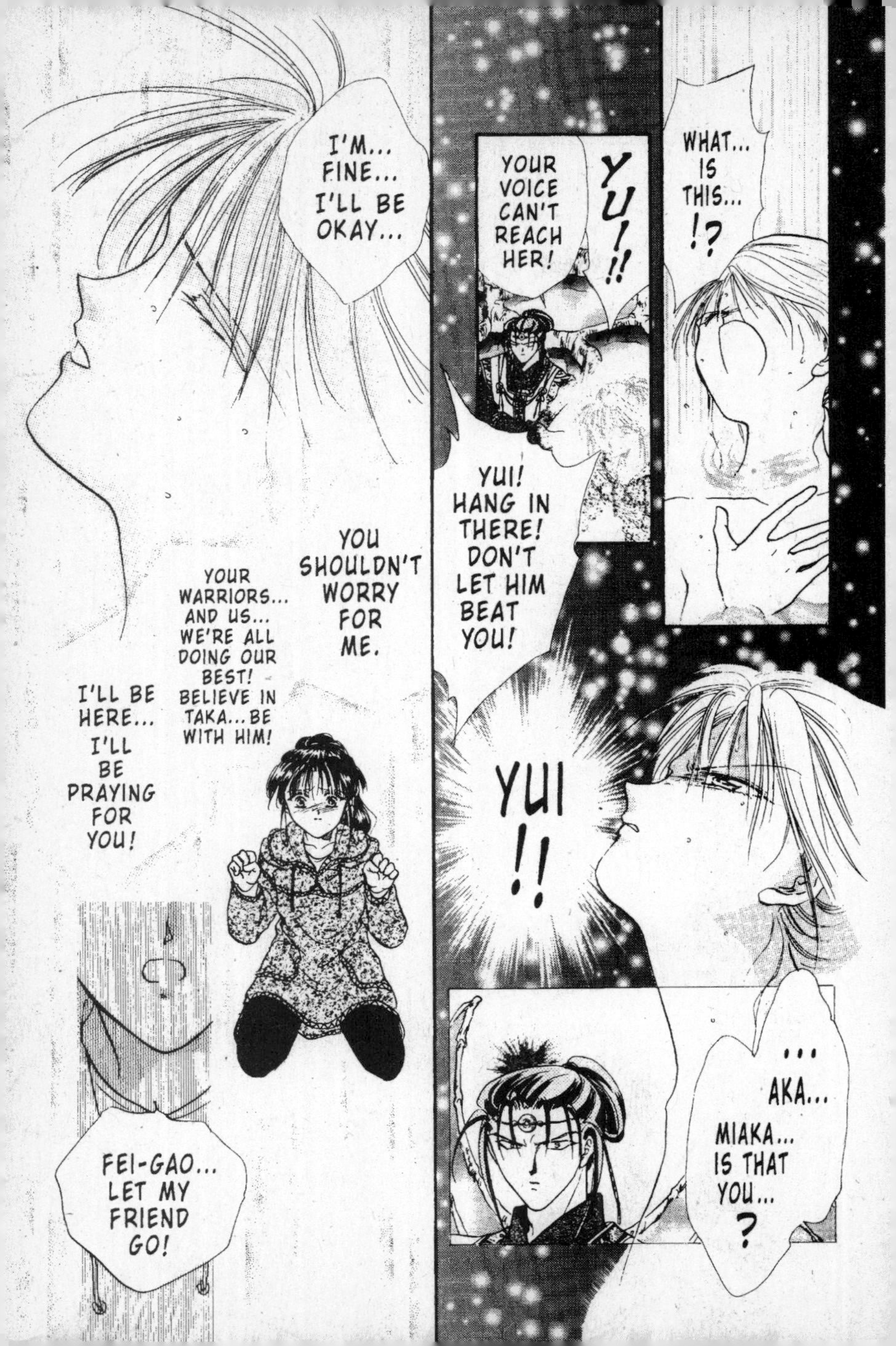
WHAT... IS THIS... !?
YUI!!
YOUR VOICE CAN'T REACH HER!
YUI! HANG IN THERE! DON'T LET HIM BEAT YOU!
YUI !!
... AKA... MIAKA... IS THAT YOU... ?
I'M... FINE... I'LL BE OKAY...
YOU SHOULDN'T WORRY FOR ME.
YOUR WARRIORS... AND US... WE'RE ALL DOING OUR BEST! BELIEVE IN TAKA... BE WITH HIM!
I'LL BE HERE... I'LL BE PRAYING FOR YOU!
FEI-GAO... LET MY FRIEND GO!

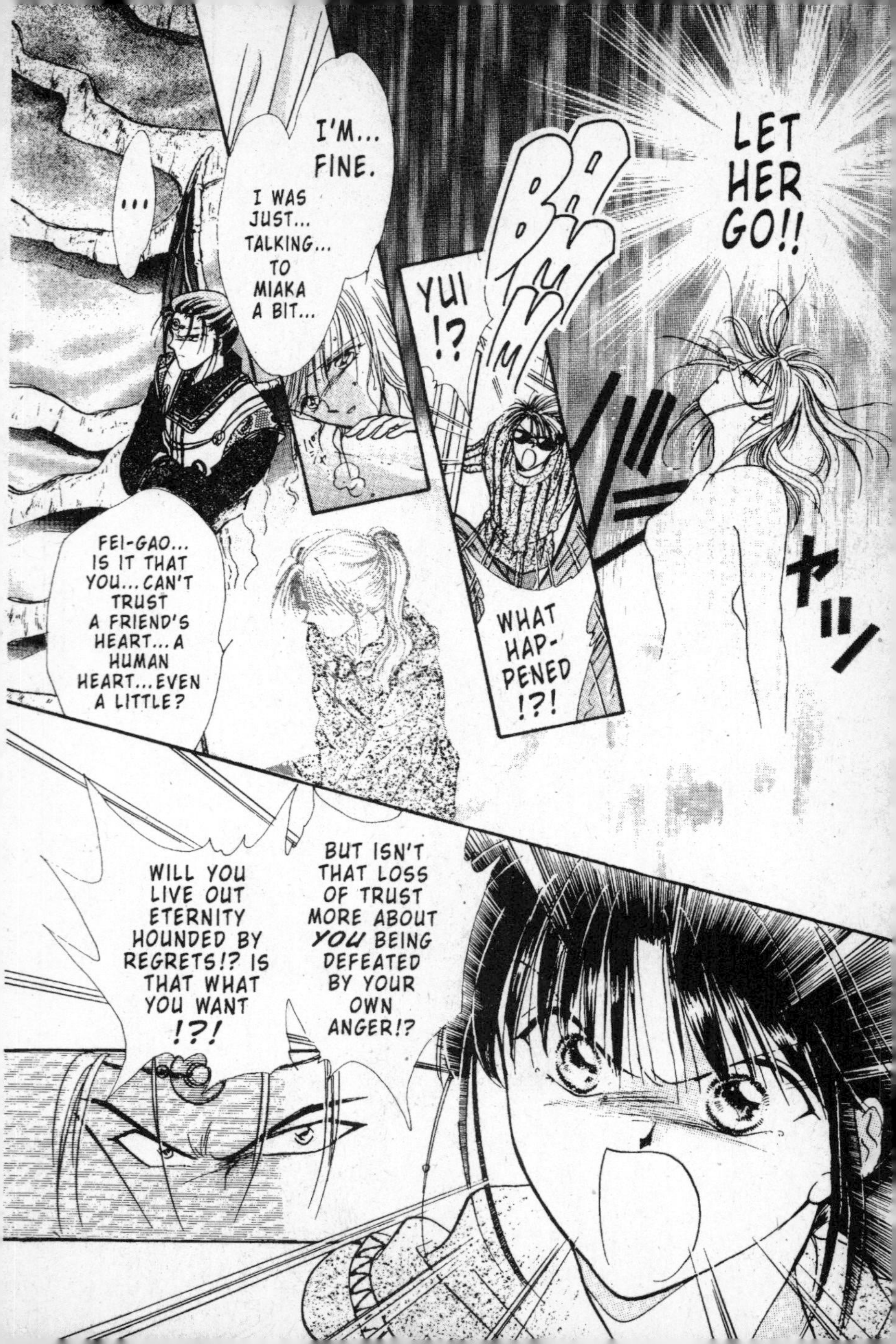
LET HER GO!!
ヤッ
BAMMM
YUI !?
WHAT HAPPENED !?!
I'M... FINE.
I WAS JUST... TALKING... TO MIAKA A BIT...
...
FEI-GAO... IS IT THAT YOU... CAN'T TRUST A FRIEND'S HEART... A HUMAN HEART... EVEN A LITTLE?
BUT ISN'T THAT LOSS OF TRUST MORE ABOUT *YOU* BEING DEFEATED BY YOUR OWN ANGER!?
WILL YOU LIVE OUT ETERNITY HOUNDED BY REGRETS!? IS THAT WHAT YOU WANT !?!

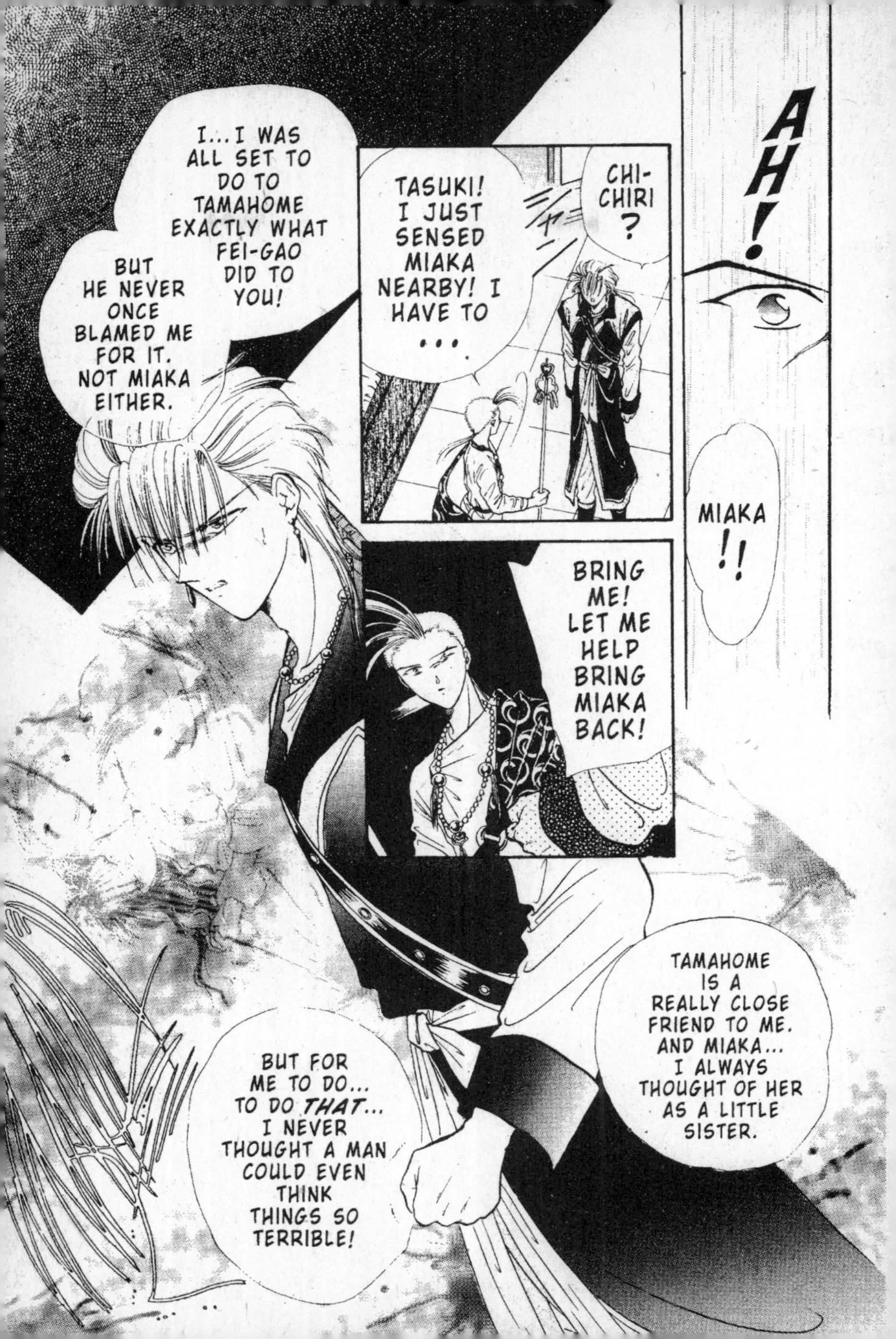
AH!
MIAKA!!
CHI-CHIRI?
TASUKI! I JUST SENSED MIAKA NEARBY! I HAVE TO . . . .
BRING ME! LET ME HELP BRING MIAKA BACK!
I...I WAS ALL SET TO DO TO TAMAHOME EXACTLY WHAT FEI-GAO DID TO YOU!
BUT HE NEVER ONCE BLAMED ME FOR IT. NOT MIAKA EITHER.
TAMAHOME IS A REALLY CLOSE FRIEND TO ME. AND MIAKA... I ALWAYS THOUGHT OF HER AS A LITTLE SISTER.
BUT FOR ME TO DO... TO DO *THAT*... I NEVER THOUGHT A MAN COULD EVEN THINK THINGS SO TERRIBLE!

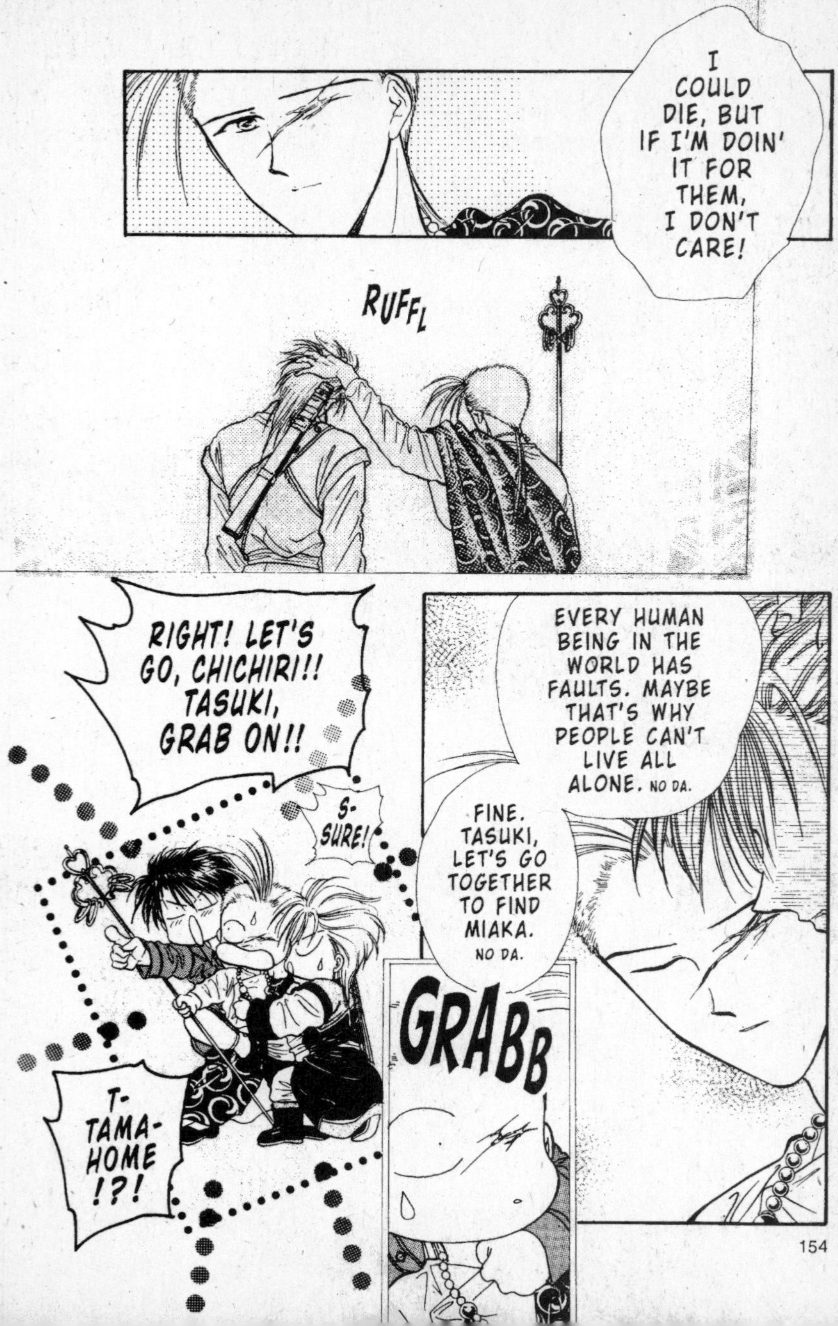
I COULD DIE, BUT IF I'M DOIN' IT FOR THEM, I DON'T CARE!
RUFFL
EVERY HUMAN BEING IN THE WORLD HAS FAULTS. MAYBE THAT'S WHY PEOPLE CAN'T LIVE ALL ALONE. NO DA.
FINE. TASUKI, LET'S GO TOGETHER TO FIND MIAKA. NO DA.
GRABB
RIGHT! LET'S GO, CHICHIRI!! TASUKI, GRAB ON!!
S-SURE!
T-TAMA-HOME !?!

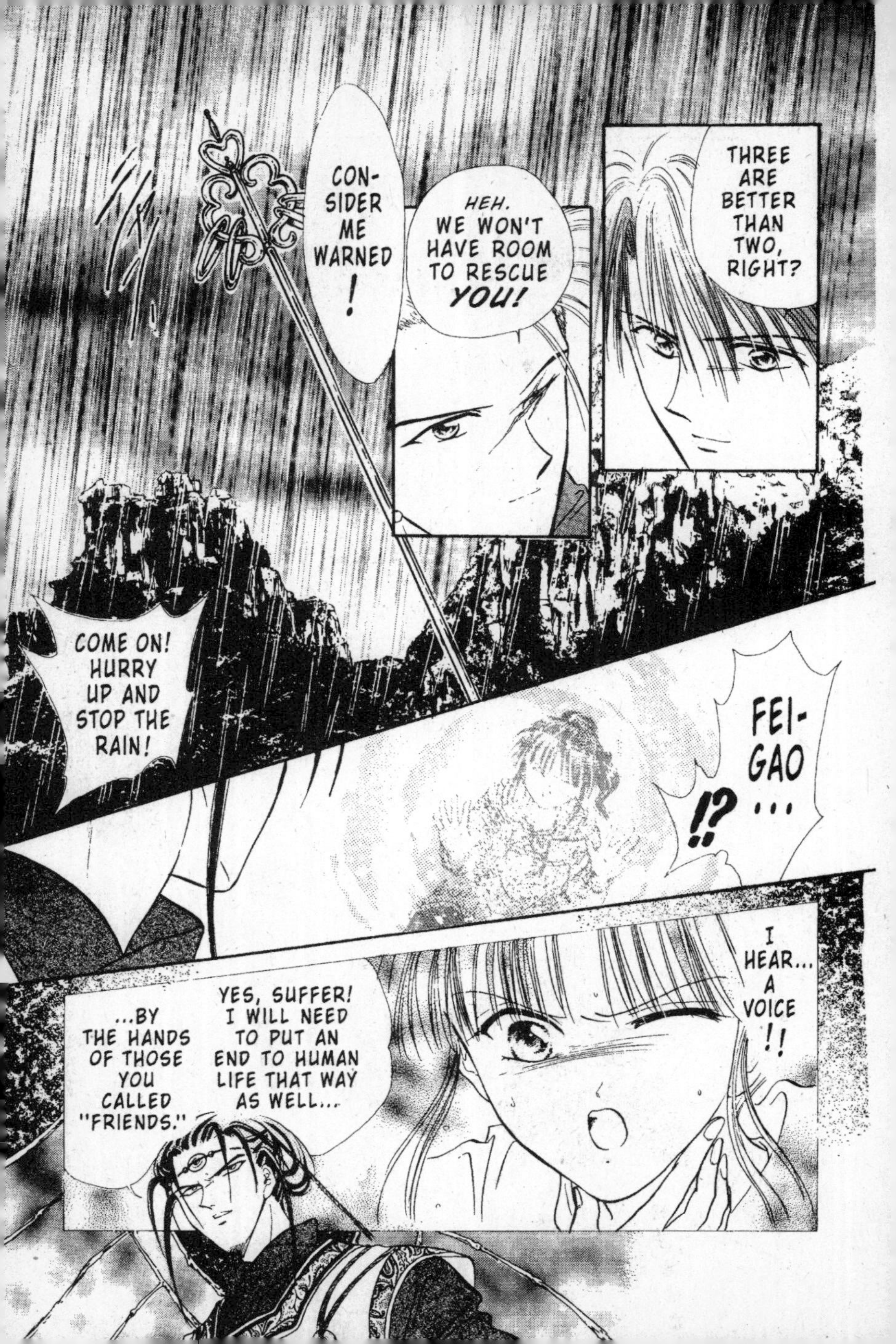
THREE ARE BETTER THAN TWO, RIGHT?
HEH. WE WON'T HAVE ROOM TO RESCUE YOU!
CON-SIDER ME WARNED!
COME ON! HURRY UP AND STOP THE RAIN!
FEI-GAO...
!?
I HEAR... A VOICE!!
YES, SUFFER! I WILL NEED TO PUT AN END TO HUMAN LIFE THAT WAY AS WELL...
...BY THE HANDS OF THOSE YOU CALLED "FRIENDS."

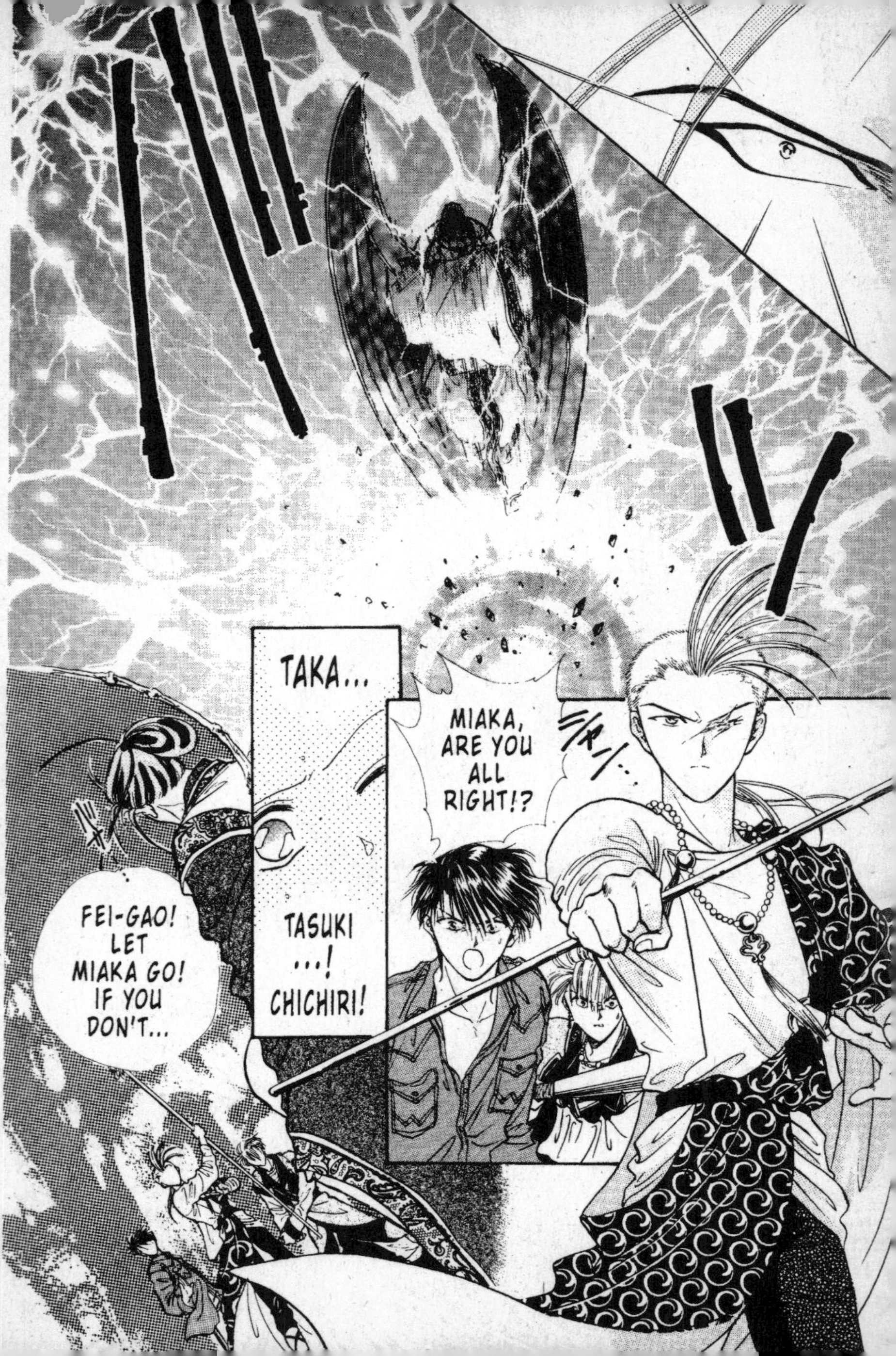
MIAKA, ARE YOU ALL RIGHT!?
TAKA...
TASUKI ...! CHICHIRI!
FEI-GAO! LET MIAKA GO! IF YOU DON'T...

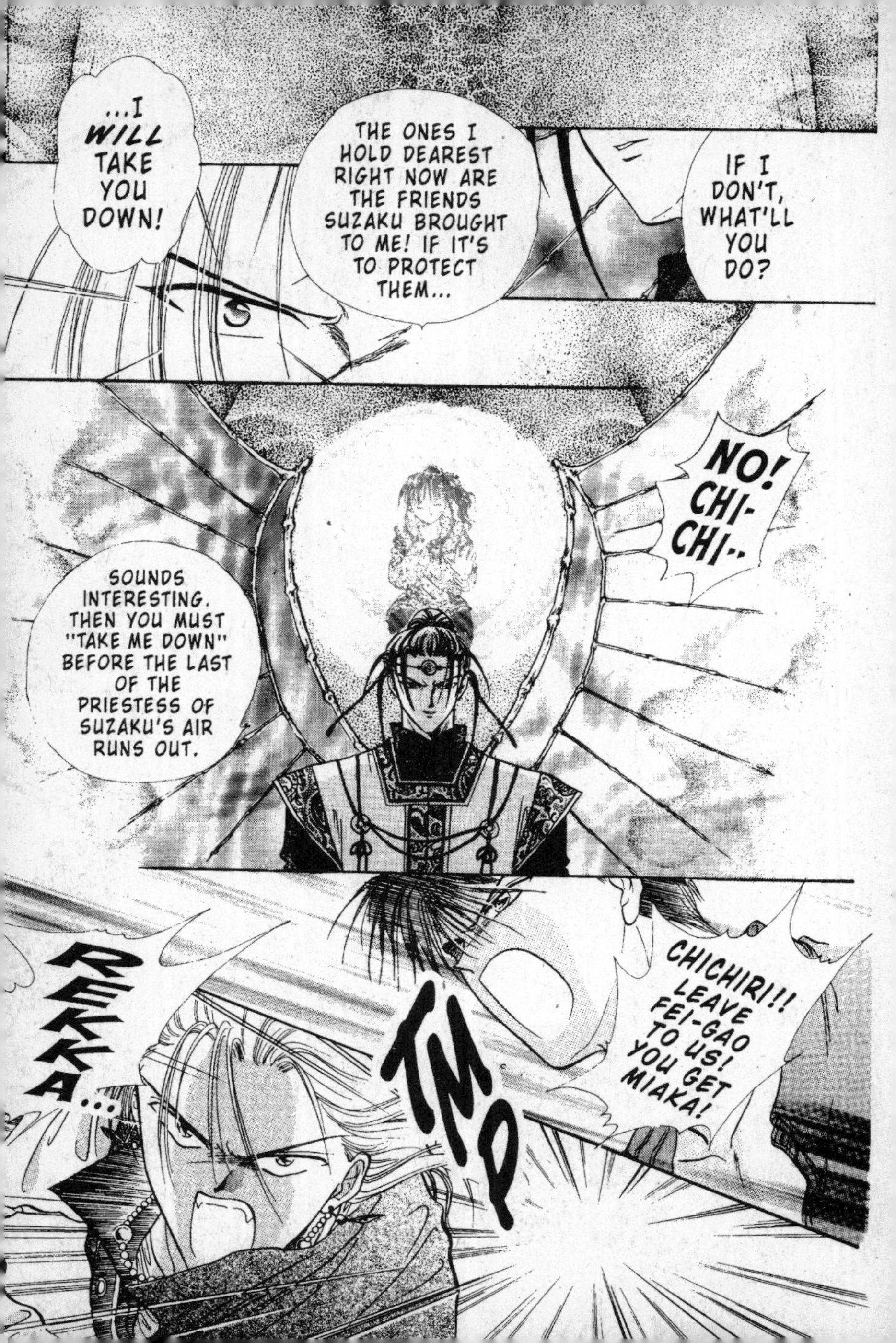
IF I DON'T, WHAT'LL YOU DO?
THE ONES I HOLD DEAREST RIGHT NOW ARE THE FRIENDS SUZAKU BROUGHT TO ME! IF IT'S TO PROTECT THEM...
...I *WILL* TAKE YOU DOWN!
NO! CHI-CHI..
SOUNDS INTERESTING. THEN YOU MUST "TAKE ME DOWN" BEFORE THE LAST OF THE PRIESTESS OF SUZAKU'S AIR RUNS OUT.
CHICHIRI!! LEAVE FEI-GAO TO US! YOU GET MIAKA!
TMP
REKKA...

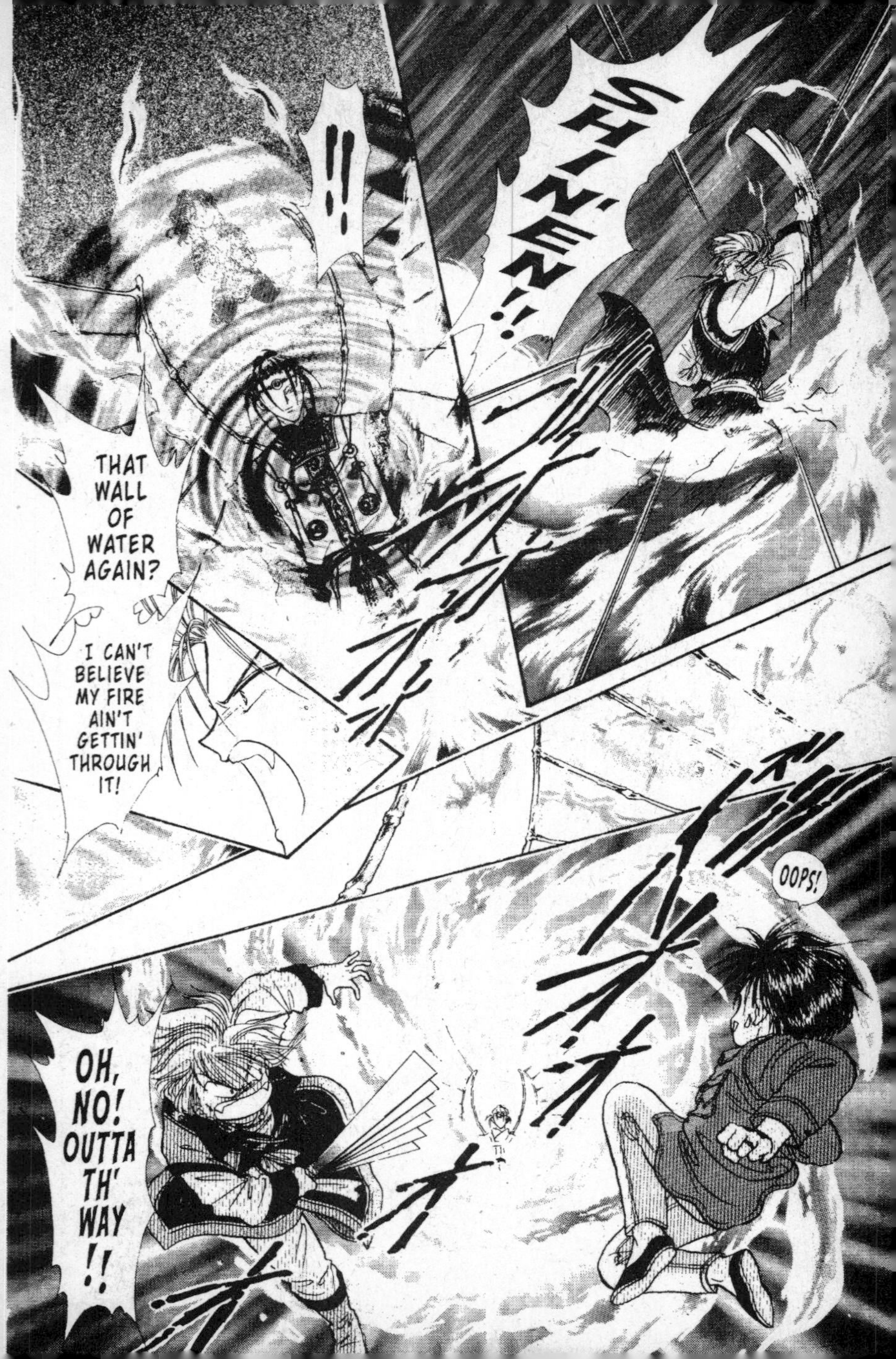
SHI-NE!!
!!
THAT WALL OF WATER AGAIN?
I CAN'T BELIEVE MY FIRE AIN'T GETTIN' THROUGH IT!
OOPS!
OH, NO! OUTTA TH' WAY!!

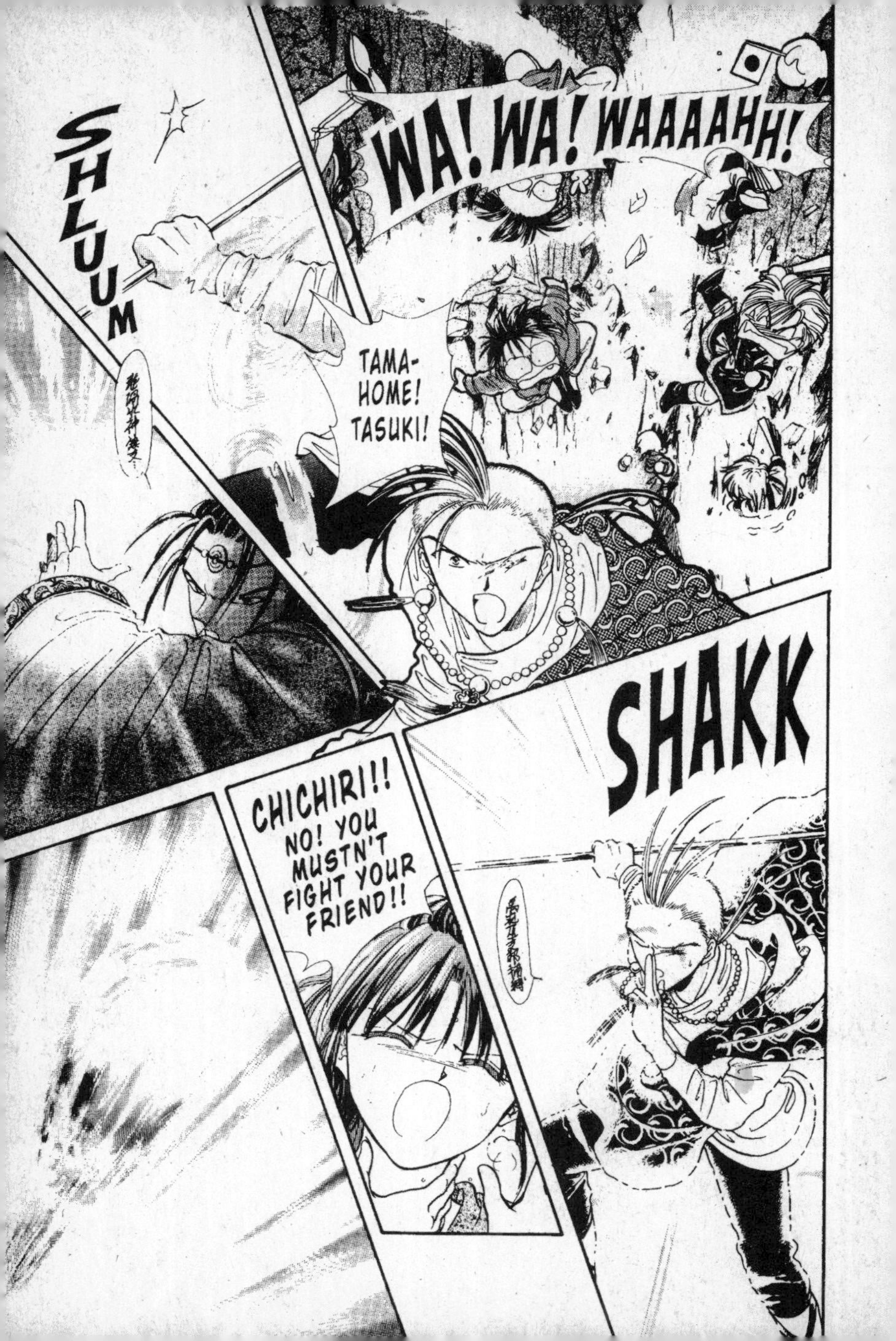
WA! WA! WAAAAHH!
TAMA-HOME! TASUKI!
SHLUUM
SHAKK
CHICHIRI!! NO! YOU MUSTN'T FIGHT YOUR FRIEND!!

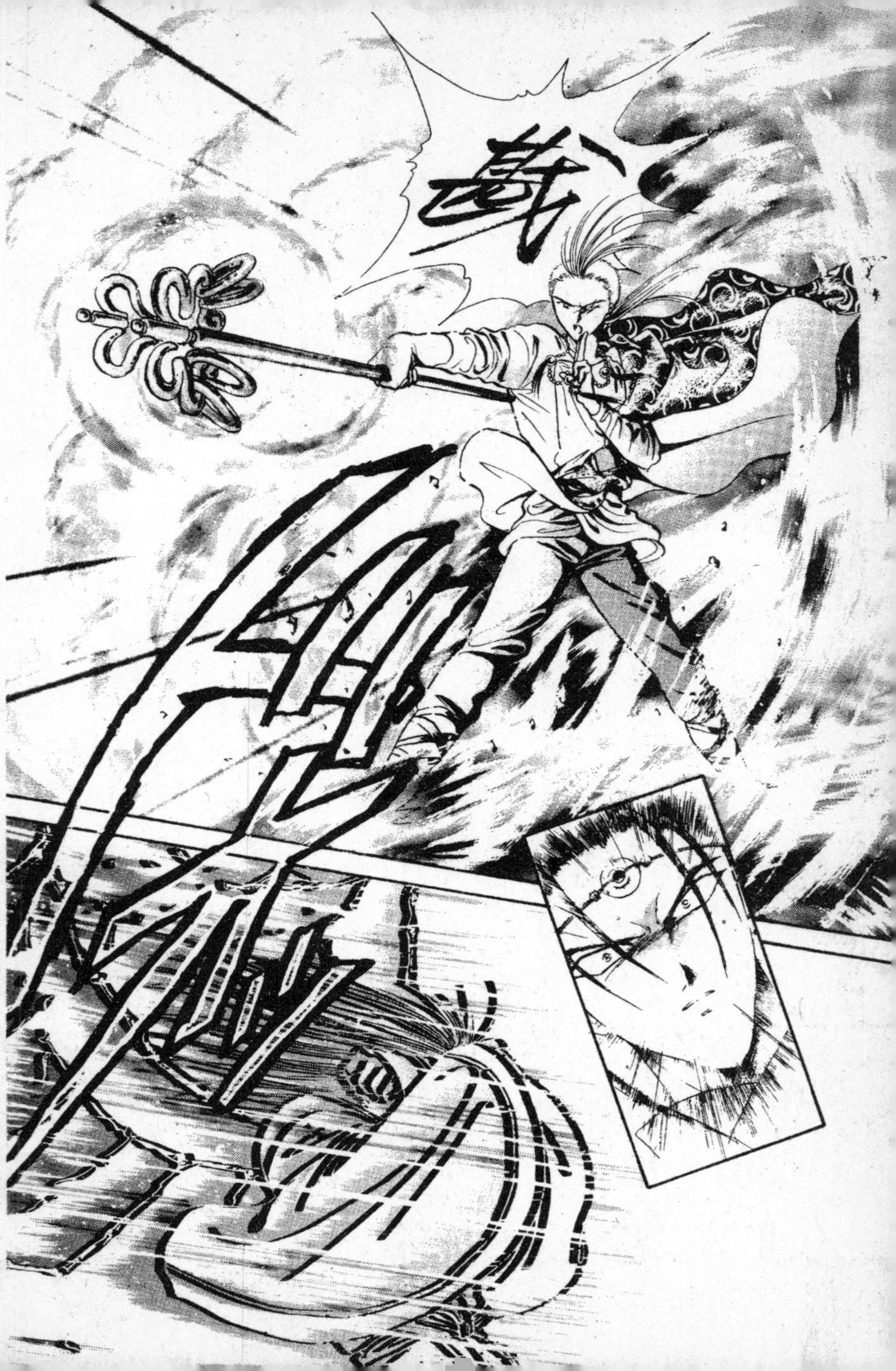

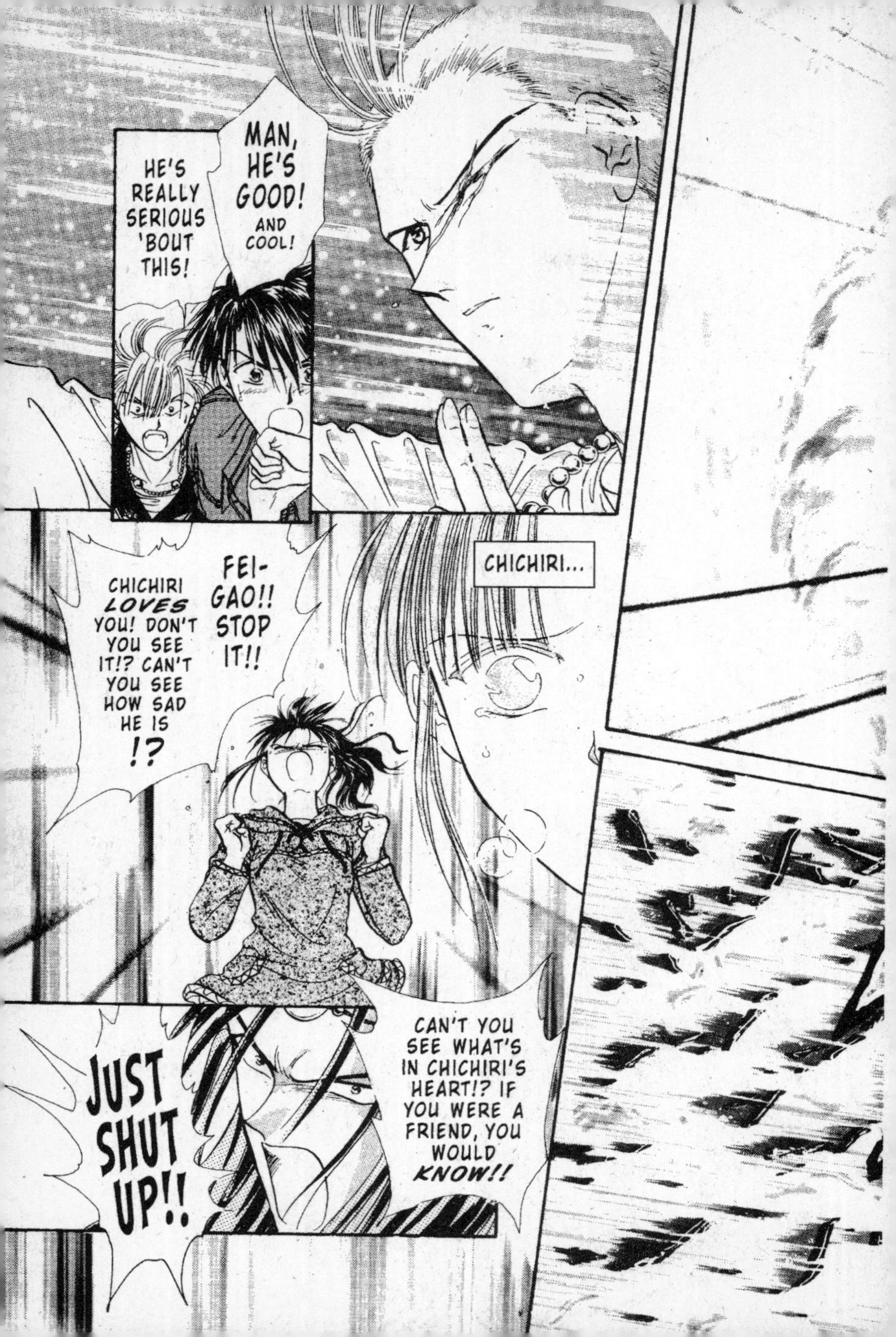
MAN, HE'S GOOD! AND COOL!
HE'S REALLY SERIOUS 'BOUT THIS!
CHICHIRI...
FEI-GAO!! STOP IT!!
CHICHIRI *LOVES* YOU! DON'T YOU SEE IT!? CAN'T YOU SEE HOW SAD HE IS !?
CAN'T YOU SEE WHAT'S IN CHICHIRI'S HEART!? IF YOU WERE A FRIEND, YOU WOULD *KNOW!!*
JUST SHUT UP!!

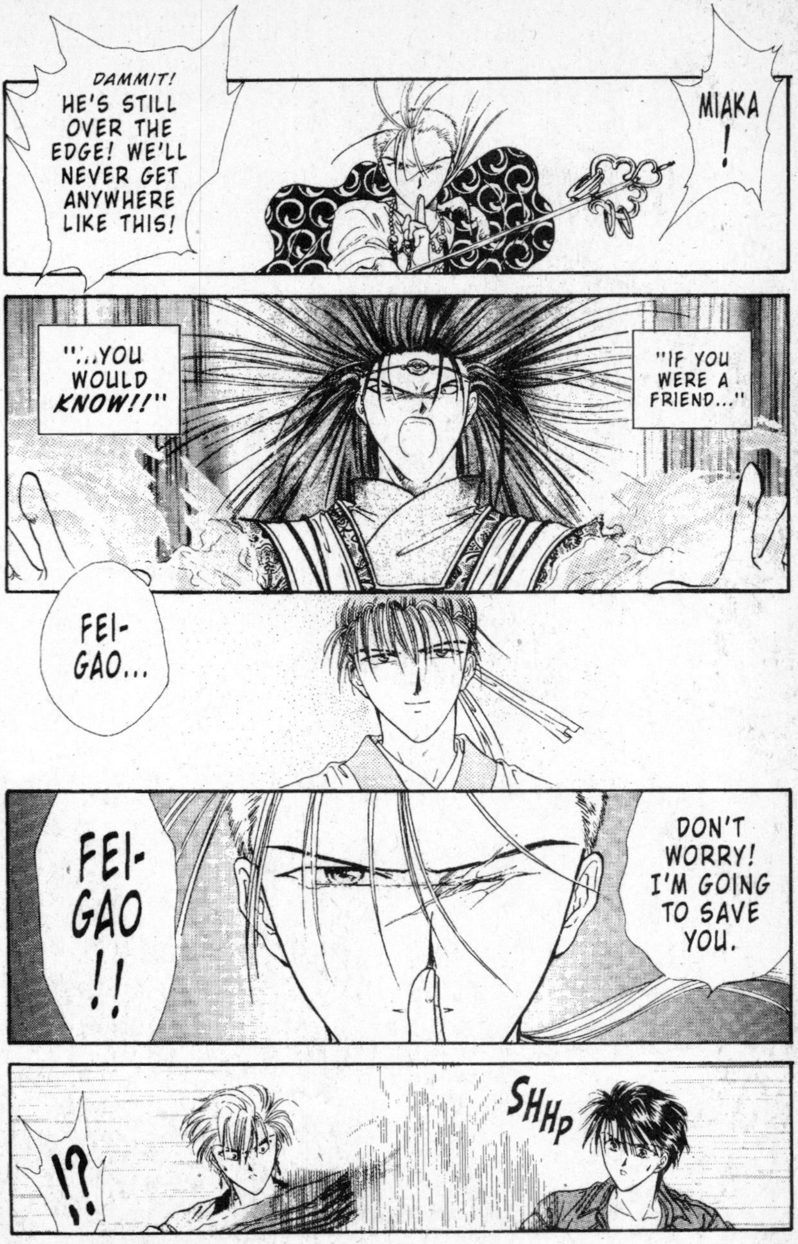
MIAKA!
DAMMIT! HE'S STILL OVER THE EDGE! WE'LL NEVER GET ANYWHERE LIKE THIS!
"IF YOU WERE A FRIEND..."
"...YOU WOULD KNOW!!"
FEI-GAO...
DON'T WORRY! I'M GOING TO SAVE YOU.
FEI-GAO!!
SHHP
!?

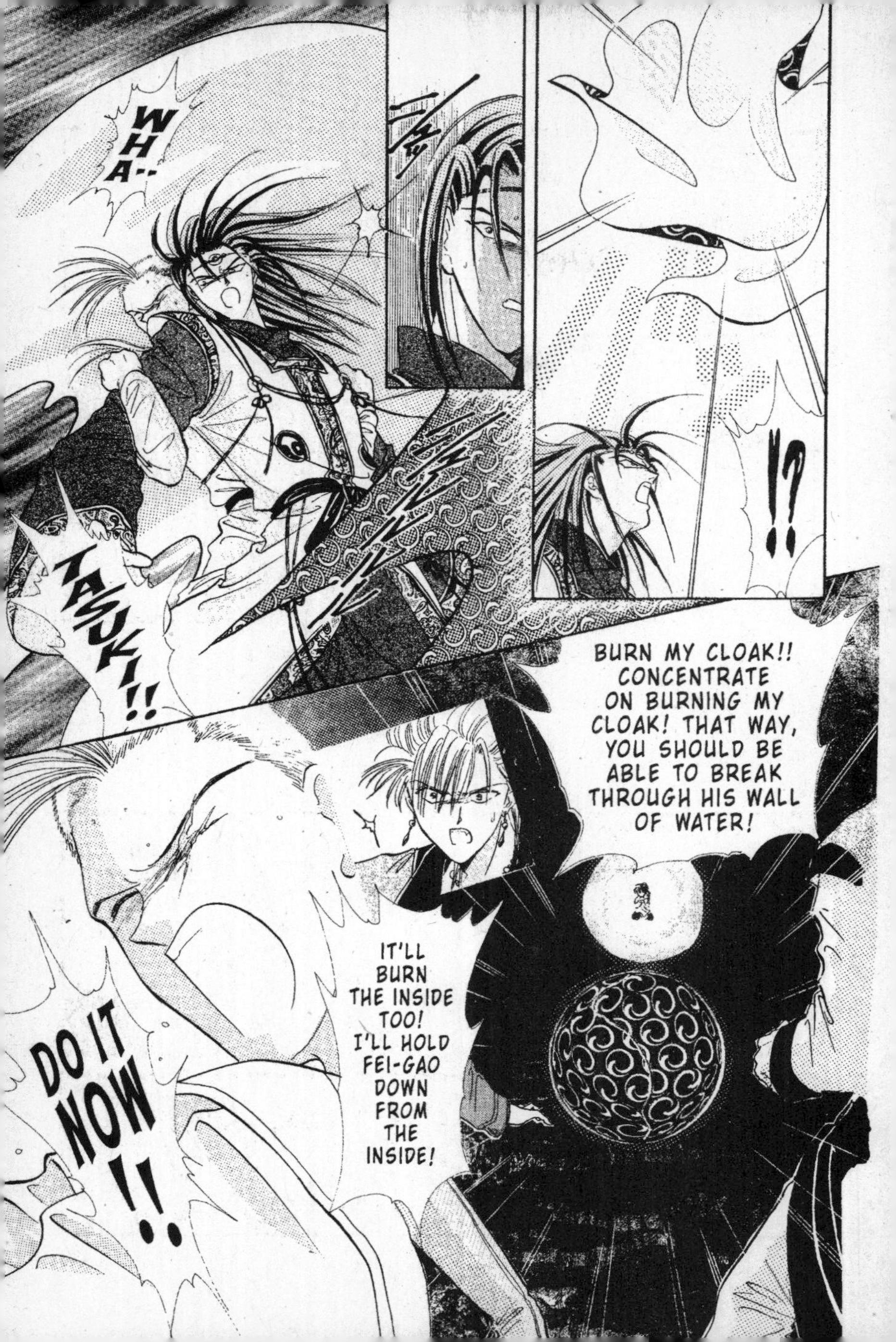
!?
WHA--
TASUKI!!
BURN MY CLOAK!! CONCENTRATE ON BURNING MY CLOAK! THAT WAY, YOU SHOULD BE ABLE TO BREAK THROUGH HIS WALL OF WATER!
IT'LL BURN THE INSIDE TOO! I'LL HOLD FEI-GAO DOWN FROM THE INSIDE!
DO IT NOW!!

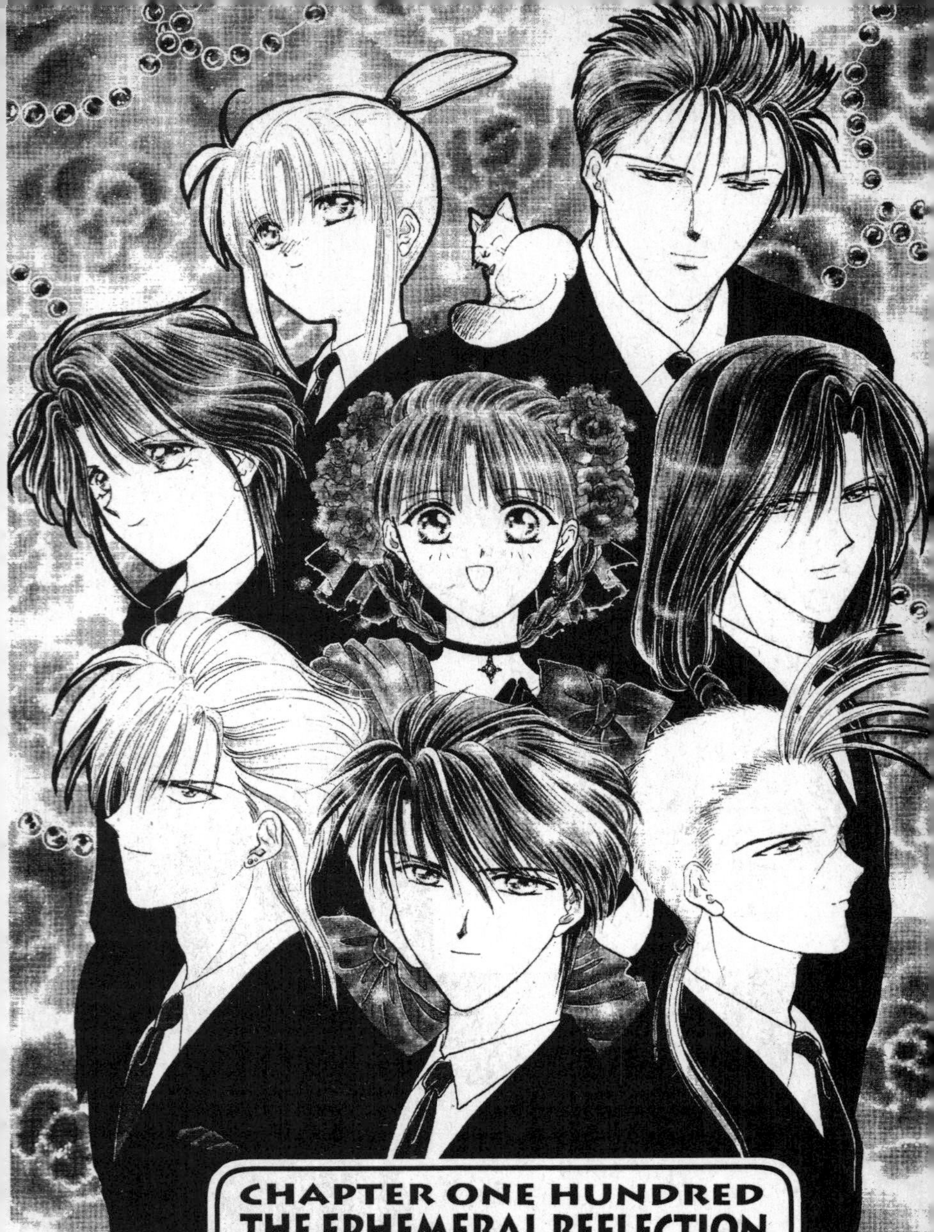
CHAPTER ONE HUNDRED
THE EPHEMERAL REFLECTION
IN THE WATER

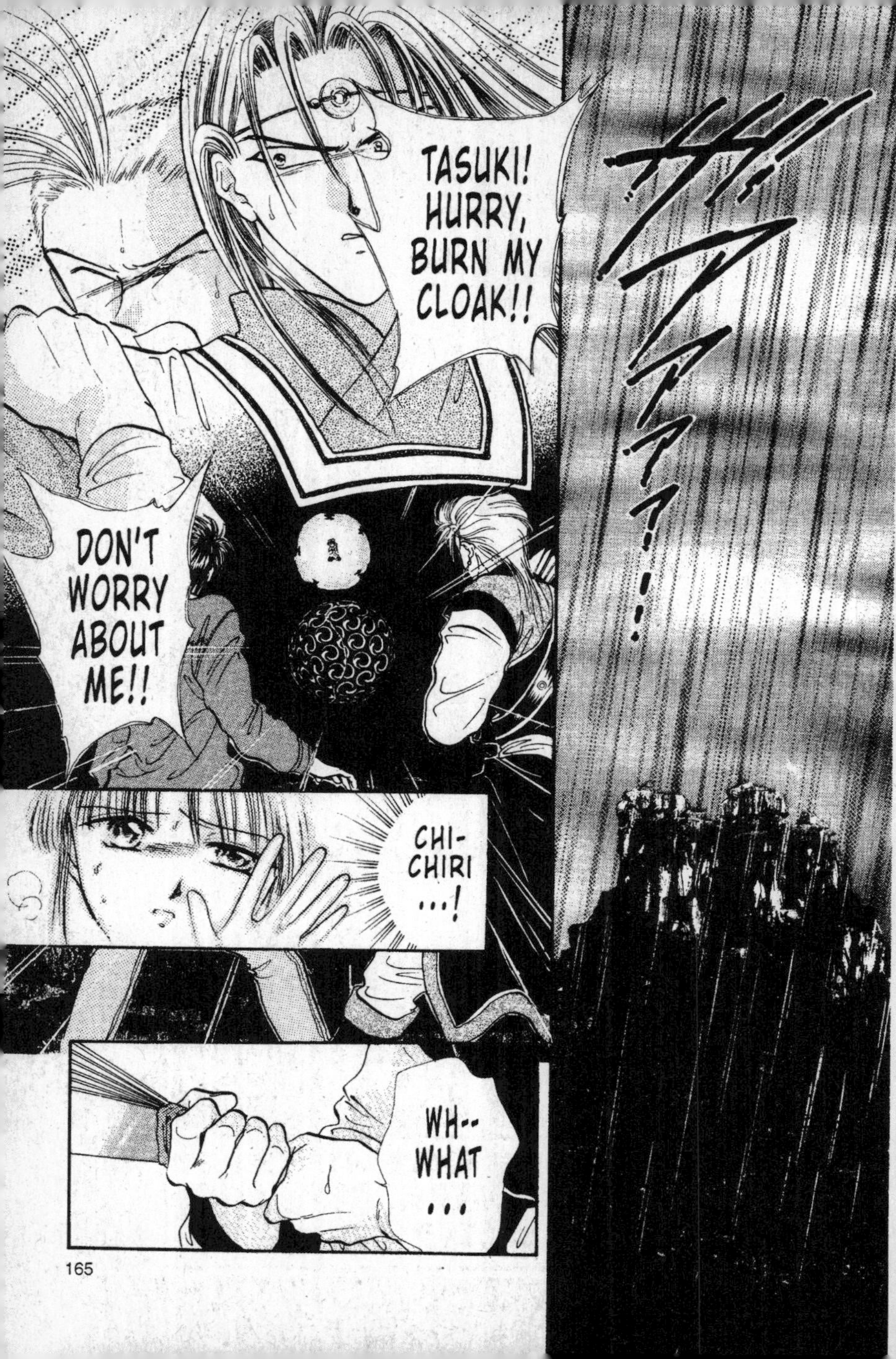
TASUKI! HURRY, BURN MY CLOAK!!
DON'T WORRY ABOUT ME!!
CHI-CHIRI ...!
WH-- WHAT ...

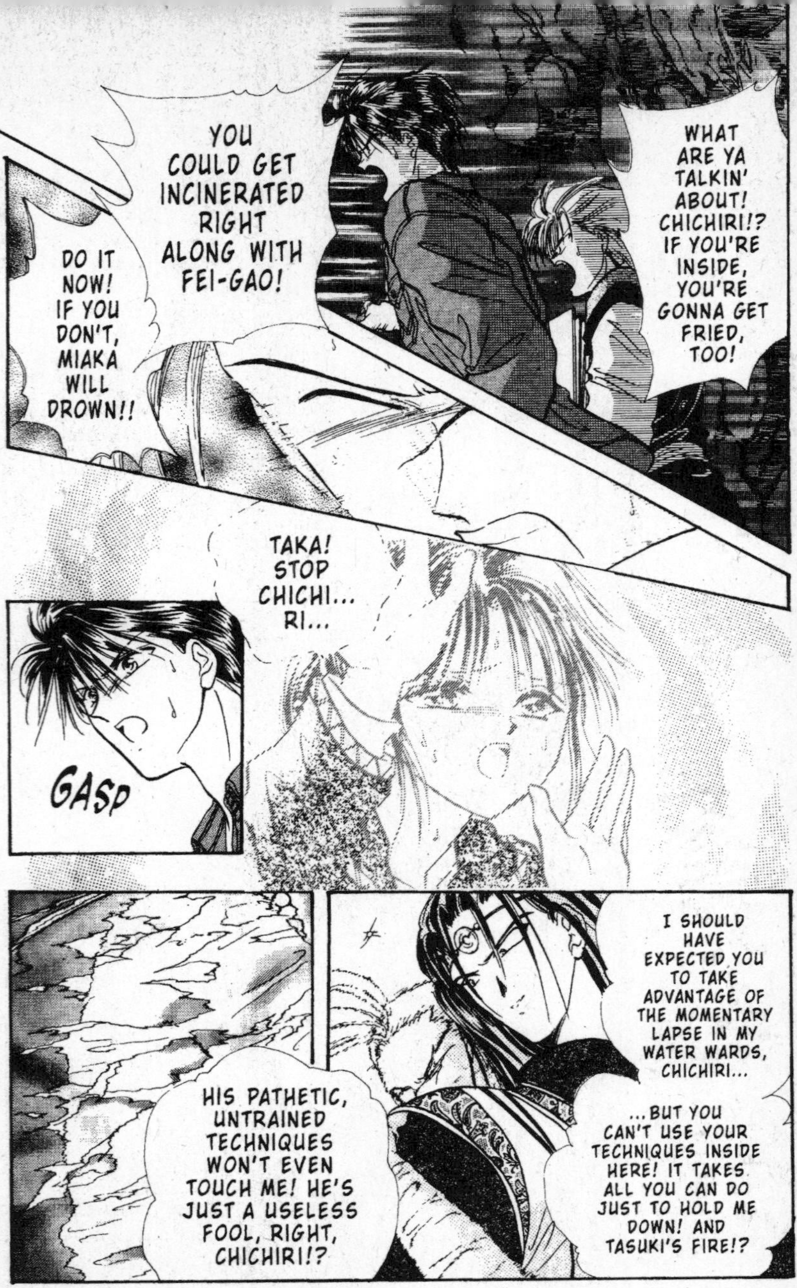
WHAT ARE YA TALKIN' ABOUT! CHICHIRI!? IF YOU'RE INSIDE, YOU'RE GONNA GET FRIED, TOO!
YOU COULD GET INCINERATED RIGHT ALONG WITH FEI-GAO!
DO IT NOW! IF YOU DON'T, MIAKA WILL DROWN!!
TAKA! STOP CHICHI... RI...
GASP
I SHOULD HAVE EXPECTED YOU TO TAKE ADVANTAGE OF THE MOMENTARY LAPSE IN MY WATER WARDS, CHICHIRI...
...BUT YOU CAN'T USE YOUR TECHNIQUES INSIDE HERE! IT TAKES ALL YOU CAN DO JUST TO HOLD ME DOWN! AND TASUKI'S FIRE!?
HIS PATHETIC, UNTRAINED TECHNIQUES WON'T EVEN TOUCH ME! HE'S JUST A USELESS FOOL, RIGHT, CHICHIRI!?

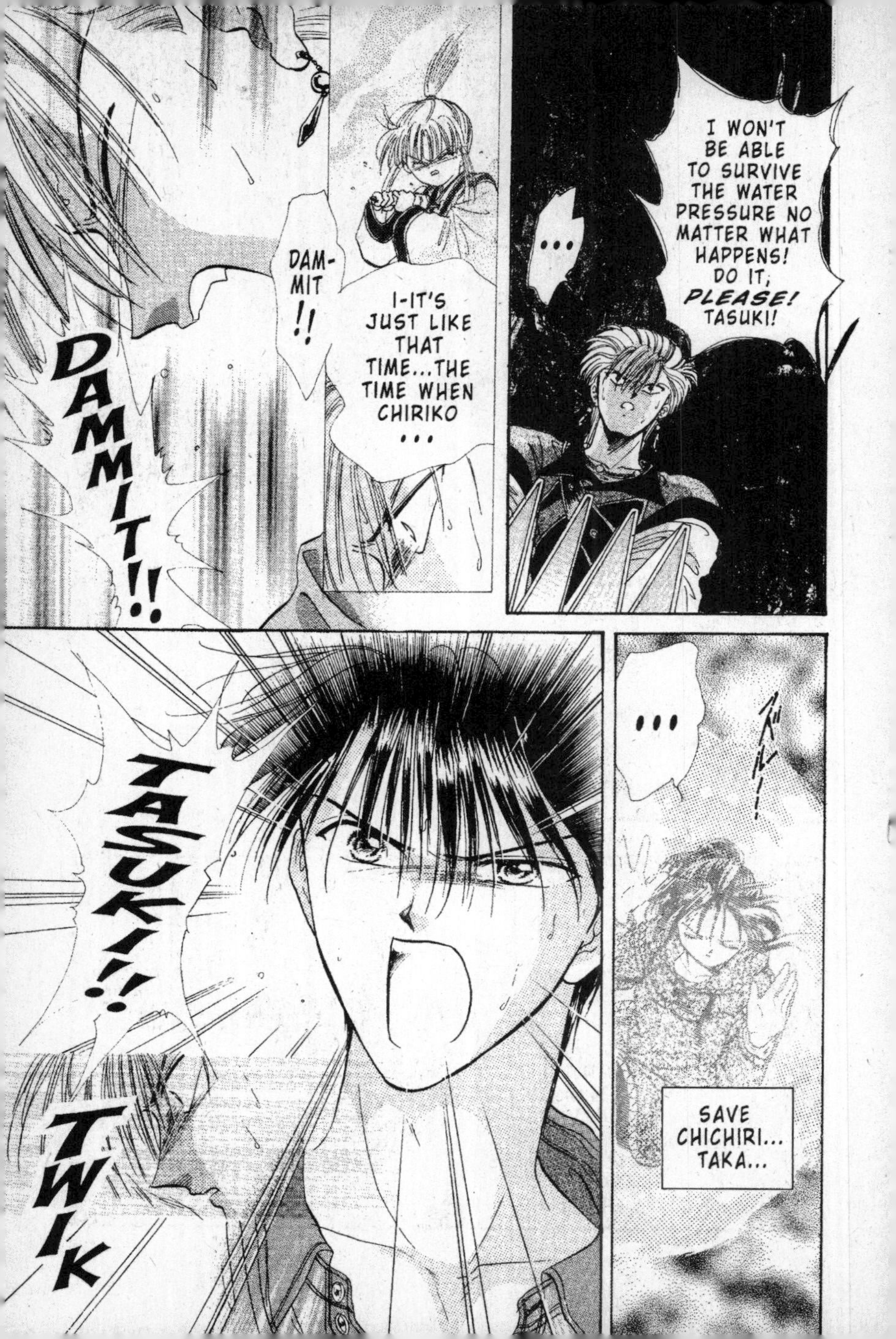
I WON'T BE ABLE TO SURVIVE THE WATER PRESSURE NO MATTER WHAT HAPPENS! DO IT, *PLEASE!* TASUKI!
...
I-IT'S JUST LIKE THAT TIME...THE TIME WHEN CHIRIKO ...
DAM-MIT !!
DAMMIT!!
...
SAVE CHICHIRI... TAKA...
TASUKI!!
TWIK

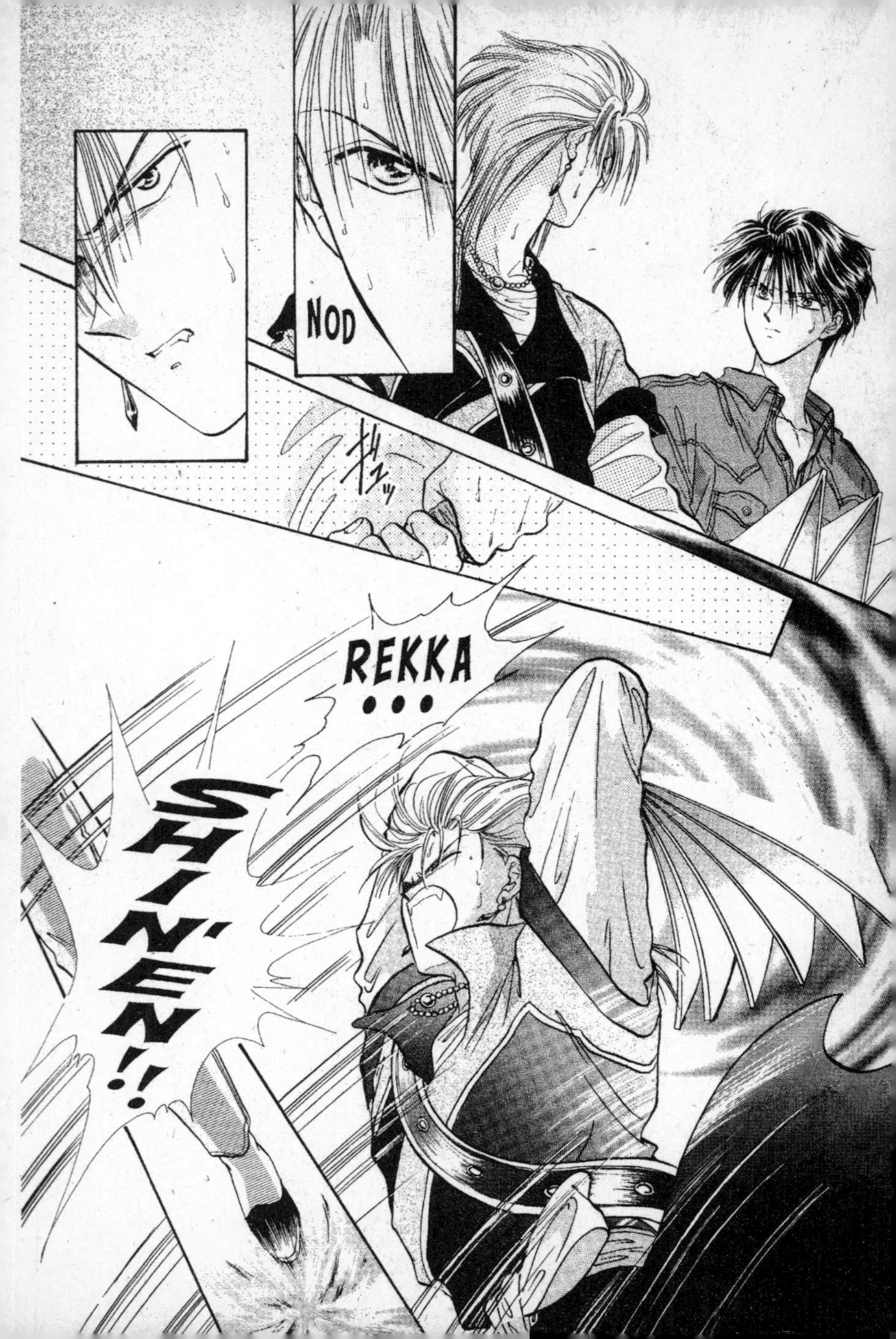
NOD
REKKA ...
SHIN'EN!!

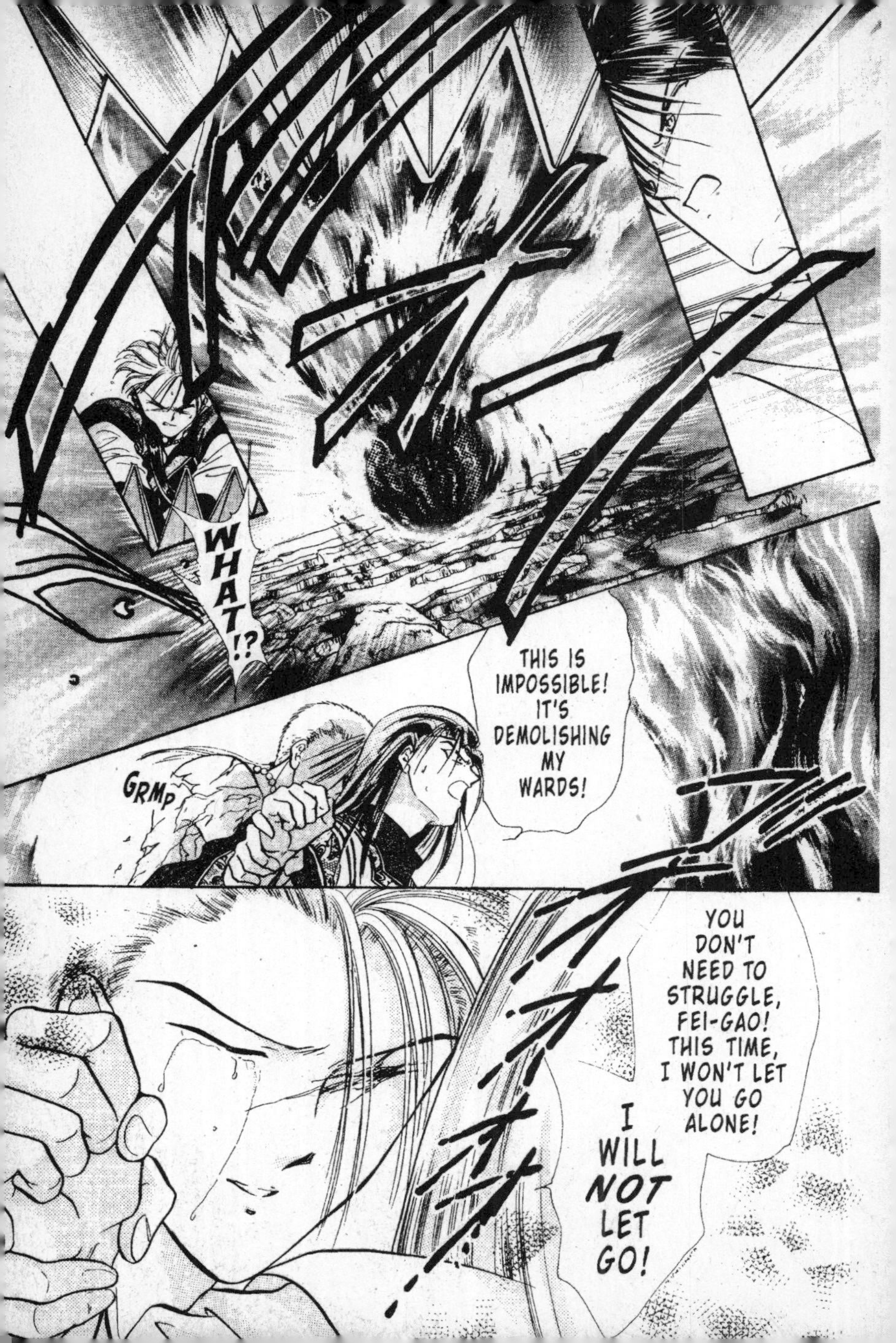
WHAT!?
THIS IS IMPOSSIBLE! IT'S DEMOLISHING MY WARDS!
GRMP
YOU DON'T NEED TO STRUGGLE, FEI-GAO! THIS TIME, I WON'T LET YOU GO ALONE!
I WILL NOT LET GO!

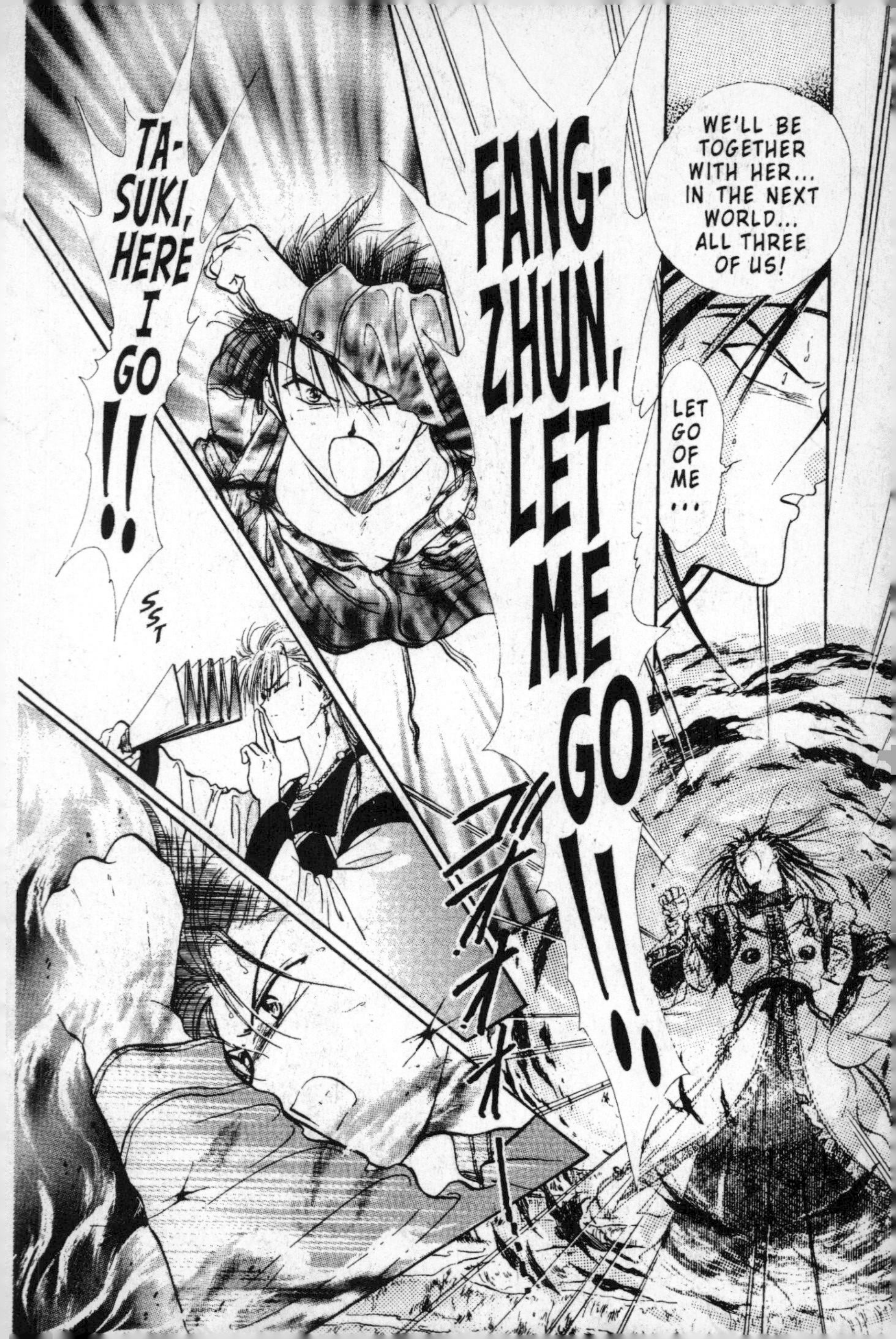
WE'LL BE TOGETHER WITH HER... IN THE NEXT WORLD... ALL THREE OF US!
LET GO OF ME...
FANG-ZHUN, LET ME GO!!
TA-SUKI, HERE I GO!!
SST

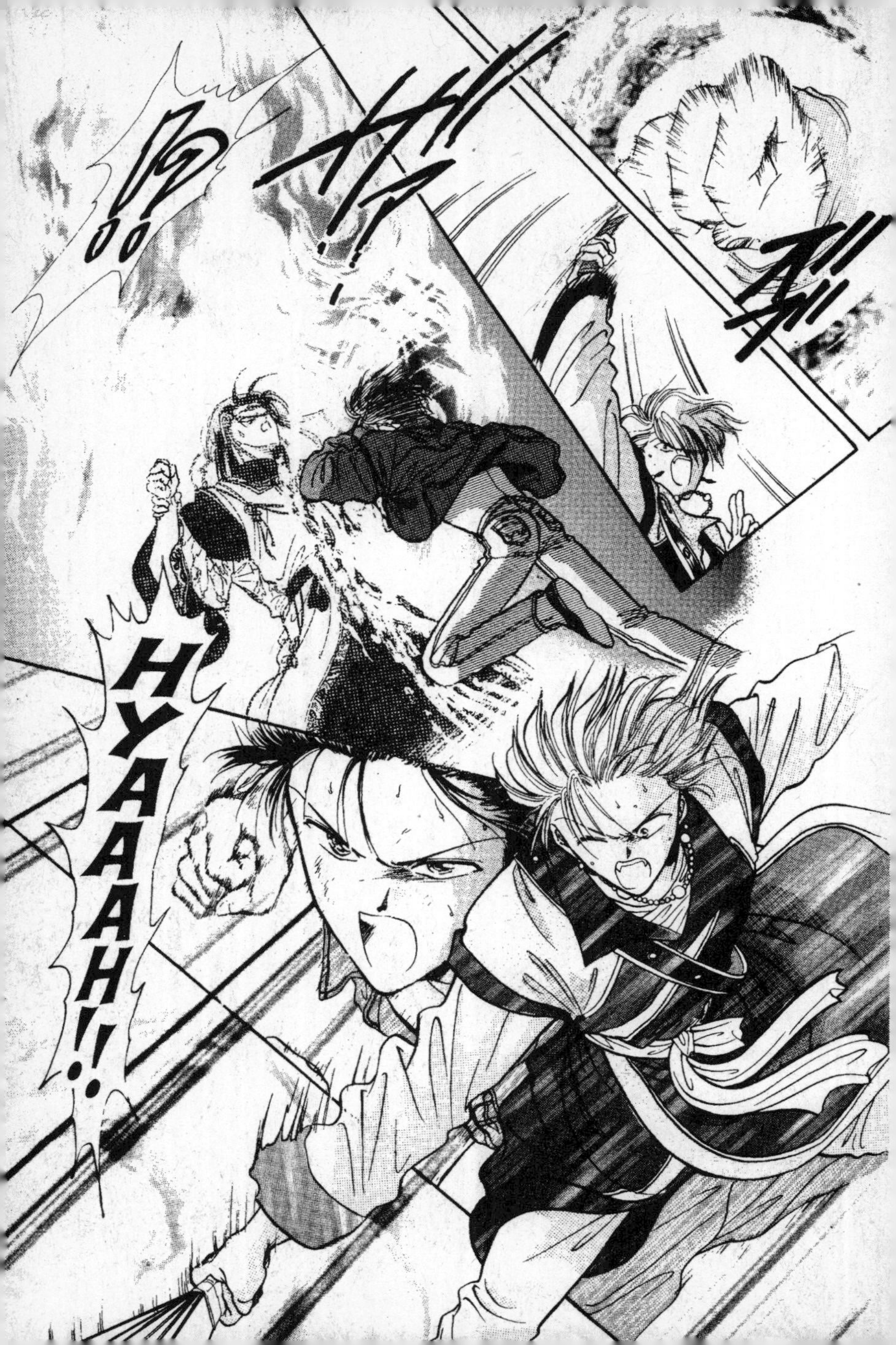
!?
HYAAAAH!!

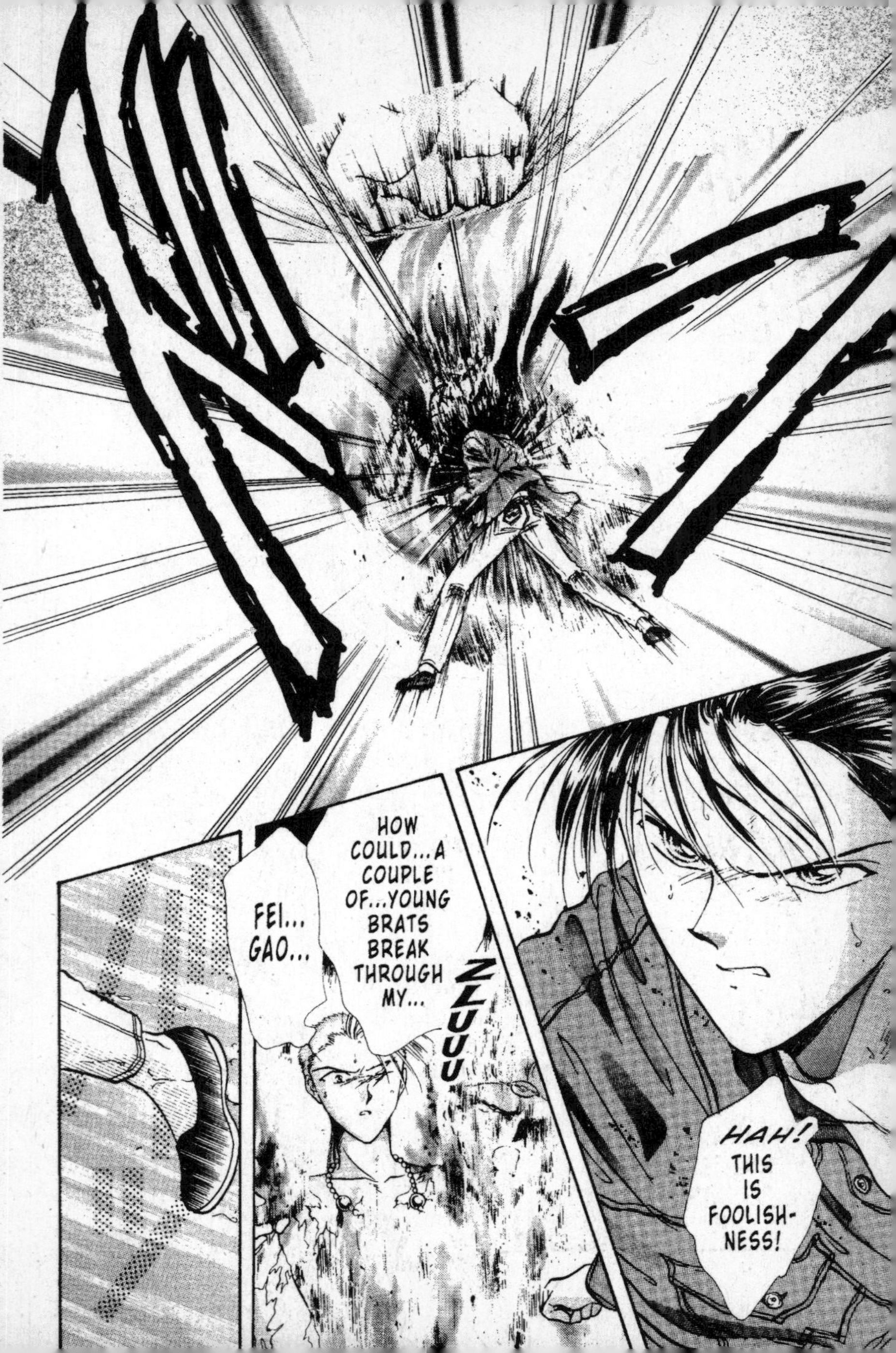
HAH! THIS IS FOOLISH-NESS!
HOW COULD...A COUPLE OF...YOUNG BRATS BREAK THROUGH MY...
ZLUUUU
FEI... GAO...

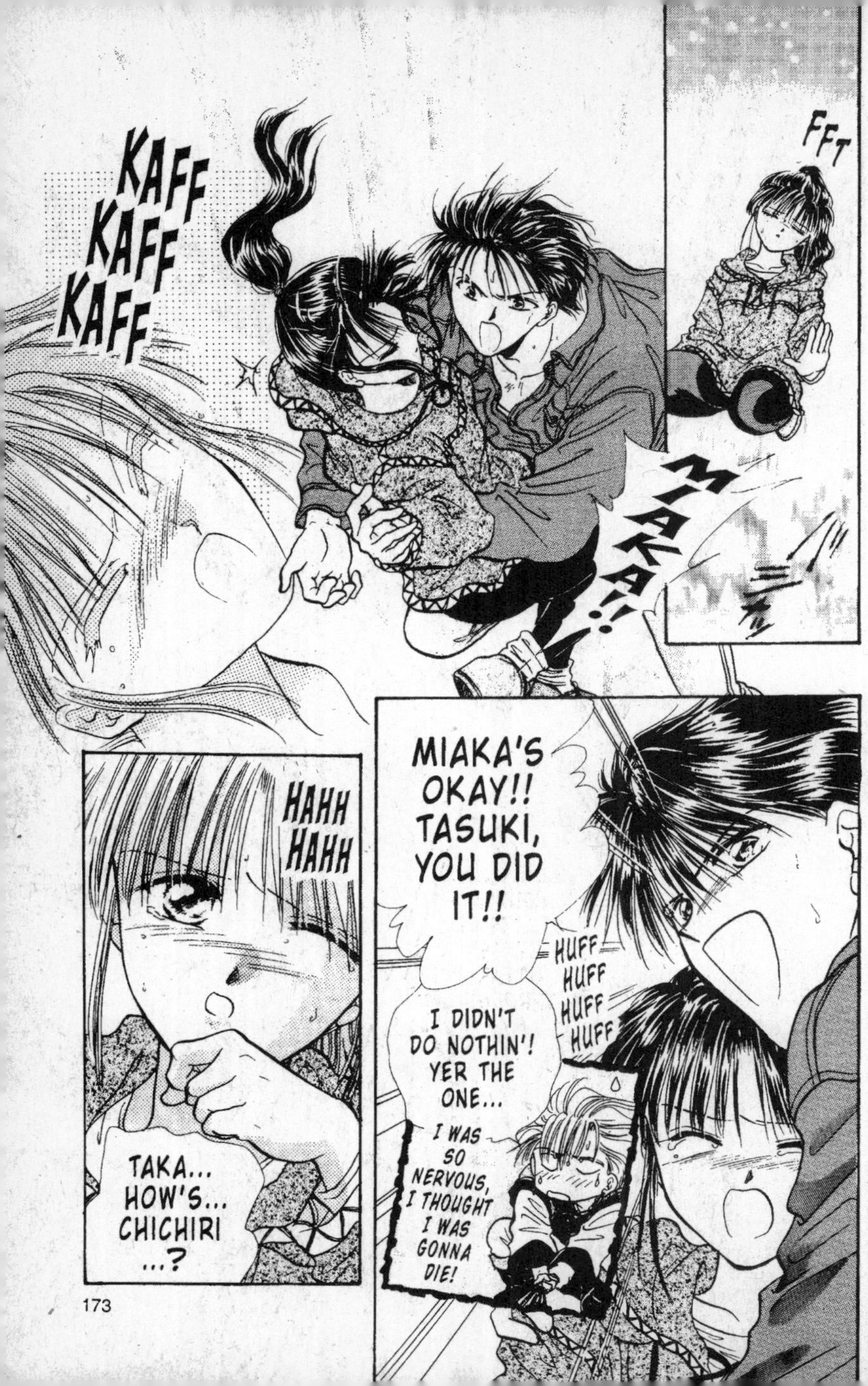
FFT
MIAKA!!
KAFF KAFF KAFF
MIAKA'S OKAY!! TASUKI, YOU DID IT!!
HUFF HUFF HUFF HUFF
I DIDN'T DO NOTHIN'! YER THE ONE...
I WAS SO NERVOUS, I THOUGHT I WAS GONNA DIE!
HAHH HAHH
TAKA... HOW'S... CHICHIRI ...?

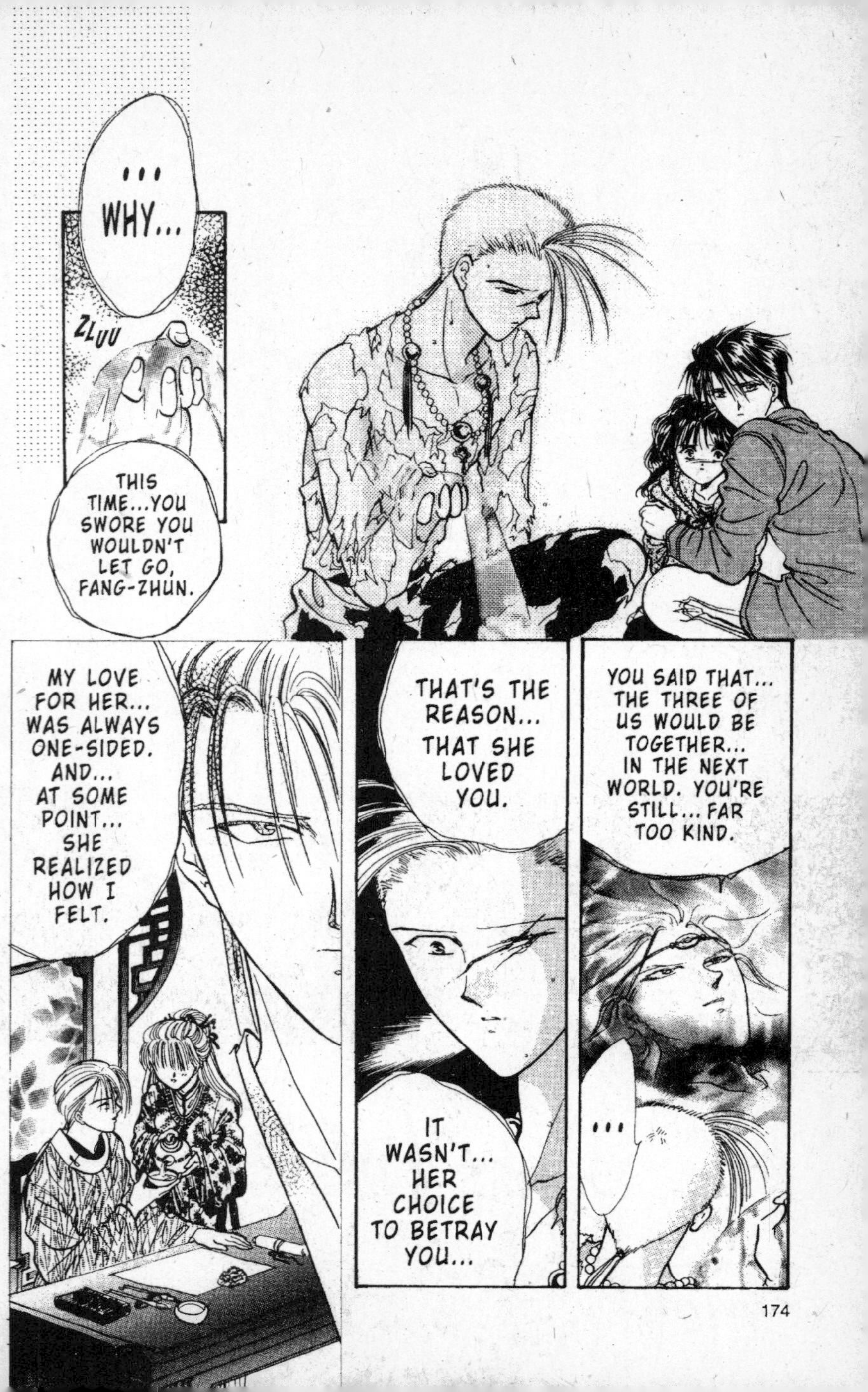
... WHY...
ZLUU
THIS TIME...YOU SWORE YOU WOULDN'T LET GO, FANG-ZHUN.
YOU SAID THAT... THE THREE OF US WOULD BE TOGETHER... IN THE NEXT WORLD. YOU'RE STILL... FAR TOO KIND.
...
THAT'S THE REASON... THAT SHE LOVED YOU.
IT WASN'T... HER CHOICE TO BETRAY YOU...
MY LOVE FOR HER... WAS ALWAYS ONE-SIDED. AND... AT SOME POINT... SHE REALIZED HOW I FELT.

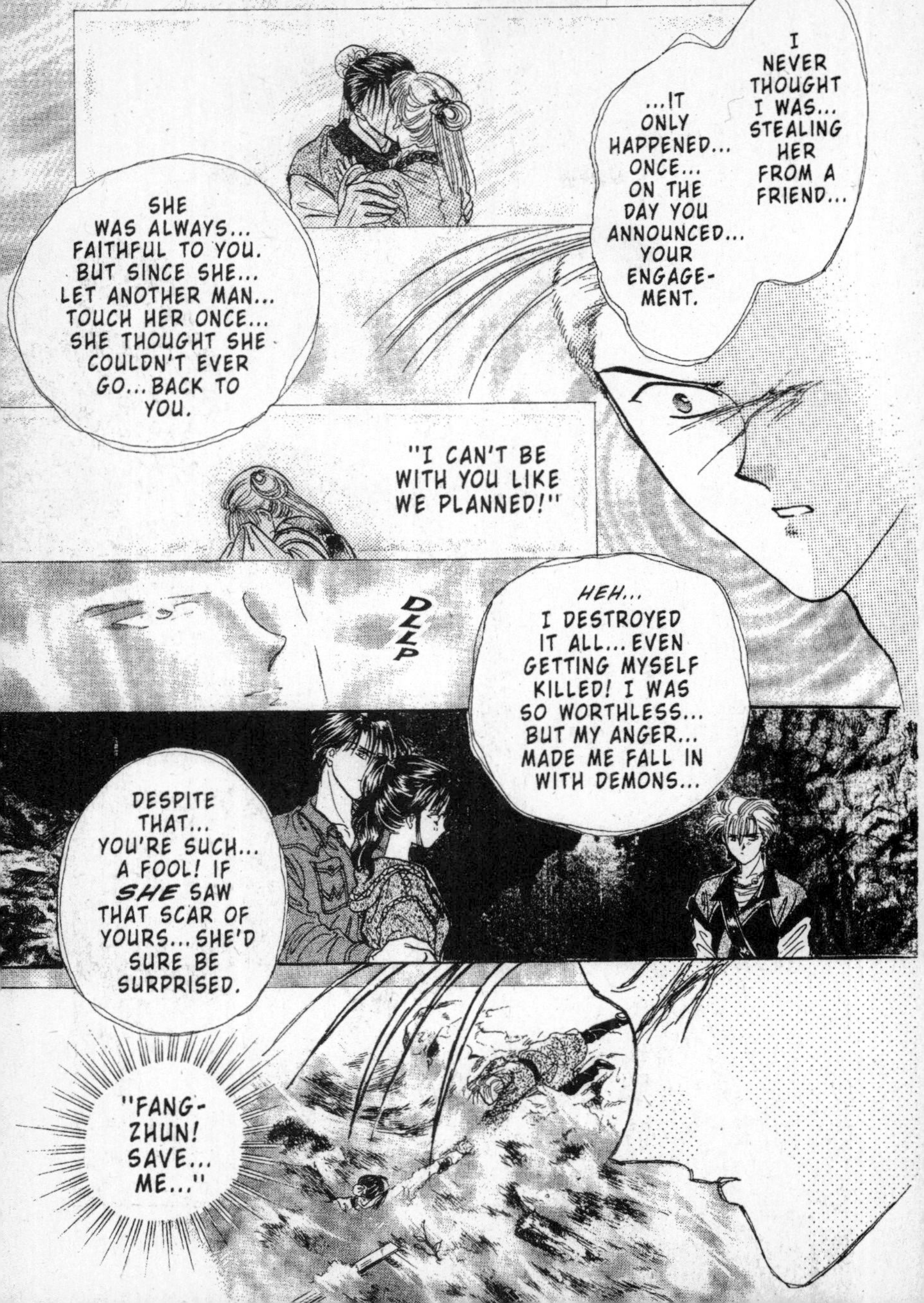
I NEVER THOUGHT I WAS... STEALING HER FROM A FRIEND...
...IT ONLY HAPPENED... ONCE... ON THE DAY YOU ANNOUNCED... YOUR ENGAGE-MENT.
SHE WAS ALWAYS... FAITHFUL TO YOU. BUT SINCE SHE... LET ANOTHER MAN... TOUCH HER ONCE... SHE THOUGHT SHE COULDN'T EVER GO... BACK TO YOU.
"I CAN'T BE WITH YOU LIKE WE PLANNED!"
DLLP
HEH... I DESTROYED IT ALL... EVEN GETTING MYSELF KILLED! I WAS SO WORTHLESS... BUT MY ANGER... MADE ME FALL IN WITH DEMONS...
DESPITE THAT... YOU'RE SUCH... A FOOL! IF SHE SAW THAT SCAR OF YOURS... SHE'D SURE BE SURPRISED.
"FANG-ZHUN! SAVE... ME..."

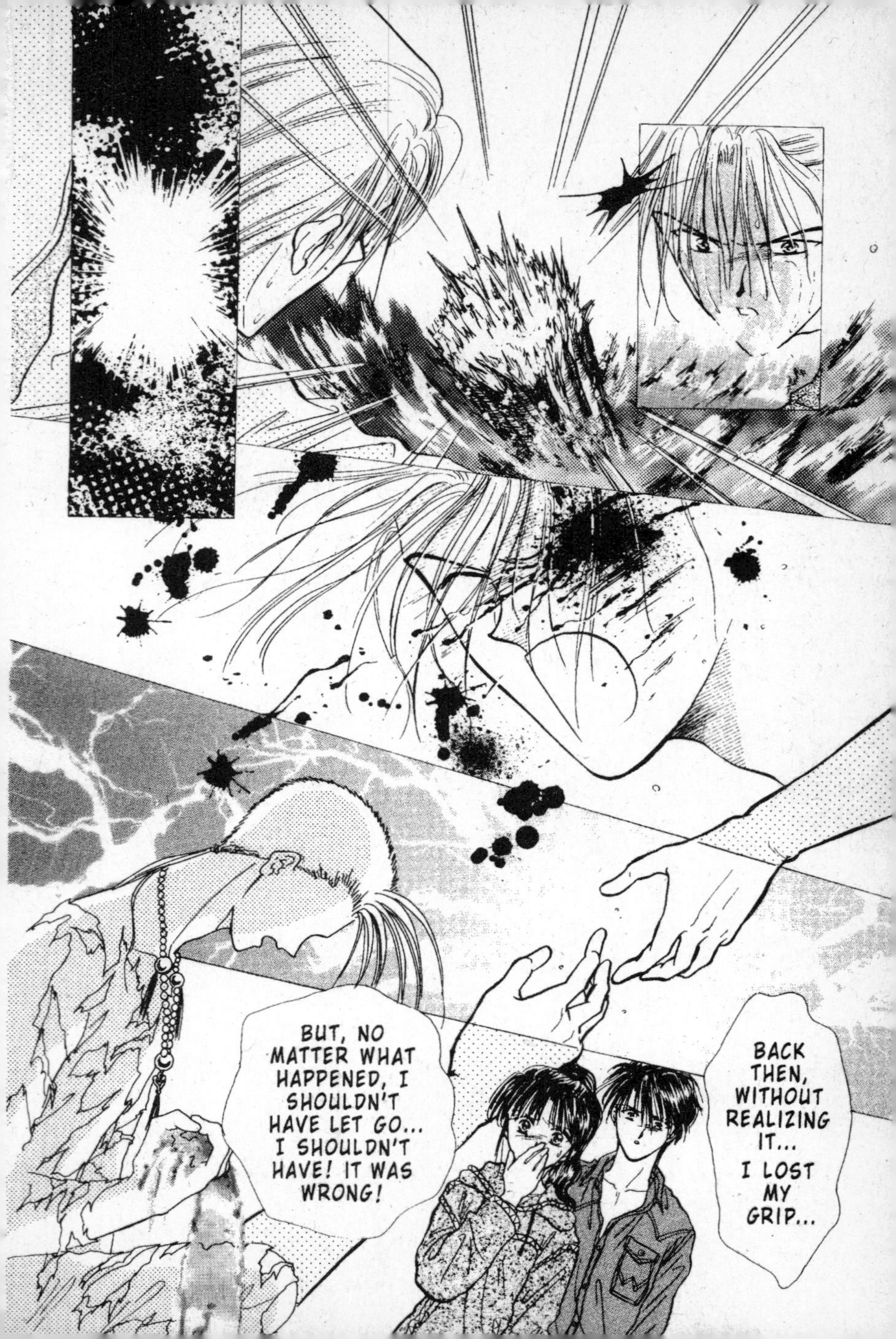
BACK THEN, WITHOUT REALIZING IT... I LOST MY GRIP...
BUT, NO MATTER WHAT HAPPENED, I SHOULDN'T HAVE LET GO... I SHOULDN'T HAVE! IT WAS WRONG!

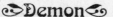

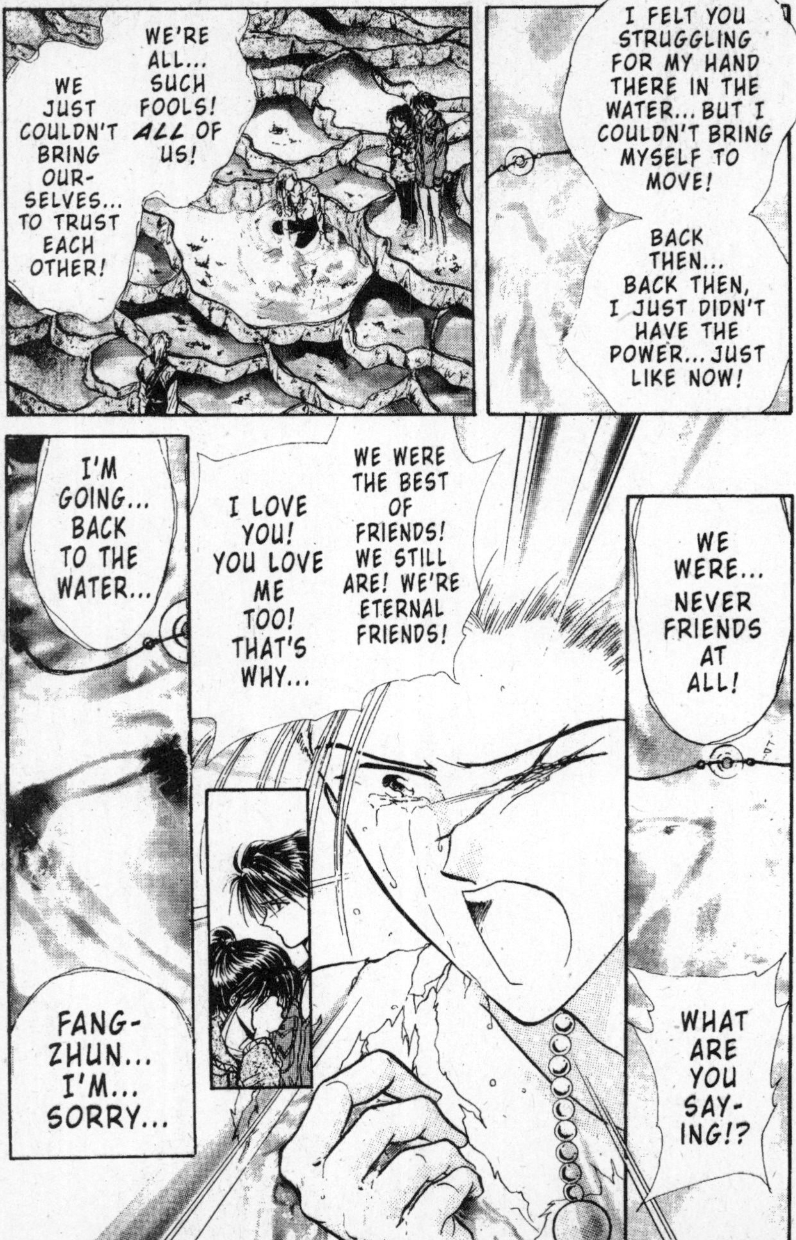
I FELT YOU STRUGGLING FOR MY HAND THERE IN THE WATER... BUT I COULDN'T BRING MYSELF TO MOVE!
BACK THEN... BACK THEN, I JUST DIDN'T HAVE THE POWER... JUST LIKE NOW!
WE'RE ALL... SUCH FOOLS! ALL OF US!
WE JUST COULDN'T BRING OUR-SELVES... TO TRUST EACH OTHER!
WE WERE... NEVER FRIENDS AT ALL!
WHAT ARE YOU SAY-ING!?
WE WERE THE BEST OF FRIENDS! WE STILL ARE! WE'RE ETERNAL FRIENDS!
I LOVE YOU! YOU LOVE ME TOO! THAT'S WHY...
I'M GOING... BACK TO THE WATER...
FANG-ZHUN... I'M... SORRY...

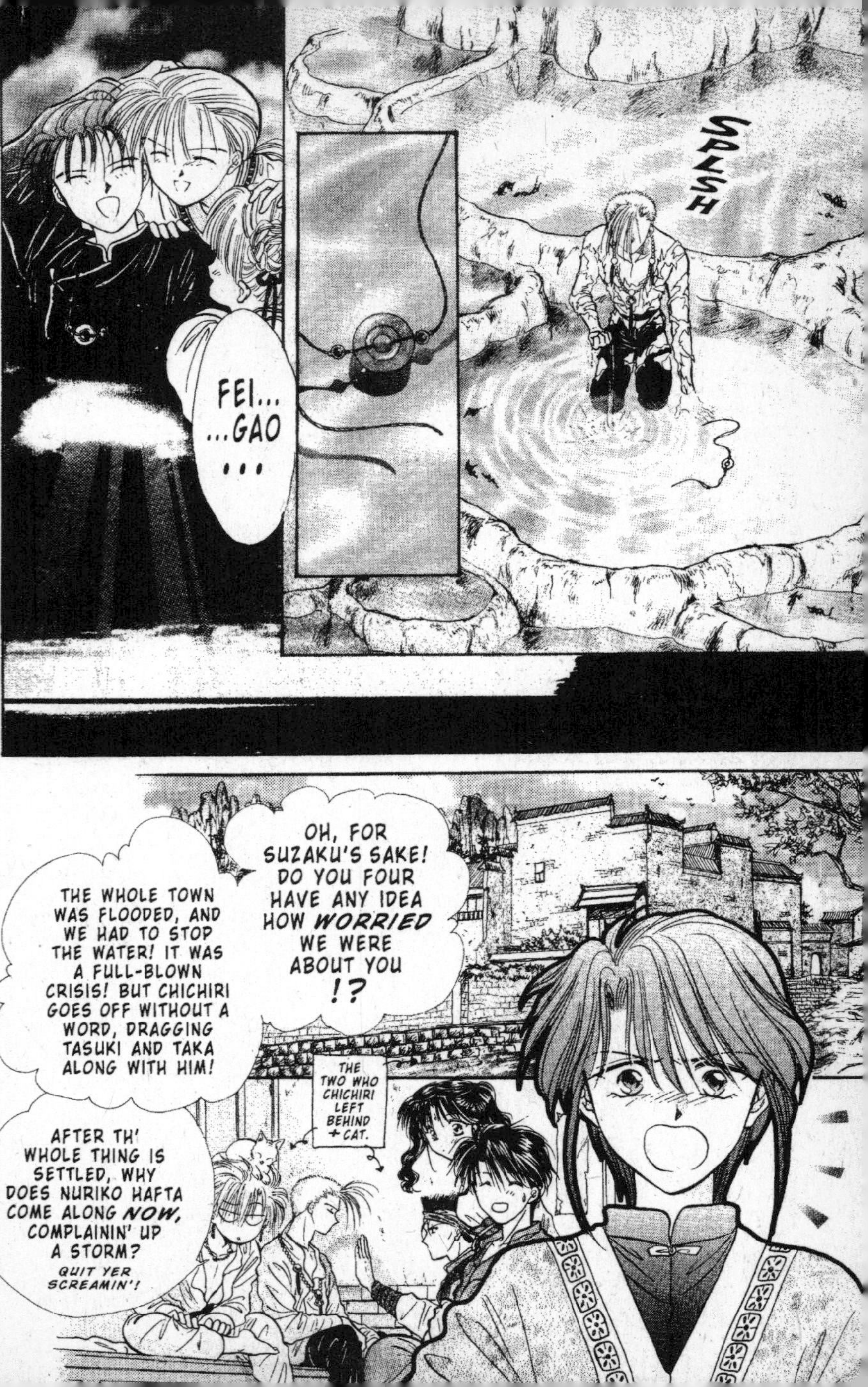
SPLSH
FEI... ...GAO ...
OH, FOR SUZAKU'S SAKE! DO YOU FOUR HAVE ANY IDEA HOW *WORRIED* WE WERE ABOUT YOU !?
THE WHOLE TOWN WAS FLOODED, AND WE HAD TO STOP THE WATER! IT WAS A FULL-BLOWN CRISIS! BUT CHICHIRI GOES OFF WITHOUT A WORD, DRAGGING TASUKI AND TAKA ALONG WITH HIM!
THE TWO WHO CHICHIRI LEFT BEHIND + CAT.
AFTER TH' WHOLE THING IS SETTLED, WHY DOES NURIKO HAFTA COME ALONG *NOW*, COMPLAININ' UP A STORM?
QUIT YER SCREAMIN'!

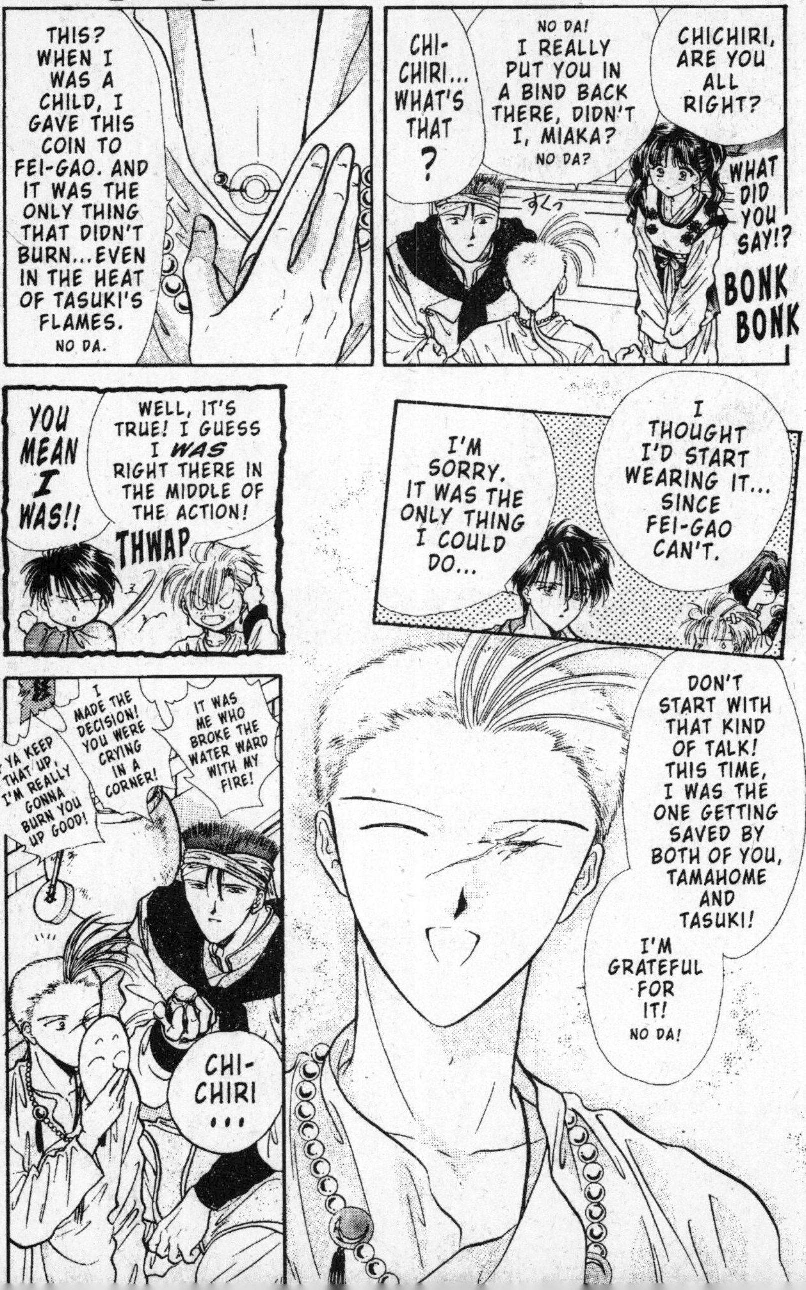
CHICHIRI, ARE YOU ALL RIGHT?
NO DA! I REALLY PUT YOU IN A BIND BACK THERE, DIDN'T I, MIAKA? NO DA?
CHI-CHIRI... WHAT'S THAT ?
すくっ
WHAT DID YOU SAY!?
BONK BONK
THIS? WHEN I WAS A CHILD, I GAVE THIS COIN TO FEI-GAO. AND IT WAS THE ONLY THING THAT DIDN'T BURN...EVEN IN THE HEAT OF TASUKI'S FLAMES. NO DA.
I THOUGHT I'D START WEARING IT... SINCE FEI-GAO CAN'T.
I'M SORRY. IT WAS THE ONLY THING I COULD DO...
WELL, IT'S TRUE! I GUESS I WAS RIGHT THERE IN THE MIDDLE OF THE ACTION!
YOU MEAN I WAS!!
THWAP
DON'T START WITH THAT KIND OF TALK! THIS TIME, I WAS THE ONE GETTING SAVED BY BOTH OF YOU, TAMAHOME AND TASUKI!
I'M GRATEFUL FOR IT! NO DA!
IT WAS ME WHO BROKE THE WATER WARD WITH MY FIRE!
I MADE THE DECISION! YOU WERE CRYING IN A CORNER!
IF YA KEEP THAT UP, I'M REALLY GONNA BURN YOU UP GOOD!
CHI-CHIRI ...

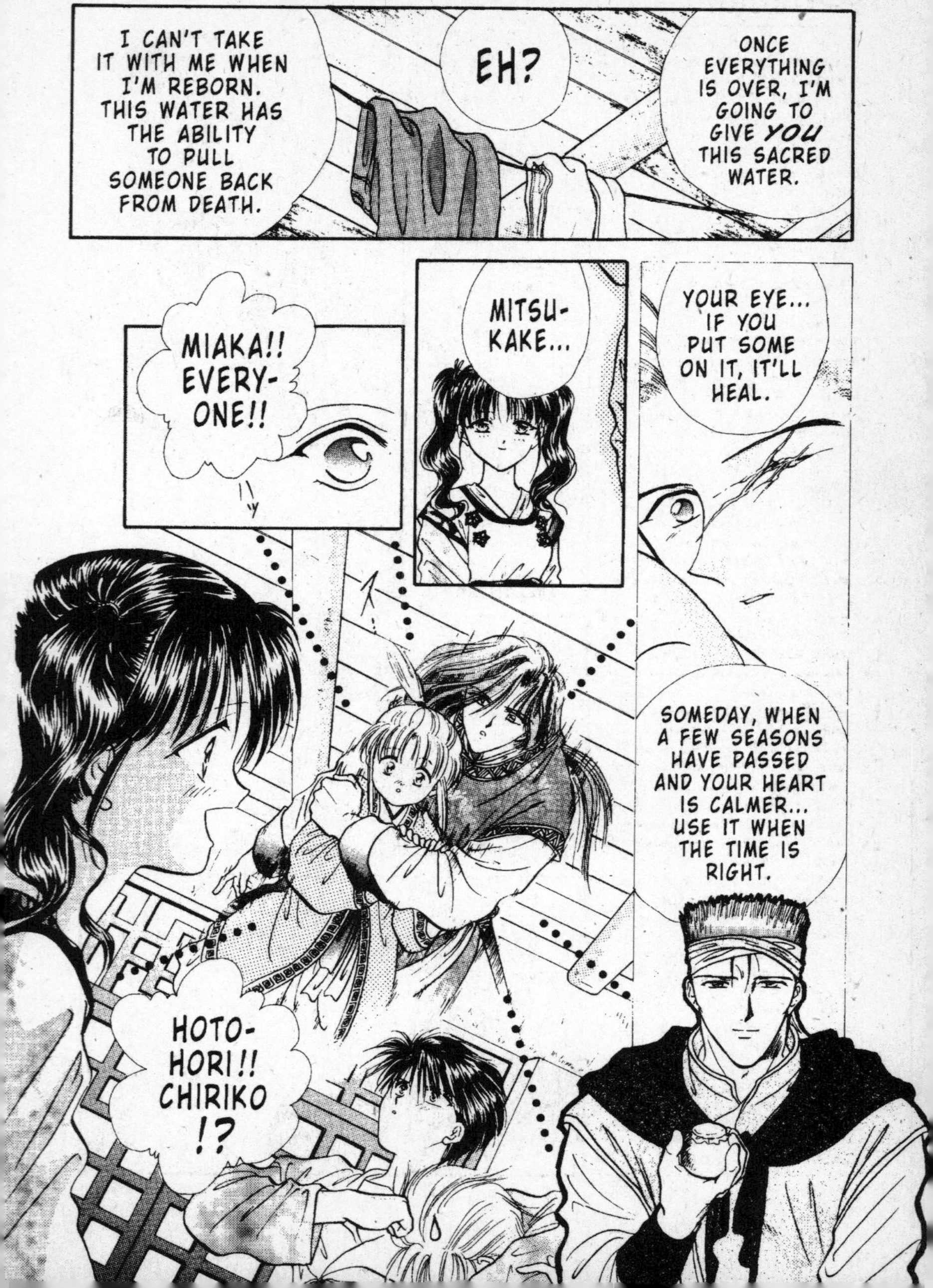
ONCE EVERYTHING IS OVER, I'M GOING TO GIVE YOU THIS SACRED WATER.
EH?
I CAN'T TAKE IT WITH ME WHEN I'M REBORN. THIS WATER HAS THE ABILITY TO PULL SOMEONE BACK FROM DEATH.
YOUR EYE... IF YOU PUT SOME ON IT, IT'LL HEAL.
SOMEDAY, WHEN A FEW SEASONS HAVE PASSED AND YOUR HEART IS CALMER... USE IT WHEN THE TIME IS RIGHT.
MITSU-KAKE...
MIAKA!! EVERY-ONE!!
HOTO-HORI!! CHIRIKO !?

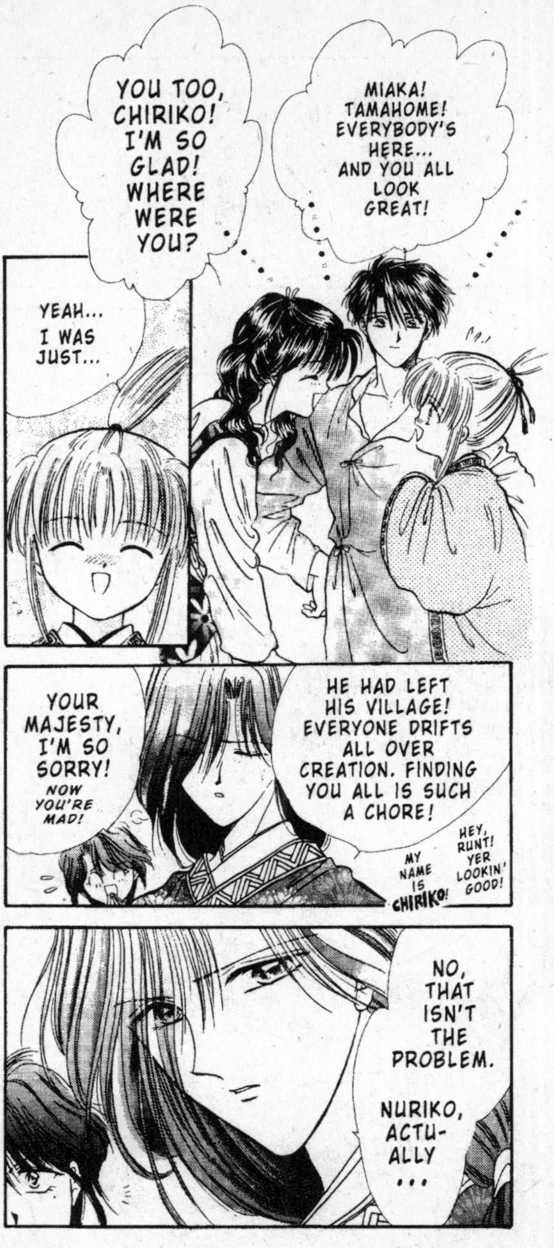
MIAKA! TAMAHOME! EVERYBODY'S HERE... AND YOU ALL LOOK GREAT!
YOU TOO, CHIRIKO! I'M SO GLAD! WHERE WERE YOU?
YEAH... I WAS JUST...
HE HAD LEFT HIS VILLAGE! EVERYONE DRIFTS ALL OVER CREATION. FINDING YOU ALL IS SUCH A CHORE!
HEY, RUNT! YER LOOKIN' GOOD!
MY NAME IS CHIRIKO!
YOUR MAJESTY, I'M SO SORRY!
NOW YOU'RE MAD!
NO, THAT ISN'T THE PROBLEM.
NURIKO, ACTU-ALLY...

Demon

One of my assistants saw Chichiri unconscious and said, "Big brother's passed out!!" ☺ It's what made the rest of the "family" (Miaka and the warriors) realize just how valuable he is. Well, everybody comments on how they all resemble a family. (But at first glance, Mitsukake seems like the eldest brother -- or maybe the father!) ☺
Mitsukake had a small but good part to play this time.
Assistant H said, "Mitchi was so cool!" when he rescued Tasuki, but actually I think she was paying closer attention to Chichiri.
There are so many scenes in this volume that I just love! But the scene where Chichiri ruffled up Tasuki's hair (p. 154) is among my absolute favorites! I think that is where Chichiri is the coolest character! "Big brother!!" *I'm going to start calling him that, too!* ☺ Tasuki is so tall, but he still acts like a child. From volume 14 on, I'm sure there are people following each character, but in Part Two, you can see how I've reached the pinnacle of my love for these characters. ☺ Even if they don't have much of a part in the story, that doesn't mean that my love for them is any less! *Ah, how I love Chiriko! Nuriko, too!* It's true that Nuriko showed just how cool a character can be up until volume 8, so for this time I wanted to draw "Childlike Nuriko" a little! The relationship of Lu-Hou to Nuriko was the same as Nuriko's to Kang-Lin, right? I tried to make that clear in the drawings. Hotohori affirmed his love for his child, wife, and himself. Mitsukake finally was able to save the life of each warrior. Tasuki and Taka fired up their friendship. (Actually Taka is a fan of Tasuki. Once again it was an assistant who said, "In that scene where he nodded to Tasuki, Taka was seeing his father there." Oh, come on! At least say, "big brother"!) And Chichiri, who was saved by the two of them, is also happy from the bottom of his "big brother" heart. And finally there's Chiriko. Go to it, Chi-ri-ko!! You too, Miaka and Taka! Your final trials are almost here! *Since we're nearing the end.*
Now... Will "love"... I mean... "The Human Race" win the day? Everything depends on what's inside your heart!!
So, I'll see you all in volume 18!

96.3/3

I always wanted to have a fight scene where the two of them act as a combo!

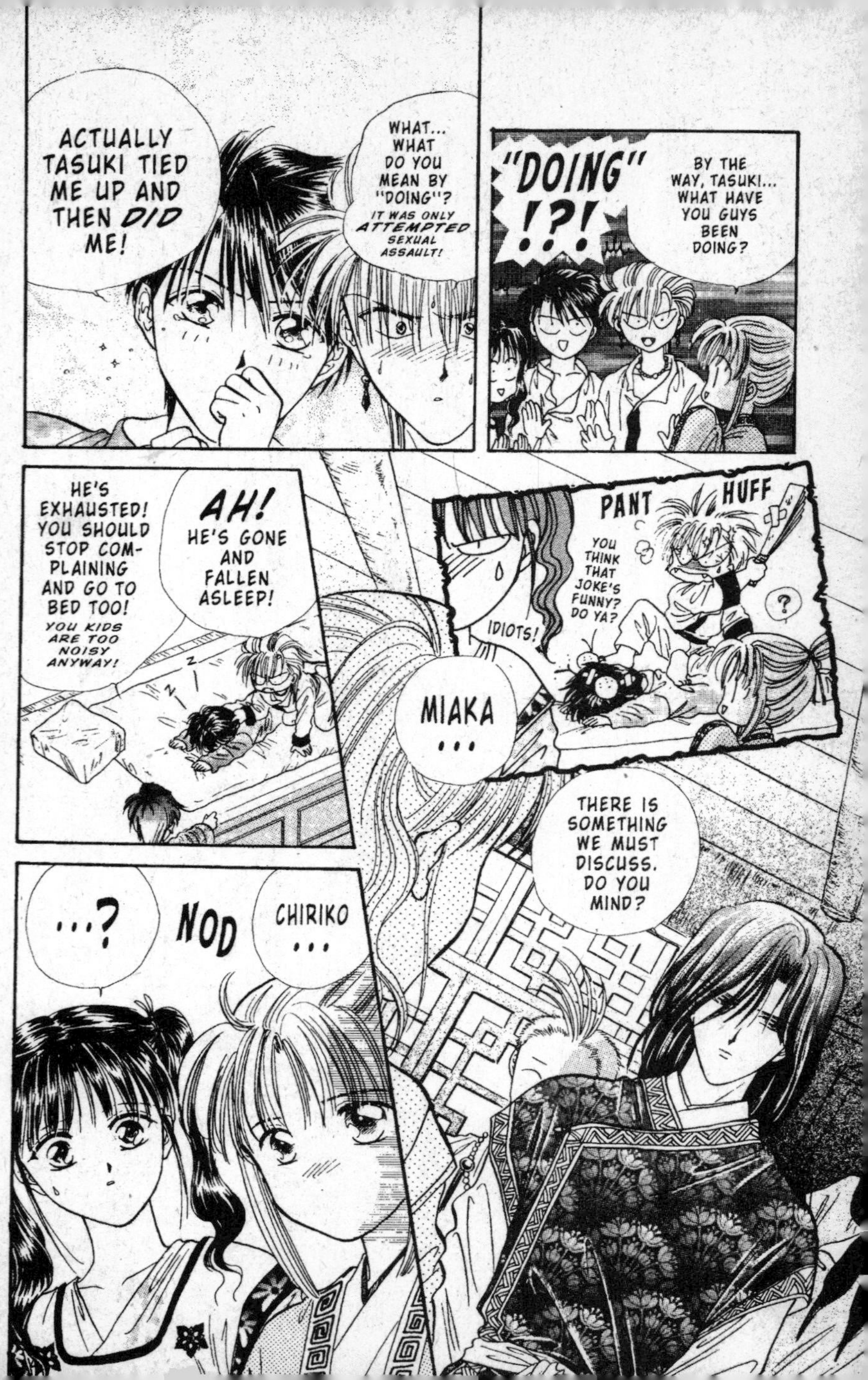
BY THE WAY, TASUKI... WHAT HAVE YOU GUYS BEEN DOING?
"DOING" !?!
ACTUALLY TASUKI TIED ME UP AND THEN DID ME!
WHAT... WHAT DO YOU MEAN BY "DOING"? IT WAS ONLY ATTEMPTED SEXUAL ASSAULT!
PANT HUFF
YOU THINK THAT JOKE'S FUNNY? DO YA?
?
IDIOTS!
AH! HE'S GONE AND FALLEN ASLEEP!
HE'S EXHAUSTED! YOU SHOULD STOP COM-PLAINING AND GO TO BED TOO! YOU KIDS ARE TOO NOISY ANYWAY!
MIAKA ...
THERE IS SOMETHING WE MUST DISCUSS. DO YOU MIND?
CHIRIKO ...
NOD
...?

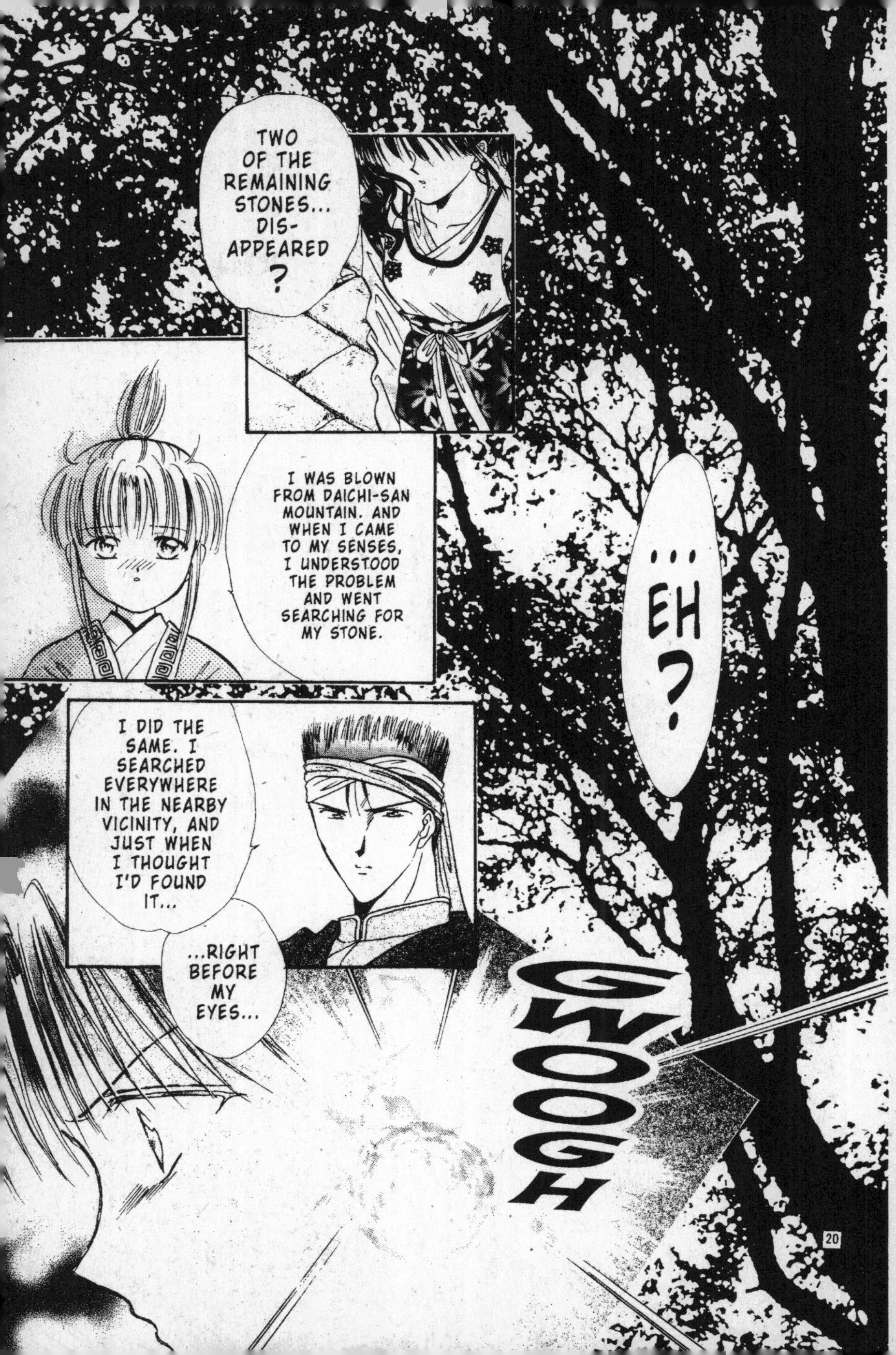
TWO OF THE REMAINING STONES... DIS-APPEARED?
...EH?
I WAS BLOWN FROM DAICHI-SAN MOUNTAIN. AND WHEN I CAME TO MY SENSES, I UNDERSTOOD THE PROBLEM AND WENT SEARCHING FOR MY STONE.
I DID THE SAME. I SEARCHED EVERYWHERE IN THE NEARBY VICINITY, AND JUST WHEN I THOUGHT I'D FOUND IT...
...RIGHT BEFORE MY EYES...
GWOOGH

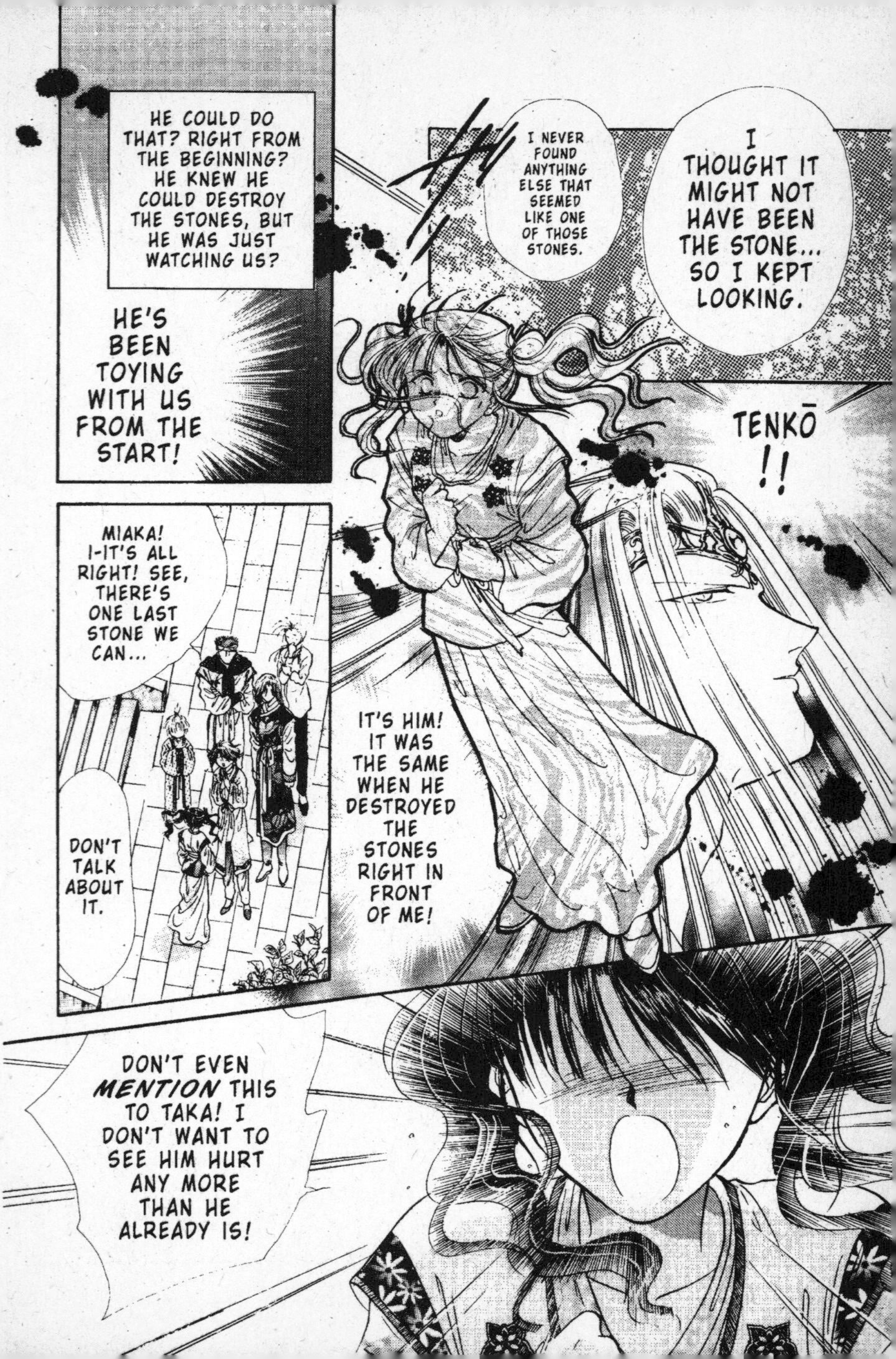
I THOUGHT IT MIGHT NOT HAVE BEEN THE STONE... SO I KEPT LOOKING.
I NEVER FOUND ANYTHING ELSE THAT SEEMED LIKE ONE OF THOSE STONES.
HE COULD DO THAT? RIGHT FROM THE BEGINNING? HE KNEW HE COULD DESTROY THE STONES, BUT HE WAS JUST WATCHING US?
HE'S BEEN TOYING WITH US FROM THE START!
TENKŌ !!
IT'S HIM! IT WAS THE SAME WHEN HE DESTROYED THE STONES RIGHT IN FRONT OF ME!
MIAKA! I-IT'S ALL RIGHT! SEE, THERE'S ONE LAST STONE WE CAN...
DON'T TALK ABOUT IT.
DON'T EVEN *MENTION* THIS TO TAKA! I DON'T WANT TO SEE HIM HURT ANY MORE THAN HE ALREADY IS!

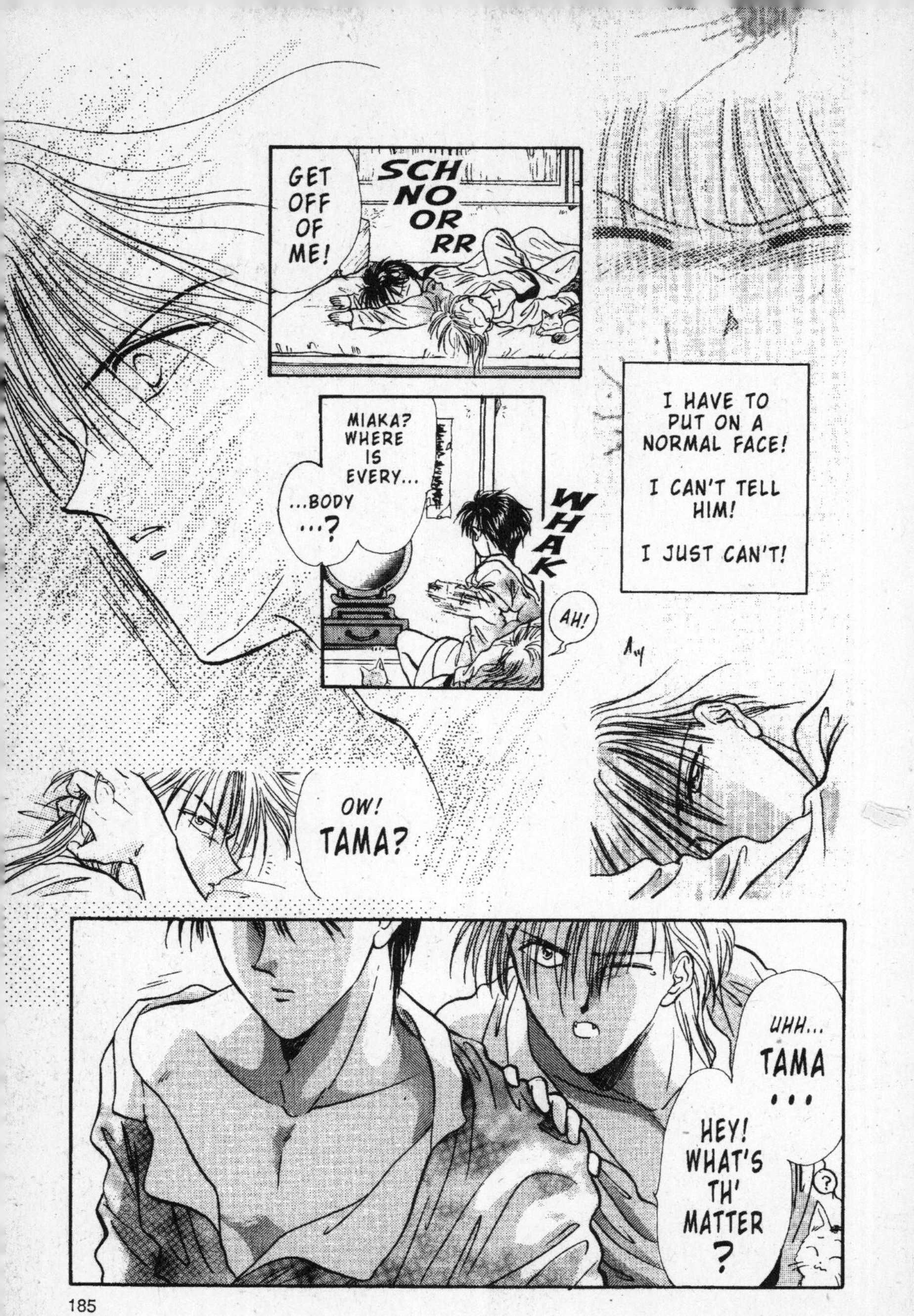
I HAVE TO PUT ON A NORMAL FACE!
I CAN'T TELL HIM!
I JUST CAN'T!
SCH NO OR RR
GET OFF OF ME!
WHAK
AH!
MIAKA? WHERE IS EVERY...
...BODY ...?
OW! TAMA?
UHH... TAMA ...
HEY! WHAT'S TH' MATTER ?

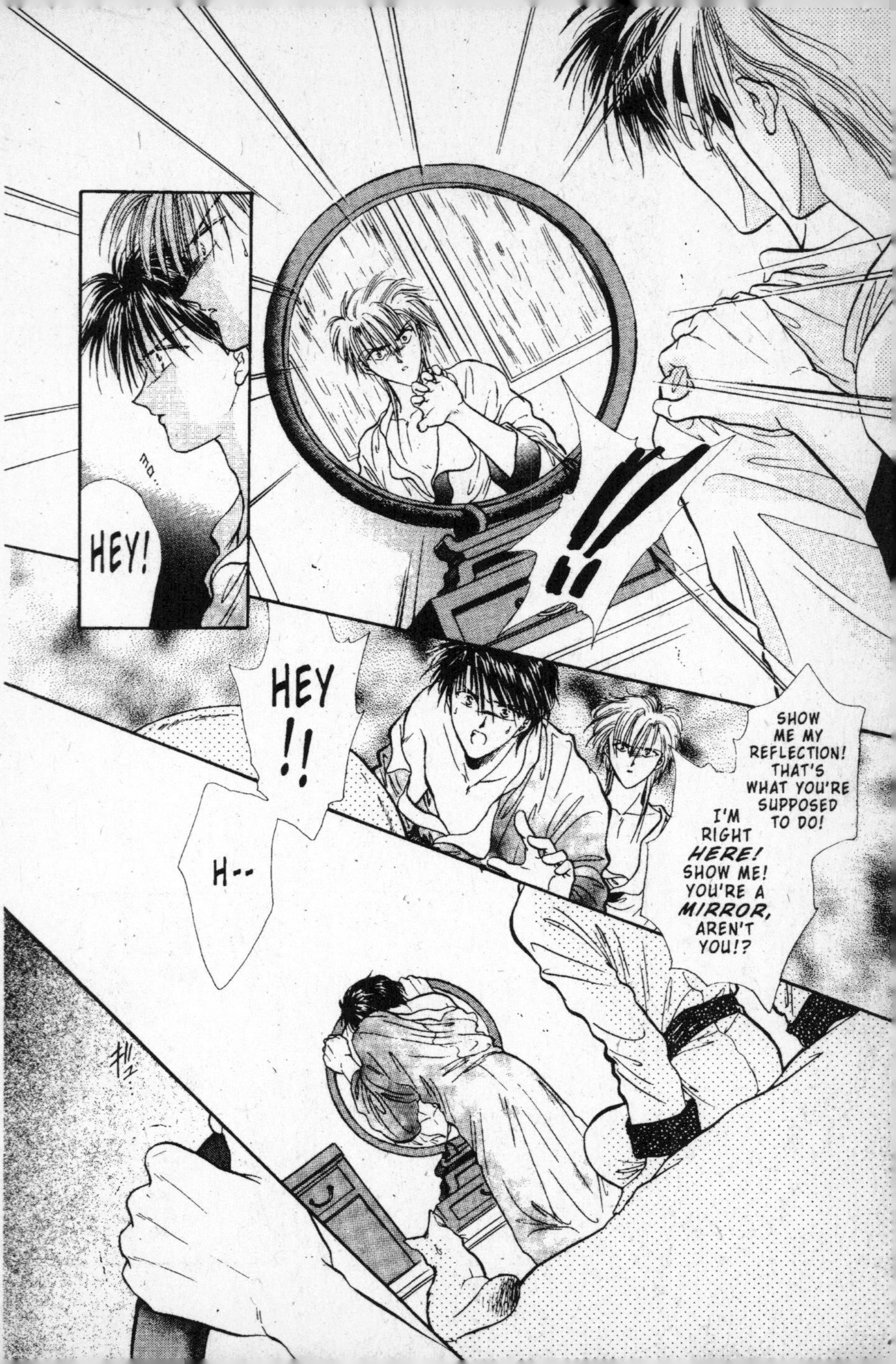
mo...
HEY!
SHOW ME MY REFLECTION! THAT'S WHAT YOU'RE SUPPOSED TO DO!
I'M RIGHT *HERE!* SHOW ME! YOU'RE A *MIRROR,* AREN'T YOU!?
HEY !!
H--

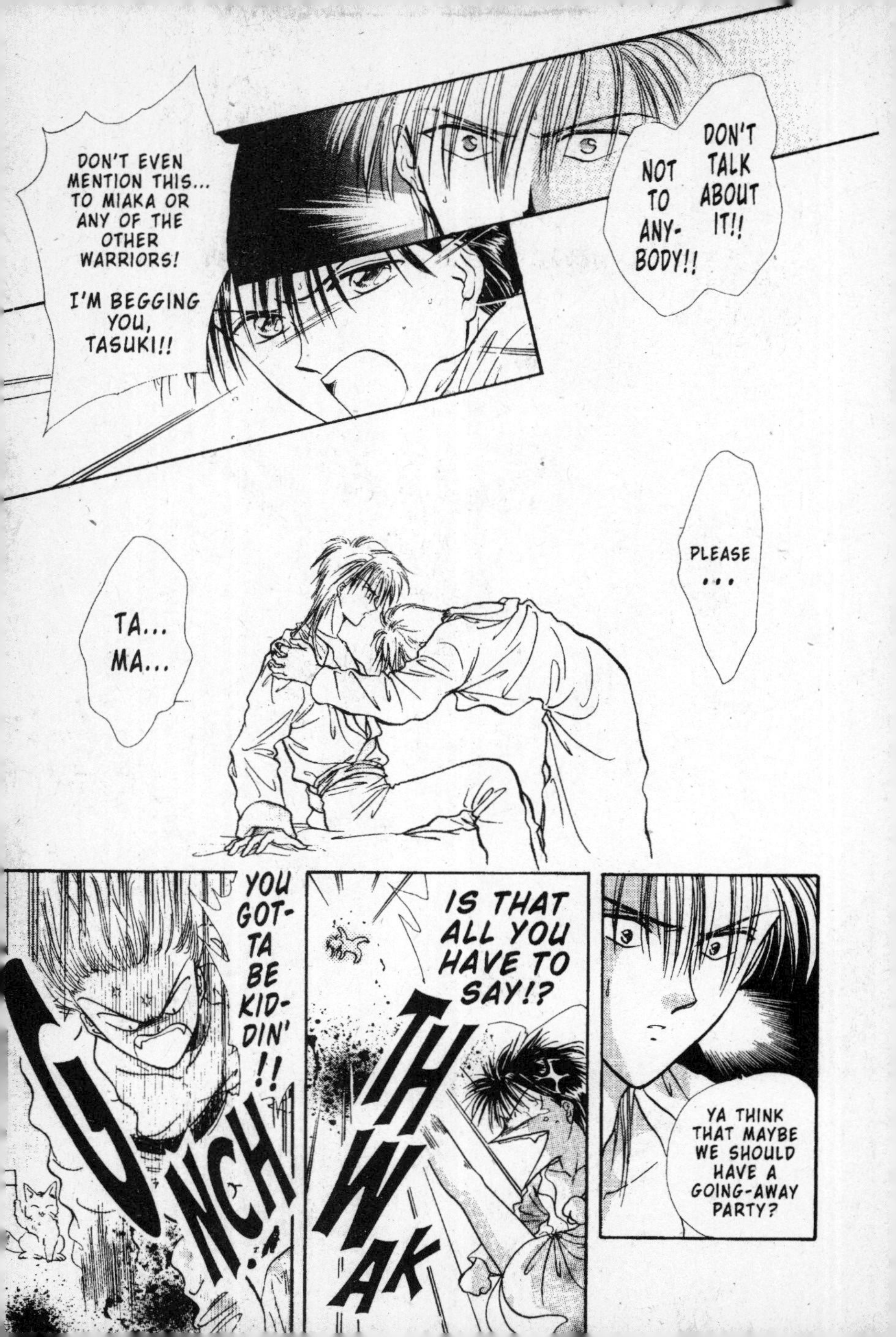
DON'T TALK ABOUT IT!! NOT TO ANY-BODY!!
DON'T EVEN MENTION THIS... TO MIAKA OR ANY OF THE OTHER WARRIORS!
I'M BEGGING YOU, TASUKI!!
PLEASE...
TA... MA...
YA THINK THAT MAYBE WE SHOULD HAVE A GOING-AWAY PARTY?
IS THAT ALL YOU HAVE TO SAY!?
THWAK
YOU GOT-TA BE KID-DIN'!!
NCH!

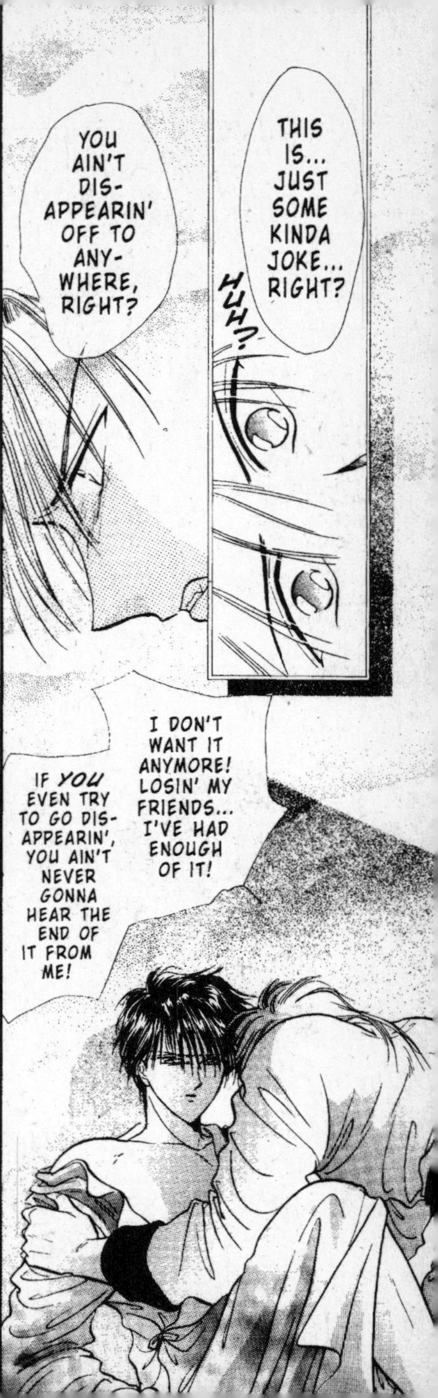
THIS IS... JUST SOME KINDA JOKE... RIGHT?
HUH?
YOU AIN'T DIS-APPEARIN' OFF TO ANY-WHERE, RIGHT?
I DON'T WANT IT ANYMORE! LOSIN' MY FRIENDS... I'VE HAD ENOUGH OF IT!
IF *YOU* EVEN TRY TO GO DIS-APPEARIN', YOU AIN'T NEVER GONNA HEAR THE END OF IT FROM ME!

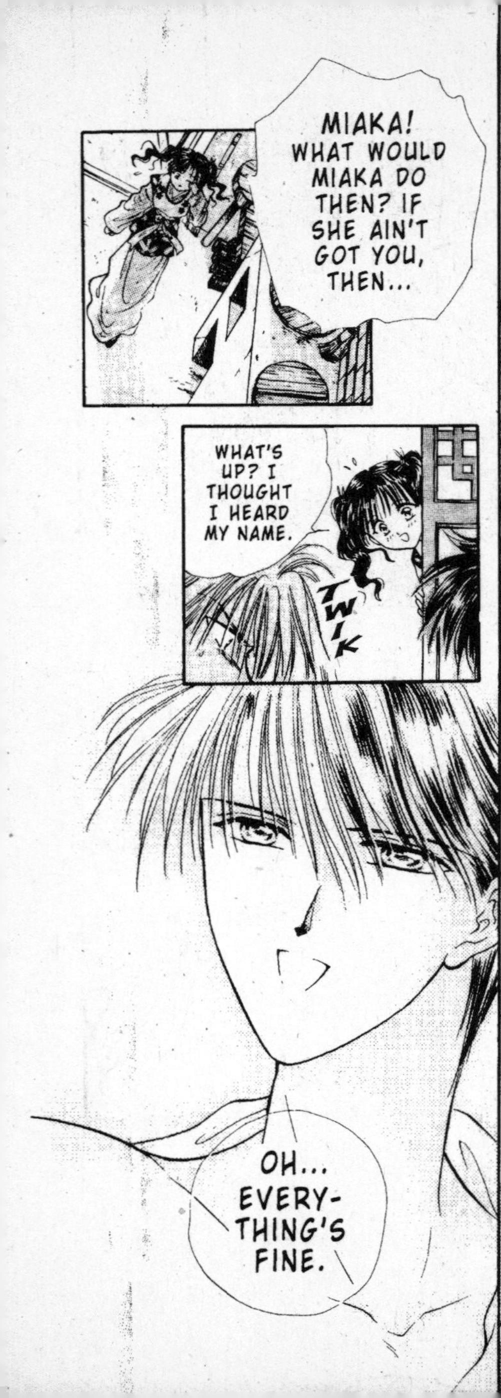
MIAKA! WHAT WOULD MIAKA DO THEN? IF SHE AIN'T GOT YOU, THEN...
WHAT'S UP? I THOUGHT I HEARD MY NAME.
TWIK
OH... EVERY-THING'S FINE.

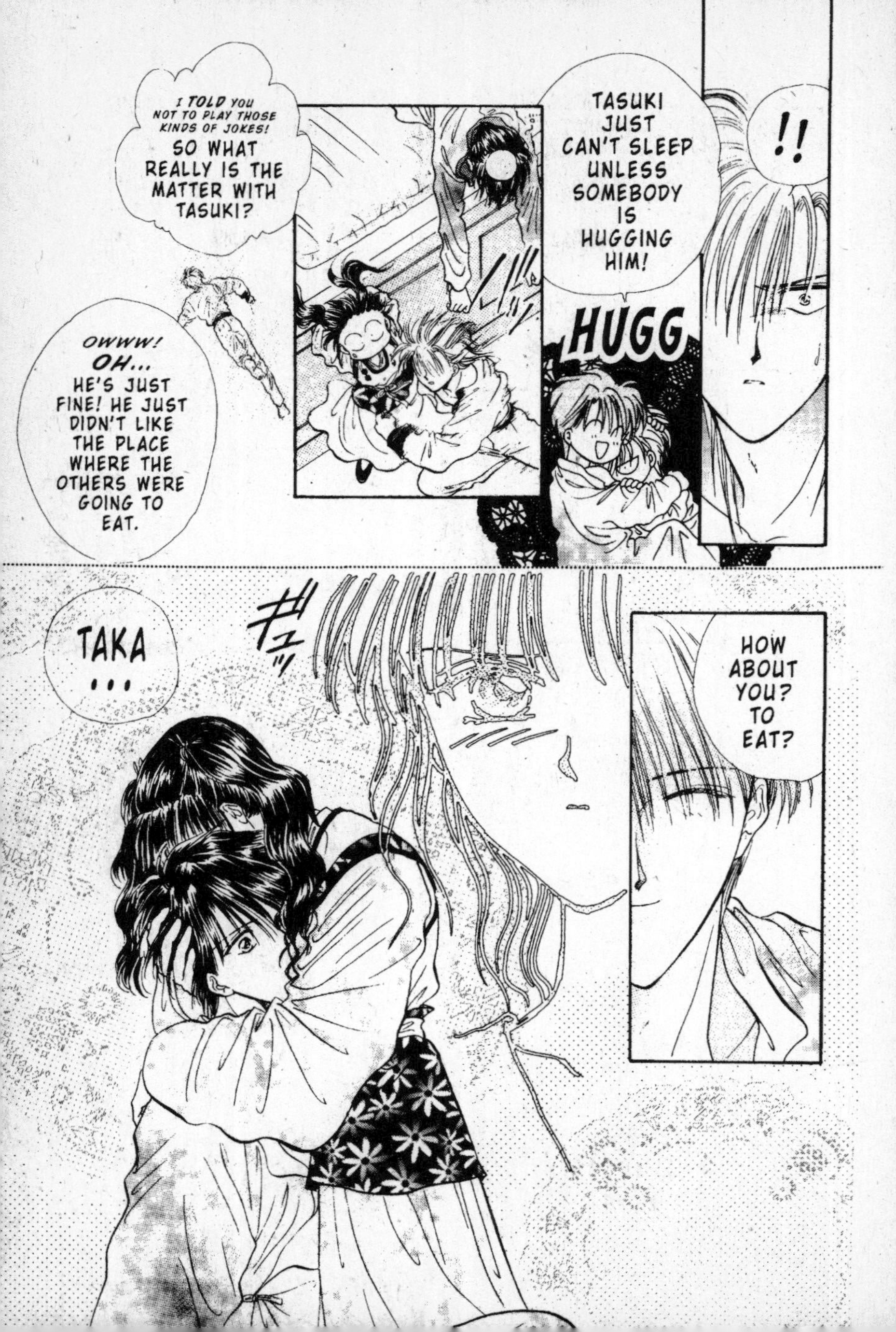
!!
TASUKI JUST CAN'T SLEEP UNLESS SOMEBODY IS HUGGING HIM!
HUGG
I TOLD you not to play those kinds of jokes! SO WHAT REALLY IS THE MATTER WITH TASUKI?
OWWW! OH... HE'S JUST FINE! HE JUST DIDN'T LIKE THE PLACE WHERE THE OTHERS WERE GOING TO EAT.
HOW ABOUT YOU? TO EAT?
TAKA ...

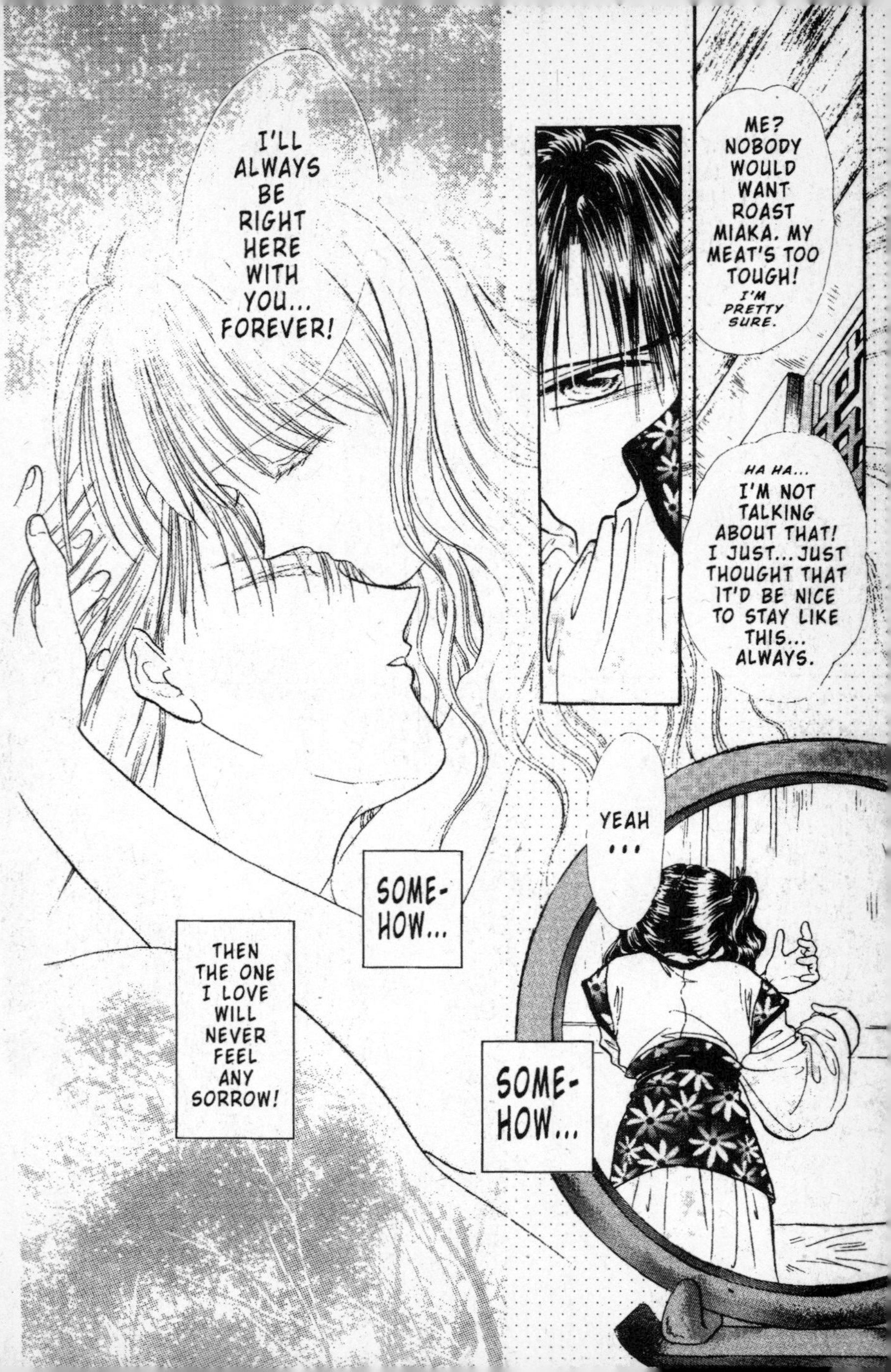
ME? NOBODY WOULD WANT ROAST MIAKA. MY MEAT'S TOO TOUGH!
I'M PRETTY SURE.
HA HA... I'M NOT TALKING ABOUT THAT! I JUST... JUST THOUGHT THAT IT'D BE NICE TO STAY LIKE THIS... ALWAYS.
YEAH...
SOME-HOW...
I'LL ALWAYS BE RIGHT HERE WITH YOU... FOREVER!
SOME-HOW...
THEN THE ONE I LOVE WILL NEVER FEEL ANY SORROW!

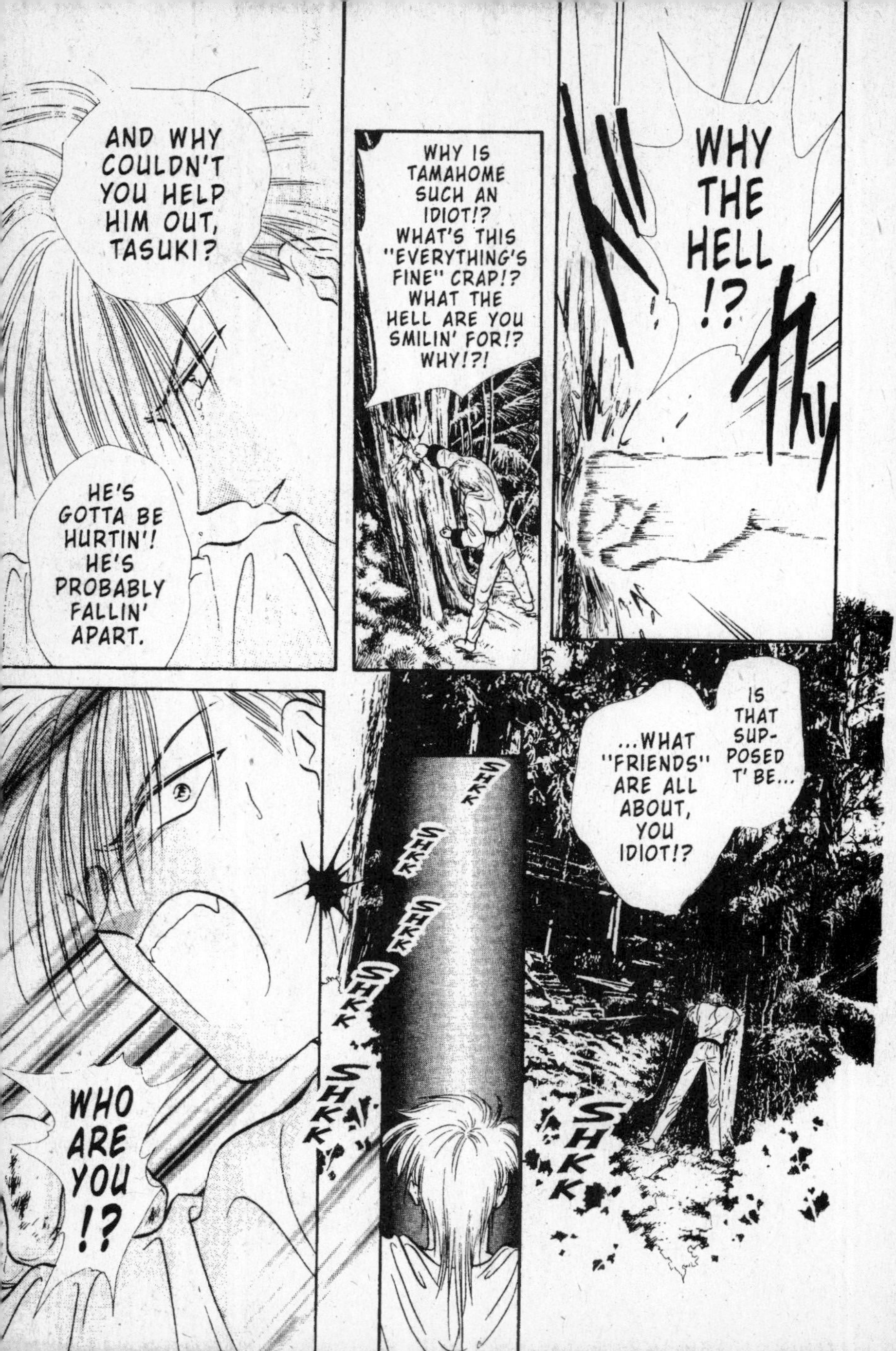
WHY THE HELL!?
WHY IS TAMAHOME SUCH AN IDIOT!? WHAT'S THIS "EVERYTHING'S FINE" CRAP!? WHAT THE HELL ARE YOU SMILIN' FOR!? WHY!?!
AND WHY COULDN'T YOU HELP HIM OUT, TASUKI?
HE'S GOTTA BE HURTIN'! HE'S PROBABLY FALLIN' APART.
IS THAT SUP-POSED T' BE...
...WHAT "FRIENDS" ARE ALL ABOUT, YOU IDIOT!?
SHKK
SHKK
SHKK
SHKK
SHKK
SHKK
SHKK
WHO ARE YOU!?

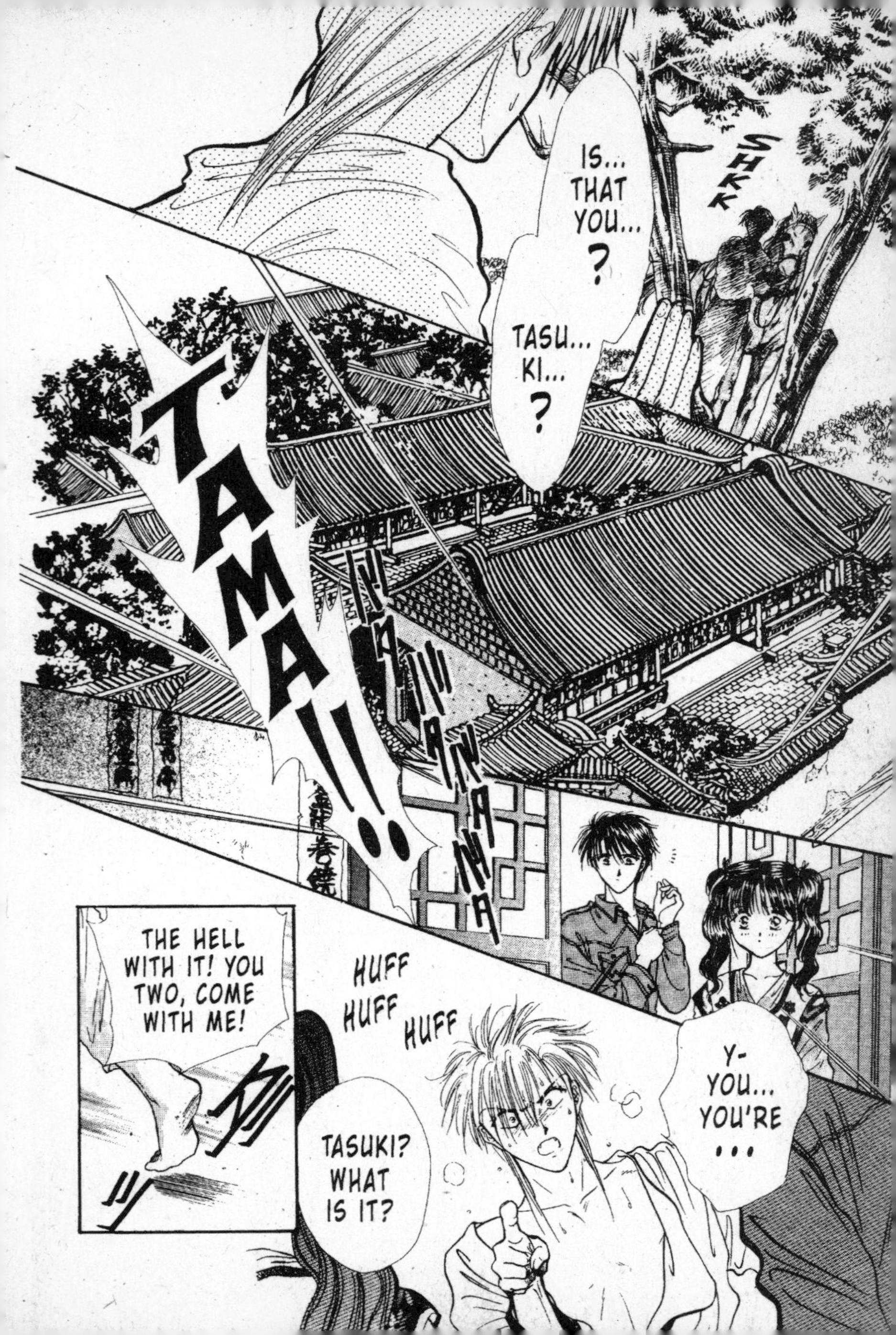
IS... THAT YOU...?
TASU... KI...?
SHKK
TAMA!!!
Y- YOU... YOU'RE...
TASUKI? WHAT IS IT?
HUFF HUFF HUFF
THE HELL WITH IT! YOU TWO, COME WITH ME!

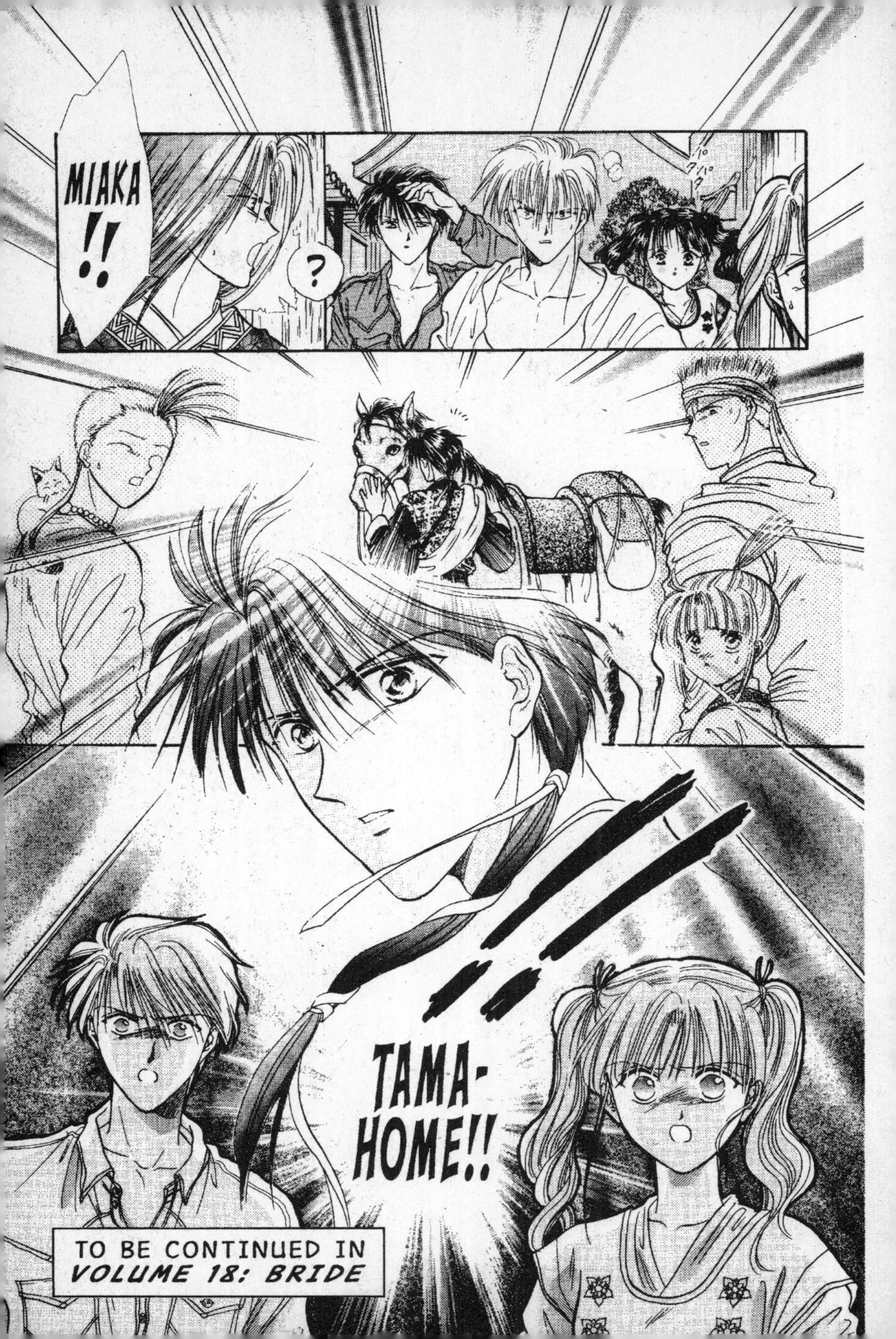
MIAKA!!
?
TAMA-HOME!!
TO BE CONTINUED IN VOLUME 18: BRIDE

ABOUT THE AUTHOR

Yuu Watase was born on March 5 in a town near Osaka,
Japan, and she was raised there before moving to Tokyo
to follow her dream of creating manga. In the decade
since her debut short story, "Pajama De Ojama" (An
Intrusion in Pajamas), she has produced more than 50
compiled volumes of short stories and continuing series.
Watase's beloved works *Ceres: Celestial Legend*, *Imadoki!*
(Nowadays), *Alice 19th*, *Absolute Boyfriend*, and *Fushigi*
Yûgi: Genbu Kaiden are now available in North America
in English editions published by VIZ Media.

The Fushigi Yûgi Guide to Sound Effects

Most of the sound effects in FUSHIGI YÛGI are the way Yuu Watase created them, in their original Japanese.

We created this glossary for a page-by-page, panel-by-panel explanation of the action and background noises. By using this guide, you may even learn some Japanese.

The glossary lists page and panel number. For example, page 1, panel 3, would be listed as 1.3.

28.4 FX: DOOOOO (explosion)
29.2 FX: ZURU (slipping)
30.3 FX: KA (flash of light)
30.4 FX: DOUU (engulfed in flame)
30.6 FX: GOOOOOO (burning)
31.6 FX: BA (rush of air)
32.3 FX: KAAAAA (light)
37.2 FX: DAN (slamming)
38.1 Note: Genbon is a book of ancient Chinese and Japanese documents. The Asuka period is between 600-710 AD.
41.2 FX: GYAA (kaw)
41.3 FX: GYAA (kaw)
43.5 FX: SU (rising)

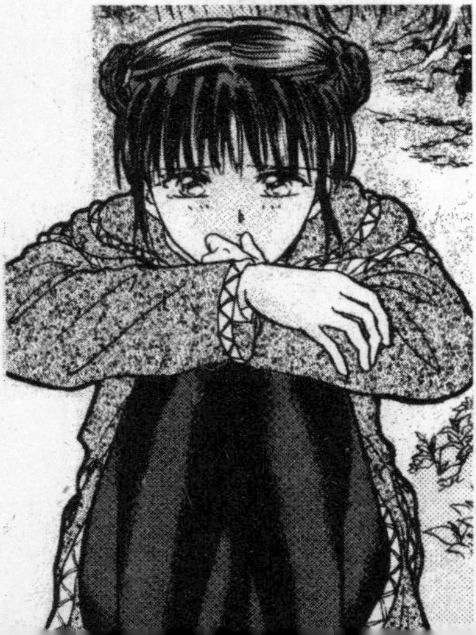

6.2 FX: UUUUUU (truck engine running)
6.3 FX: PIII POOO PIII POOO (siren)
7.2 FX: BIKU (surprised twitch)
7.3 FX: SHUUUUU (sizzling)
10.3 FX: HA (sudden realization)
10.6 FX: BA (rush of air)
12.2 FX: BASHA BASHA (splashing)
13.2 FX: ZAWA (rustling in the trees)
13.3 FX: KA (flash of light)
13.4 FX: DOSA (falling with a thud)
13.5 FX: SAPA (rushing out of water)
17.3 FX: BURU BURU (trembling)
17.5 FX: KA (sudden anger)
18.3 FX: ZUUUU (radiating energy)
18.5 FX: KA (sudden release)
19.1 FX: DO (hitting)
20.2 FX: DOKUN (heartbeat)
20.4 FX: DOKUN DOKUN (heartbeats)
20.5 FX: DOKUN DOKUN DOKUN (heartbeats)
21.5 FX: SHIKU SHIKU (sniffling)
21.6 FX: WAKU WAKU (excitement)
23.1 Note: What Lai Lai says means "Opening Wave."
23.1 FX: KA (flash of light)
24.1 FX: GAKUN (being released)
27.4 FX: YORO (wobble)

64.2 FX: ZAWA ZAWA (rustling)
70.2 FX: GAKU (slumping over)
70.3 FX: BO (flame)
70.4 FX: ZURU (slipping)
71.1 FX: DOKI (heartbeat)
72.3 FX: ZUUUU (radiating energy)
74.2 FX: SAWA SAWA (rustling)
75.1 FX: BYUN (fast movement)
75.2 FX: REEEE REEEE (crickets chirping)
75.6 FX: ZAKU ZAKU ZAKU (footsteps)
76.1 FX: ZAWA (rustling)
76.3 FX: ZAZA (wind)
77.3 FX: HA (realization)
77.4 FX: YORO (wobble)
77.5 FX: HA (realization)
80.4 FX: BO (burning)
84.3 FX: HA (realization)
86.4 FX: PAN (clap)
87.2 FX: YORO (wobble)
87.2 FX: DON (thud)
90.2 FX: JARA (chinking of beads)
90.3 FX: ZOKU (shock)
90.4 FX: GI (shifting weight)
90.5 FX: BA (sudden movement)
91.1-3 FX: DOKUN DOKUN DOKUN DOKUN DOKUN DOKUN (heavy heartbeats)
93.1-2 FX: ZA ZA ZA (running footsteps)
95.3 FX: BA (a rush)
97.5 FX: NYA (a grin)
100.2 FX: BOTA BOTA (dripping blood)
100.3 FX: ZURU (lifting himself)
102.1 FX: GYAA GYAA (crows cawing)

44.4 FX: BASA BASA BASA (flapping)
44.5 FX: BASA BASA (flapping)
45.2 FX: BYOOOOOO (whirlwind)
45.3 FX: ZAWA ZAWA (rustling)
46.5 FX: PO (frustration)
47.4 FX: BAKI (twigs snapping)
48.3 FX: DOKUN DOKUN (heavy heartbeats)
48.4 FX: DOKUN DOKUN DOKUN DOKUN (heavy heartbeats)
49.5 FX: JABABABABABA (swimming back)
50.1 FX: DOKI (heartbeat)
54.2 FX: SAWA (rustling)
58.4 FX: ZAKU ZAKU (walking)
58.5 FX: PITA (sudden stop)
59.5 FX: BA (explosion)
60.4 FX: BASHI (attack hitting)
62.1 FX: BUWA (high wind)
63.2 FX: BASA (wings flapping)

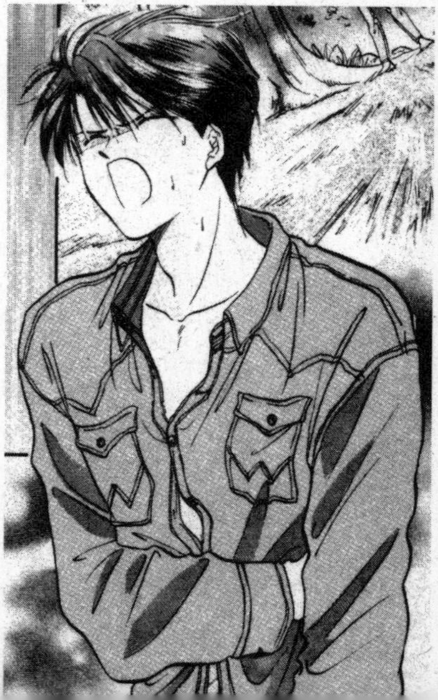

103.4 FX: GATA GATA GATA (shaking)
104.1 FX: BASHA (splash)
104.2 FX: GATA GATA GATA GATA (shaking)
104.2 FX: BASA BASA (books falling)
104.4 FX: ZUZUZU (rumbling)
104.6 FX: ZUZUZU (rumbling)
105.1 FX: ZUZUZU (rumbling)
105.4 FX: ZUZUZU (rumbling)
106.2 FX: ZUZUZU (rumbling)
111.3 FX: KA (sudden anger)
111.4 FX: BA (quick movement)
112.1 FX: BAKI BAKI (things breaking)
117.2 FX: DOKUN (heavy heartbeat)
117.3 FX: DOKUN (heavy heartbeat)
117.4 FX: DOKUN (heavy heartbeat)
117.5 FX: DOKUN DOKUN (heavy heartbeats)
117.6 FX: DOKUN (heavy heartbeat)
118.2 FX: DAN (movement)
118.3 FX: HA (realization)
119.4 FX: DON (explosion)
120.1 FX: WAAA (shocked yells)
120.3 FX: BA (rushing)
120.4 FX: GARAN (clanking to the floor)
121.4 FX: KAAAA (light glowing)
122.4 FX: KAAAAA (light glowing)
128.2 Note: In Japanese "Fei-gao" is pronounced "Hikô." Miaka says that he's splitting up friends...What airplane ("hikôki") does that? And Tasuki corrects her that the name is "hikô" and not "hikôki."
128.3 FX: PIKU (becoming aware)
128.5 FX: HA (realization)
129.1 FX: DOO (explosion)
131.4 FX: GUGU (tightening)
131.5 FX: SUPA (splash)
132.1 FX: BIKU (surprise)
132.2 FX: HA (realization)
134.4 FX: DOOO (rushing)
135.2 FX: ZURU (sliding down)
135.5 FX: ZUZUZU (sliding through)
137.1 FX: DOOOOOOOO (explosion)
137.3 FX: GOOO (roaring)
137.4 FX: KARA KARA (crackling)
138.3 FX: DOKUN DOKUN DOKUN (rhythmic beating)
138.5 FX: SUUU (movement)
140.1 FX: SHAAAA (rain)
140.3 FX: DOTA DOTA (rushing about)
142.5 FX: GYU (clench)
143.1 FX: ZAAAAA (rain)

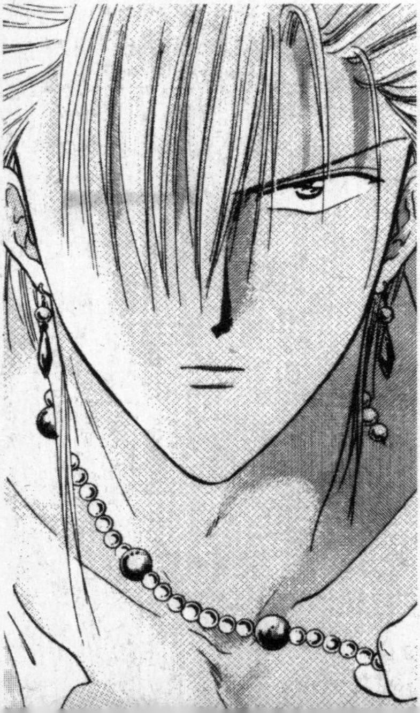

145.2 FX: GISHI (rising)
145.4 FX: ZAAAAAA (rain)
145.5 FX: DOOOO (rushing water)
146.4 FX: BIKU (surprise)
147.3 FX: KI (anger)
148.2 Note: In Japanese "Han-gui" is pronounced "Kanki." The Japanese word for "great joy" is also "kanki," but spelled with different characters. After Han-gui introduces himself, Miaka responds that there's nothing to be joyful about!
149.2 FX: GOOOO (thunder)
150.2 FX: ZAPA (water sounds)
150.3 FX: ZAAA (rushing water)
152.1 FX: BASHAA (exploding water)
152.3 FX: PASHA (splashing)
153.2 FX: SHAN (jangling of rings on staff)
155.3 FX: SHAN (jangling rings on staff)
156.2 FX: BA (explosion)
156.3 FX: SHAN (jangling rings on staff)
158.1 FX: GOOOO (fire)
158.5 FX: DOOOO (rushing water)
160.1 Note: The word that Chichiri shouts is the character for victory.
160.1 FX: DOO (explosion)
163.1 FX: BA (sudden movement)
163.2 FX: SHU (appearance)
163.3 FX: SHULULULU (wrapping)
165.1 FX: ZAAAA (rain)
168.4 FX: GYU (tight grip)
169.2 FX: DOON (explosive force)
169.4 FX: GOOO (flames)
170.3 FX: GOOOO (flames)
171.1 FX: ZUBU (rushing fist)
171.3 FX: ZAA (breaking through)
172.1 FX: DON (explosion)
172.4 FX: BA (sudden movement)
173.1 FX: BASHA (splashing water)
179.1 FX: SUKU (raising his head rapidly)
180.4 FX: HA (sudden realization)
180.5 FX: SU (appearance)
184.2 FX: ZA (shock)
186.2 FX: YORO (wobble)
186.5 FX: GYU (gripping tightly)
189.3 FX: BA (rushing)
189.6 FX: GYU (holding tight)
191.1 FX: DON (punching)
192.2 FX: BATA BATA BATA BATA (running)
192.5 FX: DA (heavy footstep)
193.1 FX: PATA PATA (footsteps)

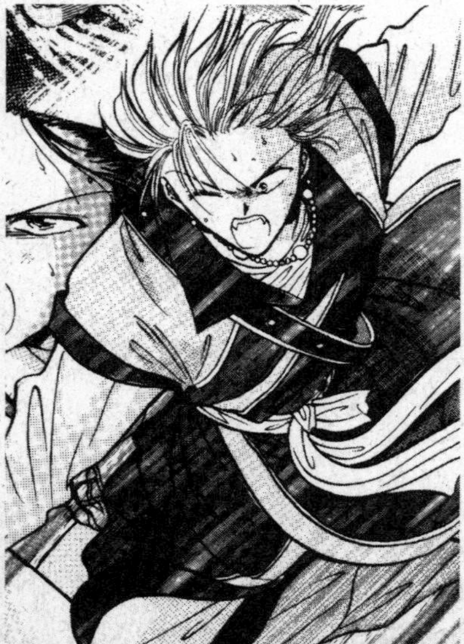

How many shojo titles have you purchased in the last year? How many were VIZ shojo titles?
(please check one from each column)

SHOJO MANGA	VIZ SHOJO MANGA
☐ None	☐ None
☐ 1 – 4	☐ 1 – 4
☐ 5 – 10	☐ 5 – 10
☐ 11+	☐ 11+

What do you like most about shojo graphic novels? **(check all that apply)**

☐ Romance ☐ Drama / conflict ☐ Fantasy

☐ Comedy ☐ Real-life storylines ☐ Relatable characters

☐ Other ______________________________

Do you purchase every volume of your favorite shojo series?

☐ Yes! Gotta have 'em as my own

☐ No. Please explain: ______________________________

Who are your favorite shojo authors / artists? ______________________________

____

What shojo titles would like you translated and sold in English? ______________________________

____

THANK YOU! Please send the completed form to:

NJW Research
ATTN: VIZ Media Shojo Survey
42 Catharine Street
Poughkeepsie, NY 12601

Your privacy is very important to us. All information provided will be used for internal purposes only and will not be sold or otherwise divulged.

LOVE SHOJO? LET US KNOW!

☐ Please do NOT send me information about VIZ Media products, news and events, special offers, or other information.

☐ Please do NOT send me information from VIZ' trusted business partners.

Name: _____

Address: _____

City: _____ State: _____ Zip: _____

E-mail: _____

☐ Male ☐ Female   Date of Birth (mm/dd/yyyy): ___ / ___ / ___   (Under 13? Parental consent required)

What race/ethnicity do you consider yourself? (check all that apply)

☐ White/Caucasian   ☐ Black/African American   ☐ Hispanic/Latino

☐ Asian/Pacific Islander   ☐ Native American/Alaskan Native   ☐ Other: _____

What VIZ shojo title(s) did you purchase? (indicate title(s) purchased)

_____

What other shojo titles from other publishers do you own? _____

_____

Reason for purchase: (check all that apply)

☐ Special offer   ☐ Favorite title / author / artist / genre

☐ Gift   ☐ Recommendation   ☐ Collection

☐ Read excerpt in VIZ manga sampler   ☐ Other _____

Where did you make your purchase? (please check one)

☐ Comic store   ☐ Bookstore   ☐ Mass/Grocery Store

☐ Newsstand   ☐ Video/Video Game Store

☐ Online (site:_____)   ☐ Other _____

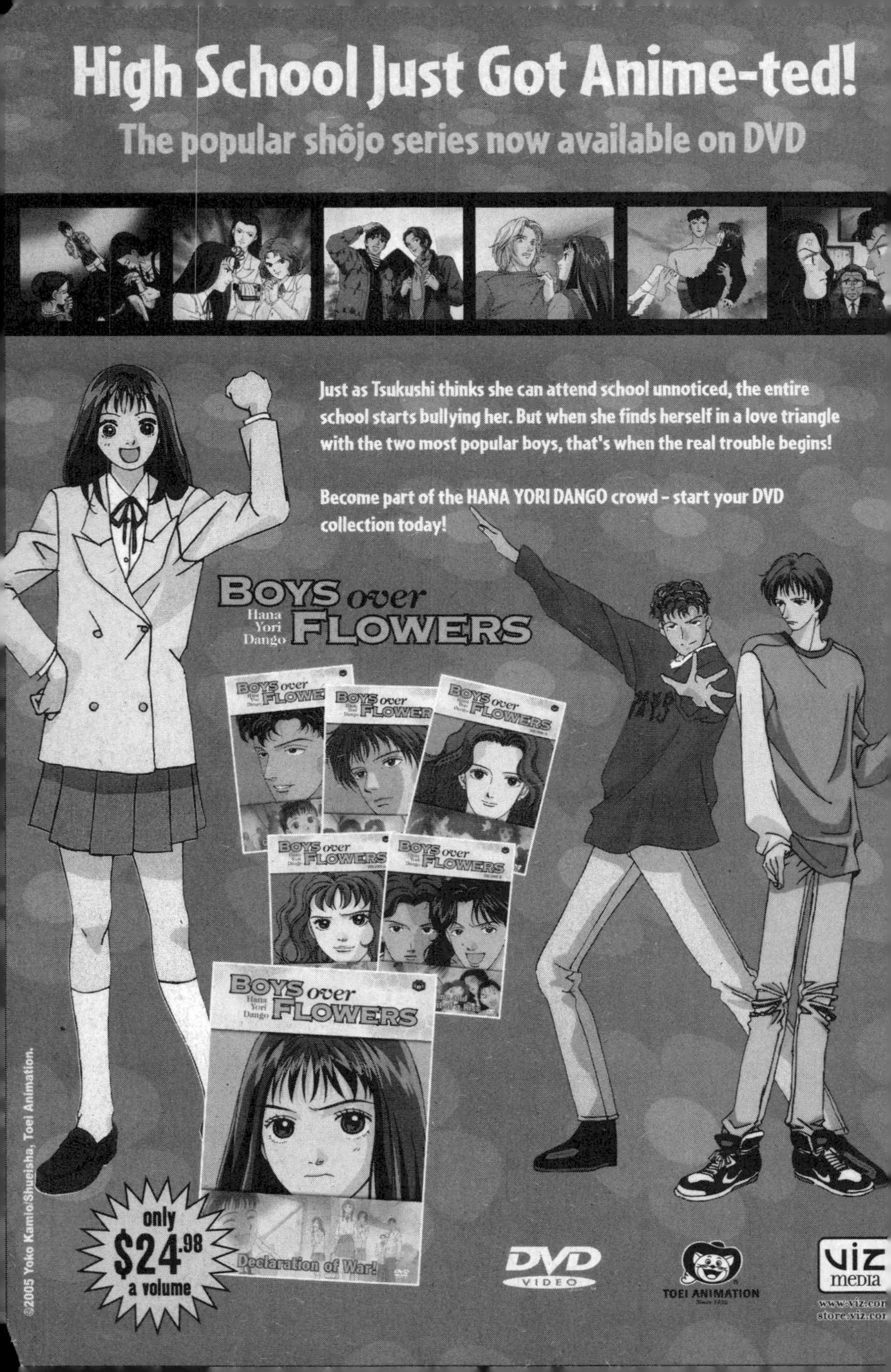
High School Just Got Anime-ted!
The popular shôjo series now available on DVD
Just as Tsukushi thinks she can attend school unnoticed, the entire school starts bullying her. But when she finds herself in a love triangle with the two most popular boys, that's when the real trouble begins!
Become part of the HANA YORI DANGO crowd – start your DVD collection today!
BOYS over FLOWERS
Hana Yori Dango
Declaration of War!
only $24.98 a volume
DVD VIDEO
TOEI ANIMATION
viz media
www.viz.com
store.viz.com
©2005 Yoko Kamio/Shueisha, Toei Animation.

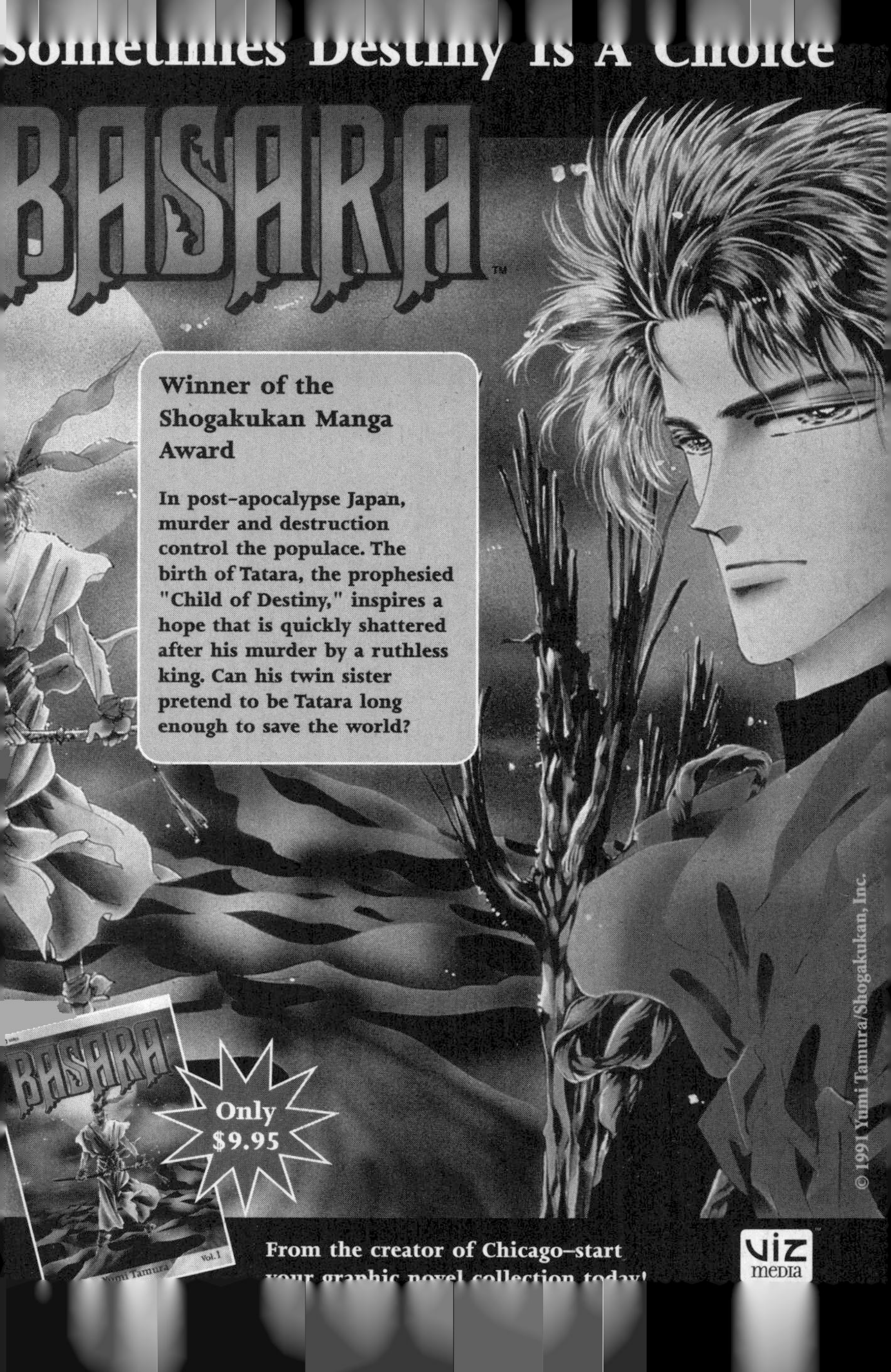
Sometimes Destiny Is A Choice
BASARA™
Winner of the Shogakukan Manga Award
In post-apocalypse Japan, murder and destruction control the populace. The birth of Tatara, the prophesied "Child of Destiny," inspires a hope that is quickly shattered after his murder by a ruthless king. Can his twin sister pretend to be Tatara long enough to save the world?
BASARA
Yumi Tamura
Vol. 1
Only $9.95
© 1991 Yumi Tamura/Shogakukan, Inc.
From the creator of Chicago–start
your graphic novel collection today!
VIZ media

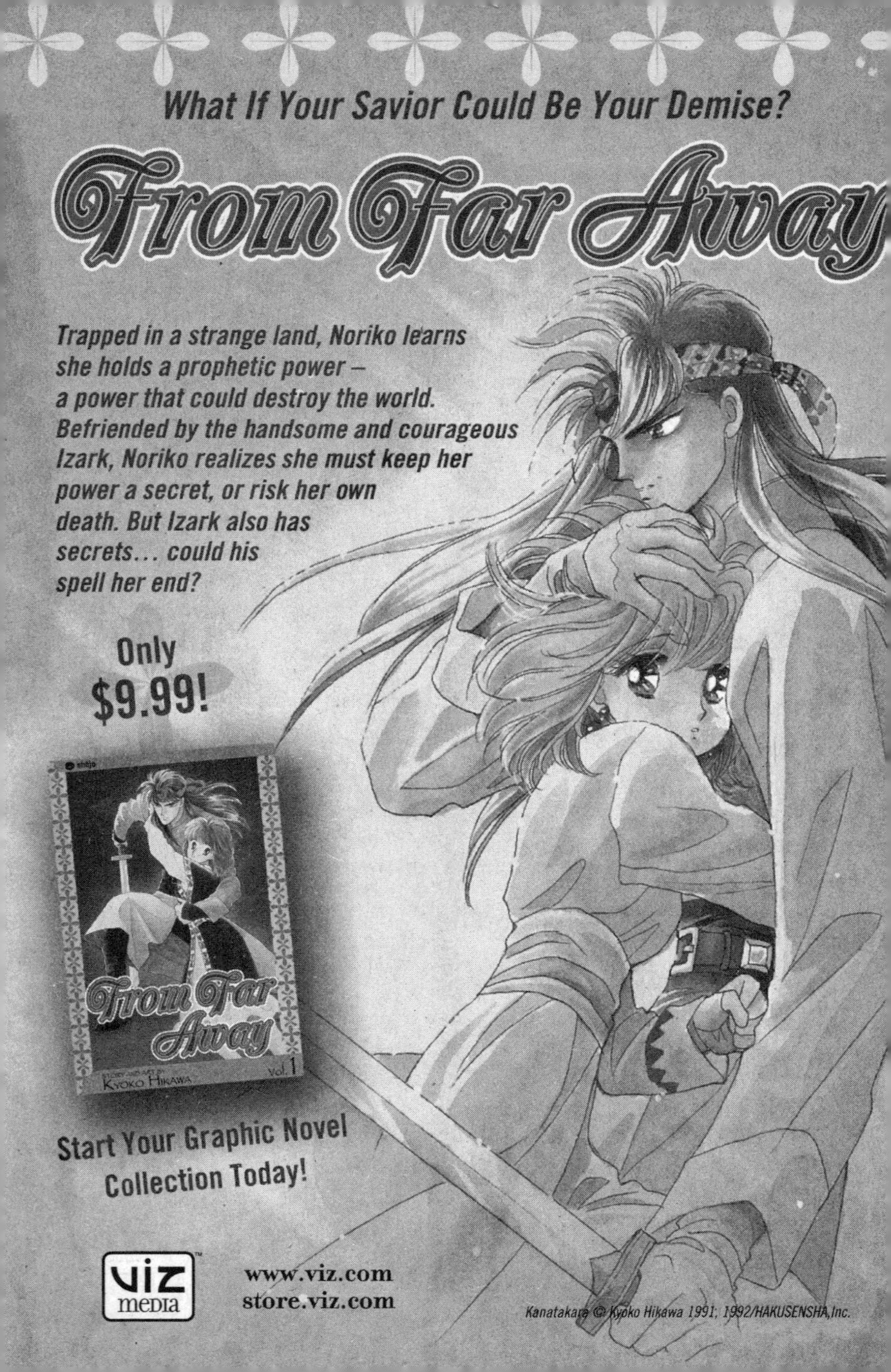
What If Your Savior Could Be Your Demise?
From Far Away
Trapped in a strange land, Noriko learns she holds a prophetic power – a power that could destroy the world. Befriended by the handsome and courageous Izark, Noriko realizes she must keep her power a secret, or risk her own death. But Izark also has secrets… could his spell her end?
Only $9.99!
From Far Away
Kyoko Hikawa
Vol. 1
Start Your Graphic Novel Collection Today!
viz media
www.viz.com
store.viz.com
Kanatakara © Kyoko Hikawa 1991, 1992/HAKUSENSHA,Inc.

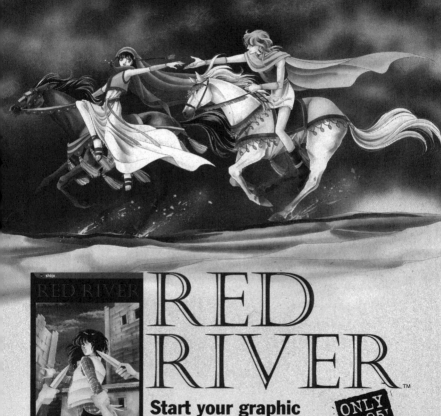

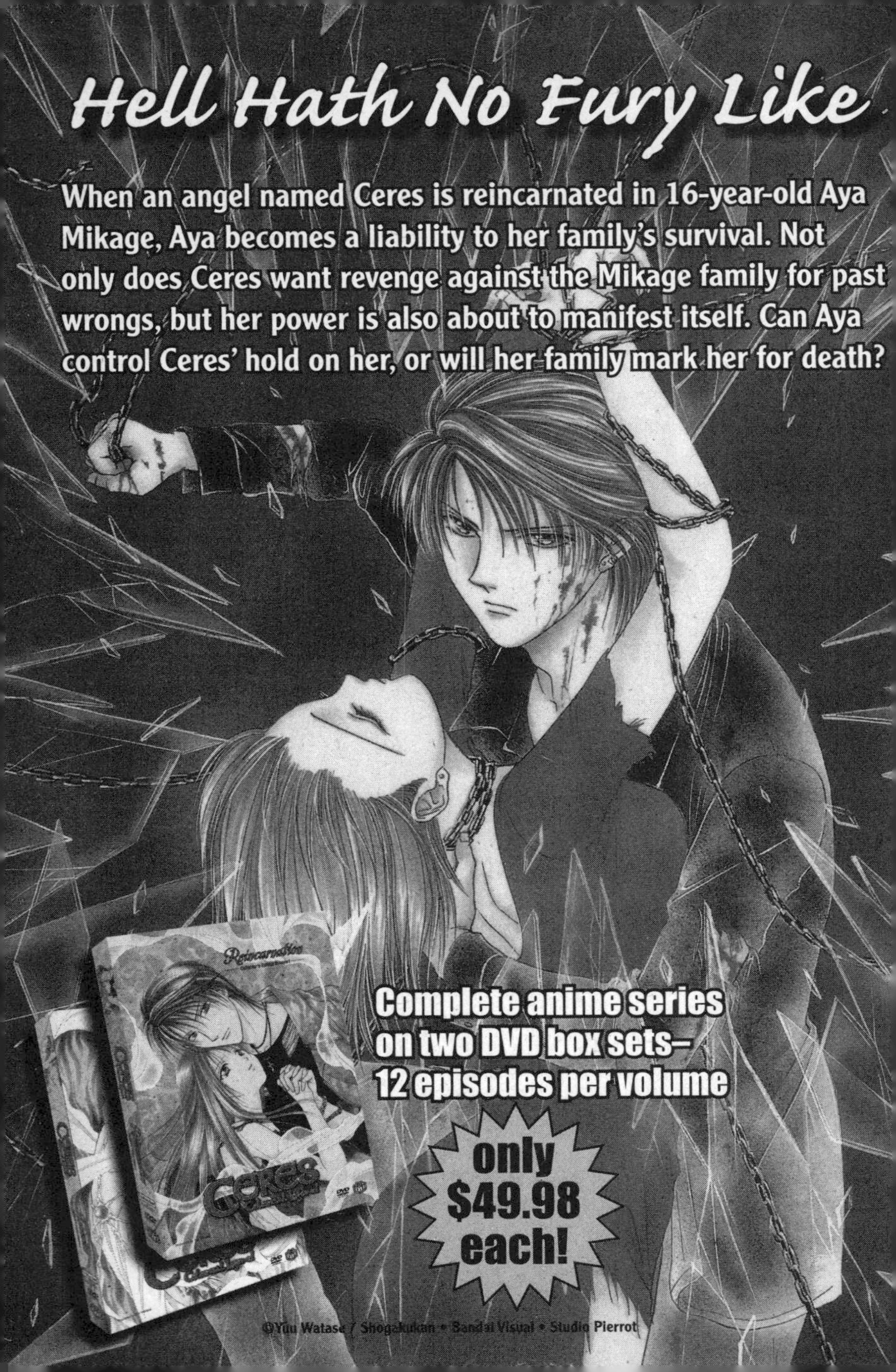

Hell Hath No Fury Like
When an angel named Ceres is reincarnated in 16-year-old Aya Mikage, Aya becomes a liability to her family's survival. Not only does Ceres want revenge against the Mikage family for past wrongs, but her power is also about to manifest itself. Can Aya control Ceres' hold on her, or will her family mark her for death?
Complete anime series on two DVD box sets– 12 episodes per volume
only $49.98 each!
©Yuu Watase / Shogakukan • Bandai Visual • Studio Pierrot

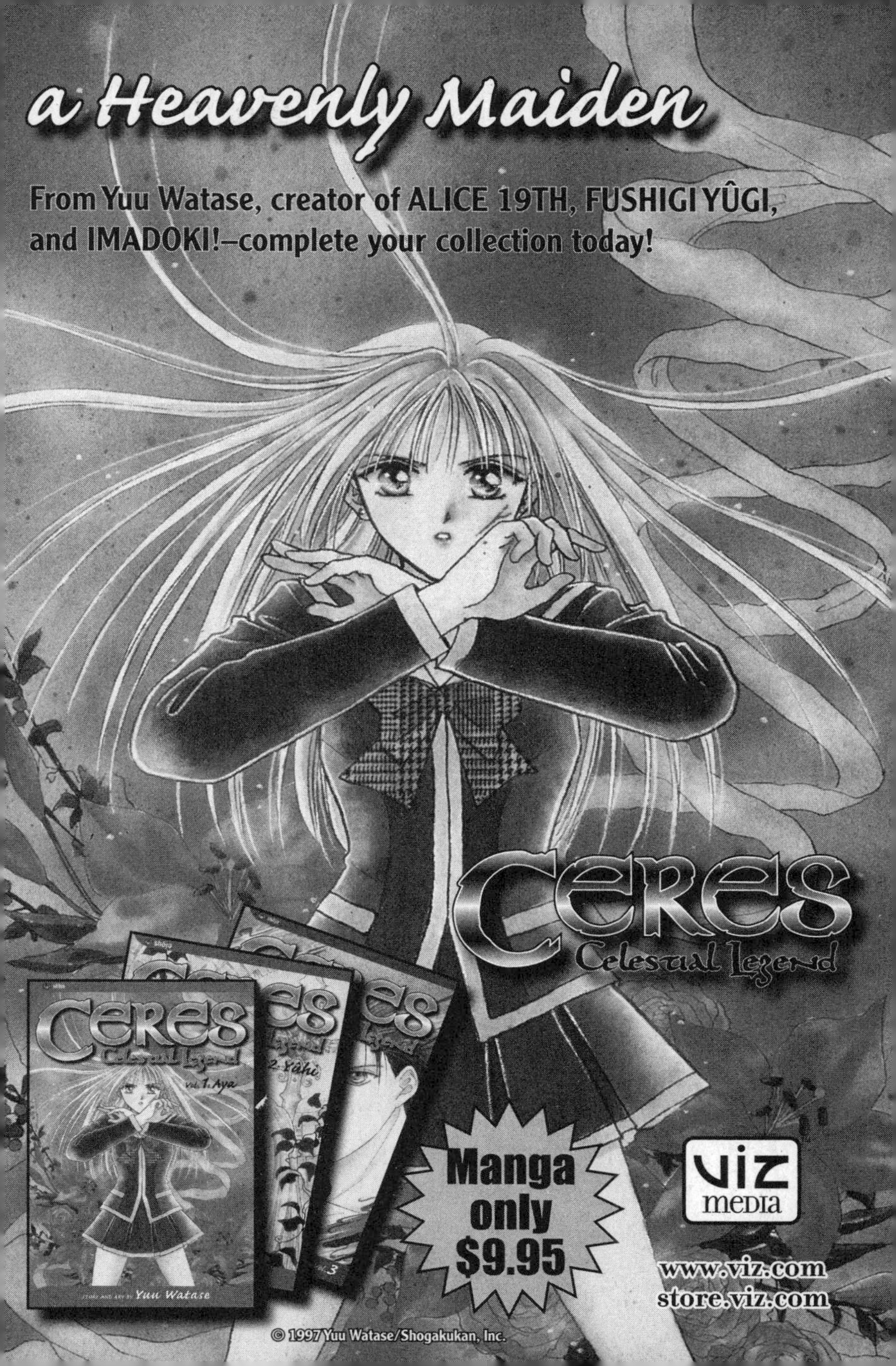
a Heavenly Maiden
From Yuu Watase, creator of ALICE 19TH, FUSHIGI YÛGI, and IMADOKI!–complete your collection today!
Ceres
Celestial Legend
Manga only $9.95
viz media
www.viz.com
store.viz.com
© 1997 Yuu Watase/Shogakukan, Inc.